Raising Capital on Arab Equity Markets

SHORT LOAN

This book may not be issued overnight
It is issued for 1hrsonly, and is
due for return on/before the last time
shown. Fines 50p per hour, or part hour
overdue.

BPP
UNIVERSITY

~~1.23~~	~~20.10~~	~~20:22~~
~~12.24~~	~~3.20~~	~~06.08~~
~~19:30~~	~~11.48~~	~~12.17~~
~~12:05~~	~~12.42~~	~~1.08~~
~~14/10/2015~~	~~19:37~~	~~2.12~~
~~3.51~~	~~19:43~~	~~5.27~~
~~4.56~~	~~3.35~~	19.31
~~1:25~~	~~1.49~~	
~~17.05~~		

Raising Capital on Arab Equity Markets

Legal and Juridical Aspects of Arab Securities Regulation

Lu'ayy Minwer Al-Rimawi

Wolters Kluwer
Law & Business

Published by:
Kluwer Law International
PO Box 316
2400 AH Alphen aan den Rijn
The Netherlands
Website: www.kluwerlaw.com

Sold and distributed in North, Central and South America by:
Aspen Publishers, Inc.
7201 McKinney Circle
Frederick, MD 21704
United States of America
Email: customer.service@aspenpublishers.com

Sold and distributed in all other countries by:
Turpin Distribution Services Ltd.
Stratton Business Park
Pegasus Drive, Biggleswade
Bedfordshire SG18 8TQ
United Kingdom
Email: kluwerlaw@turpin-distribution.com

Printed on acid-free paper.

ISBN 978-90-411-2837-9

Printed and Bound by CPI Group (UK) Ltd, Croydon, CR0 4YY.

The Author

Dr Lu'ayy Minwer Al-Rimawi hails from the 'Al-Rimawi' clan which finds its historic roots in the picturesque town of Beit Rima [believed to be known by its Roman name '*Remeth*' which means 'heights' or the 'great cliff'] and the Syrian city of Aleppo, some of whose Arab Muslim fighters came to Palestine with Saladin in the Twelfth Century, residing in Beit Rima. The town of the Al-Rimawi clan, Beit Rima or *Remeth*, may have also been one of the historic towns mentioned in the Bible as another form of '*Ramah*' (q.v.) or '*Ramoth*' (1 Chr. 6:73; Josh. 19:21), and probably also of Jarmuth (Josh. 21:29).

Over many generations, the Al-Rimawi clan has boasted of poets who performed at the Court of the Ottoman Sultan, intellectuals, prominent journalists, eminent religious scholars, university professors, members of the judiciary as well as founders of non-profitable Jordanian orphanage organisations – the Jordan Joud Foundation (JJF). The Al-Rimawi clan has also boasted of talented musicians (Syria), innovative movie producers (USA), award-winning short story Arab novelists (Jordan), chess Arab championships finalists (Jordan) and regionally acclaimed technology and non-technology entrepreneurs (Jordan, Palestine, Latin America, Canada, USA). It has equally boasted of world-class technical professionals in nuclear physics (including a former Head of the Bureau of Environmental Radiation Protection of the State of New York) and competent medical doctors (Jordan, Palestine, USA, Canada). Added to the above is the Al-Rimawi clan's deep history of involvement in regional pan-Arab nationalist movements, with some of its members having been significant leaders in the Palestinian national movement as well as ministers of state (Jordan), parliamentarians (Jordan), senators (Jordan), members of the National Consultative Council (Jordan), Speaker of the Jordanian Parliament (1967) as well as Prime Minister of the Hashemite Kingdom of Jordan (1980).

Dr Lu'ayy Al-Rimawi is well known for his strong views against the manner in which the majority of so-called Arab elites have lacked the courage, confidence or the goodwill to set true examples in self-reliance – (as he puts it) capitalising lethargically instead on a heavily skewed Arab status quo that entrenches nepotism at the expense of transparency and open competition. This, he adds, has devalued the worth of genuine hard work across the Arab world – resulting in unfair dominance of the unpalatable few whose *raison d'être* has, over many decades, been to suffocate hope, instil fear, cynicism and corruption while wilfully destroying noble values and high ideals that ordinary Arab citizens have long coveted to espouse. His motto is '*No matter how high it may leap, a frog can never reach an eagle's sky*', quoted from an English short story entitled 'Did the Eagle Ever Fly Again?', which he wrote and published during his early studies at the London School of Economics (LSE).

Dr Lu'ayy Al-Rimawi finished his bachelor of law (LLB) in Amman – being the first Jordanian from the Law Faculty in the University of Jordan to study for the Master's in Law (LLM) at Cambridge University. He then finished his Master's of Science (MSc) in International Relations from the Faculty of Economics and Political Science at the LSE, where he was a Chevening Scholar – a distinguished international scholarship awarded by the UK Foreign & Commonwealth Office. He then proceeded to study for his Ph.D in law in comparative aspects of financial services regulation at the LSE – having been awarded by the LSE (through open competition with UK, EU and international doctoral researchers) a prestigious teaching scholarship to teach public international law. During his doctoral studies at the LSE he was also awarded (through open competition) the very prestigious Lord Wedderburn Scholarship, granted by the Law Department at the LSE, for 'excellence' in doctoral research in areas including capital market studies and financial services law. His Ph.D in law is considered among the top doctorates, having been awarded outright by the LSE without the requirement of a single change or amendment.

Dr Lu'ayy Al-Rimawi has been a part-time lecturer in public international law at the LSE, a guest lecturer in Islamic financial law at Cambridge University and is a former executive civil servant at the UK Home Office in London. He is a Senior Research Fellow in comparative law at the British Institute of Securities Law and the Director of the Master's programme in Islamic financial law (LLM) at the prestigious BPP University, London – one of EU's largest academic institutions that specialises in professional legal education. He is also scheduled to be a Visiting Fellow in Islamic legal studies at Harvard University.

He has submitted a number of legal reports to various UK immigration tribunals that examined in detail various aspects of nationality laws in the Arab region. At the invitation of Mr Peter Harris, the then Official Solicitor to the UK Supreme Court, and in conjunction with the Institute of Advanced Legal Studies in London, Dr Lu'ayy Al-Rimawi has chaired a working group (comprised of eminent UK lawyers, academics and senior enforcement officers) to advise UK judges on cross-border issues pertaining to child abduction in the Middle East. He is also the founder, proprietor and director of the *Cambridgeshire Multimillion Residential Fund* – a project that was set up through the ethos of self-reliance, while at the same time highly valuing the human input of staff. It has now grown exponentially since its short inception, spanning various English counties in Cambridgeshire, Lincolnshire and Cumbria.

Dr Lu'ayy Al-Rimawi has published extensively in UK/EU financial legal journals and books on various areas pertaining to comparative aspects of Arab/EU financial services regulation, international law and Islamic financial law in *The Yearbook of Islamic and Middle Eastern Law*, *Journal of Money Laundering Control*, *Arab Bank Review*, *CCH: Financial Services Reporter*, *European Business Law Review*, *European Financial Services Law*, *International and Comparative Corporate Law Journal*, *Journal of Financial Crime*, *Journal of Financial Regulation and Compliance*, *Millennium: Journal of International Studies* and *The Company Lawyer*. He has particularly published on the illegality under international law of Israeli civilian settlements on the Occupied Arab Palestinian Territories (including Arab East Jerusalem and the Arab Syrian Golan Heights) – where such papers were taught to his LSE undergraduate students during the various seminars he had conducted when teaching public international law at the LSE. Many of his published UK papers on Islamic financial law and comparative aspects of Arab/EU financial services regulation have equally been taught to postgraduate students during his seminars/lecturers at Cambridge University as well as BPP. Much of his academic work and published papers are found in many EU universities as well as the LSE, Senate House (University of London), Institute of Advanced Legal Studies in London, the British (National) Library, etc.

Dr Lu'ayy Al-Rimawi is also a strong proponent and a well-known advocate of democracy, socio-economic reform and equitable applicability of the rule of law in Arab countries. He has had a considerable number of articles, letters to the press and opinions published in various Arab and international newspapers including *The Times*, *The Guardian*, *The Observer*, *The Independent*, *The Independent on Sunday*, *The Sunday Times*, *The Manchester Guardian Weekly*, *The International Herald Tribune*, *The New York Times*, *The Washington Post*, *The Jerusalem Post*, *Al-Hayat* (London), *Al-Sharq Al-Awsat* (London), *Al-Quds Al-Arabi* (London), and *The Jordan Times*.

Dr Lu'ayy Al-Rimawi is a regular speaker at the Cambridge International Symposium on Economic Crime, held annually at Jesus College/University of Cambridge. His latest presentation there was in September 2011, when he spoke on the question of *Shari'a* and its protection of investors in financial services. In September 2010 he had spoken on *Shari'a* as a constitutional source to Arab legislation (civil and commercial), delineating the practical legal implications that stem from this. He has made various televised and radio appearances in the UK commenting on diverse aspects pertaining to the Middle East on the BBC, MBC, Sky News, Press TV and various London-based Arab satellite stations. He enjoys enduring physical exercise and disciplined training and has briefly trained with the UK Territorial Army – the Royal Marine Commando SBS (Special Boat Service) and the Royal British Navy.

Table of Contents

List of Abbreviations

AC	Appeal Cases, UK
ABR	Arab Bank Review
ADR	American Depository Receipts
ADX	Abu Dhabi Securities Exchange, UAE
AFM	Amman Financial Market, Jordan
AFML	Amman Financial Market Law
AIBD	Association of International Bond Dealers
AIM	Alternative Investment Market, UK
All ER	All England Law Report, UK
ALQ	*Arab Law Quarterly*
AMF	Arab Monetary Fund
AML/CFT	Anti Money Laundering/Combating the Financing of Terrorism
Art.	Article
Arts	Articles
ASE	Amman Stock Exchange, Jordan
BSE	Baghdad Stock Exchange, Iraq Bahrain Stock Exchange, Bahrain Beirut Stock Exchange, Lebanon
BVMT	Bourse des Valeurs Mobilières de Tunis, Tunisia
CA	Companies Act, UK Court of Appeal, UK
CBJ	Central Bank of Jordan
CCD	Court of Cassation Decision, Jordan
CDVM	Conseil deontologique des valeurs mobilieres, Morocco

CEBS	Committee of European Banking Supervisors
CEIOPS	Committee of European Insurance and Occupational Pensions Supervisors
CESR	Committee of European Securities Regulators
Ch. D.	Chancery Division, UK
CLR	Commonwealth Law Reports Company Law Review
CMA	Capital Market Authority, Kingdom of Saudi Arabia
CMF	Conseil du Marche Financier, Tunisia
CP	Commercial Paper Consultation Paper, FSA
DFSA	Dubai Financial Services Authority, UAE
DIFC	Dubai International Financial Centre, UAE
DIFX	Dubai International Financial Exchange, UAE
DFM	Dubai Financial Market, UAE
DSM	Doha Securities Market
EASRA	East African Securities Regulatory Authorities
EBA	The European Banking Agency
ECC	Egyptian Civil Code
ECMH	Efficient Capital Markets Hypothesis
EIOPA	European Insurance and Occupational Pensions Authority
ESA	European Supervisory Authorities
ESFS	European System of Financial Supervisors
ESMA	European Securities and Markets Authority
ESRB	European Systemic Risk Board
EU	European Union
FDI	Foreign Direct Investment
FEAS	Federation of Euro-Asian Stock Exchanges
FESCO	Forum of European Securities Commissions
FSA	Financial Services Authority, UK
FSA 1986	Financial Services Act 1986, UK
FSMA	Financial Services and Markets Act 2000, UK
FT	*Financial Times, UK*
FTSE	An independent company jointly owned by The Financial Times and the London Stock Exchange. It specialises in index calculation.
GCC	Gulf Cooperation Council: Founded on 26 May 1981. It comprises: Bahrain, Kuwait, Oman, Qatar, Saudi Arabia, United Arab Emirates

GDP	Gross Domestic Products
GDR	Global Depositary Receipts
HL	House of Lords, UK
IBTF	International Bank for Trade and Finance
ICM	Islamic Constitutional Movement
IFC	International Finance Corporation, World Bank
IMF	International Monetary Fund
IOSCO	International Organisation of Securities Commissions
IPO	Initial Public Offering
ISMA	International Securities Market Association
JACPA	Jordanian Association of Certified Public Accountants
JCA	Jordanian Commercial Act
JCC	Jordanian Civil Code
JD	Jordanian Dinar (1 USD: 0.71 JD)
JSC	Jordanian Securities Commission
KB	King's Bench, UK
KCC	Kuwaiti Civil Code
KIA	Kuwait Investment Authority
KSE	Khartoum Stock Exchange, Sudan Kuwait Stock Exchange
LQR	*Law Quarterly Review*
LSJ	*Law Society Journal*, Jordan
MENA	Middle East and North Africa
MENAP	Middle East, North Africa, Afghanistan and Pakistan
MENAP oil exporting countries	Algeria (ALG), Bahrain (BHR), Iran (IRN), Iraq (IRQ), Kuwait (KWT), Libya (LBY), Oman (OMN), Qatar (QAT), Saudi Arabia (SAU), Sudan (SDN), the United Arab Emirates (UAE), and Yemen (YMN)
MENAP oil importing countries	Afghanistan (AFG), Djibouti (DJI), Egypt (EGY), Jordan (JOR), Lebanon (LBN), Mauritania (MRT), Morocco (MAR), Pakistan (PAK), Syria (SYR), and Tunisia (TUN)
MLR	*Modern Law Review*
MMoU (IOSCO)	Multilateral Memorandum of Understanding Concerning Consultation and Cooperation and the Exchange of Information

MSCI	MSCI is an index created by Morgan Stanley Capital International (MSCI), designed to measure equity market performance in global emerging markets. In this respect, one states that the Emerging Markets Index is a float-adjusted market capitalisation index. As of March 2011, it consisted of indices in twenty-two Emerging Economies: Brazil, Chile, China, Colombia, Czech Republic, Egypt, Hungary, India, Indonesia, Malaysia, Mexico, Morocco, Peru, Philippines, Poland, Russia, South Africa, South Korea, Taiwan, Thailand, Turkey and Ukarine
MSM	Muscat Securities Market, Oman
No.	Number
OECD	Organisation for Economic Construction and Development
OTC	Over-the-counter
PADICO	Palestine Development and Investment Company
para.	Paragraph
paras	Paragraphs
PCS	Potash Corporation of Saskatchewan
PRGF	Poverty Reduction and Growth Facility
PSE	Palestinian Securities Exchange
Pt.	Part
QB	Queen's Bench, UK
QFC	Qatar Financial Centre
QFMA	Qatar Financial Market Authority
s.	Section
ss	Sections
SA 1933	Securities Act 1933, USA
SA 1997	Securities Act 1997, Jordan
SA 2002	Securities Act 2002, Jordan
SAMA	Saudi Arabian Monetary Agency
SCA	Securities and Commodities Authority, UAE
SCFMS	Syrian Commission on Financial Markets, Syrian Arab Republic
SCC	Supreme Constitutional Court, Egypt
Sched.	Schedule
SDC	Securities Depository Centre, Jordan
SE 1934	Securities and Exchange Act 1934, USA
SEC	Securities Exchange Commission, USA

SIB	Securities Investment Board, UK
SMC	Securities Market Commission, Kuwait
S&P	Standard and Poor's
SSC	Social Security Corporation, Jordan
UAE	United Arab Emirates
UKLA	United Kingdom Listing Authority
USD	United States Dollar
UNCTAD	United Nations Conference on Trade and Development
VAT	Value Added Tax
WB	World Bank
WLR	*Weekly Law Reports*
WP	Working Paper
XBRL	Extensible Business Reporting Language: A global standardised technology for financial information, widely recognised and promoted across the world because it is readable and comparable in computers and easy for data flow and data treatment

Foreword

Foreword by the Honourable Mr Justice Blair, High Court Judge in England and Chairman of the Qatar Financial Centre Regulatory Tribunal.

Because 2011 has been the year of the 'Arab Spring', it is good to be able to welcome a new book that (at least so far as publications in the English language are concerned) takes a fresh look at securities markets in the Arab world, and their regulation. The book discusses in particular the role of investor protection as regards disclosure when issuers are offering securities to the public, taking Jordan as its primary point of reference.

However, the book goes beyond any one country. It contains a description of Arab securities markets through the stock exchanges of seventeen countries (eighteen including both Abu Dhabi and Dubai), of which the Saudi Stock Exchange (*Tadawul*) is the largest in terms of capitalisation, and those in Iraq, Libya and Syria are relatively new, offering, as the author puts it, 'promising potential'.

There follows a discussion of the regulation of the markets, with an eye to international standards, and the policy issues involved. There is a discussion of the relationship between the secular law and the principles of the *Shari'a*, showing both how full and frank disclosure has played an important role in Islamic law, and also how conventional regulation along modern lines is essential.

More generally, in the wide-ranging chapter entitled '*Shari'a*'s Juridical Risks in the Context of Arab Securities Regulation', the author expresses the view that the relationship between the *Shari'a* and contrary provisions in modern commercial laws (e.g., as to the charging of interest) remains unresolved.

Finally, there is a detailed analysis of the Jordanian regime for public offers and the listing of securities. This is considered from the perspective of the regulatory law and general civil law of Jordan, as well as that of the *Shari'a*. The author suggests various changes that should be made to the securities laws in order to provide better investor protection for shareholders.

Among the strengths of Dr Lu'ayy Minwer Al-Rimawi's book is the fact that at all times he adopts a comparative approach, not only as between different Arab systems, but also with an appreciation of the legal position in the UK and the European Union and elsewhere. This book will commend itself to all those with an interest in securities markets in the Arab world, and in particular to those concerned with a central question in all such markets – how the law can properly protect investors.

Sir William Blair
London
January 2012

Acknowledgements

. . . This book is dedicated to the Almighty God from a deeply grateful heart for His very many gracious blessings: generously granting health and strength; benevolently tipping the balance in favour of beautiful and noble values which I have always wholeheartedly espoused . . . .

. . . To the memory of HM King Hussein of Jordan (may the Almighty rest his soul) in deep appreciation for all his gentle messages of 'friendship' as officially then conveyed to me during my early studies at the LSE . . . His Late Majesty's formal appreciation of my national efforts on behalf of Jordan and the defence of His Late Majesty in the international press (even though I was only in my early 20s) has always been deeply cherished . . .

. . . To HM King Abdullah II for his genuine efforts to build an exemplary Jordan hallmarked by the rule of law within an institutionalised setting. His Majesty's gracious personal appreciation of my national efforts has always been deeply relished . . . May the Almighty God grant His Majesty continued strength and grit to solidify Jordan's national unity, bringing about justice, equality and meaningful change . . .

. . . To HRH Prince El-Hassan bin Talal of Jordan for his precious interest over the years in my activities in the UK: My intellectual role model, well before I embarked on my existentialist UK odyssey; a toweringly substantial Arab and Jordanian national asset . . . It was no surprise that I have always deeply treasured His Royal Highness' warm congratulations upon obtaining my doctorate from the LSE in 2004 . . .

. . . To HRH Prince Ghazi bin Muhammad of Jordan for being a genuine older brother during our studies at Cambridge University and beyond: A redoubtable spirit and a conglomerate of dignified humility rapped in assertively noble self-deprecation that has resonated deeply with my own ethos. . . . Thank you for being a genuinely caring older brother when I needed an older brother the most . . .

. . . To HRH Princess Rahma bint El-Hassan of Jordan and HRH Prince Zeid bin Ra'ad of Jordan for being graceful colleagues in Cambridge . . .

...To my (Greek) family in London: Michael, Tona, Eleni, George and Kat...It is really hard to imagine that I would for one second ever forget Michael's and Tona's precious hearts: Thank you both most heartily for all you have done for me...To my (Greek) family in Cyprus: Demetra, Stavroulla, Kostas, Yorgus, Antonis and Didi...My (Jordanian) family in Amman: My parents for their unshakable confidence and gracious love. My brother Rami, his wife Majida and their children: Taleen and 'Little' Lu'ayy... My sister Hadeel, her husband Majdi and their children: Yzen, Rahaf, Razan, Rawan and Ya'eesh...

...To Professor John Tiley Q.C. of Cambridge University, Professor Christopher Forsyth of Cambridge University, Dr Martin Dixon of Cambridge University, Dr Peter Brooks of Cambridge University, Dr Christopher Constable of Cambridge University, Dr Christopher Hughes formerly of Cambridge University, Professor Michael Zander, Q.C. of the LSE, Professor Christopher Greenwood, Q.C. of the LSE: Thank you all for entrenching my staunch belief in the value of hard work at such an early stage of my life...

...To Sir (Professor) Ross Cranston, Q.C. (Judge of the High Court, ex-MP, ex-Solicitor General/UK government, my first doctoral supervisor) and Professor Paul Davies, Q.C. of Oxford University (my second doctoral supervisor), a distinguished academic and a family friend. Thank you both most heartily for your critical and stimulating legal input that ensured my legal-intellectual development...

...To the memory of a tutor and a friend, Professor Fred Halliday of the LSE: A highly respected international intellectual figure, with whom I enjoyed numerous personal and academic discussions...

...To all my friends and colleagues from Cambridge University, the LSE and beyond who shared their most inner thoughts with me, particularly Ms Alissa Katherine Bell and Ms Sally Thelma Woodford...My 'Robinsonian' Cambridge colleagues for their true friendship during our mutual studies at Robinson College/Cambridge University: Dr Jonathan Greenland (formerly of the Brooklyn Museum, NY), Ms Anna Borzello (formerly of the BBC), Mr Andy Lewis (of HM Treasury, UK), his wife Rose, the Rev. Dr. Ashley Null, Canon Theologian of the Diocese of Western Kansas (USA), Mr Andy Davies...

...To my staff and friends who have supported the *Cambridgeshire Multimillion Residential Fund*, particularly my dearest friend Ms Justyna Gwozdz, Ms Klaudia Kawalik, Mr Pawel Cyniak, his wife Malgorzata and their daughter my little Olivia, Mr Zbigniew Ogonek, Mr Hubert Ogonek, Mr Piotr Czumak, Mr Rafal Werkus, my friend Magda, her mother Krestina and little daughter Emilia...Mr Nick Wilson, my accountant Mr John Allen of Harvey Winning & Co., Mr Angus Adams of Forresters Solicitors, his efficient team, especially Emma and Helen...

...To all former colleagues and my staff at HM Home Office: Thank you all for your friendship...

...To His Excellency Mr Muhammad Tash, the new Chairman of the Jordanian Securities Commission (JSC), a true friend with whom I have shared many Jordanian regulatory concerns; both courageously enduring the wrath of vested interests yet representing a genuine hope for a fresh and world-class performance that restores integrity and dynamism...

. . . To Professor Barry AK Rider of Cambridge University for being a deeply trusted friend: a most congenial and very dear colleague . . .

. . . To all my students in the various UK universities I have been teaching for their input and constant enthusiasm . . .

Lu'ayy Minwer Al-Rimawi
January 2012

Introduction: Methodology and Structure

This book investigates the role of investor protection, with particular reference to disclosure, when offering securities to the public. What motivates it is the lack of attention to examining juridical and legal aspects pertaining to Arab securities markets. Moreover, despite the well-developed literature on Islamic banking, for example, no parallel literature exists on regulatory aspects of Islamic and Arab capital markets. This is somewhat surprising, given Islam's active encouragement of equity holdings and entrepreneurship.

Generally speaking, securities regulation is geared towards ensuring investor protection rather than maintaining systemic stability. As opposed to merit regulation, which entails direct regulatory interference, mandatory disclosure offers a less burdensome regulatory tool. When offering shares to the public, mandatory disclosure aims at providing investors (and their investment advisors) with sufficient information on issuers and offered securities, in order to help them reach an *informed* decision. In the process, it performs a number of functions. These include providing equal access to information, enhancing price accuracy, reducing price volatility and achieving 'standardisation' of disclosure. Accordingly, not only is mandatory disclosure considered as the primary regulatory tool in the UK/EU regulatory model, it is also increasingly becoming the main international tool adopted by almost all national systems.

Given the dearth of research in this important area, a number of underlying juridical questions cannot be taken for granted. Indeed, this book will produce a truncated analysis if it proceeds only to examine black letter questions. Neither will the discussion be complete if it adopts a vertical methodology that only focuses on the selected Arab jurisdiction to the horizontal exclusion of the regional macro-economic matrix. The book shall accordingly be subdivided into two major sections. The first looks *horizontally* at underlying relevant questions in the Arab region. The second looks *vertically* at the case study in order to give a detailed analysis of the development of an Arab regulatory model.

The book shall therefore proceed in the following sequence:

Part I: Horizontal Account of Legal, Juridical and Macroeconomic Issues When Contextualising Arab Securities Markets

This part shall be divided into seven chapters tackling various underlying macroeconomic, statistical and regulatory aspects as follows:

Chapter 1: This chapter introduces basic concepts like 'securities markets' and 'securities'. It establishes a basic understanding of 'emerging markets' through introducing the relevant quantitative indicators. It equally explains the benefits of securities markets both generally and in the particular context of emerging economies.

Chapter 2: This chapter explains the meaning of the term 'Arab securities markets', looking into their division in terms of capitalisation as well as according to legal sophistication and underlying macroeconomic conditions.

Chapter 3: This chapter looks at the reasons for recent Arab interest in regulating domestic securities markets – which largely stem from belated Arab recognition of the importance of capital markets as engines of economic growth and alternative means of funding. Such reasons should not be taken for granted when explaining the above. Unlike many other countries, the regulation of Arab securities markets is a relatively new phenomenon. Understanding the recent factors that have generated this unprecedented Arab interest in regulating its securities markets is therefore important in order to draw an overall picture of underlying conditions.

Chapter 4: This chapter looks at the relationship between securities regulation and investor protection. For, unlike banking regulation, which is essentially prudential, securities regulation is generally more concerned with investor protection and conduct of business rules. In developing the theme of mandatory versus voluntary disclosure, it presents the major arguments of why mandatory disclosure is considered as the main regulatory tool for ensuring investor protection.

Chapter 5: This chapter looks at the relevance of international regulatory standards to Arab securities markets and why Arab regulators have been so keen to catch up with such international standards. This is especially important to explain as, historically speaking, Arab securities markets were traditionally considered something akin to speculative tools far removed from their roles in national economies as economic engines for growth and reallocation of funds.

Chapter 6: A recent phenomenon that has been developing in Arab countries is gingerly to gravitate towards Islamic banking and Islamic finance. However, although in some respect this has been motivated by ideological reasons, such gravitation has equally been generated by pecuniary objectives. This chapter therefore discusses some juridical aspects by presenting a detailed discussion of the relevant general law, seen through the juridical influence of *Shari'a*. It starts by explaining *Shari'a's* contemporary juridical relevance, before briefly looking into the sources of Islamic law. However, Islam is jurisprudentially permissive of equity trading, and its socio-economic theory is based on social justice and profit sharing. Yet, it is *Shari'a's* overprotection of the weaker party to a transaction that can often be seen as presenting juridical risks to the functioning of capital markets and their regulation. Chapter 6 therefore concludes by investigating the nature and impact of *Shari'a's* unquantifiable juridical risks on both the selected Arab jurisdiction (commercial and civil) codes and the *modus operandi* of its securities markets.

In advanced jurisdictions, such as the UK, the question of why the general law is not enough to produce an adequate securities disclosure regime has been answered in the literature. Nevertheless, surprising as it may be, this question has *never* been answered in relation to Arab jurisdictions – for which *Shari'a* remains a primary legislative and jurisprudential source. This is therefore tackled in the next chapter.

Chapter 7: This chapter accordingly addresses the question of why *Shari'a's* general principles would not be enough to produce an effective securities disclosure regime. However, as the question of securities disclosure under *Shari'a* has *not* been discussed in the literature before, Chapter 7 constructs a model of such a regime. It uses the methodology of looking at relevant general *Shari'a* principles, particularly whether they would differ from those of the Common Law under the doctrine of *caveat emptor*. In order to ascertain the main informational requirements of a *Shari'a* disclosure regime, Chapter 7 investigates *Shari'a's* full disclosure requirements under contracts of sale vis-à-vis the question of defect. It concludes by assessing the *Shari'a* securities disclosure model, in terms of whether it would withstand the scrutiny of contemporary arguments in favour of mandatory disclosure when offering securities to the public.

Part II: Vertical Case Study of the Evolvement of Public Offering Regime and Resultant Legal Liabilities in an Arab Jurisdiction, the Case of Jordan

Having addressed the above in a horizontal manner, the book then looks vertically at the Arab regulatory regime for public offers and equity listing. One however cautions that the experience of Arab countries is not necessarily identical in this area. In order to develop a better understanding of the regulatory phenomenon, it is important to take a closer look at the practical level in which an Arab country addresses some of the relevant questions. The book shall therefore take the Jordanian regulatory model as a case study in order to provide an in-depth analysis. When examining the case study the book:

(1) explains the legal development of public offers and equity listing, identifying and assessing the techniques deployed to ensure investor protection;
(2) if any, identifies the role of mandatory disclosure. One here looks at the substantive disclosure requirements, particularly assessing: (a) the legal understanding of public offers; (b) the general regulatory principles

governing disclosure; and (c) the instruments deployed to disseminate disclosure; and
(3) looks at liability for misleading or inaccurate disclosure.

However, as the development of the Jordanian regulatory regime can be divided into two historically discrete parts, the treatment of the case study is subdivided into two separate chapters.

Chapter 8: This chapter tackles the development of public offer regime in Jordan up until 1997. It accordingly looks at the legal framework for regulating public offers and listing in that period. It proceeds to explain the Jordanian regulatory techniques for ensuring investor protection when offering/listing shares. It assesses whether or not such techniques provided adequate levels of investor protection.

Chapter 9: This chapter follows up the discussion by addressing the regulatory developments after 1997. It first explains the microstructure of Jordanian equity markets. It then follows up the discussion by looking at the Jordanian regulatory regime after 1997. It explains the catalysts for this structural change, before looking at the question of why mandatory disclosure is needed in Jordan. It then discusses both the general regulatory changes as a whole and the specific changes vis-à-vis the legal framework of public offers and equity listing.

It discusses the disclosure regime in terms of the applicable laws and regulations, substantive disclosure requirements and the instruments deployed for conveying securities disclosure. It concludes by assessing the new regulatory regime in terms of whether or not it achieves better standards of investor protection – focusing on: (i) the new legal understanding of public offers; (ii) Jordanian general principles regarding disclosure; and (iii) the instruments deployed for disseminating securities disclosure.

After having considered and critiqued the legal structure of public offers and listing in Jordan, the book then moves to consider the question of remedies both under the general law and under the regulatory regime. When addressing this, reference shall comparatively be made to EU/UK relevant aspects.

Chapter 10: This chapter looks at underlying relevant questions vis-à-vis the general law. Indeed, as aspects of liability are at the heart of questions related to investor protection, this chapter starts the discussion by looking at liability for fraudulent and negligent misstatements under the general law in the selected case study. It first looks at liability for fraudulent misstatements arising from the *Shari'a* concepts of *ghubin fahish* and *taghreer*, which are fully enshrined in a number of Arab civil codes. It addresses in the process the question of how effective shareholders remedies are under such concepts. It then looks at liability for negligent misstatements under the jurisdiction of the selected Arab general law. When tackling this area, this chapter looks at some comparative aspects found in the Common Law in order to flesh out comparable similarities and dissimilarities between these diverse legal systems.

However, as tortious liability regime under some Arab civil codes is simultaneously based on contradictory *Shari'a* and non-*Shari'a* sources (such as

Jordan), Chapter 10 briefly discusses tortious liability under *Shari'a*. It concludes by discussing the constituent elements of liability that shareholders need to establish in order to sue for negligent misstatements in the prospectus, before assessing whether or not shareholders' remedies are effective under negligence. In ferreting out the position of the general law in the selected Arab jurisdiction on fraudulent and negligent liabilities, this chapter looks extensively at relevant rulings as enunciated by an Arab court of cassation – focusing on Jordan.

Having addressed the above, the book then moves to address the question of liability (civil and criminal) under the specific regulatory regime in the selected Arab jurisdiction. When addressing this question, the book looks at comparative aspects with EU law as implemented in the UK.

Chapter 11: This chapter therefore concludes this book by looking at the question of liability as constructed by the new regulatory regimes in the selected Arab jurisdiction for misleading or inaccurate disclosure. It assesses the civil and criminal liabilities that arise from diluting the impact of the prospectus and equally from undermining its informational probity. It critically looks at the administrative remedies enjoyed by the Arab regulatory body in the selected Arab jurisdiction. It concludes by discussing the case study of the regulatory body's disciplinary and civil enforcement powers. In conducting the above analysis, Chapter 11 looks at comparative legal aspects regarding that of the UK, as it implements EU law in this area.

Part I

Horizontal Account of Legal, Juridical and Macroeconomic Issues When Contextualising Arab Securities Markets

Chapter 1

Securities Markets and Their Benefits

INTRODUCTION

Chapter 1 explains the terms 'securities markets' and 'securities', before it discusses the term 'emerging markets'. It also looks at the benefits of securities markets in emerging markets. This has interesting implications; especially as shall be seen in Chapter 2, some Arab capital markets are actively seeking to be classified as emerging markets.

1. SECURITIES MARKETS AND THEIR INSTRUMENTS

This subsection discusses the connotations of the terms 'securities markets' and 'securities'.

1.1. Securities Markets

For the purposes of this book, securities markets refer to mechanisms that facilitate the offering of securities to the public and secondary trading. An example of a statuary definition of a securities exchange would be:

> Any organisation, association, or group of persons, whether incorporated or unincorporated, which constitutes, maintains or provides a market place or facilitates for bringing together purchasers and sellers of securities or for otherwise performing with respect to securities the functions commonly

> performed by a stock exchange as the term is generically understood, and includes the market place and the market facilities maintained by such exchange.[1]

From a microstructural viewpoint,[2] securities markets are a composite of broker-dealer firms, physical (or electronic) exchanges, clearance and settlement houses, agents for issuing securities and institutional underwriters.[3] Brokers act as agents (with no financial interest) buying and selling on behalf of their clients. Dealers (market-makers), on the other hand, are principals making their profit from a 'mark-up' on the securities sold and a 'mark-down' on the securities purchased – with often an inventory in which they take long or short positions.[4]

Securities markets arc also divided into money, capital, primary and secondary.[5] On money markets, trading takes place in financial debt securities such as treasury bills and notes such as commercial papers.[6] Capital markets, on the other hand, facilitate trading in securities with a longer maturity span. There is, however, no fixed time to distinguish between money and capital markets. But it is generally accepted that securities traded on money markets mature within one year or less, while securities that mature in more than one year are traded on capital markets.[7]

Primary markets simply refer to markets of newly issued securities, while secondary markets refer to markets on which issued securities are traded (e.g., bought or sold). Primary markets are of vital importance to issuers (financial or non-financial corporations) as a source of finance. They are equally of crucial importance to the economy as a whole as they act as conduits for transferring investment risks among investors, thus stimulating economic growth.[8]

---

1. Section 3(a)(1) of the Securities Exchange Act 1934.
2. Put briefly, microstructure theory examines how trading systems and traded securities influence market behaviour. See J Glen, 'An Introduction to the Microstructure of Emerging Markets', Discussion Paper No. 24, IFC, Washington, (November 1994), p. 2.
3. See J Norton et al., 'Securities Law Models in Emerging Economies', in J Norton & M Andenas, *Emerging Financial Markets and the Role of International Financial Organisations*, Kluwer, 1996, pp. 344–349. Securities markets can also be dealer or auction, periodic (call) or continuous, floor or electronic markets.
4. See E Willett, *Fundamentals of Securities Markets*, New Century (New York), 1971, p. 21; P Dattels, 'The Microstructure of Government Securities Markets', Monetary and Exchange Affairs Department, IMF, WP/95/117, (November 1995), p. 6.
5. Securities markets are divided into an exchange or over-the-counter (OTC). See R Pardy, 'Regulatory and Institutional Impacts of Securities Market Computerization', Country Economic Department, World Bank, WPS 866, (February 1992), p. 5.
6. Commercial papers (CPs) are (unsecured) short-term promissory notes issued at a discount in bearer form. They are often used as a substitute for bank borrowing by large corporations which enjoy high credit ratings. See T Smith, 'Markets for Corporate Debt Securities', Research Department, IMF (July 1995), pp. 3–4; A Agtmael, *Emerging Securities Markets: Investment Banking Opportunities in the Developing World*, Euromoney Publications (London) 1984, p. 2.
7. See F Fabozzi, *Capital Markets: Institutions and Instruments*, Prentice Hall (New Jersey), 1996, p. 12.
8. See J Rutterford, *Introduction to Stock Exchange Investment*, Macmillan, 1993, pp. 8–9.

For their part, secondary markets are of more importance to investors as they facilitate converting securities (future financial claims) into cash. Thus, transferring property rights between investors *inter se* providing them with liquidity.[9] They perform an important function, without which investment on primary markets would prove to be limited at best. For, they transfer 'waiting' from one investor to another, in terms of transforming long-term securities into short-term ones by offering both immediate and permanent marketability.[10] Indeed, without secondary markets, issuers of securities may well have to offer investors 'liquidity premiums' in the form of higher returns in order to compensate them for not being able to realise (liquidate) their security before the end of their investment life.[11]

Securities markets' structure in emerging markets is not substantially dissimilar from those in developed economies. Overall framework of issuers of securities, financial intermediaries, marketplace and investors (individual or institutional) remain structurally the same, whether in emerging markets or developed economies.[12]

1.2. Instruments of Securities Markets

The concept of securities is often complex and subject to varying judicial interpretations. Due to market innovations it cannot be completely fixed by statute.[13] Equities refer to securities 'which are an evidence of ownership' comprising common stocks[14] and preferred stocks.[15] For a regulatory definition of 'equities' one can look at Directive No. 2003/71/EC,[16] which defines 'equity securities' as:

> Shares and other transferable securities equivalent to shares in companies, as well as any other type of transferable securities giving the right to acquire any of the aforementioned securities as a consequence of their being converted or the rights conferred by them being exercised, provided that securities of the

9. See K Garbade, *Securities Markets*, McGraw-Hill (USA), 1982, p. 1.
10. See Rutterford, *supra* note 8, pp. 10–11.
11. *Ibid.*
12. See Agtmael, *supra* note 6, p. 2.
13. US definitions recognise that securities are an ever-expanding financial specie. The US Securities Act 1933 and the US Securities Exchange Act 1934 opted for open-ended definitions. Section 2(1) defines a 'security' as: 'note, stock, treasury stock, bond, debenture, evidence of indebtedness, certificate of interest or participation in any profit-sharing agreement, collateral-trust certificate', etc. This definition is also repeated in the Investment Advisors Act 1940 and the Investment Company Act 1940. See generally: *Tchereonin v. Knight* (1967) 389 US 332, 336; *United Housing Foundation Inc. v. Forman* (1975) 421 US 837, 847. Similarly, the UK's s. 14(7) of the Financial Services and Market Act 2000 (FSMA) defines listed securities as anything which has been admitted to the official list under Part VI. Section 74(5) of the FSMA refers to securities as anything which has been, or may be, admitted to the official list. Sched. 2 defines securities as 'shares or stock in the share capital of a company'.
14. With voting rights, whose dividends do not have priority over other claims.
15. Whose dividends have priority claim over common stocks. See Willett, *supra* note 4, pp. 89, 96.
16. I.e.: The Prospectus Directive of November 2003.

latter type are issued by the issuer of the underlying shares or by an entity belonging to the group of the said issuer.[17]

For their part, debt securities refer to bonds or debentures issued by a corporation, public body or even individuals, in which the issuer normally promises interest and full redemption of the instrument upon maturity.[18] A marked difference between equity and debt instruments is that the former may entitle the holder to an ownership share in the company, while the holder of the latter is generally a creditor.

'Derivatives' is a collective term that refers to financial products that are 'derived' from other financial instruments utilised for the purpose of hedging, speculation, arbitrage or asset liability management.[19] They include a number of financial products such as swaps (currency, interest rates or equity), options (currency or equity), convertibles, warrants, forwards and futures contracts.

2. EMERGING MARKETS AND BENEFITS OF SECURITIES MARKETS

Before examining the benefits of securities markets in emerging markets, this subsection first explains what 'emerging markets' are.

2.1. Emerging Markets

The use of the term emerging markets as a collective term denoting a varying spectrum of developing economies is not without criticism for lack of precision. Nevertheless, the borderline between an 'emerging' and a 'developed' market can be delineated quantifiably, relying on two broad indicators.

First, traditional indicators such as number of listed companies, total capitalisation divided by gross domestic product (GDP), total value traded divided by GDP, new issues, etc. Second, institutional indicators such as sophistication of underlying accounting rules, lack (or existence) of well-functioning prudential regulation and supervisory bodies, etc.[20] In this context, a developed market is one which, *inter alia*, enjoys low transaction costs, short settlement periods, together with favourable externalities such as free convertibility of currency, easy entry, etc.[21] Yet, although such indicators may on occasions be criticised as subjective and/or qualitative, they nevertheless remain useful in providing guiding variables that distinguish quantitatively between emerging and developed securities markets.

17. See Art. 2(b) of EU Directive No. 2003/71/EC.
18. See P Davies, *Gower's Principles of Modern Company Law*, Sweet & Maxwell, 1997, pp. 321–326. Upon liquidation, debt instruments have priority over share claims.
19. See generally A Hudson, *The Law on Financial Derivatives*, Sweet & Maxwell, 1998.
20. A Demirguc et al., 'Stock Market Development and Financial Intermediary Growth: A Research Agenda', Policy Research Department, World Bank, WPS 1159, (July 1993), pp. 5–6.
21. *Ibid.*

Neither are securities markets in emerging economies a homogenous group. For, one can broadly speak of substantial differences between them *inter se*. These differences include market capitalisation, structure and number of listed companies. Dissimilarities also relate to the role and size of the private sectors, entry to markets, clearing and settlement arrangements, accounting standards, etc.[22] However, a number of 'common characteristics' have been advanced collectively to identify emerging securities markets. These include thinness[23] (even when they are relatively old), high illiquidity, concentration of trading in a small number of listed corporations, high volatility and proneness to excessive speculative bubbles and high susceptibility to fraudulent activities.[24] Another general characteristic of emerging securities markets is low equity ratio earnings.[25]

Despite this lack of homogeneity, quantitative indicators have been used to justify a division of emerging markets into four broad groups.[26] The first includes markets in early stages of development. These exhibit limited numbers of quoted companies, limited capitalisation, high concentration and volatility, low liquidity and rudimentary institutional setting. The second has a wider variety of quoted companies, increased liquidity, and despite their small size in relation to the overall economy, the corporate sector relies more increasingly on equity financing.

The third is less volatile, with increased issuance and trading activities. They enjoy more considerable market activity and capitalisation, together with reasonably developed risk transfer mechanisms such as equity and currency hedging instruments. The fourth group is relatively mature markets with high levels of liquidity and trading activities, substantial breadth and equity risk *premia*[27] that approaches internationally competitive levels. However, as such division of emerging markets into four groups depends on quantitative indicators; it should not be considered as conclusive.[28] Needless to say, it merely provides a helpful tool to identifying emerging markets.

For their part, Arab emerging securities markets generally belong to the second and third groups (depending on the aforementioned quantitative indicators), though some studies pointed to the Amman Financial Market as a regional example of a 'relatively highly developed' equity market.[29] However, a helpful

22. See R Feldman et al., 'Emerging Equity Markets: Growth, Benefits and Policy Concerns', Research Department, IMF, PPAA/94/7, (March 1994), p. 6.
23. Thinness generally refers to low numbers of listed companies and traded securities.
24. See H Blommestein et al., 'The Role of Financial Institutions in the Transition to a Market Economy', Research Department, IMF, WP/93/75, (October 1993), p. 24.
25. See K Kalotay, 'Emerging Markets and the Scope for Regional Cooperation', United Nation's Conference on Trade and Development, UNCTAD/OSG/DP/79, (February 1994), pp. 17–18.
26. See Blommestein et al., *supra* note 24, pp. 6–8.
27. *Premia* can be defined as risk adjusted returns relative to short-term money market interest rates. *Ibid.*
28. See Kalotay, *supra* note 25, pp. 17–18, where emerging capital markets are divided into three broad categories. The *first* includes Malaysia, Mexico, Taiwan and Thailand. The *second* includes Argentina, Brazil, India, Nigeria and the Philippines. The *third* includes the rest of the emerging markets including Central and Eastern Europe, African and Middle Eastern countries.
29. See M Kumar et al., 'Emerging Equity Markets in Middle Eastern Countries', Middle Eastern and Research Departments, IMF, WP/94/103, (September 1994), p. 16.

indicator to emerging markets is a number of international indices that list a number of Emerging Economies. These, for example, include the MSCI, which among its twenty-two emerging economies includes Morocco and Egypt,[30] S&P which includes twenty-one emerging economies among which is also Egypt and Morocco[31] as well as the Dow Jones list of emerging economies which comprises thirty-five countries, including a number of Arab countries; namely, Bahrain, Egypt, Jordan, Kuwait, Morocco, Oman, Qatar and United Arab Emirates.[32]

2.2. Benefits of Securities Markets

Benefits of securities markets should not be taken for granted as opinions vary concerning their role in national economies – though the majority of literature is overwhelmingly in favour of them as shall be seen below.

2.2.1. Benefits Generally

Equity markets decentralise ownership by spreading risk between corporations and investors in a manner that stimulates investment and lowers the cost of raising capital in the long term.[33] Securities markets also link 'deficit units' with 'surplus units' in the economy, providing alternative funding sources for governments and private corporations. However, their role is not only restricted to private financing.[34]

2.2.2. Benefits in Emerging Markets

Equity-related inflows to emerging markets comprise of direct flows to local equity markets, purchases through country regional and sector-specific mutual funds, and

30. MSCI is an index created by Morgan Stanley Capital International (MSCI), designed to measure equity market performance in global emerging markets. In this respect, one states that the Emerging Markets Index is a float-adjusted market capitalisation index. As of March 2011, it consisted of indices in twenty-two Emerging Economies: Brazil, Chile, China, Colombia, Czech Republic, Egypt, Hungary, India, Indonesia, Malaysia, Mexico, Morocco, Peru, Philippines, Poland, Russia, South Africa, South Korea, Taiwan, Thailand, Turkey and Ukarine.
31. As of September 2011, Standard and Poor's list of Emerging Economies comprised twenty-one countries: Brazil, Chile, China, Colombia, Czech Republic, Egypt, Hungary, India, Indonesia, Malaysia, Mexico, Morocco, Peru, Philippines, Poland, Russia, South Africa, South korea, Taiwan, Thailand, Turkey.
32. As of May 2010 the Dow Jones list of Emerging Economies comprised thirty-five countries: Argentina, Bahrain, Brazil, Bulgaria, Chile, China, Colombia, Czech Republic, Egypt, Estonia, Hungary, India, Indonesia, Jordan, Kuwait, Latvia, Lithuania, Malaysia, Mauritius, Mexico, Morocco, Oman, Peru, Philippines, Poland, Qatar, Romania, Russia, Slovakia, South Africa, Sri Lanka, Taiwan, Thailand, Turkey, United Arab Emirates.
33. See R Pardy, 'Institutional Reform in Emerging Securities Markets', Country Economic Department, World Bank, WPS 907, (May 1992), pp. 8, 12.
34. Research has even pointed to securities markets' potential public role in supporting overall price stability in the economy through acting as intermediate 'channels' of monetary and fiscal policies. See generally R Chami et al., 'The Stock Market Channel of Monetary Policy', IMF Institute, WP/99/22, (February 1999).

private placements.[35] However, high fiscal deficits, overvalued exchange rates, together with barriers to inflows of foreign capital, have all discouraged the growth of equity markets in emerging economies.[36] Additionally, adverse local tax systems that levy high capital gains tax on dividends are among the important factors that have made securities markets in emerging economies less enticing to investors.[37]

General arguments in support of setting up securities markets in emerging economies have, on the whole, been categorised into favourable macro-, micro-, social equality and productivity arguments. [Macro-arguments include: more efficient and competitive financial systems; better saving mobilisation; and better resource allocation. Micro-arguments include: having private sector not crowded out by favourable government treatment and stronger corporate balance sheets. Social equality arguments include: wider participation in attractive opportunities; de-concentration of ownership and more equitable tax collection. Productivity arguments include: improved access to finance for young companies; easier owner/non-owner management transition and better management of information.[38]]

Securities markets in emerging markets can particularly play a favourable role in financial liberalisation.[39] They also promote a number of sectoral interrelations that can galvanise wider aspects of the financial system, such as better allocation of resources in contractual saving institutions.[40] In this context, objectives of financial sector reforms in emerging markets can be identified as striving to achieve three chief aims: improving monetary control; raising the efficiency of financial intermediation; and overhauling the overall safety and soundness of the financial system.[41] Empirical evidence has especially pointed to equity markets' vital role in promoting financial liberalisation in emerging markets.[42] Indeed, strengthening securities markets' prudential and supervisory regulation is often viewed as a necessary ingredient in any attempt at financial reforms undertaken by emerging markets.[43]

---

35. *Ibid.*, p. 6. The long-term favourable impact of equity-related inflows to emerging economies is however occasionally viewed with suspicion due to their short-termism. See, for example, G Underhill, 'Keeping Governments Out of Politics: The Internationalisation of Securities Markets and the Question of Regulation', Working Paper No. 118, University of Warwick, (August 1993).
36. See P Cashin et al., 'Informational Efficiency in Developing Equity Markets', WP/95/58, Research Department and Middle Eastern Department, IMF, (June 1995), p. 2.
37. See D He, 'Stock Market Development and Financial Deepening in Developing Countries: Some Correlation Patterns', Country Economic Department, World Bank, WPS 1084, (February 1993), p. 1; Pardy, *supra* note 33, pp. 2–3.
38. See Agtmael, *supra* note 6, p. 5.
39. For a general discussion of the benefits of securities markets in emerging economies see, for example, L Al-Rimawi, 'Securities Markets: Instruments, Globalization and Benefits for Emerging Economies', *Arab Bank Review* (*ABR*), Vol. 3, No. 2, (October 2001), pp. 33–44.
40. For an analysis of the interplay between securities markets development and liberalisation, see Pardy, *supra* note 33, pp. 7–12.
41. See V Galibs, 'Financial Sector Reforms in Eight Countries: Issues and Results', Policy Development and Review Department, IMF, WP/95/141, (December 1995), p. 18.
42. For example, Korea's securities markets. See A Amsden et al., 'Republic of Korea's Financial Reforms: What are the Lessons?', UNCTAD Discussion Paper No. 30, (April 1990), pp. 49–53.
43. *Ibid.* See also Cashin et al., *supra* note 36, p. 3.

Securities markets in emerging economies can particularly facilitate privatisation, provide alternative investment venues for national savings and represent a medium that attracts foreign capital.[44] In this context, empirical work done on South Korea, Brazil and Nigeria pointed clearly to securities markets' favourable role in channelling savings into real investments. In this sense, securities markets are seen as credible substitutes to debt financing, which often overburden the economy and stem economic growth.[45] Thus, providing individual and institutional investors with attractive ranges of investment opportunities.

Indeed, emerging securities markets' importance in financing local corporations has been particularly highlighted in a manner that exceeds their importance in industrialised countries.[46] This is especially relevant in the context of venture capital. It has also been argued that securities markets in emerging economies contribute to a more competitive and solvent financial system, improve allocative efficiency of investments and eventually lead to raising accounting and auditing standards.[47]

Moreover, in their role as facilitators of the provision of capital, securities markets have also been likened to banks in their lending role, especially their potential contribution to corporate control.[48] For, it has been argued that properly regulated securities markets can enhance the overall soundness of the financial system through imposing market accountability through various requirements of disclosure and transparency.[49] This in turn creates incentives for better internal governance, as equity markets can potentially discipline weakly managed firms by depressing their equities. Thus, exposing their managers and directors to the threat

44. See Norton et al., *supra* note 3, pp. 335–38; R Atje et al., 'Stock Markets and Development', *European Economic Review*, Vol. 37, (June 1993), pp. 632–640.
45. See generally A Abdel-Hadi, 'The Role of Capital Markets in Underdeveloped Countries with Particular Reference to South Korea, Brazil and Nigeria', Ph.D. thesis, Exeter University, 1989.
46. Corporations in emerging economies tend to utilise non-internal sources relying more on long-term debt and equity, while corporations in developed economies place higher emphasis on internal sources such as retained profits. See generally A Singh et al., 'Corporate Financial Structure in Developing Countries', Technical Paper No. 1, IFC, (May 1992); Blommestein, *supra* note 24; Feldman et al., *supra* note 22; Kumar, *supra* note 29; Demirguc, *supra* note 20; C Mayer, 'Myths of the West: Lessons from Developed Countries for Development Finance', Policy, Planning and Research in Development Economics, IMF, (November 1989) and J Mullin, 'Emerging Equity Markets in the Global Economy', *Federal Reserve Bank of New York Quarterly Review*, Summer 1993.
47. See Agtmael, *supra* note 6, pp. 5–9.
48. See M Harris et al., 'The Theory of Capital Structure', *Journal of Finance*, Vol. 46, (1991), pp. 297–355; B Holmstron et al., 'The Theory of the Firm' in R Schmalensee et al., *Handbook of Industrial Organisation*, Vol. 1 (Amsterdam), 1989, pp. 61–133.
49. See generally S Claessens, 'Corporate Governance and Equity Prices: Evidence from the Czech and Slovak Republics', World Bank, Policy Research Working Paper No. 1427, (February 1995); R Egerer, 'Capital Markets, Financial Intermediaries and Corporate Governance: An Empirical Assessment of the Top Ten Voucher Funds in the Czech Republic', World Bank, Policy Research Working Paper No. 1555, (December 1995); P Dittus et al., 'Corporate Control in Central Europe and Russia: Should Banks Own Shares?', Transition Economics Division, World Bank, Policy Research Working Paper No. 1481, (June 1995).

of mergers and acquisitions.[50] Equity markets' role in enhancing corporate governance in emerging markets was also highlighted as one of the three key areas that need 'urgent action' by a joint report issued by the G-10 countries. The report, *Financial Stability in Emerging Market Economies*, called for complementing market discipline by creating effective regulatory and supervisory bodies.[51]

However, although much of the literature has highlighted their benefits in emerging markets, some studies have also alluded to the drawbacks that affect both national economies and investors.[52] Drawbacks are mainly seen through harming national economies through excessive short-term volatility of securities prices and potential speculative bubbles. These could spell over precipitating systemic risks that could destabilise the entire financial system.[53] However, one retorts by saying that this general argument is premised on securities markets occupying a large proportion of an emerging country's GDP. They therefore may not necessarily apply to all emerging markets under all circumstances.

3. CONCLUSION

There remains intense debate about the pros and cons of securities markets. This debate about the benefits (or not) of securities markets has not been exclusive to advanced economies or emerging markets. Nevertheless, an overwhelming amount of literature clearly demonstrates the benefits of securities markets, outweighing their drawbacks.

These benefits, *inter alia*, include playing a favourable role in financial liberalisation and channelling funds from 'surplus units' in the economy to 'deficit units'. In emerging economies, securities markets can particularly facilitate privatisation,

---

50. Such a role must not however be exaggerated. For, the mechanisms for monitoring and controlling corporate management can often be less 'explicit' than is the case in banking debt contracts. See Blommestein, *supra* note 24, pp. 18–19. Moral hazards may not always work, as managers may prepare for dismissal by generous severance packages. See Dittus et al., *supra* note 49, p. 7. Additionally, disciplinary power of take-overs is still untested in emerging markets. See Pardy, *supra* note 33, p. 15; P Davies, 'Institutional Investors in the United Kingdom' in D Prentice *Contemporary Issues in Corporate Governance*, Oxford University Press, Oxford, 1993, pp. 74–78. Hostile take-over bids, as a means to replacing weak management, is equally at best infrequent. See M Knight, 'Developing Countries and the Globalization of Financial Markets', Monetary and Exchange Affairs Department, IMF, WP/98/105, (July 1998), pp. 18–26; Feldman, *supra* note 22, p. 14; M Kumar, *Growth, Acquisition and Investment*, Cambridge University Press, Cambridge, 1984.
51. See generally Group of Ten, 'Financial Stability in Emerging Market Economies – A Strategy for the Formulation, Adoption, and Implementation of Sound Principles and Practices to Strengthen Financial Systems: Report of the Working Party on Financial Stability in Emerging Markets Economies'. Basle, Bank of International Settlements, (April 1997).
52. On the costs and benefits of securities markets, see Pardy, *supra* note 33, pp. 7–12; A Bernham et al., 'The Securities Markets: Findings and Recommendations of a Special Staff of the Twentieth Century Fund', Twentieth Century Fund, Inc. (New York), 1935, pp. 19–32.
53. See Feldman, *supra* note 22, pp. 17–18; Kumar, *supra* note 50, p. 14.

provide alternative investment venues for national savings and represent a medium that attracts foreign capital.

The above benefits are especially relevant in the contemporary context of Arab countries. Yet, although the underlying economic conditions vary between Arab countries *inter se*, the majority of them now demonstrate increased interest in deepening their domestic securities markets. For, capital-surplus and capital-deficit Arab countries are now similar in awakening to the benefits of securities markets – particularly their role in attracting foreign investors to provide much needed foreign capital.

Chapter 2
Arab Securities Markets

INTRODUCTION

This chapter explains the term 'Arab securities markets'. It looks at the division of Arab capital markets first in terms of capitalisation and then on the basis of broad regulatory and macroeconomic conditions.

1. ARAB SECURITIES MARKETS: WHAT ARE THEY?

This subsection looks at the term 'Arab securities markets' and identifies the markets included therein. The term 'Arab securities markets' generally refers to an increasing number of securities markets in Arab countries that have established formal stock exchanges. There are currently eighteen of such exchanges, with considerably varying levels of activity, legal sophistication and capitalisation. Arranged alphabetically, these Arab capital markets are:

(1) Algeria (Bourse d'Alger);
(2) Bahrain (Bahrain Stock Exchange);
(3) Egypt (The Egyptian Exchange);
(4) Iraq (Iraqi Stock Exchange);
(5) Jordan (Amman Stock Exchange);
(6) Kuwait (Kuwait Stock Exchange);
(7) Lebanon (Beirut Stock Exchange);
(8) Libya (Libyan Stock Exchange);
(9) Morocco (Casablanca Stock Exchange);
(10) Oman (Muscat Securities Market);

(11) Palestinian Authority (The Palestine Exchange);
(12) Qatar (The Qatar Exchange);
(13) Saudi Arabia (*Tadawul*);
(14) Sudan (Khartoum Stock Exchange);
(15) Syria (Damascus Stock Exchange);
(16) Tunisia (Tunis Stock Exchange);
(17) United Arab Emirates (Abu Dhabi Securities Market); and
(18) United Arab Emirates (Dubai Financial Market).

2. DIVISION IN TERMS OF CAPITALISATION

Similar to the international downward trend in the aftermath of the credit crunch, capitalisation of Arab securities markets ebbed significantly. This can clearly be demonstrated when comparing current figures with those of the second quarter in 2008.

Indeed, from highs of roughly USD 1,390 billion in June 2008, the capitalisation of Arab stock exchanges tumbled roughly to USD 870 billion in the second quarter of 2010.[54] Total capitalisation of Arab stock markets in June 2011 (excluding the Libyan and Iraqi stock exchanges) reached USD 959.64 billion.[55] It however must be stated that most of these statistics regarding the overall capitalisation of Arab capital markets exclude the three recently established Arab stock exchanges in Iraq, Libya and Syria – which in 2010 were collectively capitalised at (roughly) USD 8.712 billion, as shall be seen from the discussion below.

In terms of their relative capitalisation by June 2011, Arab stock exchanges were arranged as following: (1) The Saudi Securities Market (*Tadawul*); (2) The Qatar Exchange; (3) The Kuwait Stock Exchange; (4) The Abu Dhabi Securities Market; (5) The Casablanca Stock Exchange; (6) The Egyptian Exchange; (7) The Dubai Financial Market; (8) The Amman Stock Exchange; (9) The Muscat Securities Market; (10) The Bahrain Stock Exchange; (11) The Beirut Stock Exchange; (12) The Tunis Stock Exchange; (13) The Palestine Exchange; (14) Khartoum Stock Exchange; and (15) Bourse d'Alger.

Added to the above are the relatively three new stock exchanges in Iraq, Libya and Syria – the Iraqi Stock Exchange, the Libyan Stock Exchange and the Damascus Stock Exchange, respectively.

The capitalisation of these stock exchanges is discussed as follows:

(1) *The Saudi Securities Market (Tadawul)*. It is the largest in the Arab world in terms of capitalisation, constituting 42.05% of total Arab capitalisation – having capitalised at USD 319.56 billion in June 2010.[56] Its

54. See *Quarterly Bulletin*, Arab Monetary Fund, No. 61, (1st & 2nd Quarter, 2010), pp. 9, 109.
55. Information provided by the Damascus Stock Exchange.
56. See *Quarterly Bulletin*, Arab Monetary Fund, No. 61, (1st & 2nd Quarter, 2010), p. 109.

capitalisation reached USD 348.63 billion in June 2011.[57] However, the June 2010 percentage of market share is significantly higher than in June 2008 when it constituted 36.73% of total value of Arab stock exchanges.[58] This is despite the fact that in terms of pure monetary value, *Tadawul* in June 2008 was significantly higher than in June 2010 – capitalising at USD 473.24 billion.[59]

The obvious explanation for this apparent contradiction in terms of monetary value is the significant depreciation of the total value of Arab securities markets in June 2010 when compared to its much higher overall capitalisation in June 2008 – having depreciated by nearly USD 520 billion between June 2008 and June 2010. *Tadawul* also ranked first in the previous year representing 33.95% of the total Arab capital markets capitalisation – having capitalised in September 2007 at USD 355.416 billion.[60]

(2) *The Qatar Exchange*. Relative to the position of other Arab securities markets, the Qatar Exchange made significant progress in June 2010. Indeed, its capitalisation in that period reached USD 100.318 billion representing 11.53% of the total value of Arab capital markets in June 2010.[61] In June 2011, its capitalisation was even higher having increased to USD 122.22 billion.[62] This can be contrasted to its position in June 2008 when it was the fourth largest – constituting 9.77% of total capitalisation of Arab securities markets, with a value reaching USD 135.722 billion.[63]

However, this still represented a significant improvement on the previous year, where the Doha Stock Exchange (as it was known then) ranked sixth in terms of its relative capitalisation among Arab stock exchanges. For, in September 2007, the Doha Stock Exchange percentage of the total capitalisation of Arab securities markets reached 7.27%, capitalising at USD 76.112 billion.[64]

(3) *The Kuwait Stock Exchange (KSE)*. By June 2011, its capitalisation appreciated to USD 120.87 billion,[65] having also been the third largest in June 2010, with capitalisation constituting 10.22% of total value of Arab stock exchanges – capitalising at USD 88.920 billion.[66] However, despite this relatively low capitalisation in June 2010, the Kuwaiti Stock Exchange represented an improvement on its ranking when compared

57. See *Quarterly Bulletin*, Arab Monetary Fund, No. 65, (2nd Quarter, 2011), p. 109.
58. See *Quarterly Bulletin*, Arab Monetary Fund, No. 54, (2nd Quarter, 2008), p. 81.
59. *Ibid.*
60. See *Quarterly Bulletin*, Arab Monetary Fund, No. 51, (3rd Quarter, 2007), pp. 77–78.
61. See *Quarterly Bulletin*, Arab Monetary Fund, No. 61, (1st & 2nd Quarter, 2010), p. 109.
62. See *Quarterly Bulletin*, Arab Monetary Fund, No. 65, (2nd Quarter, 2011), p. 109.
63. See *Quarterly Bulletin*, Arab Monetary Fund, No. 54, (2nd Quarter, 2008), p. 81.
64. See *Quarterly Bulletin*, Arab Monetary Fund, No. 51, (3rd Quarter, 2007), pp. 77–78.
65. See *Quarterly Bulletin*, Arab Monetary Fund, No. 65, (2nd Quarter, 2011), p. 109.
66. See *Quarterly Bulletin*, Arab Monetary Fund, No. 61, (1st & 2nd Quarter, 2010), p. 109.

with the years before. For example, in June 2008 it ranked sixth largest having capitalised at USD 119.562 billion – representing 8.6% of total value of Arab stock exchanges.[67]

Nevertheless, it must be stated here that the Kuwaiti Stock Exchange has traditionally ranked second largest in terms of its capitalisation relative to the total capitalisation of Arab securities markets. This was evident, for example, in September 2007 when it was the second largest representing 13.21% of the total value of Arab stock exchanges, capitalising at USD 138.249 billion.[68]

(4) *The Abu Dhabi Stock Exchange.* It was the fourth largest in June 2011, capitalising at USD 78.34 billion.[69] This is indeed significant progress as, in terms of its relative capitalisation, this market appeared consistently to be holding the fifth largest position among Arab securities markets. For example, in June 2010, it accounted for 8.49% of total value of Arab securities markets, capitalising at USD 73.828 billion.[70] This ranking was similar to that achieved in previous years – when, for example, in June 2008 (despite the fact that its capitalisation reached USD 133.923 billion, constituting 9.64% of total value of Arab capital markets) it still ranked fifth.[71] This is also similar to its ranking in the previous year, when in September 2007 it also ranked fifth – constituting 9.14% of the total value of Arab stock exchanges, capitalising at USD 95.681 billion.[72]

(5) *The Casablanca Stock Exchange.* This market improved its ranking to the fifth position – as it normally used to occupy the seventh largest in terms of its relative capitalisation. Indeed, its capitalisation in June 2011 reached USD 67.14 billion.[73] This is a considerable improvement on its position in June 2010 when ranked sixth having capitalised at USD 63.571 billion, constituting 7.31% of the total value of Arab stock exchanges.[74] This was also an improvement on its ranking in 2008. For example, although in June 2008 it capitalised at the significantly higher USD 90.591 billion, it still ranked seventh – constituting 6.52% of the total value of Arab stock exchanges.[75] This ranking was similar to the previous year, when in September 2007 it also ranked seventh – having constituted 6.92%, with capitalisation of USD 72.478 billion.[76]

---

67. See *Quarterly Bulletin*, Arab Monetary Fund, No. 54, (2nd Quarter, 2008), p. 81.
68. See *Quarterly Bulletin*, Arab Monetary Fund, No. 51, (3rd Quarter, 2007), pp. 77–78.
69. See *Quarterly Bulletin*, Arab Monetary Fund, No. 65, (2nd Quarter, 2011), p. 109.
70. See *Quarterly Bulletin*, Arab Monetary Fund, No. 61, (1st & 2nd Quarter, 2010), p. 109.
71. See *Quarterly Bulletin*, Arab Monetary Fund, No. 54, (2nd Quarter, 2008), p. 81.
72. See *Quarterly Bulletin*, Arab Monetary Fund, No. 51, (3rd Quarter, 2007), pp. 77–78.
73. See *Quarterly Bulletin*, Arab Monetary Fund, No. 65, (2nd Quarter, 2011), p. 109.
74. See *Quarterly Bulletin*, Arab Monetary Fund, No. 61, (1st & 2nd Quarter, 2010), p. 109.
75. See *Quarterly Bulletin*, Arab Monetary Fund, No. 54, (2nd Quarter, 2008), p. 81.
76. See *Quarterly Bulletin*, Arab Monetary Fund, No. 51, (3rd Quarter, 2007), pp. 77–78.

(6) *The Egyptian Exchange.* In June 2011, it was the sixth largest having capitalised at USD 66.99 billion.[77] This however represented a downgrade as it used to be the fourth largest in terms of its share in the total capitalisation of Arab securities markets in June 2010. Its capitalisation in that period reached USD 74.780 billion, constituting 8.60% of the total capitalisation of Arab capital markets.[78] This performance was, for example, in marked contrast to the position the Egyptian Exchange held in June 2008 when it was second largest capitalising at USD 152.817 billion – which then comprised 11.00% of the total capitalisation of Arab capital markets.[79] This performance in 2008 also represented a step forward when compared with the previous year. For, in September 2007, it held the third largest position in terms of capitalisation – constituting 11.04% of the total value of Arab stock exchanges, capitalising at USD 115.546 billion.[80]

(7) *The Dubai Stock Exchange.* In June 2011, it was the seventh largest, having capitalised at USD 53.07 billion.[81] This ranking was not too dissimilar to the position in the previous year when in June 2010 it had capitalised at USD 52.259 billion comprising 6.01% of total capitalisation of Arab stock exchanges.[82] However, this represented a steep downgrade from, for example, June 2008 when it ranked third largest – representing 9.87% of total capitalisation of Arab capital markets, having capitalised at USD 137.166 billion.[83] This ranking in June 2008 was nevertheless an improvement on its performance in September 2007 when it came fourth capitalising at USD 100.653 billion and comprising 9.62% of the total market capitalisation.[84]

(8) *The Amman Stock Exchange.* It was the eighth largest in June 2011, capitalising at USD 27.81 billion.[85] This position was equally the same the previous year when in June 2010 it also ranked eighth – having capitalised at USD 29.361 billion, representing 3.37% of total capitalisation of Arab securities markets.[86] However, this ranking relative to the total capitalisation of Arab capital markets was the same in 2008 and 2007. For example, despite a higher capitalisation of USD 57.031 billion in June 2008, the Amman Stock Exchange still ranked eighth comprising 4.10% of the total capitalisation of Arab securities markets.[87] Similarly,

77. See *Quarterly Bulletin*, Arab Monetary Fund, No. 65, (2nd Quarter, 2011), p. 109.
78. See *Quarterly Bulletin*, Arab Monetary Fund, No. 61, (1st & 2nd Quarter, 2010), p. 109.
79. See *Quarterly Bulletin*, Arab Monetary Fund, No. 54, (2nd Quarter, 2008), p. 81.
80. See *Quarterly Bulletin*, Arab Monetary Fund, No. 51, (3rd Quarter, 2007), pp. 77–78.
81. See *Quarterly Bulletin*, Arab Monetary Fund, No. 65, (2nd Quarter, 2011), p. 109.
82. See *Quarterly Bulletin*, Arab Monetary Fund, No. 61, (1st & 2nd Quarter, 2010), p. 109.
83. See *Quarterly Bulletin*, Arab Monetary Fund, No. 54, (2nd Quarter, 2008), p. 81.
84. See *Quarterly Bulletin*, Arab Monetary Fund, No. 51, (3rd Quarter, 2007), pp. 77–78.
85. See *Quarterly Bulletin*, Arab Monetary Fund, No. 65, (2nd Quarter, 2011), p. 109.
86. See *Quarterly Bulletin*, Arab Monetary Fund, No. 61, (1st & 2nd Quarter, 2010), p. 109.
87. See *Quarterly Bulletin*, Arab Monetary Fund, No. 54, (2nd Quarter, 2008), p. 81.

this position did not represent any change in its ranking in September 2007 when it also ranked the eighth largest comprising 3.01% of the total value of Arab stock exchanges, capitalising at USD 31.514 billion.[88]

(9) *The Muscat Securities Market.* It improved on its ranking in 2011, occupying the ninth largest in terms of capitalisation. This is especially as it had traditionally occupied the tenth largest. Indeed, it ranked the ninth largest in terms of capitalisation in June 2011, having capitalised at USD 26.64 billion.[89] It similarly ranked the ninth largest in June 2010, having capitalised at USD 24.031 billion, representing 2.76% of total Arab capital markets capitalisation.[90] This was an improvement on its ranking in June 2008 when it ranked the tenth largest. For, despite a higher value capitalising at USD 29.140 billion, it still ranked tenth representing 2.10% of the total value of Arab securities markets.[91] This ranking was not too dissimilar to that achieved in September 2007 when it also ranked tenth – representing 1.55% of the total value of Arab stock exchanges, having capitalised at USD 16.271 billion.[92]

(10) *The Bahrain Stock Exchange.* It made a step backward in June 2011 and June 2010, as it ranked tenth largest in terms of capitalisation – as opposed to the ninth largest position which it had traditionally occupied over a number of years. For, example it capitalised at USD 19.06 billion in June 2011.[93] Its capitalisation in June 2010 reached USD 16.24 billion, representing 1.87% of the total capitalisation of Arab capital markets.[94] In June 2008, it ranked ninth – capitalising at USD 30.471 billion, representing 2.19% of total capitalisation of Arab capital markets.[95] The same ninth position in terms of capitalisation was also maintained in September 2007 – when it represented 2.32% of the total market capitalisation of Arab capital markets, having capitalised at USD 24.289 billion.[96]

(11) *The Beirut Stock Exchange.* For a number of years, it has consistently held the position of the eleventh largest in terms of its relative capitalisation. For example, in June 2011, it was the eleventh largest, having capitalised at USD 11.33 billion.[97] In June 2010, it equally ranked the eleventh largest, constituting 1.44% of the total value of Arab stock exchanges, capitalising at USD 12.501 billion. It equally held a similar ranking in 2008.[98] Despite higher capitalisation reaching USD 16.231

88. See *Quarterly Bulletin*, Arab Monetary Fund, No. 51, (3rd Quarter, 2007), pp. 77–78.
89. See *Quarterly Bulletin*, Arab Monetary Fund, No. 65, (2nd Quarter, 2011), p. 109.
90. See *Quarterly Bulletin*, Arab Monetary Fund, No. 61, (1st & 2nd Quarter, 2010), p. 109.
91. See *Quarterly Bulletin*, Arab Monetary Fund, No. 54, (2nd Quarter, 2008), p. 81.
92. See *Quarterly Bulletin*, Arab Monetary Fund, No. 51, (3rd Quarter, 2007), pp. 77–78.
93. See *Quarterly Bulletin*, Arab Monetary Fund, No. 65, (2nd Quarter, 2011), p. 109.
94. See *Quarterly Bulletin*, Arab Monetary Fund, No. 61, (1st & 2nd Quarter, 2010), p. 109.
95. See *Quarterly Bulletin*, Arab Monetary Fund, No. 54, (2nd Quarter, 2008), p. 81.
96. See *Quarterly Bulletin*, Arab Monetary Fund, No. 51, (3rd Quarter, 2007), pp. 77–78.
97. See *Quarterly Bulletin*, Arab Monetary Fund, No. 65, (2nd Quarter, 2011), p. 109.
98. See *Quarterly Bulletin*, Arab Monetary Fund, No. 61, (1st & 2nd Quarter, 2010), p. 109.

billion in June 2008, it was also the eleventh largest, representing 1.17% of the total value of Arab stock exchanges.[99] This position was not too dissimilar to the previous year. For, in September 2007, it capitalised at USD 9.266 billion – equally being the eleventh largest, having comprised 1.89% of total value of Arab stock exchanges.[100]

(12) *The Tunis Stock Exchange*. This market is among a number of Arab stock exchanges whose ranking, over recent years, in terms of capitalisation has seen no change. This is especially as it was the twelfth largest in June 2011 capitalising at USD 9.67 billion.[101] This was similar to its position in June 2010 when it also ranked the twelfth largest having capitalised at USD 9.464 billion, representing 1.09% of the total value of Arab stock exchanges.[102] This ranking was not too dissimilar to the one reached in 2008 – having capitalised at USD 6.614 billion, representing 0.48% of the total value of Arab stock exchanges.[103] The Tunis Stock Exchange equally ranked the twelfth largest in September 2007 – forming 0.47% of the total value of Arab stock exchanges, capitalising at USD 4.903 billion.[104]

(13) *The Palestine Exchange.* It slightly improved on its ranking in 2011 and 2010 as it was the thirteenth largest in terms of capitalisation. For example, in June 2011, it capitalised at USD 2.81 billion.[105] In June 2010, it represented 0.29% of total value of Arab stock exchanges, capitalising at USD 2.545 billion.[106] However, this as mentioned above represented an improvement. For, in June 2008, it ranked the fourteenth largest despite a higher capitalisation of USD 3.118 billion, constituting 0.22% of total value of Arab stock exchanges.[107] This equally was not too dissimilar to the previous year – having capitalised at USD 2.439 billion, representing 0.23% of total value of Arab stock exchanges in September 2007.[108]

(14) *The Khartoum Stock Exchange*. Its ranking in June 2011 and June 2010 was a step backward as it reverted to the fourteenth position. For example in June 2011 it was capitalised at USD 2.61 billion.[109] In June 2010 it roughly constituted 0.29% of the total value of Arab stock exchanges, capitalising at USD 2.519 billion.[110] This is especially as it normally ranked the thirteenth largest. For example, in June 2008, it ranked the

---

99. See *Quarterly Bulletin*, Arab Monetary Fund, No. 54, (2nd Quarter, 2008), p. 81.
100. See *Quarterly Bulletin*, Arab Monetary Fund, No. 51, (3rd Quarter, 2007), pp. 77–78.
101. See *Quarterly Bulletin*, Arab Monetary Fund, No. 65, (2nd Quarter, 2011), p. 109.
102. See *Quarterly Bulletin*, Arab Monetary Fund, No. 61, (1st & 2nd Quarter, 2010), p. 109.
103. See *Quarterly Bulletin*, Arab Monetary Fund, No. 54, (2nd Quarter, 2008), p. 81.
104. See *Quarterly Bulletin*, Arab Monetary Fund, No. 51, (3rd Quarter, 2007), pp. 77–78.
105. See *Quarterly Bulletin*, Arab Monetary Fund, No. 65, (2nd Quarter, 2011), p. 109.
106. See *Quarterly Bulletin*, Arab Monetary Fund, No. 61, (1st & 2nd Quarter, 2010), p. 109.
107. See *Quarterly Bulletin*, Arab Monetary Fund, No. 54, (2nd Quarter, 2008), p. 81.
108. See *Quarterly Bulletin*, Arab Monetary Fund, No. 51, (3rd Quarter, 2007), pp. 77–78.
109. See *Quarterly Bulletin*, Arab Monetary Fund, No. 65, (2nd Quarter, 2011), p. 109.
110. See *Quarterly Bulletin*, Arab Monetary Fund, No. 61, (1st & 2nd Quarter, 2010), p. 109.

thirteenth largest, having capitalised at USD 3.772 billion, constituting 0.27% of the total value of Arab stock exchanges.[111] Khartoum Stock Exchange equally ranked the thirteenth largest in September 2007, comprising 0.37% of the total value of Arab stock exchanges, having capitalised at USD 3.877 billion.[112]

(15) *The Bourse d'Alger.* It has consistently ranked the fifteenth largest Arab securities market. For example, it was the fifteenth largest in June 2010 – constituting 0.01% of total value of Arab stock exchanges, capitalising at a meagre USD 96 million.[113] This fifteenth position was not much different from, for example, June 2008 when the Bourse d'Alger equally represented 0.01% of the total value of Arab stock exchanges, capitalising at USD 102 million.[114] This fifteenth position in terms of relative capitalisation was also the case in September 2007. For, in that year the Bourse d'Alger capitalised at USD 100 million, comprising 0.01% of the total value of Arab stock exchanges.[115]

Added to the above Arab securities markets are the newly established securities markets in Iraq, Libya and Syria. However, they have not been added to the above list due to the fact that their statistics still have not yet been fully incorporated by the Arab Monetary Fund.[116] Nevertheless, these three capital markets remain relatively active and offer promising potential, with the Damascus Stock Exchange performing well since its inception in March 2009:

(1) *The Iraqi Stock Exchange.* This stock exchange replaced the former Baghdad Stock Exchange in 2004. The Iraq Stock Exchange capitalisation is estimated to have reached roughly USD 3.0 billion by mid-June 2010.[117]

(2) *The Libyan Stock Exchange.* In April 2010, the Libyan Stock Exchange capitalisation was estimated at LYD 3,830,808,459, equating to roughly USD 3.277 billion.[118] Its capitalisation on 19 September 2010 reached LYD 3,464,241,138 or approximately USD 2.963 billion.[119] Reliable estimates put its capitalisation on 12 October 2010 to be worth LYD 3,495,658,831 (roughly USD 2.865 billion).[120]

(3) *The Damascus Stock Exchange.* This is the newest Arab capital market to be established. By 1 November 2010 it was estimated to have been

111. See *Quarterly Bulletin*, Arab Monetary Fund, No. 54, (2nd Quarter, 2008), p. 81.
112. See *Quarterly Bulletin*, Arab Monetary Fund, No. 51, (3rd Quarter, 2007), pp. 77–78.
113. See *Quarterly Bulletin*, Arab Monetary Fund, No. 61, (1st & 2nd Quarter, 2010), p. 109.
114. See *Quarterly Bulletin*, Arab Monetary Fund, No. 54, (2nd Quarter, 2008), p. 81.
115. See *Quarterly Bulletin*, Arab Monetary Fund, No. 51, (3rd Quarter, 2007), pp. 77–78.
116. It however must be mentioned that statistics on the Damascus Stock Exchange began to be included from 2011.
117. Information provided by the Iraqi Stock Exchange.
118. Information provided by the Damascus Stock Exchange.
119. *Ibid.*
120. See for example *Tripoli Post*, 'Libyan Stock Exchange up', 12 October 2010.

capitalised at roughly USD 2.847 billion.[121] In June 2011 it capitalised at USD 2.27 billion.[122] This however is a very encouraging figure having by 15 June 2009 capitalised at SYP 85,151,176.00 – roughly equating to USD 1.844 billion.[123]

Having discussed Arab stock exchanges in terms of their respective capitalisation relative to overall value, the subsection below addresses the division between Arab capital markets in terms of broad underlying macroeconomic and regulatory conditions.

It is relevant to mention here the ongoing (short-term) economic costs of the Arab Spring which took place in 2011 – largely affecting Bahrain, Egypt, Libya, Syria, Tunisia and Yemen. Indeed, by the end of September 2011 it was estimated that the combined total cost (GDP plus public finances) was roughly USD 55.88 billion – broken down in *The Cost of the Arab Spring: Roadmap for G20/UN Support?* (Geopolicity Inc., October 2011). This report on p. vi shows the combined cost as USD 55.84 billion, as follows:

1. Bahrain: USD 1.09 billion;
2. Egypt: USD 9.79 billion;
3. Libya: USD 14.2 billion;
4. Syria: USD 27.3 billion;
5. Tunisia: USD 2.52 billion; and
6. Yemen: USD 0.98 billion.

For his part, the author used the individual aggregation of the combined total (cost to GDP plus cost to public finances) as outlined by the report [i.e., USD 1.09 billion, USD 9.79 billion, USD 14.2 billion, USD 27.3 billion, USD 2.52 billion, USD 0.98 billion.] This adds up to USD 55.88 billion, not USD 55.84 billion. This is especially as the report's aforementioned figures on p. vi regarding Yemen do not appear to add up [i.e., cost to GDP quoted as USD 0.12 billion and cost to public finances also quoted as USD 0.12 billion] – marginally impacting on the total figures for cost to GDP as well as cost to public finances. Nevertheless, this report represented the first serious attempt to quantify the financial costs of the Arab Spring. Hence its inclusion in this book.

3. DIVISION IN TERMS OF BROAD UNDERLYING MACROECONOMICS AND REGULATORY STRUCTURE

Taking into account the per capita income and the capacity to export oil, Arab countries are generally divided into: *high-income oil producers* (Bahrain, Kuwait, Oman, Qatar, Saudi Arabia and the United Arab Emirates); *middle-income oil*

121. Information provided by the Damascus Stock Exchange.
122. See *Quarterly Bulletin*, Arab Monetary Fund, No. 65 (2nd Quarter, 2011), p. 109.
123. Information provided by the Damascus Stock Exchange.

producers (Algeria, Iraq, Libya, Syria and Yemen); *middle-income non-oil producers*: (Egypt, Jordan, Lebanon, Morocco, the emerging Palestinian entity and Tunisia); and *low-income non-oil producers*: (Djibouti, Mauritania[124] and Somalia).[125]

However, when examining Arab securities markets within the framework of their regulatory and macroeconomic environment, one generally speaks of four distinct groups of Arab countries.[126]

3.1. Not Likely Existence of Capital Markets in the Short to Medium Term

The first category consists of countries like Djibouti, Mauritania and Somalia. These countries either lack the requisite macroeconomic foundations or the operational infrastructure necessary for securities markets, or both. Particularly in the case of Djibouti and Mauritania, despite internal instability, these countries are not technically failed States as such. They continue in their strife to better their economic conditions and address steep problems in their underlining macroeconomic conditions.

For example, while Djibouti's average total government debt percentage of its GDP in 2000–2005 was 59.1%, it decreased to 56.8% in 2006. This however increased to 63.6%, before decreasing to 60.2% in 2007 and 2008, respectively. This was projected to decrease further to 58.8% in 2010 and to 55.4% in 2011.[127] However, Djibouti's average nominal GDP remains almost negligible. For example, in 2000–2005 it was USD 0.6 billion, increasing to USD 0.8 billion in 2006 and holding steady at USD 0.8 billion in 2007. It marginally increased to USD 1.0 billion and held steady at USD 1.0 billion in 2008 and 2009, respectively. It was projected to reach USD 1.1 billion and USD 1.2 billion in 2010 and 2011, respectively.[128]

For its part, Mauritania's new investment law was approved in December 2001. This improved opportunities for direct foreign investment in the country and provided it with a much needed legal structure. Additionally, Mauritania and the International Monetary Fund (IMF) agreed to a three-year Poverty Reduction and Growth Facility (PRGF) in 2006. Mauritania made satisfactory progress. However, following the August 2008 coup, the IMF and World Bank suspended

---

124. This is despite the fact that Mauritania became a net exporter of oil in 2006. Oil prospects initially were promising. However, they have largely failed to materialise – hence the inclusion of Mauritania in this category.
125. See for example M Fouad et al., 'Public Debt and Fiscal Vulnerability in the Middle East', IMF, WP/07/12 (January 2007), p. 5.
126. See, for example, A Abisourour, 'The Emerging Arab Capital Markets: Status, Role and Development Prospects', in S El-Naggar *Financial Policies and Capital Markets in Arab Countries*, IMF, 1994, pp. 65–66.
127. See IMF, *World Economic and Financial Surveys: Regional Economic Outlook, Middle East and Central Asia,* International Monetary Fund, Washington DC, (October 2010), p. 67.
128. *Ibid.*, p. 57.

their programmes in Mauritania. Nevertheless, after the July 2009 presidential elections, the IMF and World Bank became engaged with the new government.[129]

Having said the above, one must clearly state that such countries are now in the minority. For, as shall be seen below, the overwhelming majority of Arab countries (within the past few years) have been actively seeking to establish formal equity markets.

3.2. Newly, About To Be Set Up, or Stock Exchanges with Limited Impact in the Overall Economy

The second group consists of Arab countries that are about to establish stock exchanges, have recently set up securities markets, or those in which stock exchanges play a limited role in the wider national economy. Such group comprises countries such as Algeria, Iraq, Libya, Palestinian Authority, Sudan, Syria and Yemen. Although these countries have now set up equity markets, the role of such markets remains at best limited. Additionally, the role of the private sector (including private banking) is yet to be defined and enhanced. Nevertheless, it must be mentioned here that these countries are undergoing rapid economic reform that would have been unimaginable only a decade ago. This is particularly the case in Syria and Libya as shall be seen below.

3.2.1. Algeria

Algeria established a securities market on 28 July 1999 having initially three listed companies.[130] The number of listed companies is still in fact very thin, having reached only two at the end of September 2007. This number has not changed much during 2008 and 2010, when it equally stood at two by June 2010. As far as market capitalisation is concerned, while at the end of March 2004 it reached USD 148.5 million,[131] it was a meagre USD 95.7 million at the end of December 2006,[132] rising again to USD 100 million by the end of September 2007.[133] As seen above, capitalisation in June 2010 did not exceed USD 100 million.

Due to chronic shortage of listed companies and limiting trading days on the capital market to no more than two, the volume of trading is negligibly low. For example, daily average trading value on the Bourse d'Alger did not total more than USD 0.0048 million for the second quarter in 2006.[134] However, one must hasten to add that although still relatively very low, this volume of trading has been

129. See for example *2010 World Fact Book of the United States Central Intelligence Agency (CIA)*.
130. These are: (1) Eriad-Setif (a food processing company); (2) Saidal (a pharmaceutical company); and (3) El Aurassi Hotel.
131. See *Quarterly Bulletin*, Arab Monetary Fund, No. 37, (1st Quarter, 2004), p. 72.
132. See *Quarterly Bulletin*, Arab Monetary Fund, No. 48, (4th Quarter, 2006), p. 74.
133. See *Quarterly Bulletin*, Arab Monetary Fund, No. 51, (3rd Quarter, 2007), pp. 77–78.
134. See *Quarterly Bulletin*, Arab Monetary Fund, No. 49, (1st Quarter, 2007), p. 89.

improving recently from historical lows – having, for example, reached an average daily trading volume of USD 2.239 million for the second quarter in 2010.[135] Nevertheless, it must be stated here that Algeria's banking system is still dominated by no more than a handful of state-owned banks.[136]

3.2.2. Iraq

For its part, Iraq opened a limited stock exchange in 1992, regulated by the Baghdad Stock Exchange Law No. (24) for the year 1991. In January 1997, new listing and admission regulations were promulgated (in accordance with Article 26 of Law No. (24) for the year 1991). Nevertheless, despite the fact that the number of listed companies then exceeded an average of 100, market capitalisation was generally very small compared to the full potential of the national economy – reaching only USD 394 million in early 2001.[137]

Nevertheless, following the dislodgement of the political regime in 2003, a new stock exchange comprising of fifteen listed companies replaced the former exchange – with active trading having started on 24 June 2004. There is now a new Iraqi Securities Commission, which is responsible for all regulatory aspects. New regulations issued in March 2007 by the Iraqi Securities Commission allow foreign investors to buy and sell shares on the Iraq Stock Exchange. Although, the expectations are high, it still remains to be seen how far this new exchange will go in acting as a genuine engine for Iraqi economic growth. Setting the (present) deteriorating political and security conditions aside, early indications point to a new modern Iraqi investment law that will eventually remove most of the barriers imposed on non-Iraqis. This law came into force in March 2007, offering, *inter alia*, tax exemptions, protecting investors' assets, etc.

However, by the end of 2006, market capitalisation was estimated at USD 115 million, while the number of listed companies was 100, reducing to 94 companies by the end of November 2007.[138] As seen above in terms of its capitalisation, the Iraqi Stock Exchange continues to make relatively encouraging progress having (as seen from the discussion above) capitalised in 2010 at nearly USD 3.00 billion. Moreover, in October 2010 it had ninety listed companies, forty-five licensed brokers and a daily turnover of USD 2 million.[139] The total shares traded on the Iraqi Stock Exchange in 2009 were estimated at 211 billion shares. This

135. See *Quarterly Bulletin*, Arab Monetary Fund, No. 61, (1st & 2nd Quarter, 2010), p. 111.
136. Among such banks are: (1) Banque Nationale d'Algérie (BNA); (2) Banque Extérieure d'Algérie (BEA); (3) Banque de l'Agriculture et du Développement Rural (BADR); (4) Crédit Populaire d'Algérie (CPA); (5) Banque de Développement Local (BDL); and (6) Caisse Nationale d'Epargne et de Prévoyance (CNEP).
137. According to official statements released in early 2001 by then Baghdad Stock Exchange.
138. See *Al-Sharq Al-Awsat* (London) 6 Apr. 2007 and 12 Dec. 2007.
139. See *The National* (United Arab Emirates) 'Iraqi Stock Exchange Law before Parliament', 1 Oct. 2010.

represented an increase of nearly 40% when compared with the number of traded shares in 2008.[140]

Total volume of trading on the Iraqi Stock Exchange for 2009 was USD 368 million, representing an increase of 36% from the previous year. However, this represents a woefully small volume given the full potential of the Iraqi national economy, especially given the huge revenue achieved from its oil industry. For example, by 30 September 2010, the Iraqi government had received USD 35.60 billion in oil revenue. Given this, projections for oil revenue for the full 2010 were estimated at USD 47.47 billion – 28% more than the USD 37.02 billion revenue achieved in 2009.[141]

Having said the above, one must state that despite political and security problems, the IMF as early as 2006 acknowledged that Iraq continued to make progress. This was particularly in its fiscal policy, about which the IMF stated that it was being conducted through an appropriate budgetary process, agreeing also that fiscal targets were generally met. The IMF also accepted that the exchange rate against the US dollar was stable, and that the central bank's foreign reserves were increasing.[142] However, it was less complementary about the state of inflation and Iraq's progress in attempting structural reform. This is especially as inflation in Iraq increased to 65% in the year to December 2006.[143] For its part, Iraqi official statistics state that inflation receded to 41% by July 2007, with foreign capital reserves in the Iraqi Central Bank reaching USD 21 billion.[144] Furthermore, the situation vis-à-vis inflation improved markedly since then, especially as IMF projections for 2010 and 2011 were 5.1% and 5.0%, respectively.[145]

3.2.3. Libya

Libya is the second latest Arab country to establish a stock exchange. Following the collapse of the Gaddafi regime in 2011, it is helpful here to track historically the moves that led to the setting up of the Libyan Stock Exchange. Indeed, pursuant to Decision No. (105) on 24 May 2005, the Secretariat of the General People's Committee for Trade and Commerce was asked to *set up a stock exchange and take all necessary requirements to oversee this process in a manner that would make it take its role in facilitating investment and enlarging the base of ownership through*

140. See *Federation of Euro-Asian Stock Exchanges Annual Report June 2010*, p. 88.
141. See for example Special Inspector General for Iraq Reconstruction: Quarterly Report to the United States Congress, 30 October 2010, p. 44.
142. See *World Economic and Financial Surveys, Regional Economic Outlook: Middle East and Central Asia*, IMF, September 2006, p. 16.
143. See country report on Iraq by International Monetary Fund. IMF Country Report No. 07/115 (March 2007), p. 5.
144. See interview with the governor of the Iraqi Central Bank. *Al-Sharq Al-Awsat* (London) 27/7/2007.
145. See IMF, *World Economic and Financial Surveys: Regional Economic Outlook, Middle East and Central Asia, International Monetary Fund, Washington DC*, (October 2010), p. 25.

trading in shares and bonds . . . As a result, the Libyan Stock Exchange was established by Decision No. (134) of the General People's Committee, on 3 June 2006.[146]

The Libyan Stock Exchange was officially opened on 12 March 2007, with a handful of listed companies. Since then, the General People's Committee issued Decision No (436) on 13 July 2008 regulating the Libyan Stock Exchange. On 4 April 2008 the Libyan Stock Exchange became automated, though it must be admitted that the number of listed companies did not exceed seven. In this respect, it must be emphasised that in 2010 trading in shares took place only in the ten most actively traded listed companies. This conformed to a pattern of trading that seems at this stage to typify the Libyan Stock Exchange in terms of limited listed companies.

In this respect, one must mention June 2009, when Decision No. (14) allowed non-residential investors to own up to 5% of a listed company. Seen from a historical perspective, this undoubtedly represented a huge positive step, given Libya's traditionally dismissive stance on this matter under the former Gaddafi regime.

Following the civil conflict in Libya and NATO's involvement in the wake of UN Security Council Resolution 1973 (March 2011), the economic situation deteriorated significantly – this is especially as the Libyan economy was projected to shrink by 19% in 2011, after growing by 7.4% in 2010. Inflation rate was also projected to jump to 12.1% in 2011 from 4.7% in 2010.[147] Prior to the civil conflict, Libya exported approximately 1.7 million barrels constituting nearly 2% of the total global oil export capacity. However, Libya's oil exports dwindled by nearly 75% throughout much of 2011 and had been projected to grind to a halt should the Libyan conflict develop to a full-blown civil war – which it did not.

The dictatorial Gaddafi regime collapsed in August 2011. The international recognition of the Libyan National Transitional Council (NTC) resulted in unfreezing of substantial Libyan assets totalling billions – with only China giving some cause for concern in early September 2011. The immediate future of the Libyan Stock Exchange remained in the balance, especially as it closed for much of 2011. For its part, following the formation of the new government, Libya resumed its oil production in November 2011 to the tune of nearly 600,000 barrels – with expectations of reaching a total daily production of 800,000 barrels by the end of 2011.

3.2.4. The Palestinian Authority

For its part, the establishment of the Palestinian Securities Exchange (PSE), which later became known as the Palestinian Exchange, was initially a purely private initiative – by the Palestine Development and Investment Company (PADICO) and SAMED.[148] The PSE was incorporated as a private shareholding company in

146. Information provided by the Libyan Stock Exchange.
147. See *The 2011 African Economic Outlook*, released in Lisbon in June 2011.
148. SAMED is the Palestine Martyrs Works Society. It was set up by the Palestinian Liberation Organisation (PLO) in the 1970s. It has a large international portfolio invested worldwide.

early 1995, and commenced trading in February 1997 with eight listed companies.[149] The PSE was initially supervised by the Ministry of Finance. The private status of the PSE was since subject to examination and the PSE decided in February 2007 to convert to a public shareholding company. However, this did not materialise before February 2010 when it became a public shareholding company.

Since its inception,[150] the PSE has undergone considerable technological developments, the latest of which was in April 2007 when e-trading was launched. By the end of December 2006, PSE's capitalisation was USD 2.729 billion, while the number of listed companies was thirty-three.[151] By the end of September 2007, due to the turmoil in the underlying political conditions, market capitalisation decreased to USD 2.493 billion.[152] However, as seen above, the capitalisation of the Palestine Exchange reached USD 2,545 billion, with thirty-eight listed companies.[153] By May 2011 there were forty-six listed companies, with market capitalisation of nearly USD 2.8 billion – subdivided into five main economic sectors: banking and financial services, insurance, investments, industry, and services.[154]

The PSE remains highly vulnerable to intra-Palestinian domestic strife and the ebbing and flowing of the dynamics of the Palestinian-Israeli peace process. Additionally, when compared to the majority of Arab countries, the underlying general legal environment in the Palestinian Authority areas leaves much to be desired. Having said this, one must equally state that the Palestinian National Authority promulgated *The Laws on the Encouragement of Investment.* These laws stipulate various categories of investment projects which are exempt from tax and custom duties. For example, projects with paid up capital of more than USD 500,000 and for projects, which permanently employ at least twenty-five Palestinians and expected to stay in business for at least ten years, will be exempt from taxes and duties for five years. Projects with a paid-up capital of more than USD 150,000 and less than USD 500,000 and/or projects which permanently employ at least twenty-five Palestinians and expected to stay in business for at least six years, will be exempt from taxes for the first three years.

Palestinian financial laws also guarantee against 'nationalisation, expropriation, and confiscation'. They also accept the admissibility of dispute resolution through arbitration. Property rights are defined in laws dealing with land, immovables, tangible and intellectual property. The Civil Code covers exchange of property rights. Company law and new foreign investment laws govern business entry and exit. There are also some bankruptcy and liquidation measures, together with trade rules, labour, tax, banking and insurance laws. The registration of companies comes under the Jordanian Companies law of 1964, applicable in the West Bank and the Companies Law of 1929 applicable in Gaza.

---

149. This took place through the sale of 100 shares of the Arab Insurance Company for JD 4 per unit.
150. EFA Software Services, a Canadian company provided both the trading, settlement and clearing systems for the PSE.
151. See *Quarterly Bulletin*, Arab Monetary Fund, No. 48, (4th Quarter, 2006), p. 79.
152. See *Quarterly Bulletin*, Arab Monetary Fund, No. 51, (3rd Quarter, 2007), pp. 77–78.
153. See *Quarterly Bulletin*, Arab Monetary Fund, No. 61, (1st & 2nd Quarter, 2010), p. 109.
154. Information provided by the Palestinian Stock Exchange in June 2011.

In terms of specific legal development pertaining to the PSE, one states that a Palestinian securities law was drafted in close cooperation between the Ministry of Finance, and the International Finance Corporation, World Bank (IFC). This later became known as *Law No. (12) for the year 2004.*[155] This law set up a securities exchange,[156] depositary centre,[157] and tackled the power of the proposed regulatory agency. The PSE's bylaws were issued in 2005 and became effective on 15 July 2005.[158] Additionally, disclosure,[159] listing[160] and trading[161] regulations were also issued in the same year and equally became effective on 15 July 2005. All or some of the disputes that arise involving the PSE can be referred to arbitration,[162] where a set of specialised regulations were also issued in 2005 to deal with dispute resolution.[163] Another important Palestinian legislation was *Law No. (13) for the year 2004*, which specifically set up a designated regulatory authority, known as the

---

155. Article (1) *Law No. (12) for the year 2004* states: 'This Law applies to: 1. The activities of the securities exchanges, authorised members, those dealing in securities and any new activities authorised by the Capital Market Authority. 2. Issuance and offering of securities and trading thereon. 3. Securities companies, investment advisors, financial managers, investors, securities experts depositary and settlement centres, fund managers, custody services, issuers, major holders and any activity authorised by the Authority pursuant to this Law.'
156. Article (5) of *Law No. 12 for the year 2004* states: '1. One or more securities exchanges shall be established in Palestine, which shall be autonomous and shall have financial and management independence. 2. Securities exchanges shall be the only entities authorised to operate trading in securities in Palestine 3. The management of the securities exchange shall be carried out by a board of directors and a full time general manager and an organizational structure and systems approved by the Authority. 4. The chairman of the board of directors or his deputy shall be prohibited from being a partner or a member of a board of directors or managers or employees of any entity which is a member of the securities exchange or be its representative. 5. A securities exchange may be restructured subject to the approval of the Authority. 6. The securities exchange shall be regulated by the Authority, its supervision and inspection. The Authority may audit its records.'
157. Article (5) of *Law No. 12 for the year 2004* states: 'The Centre conducts the following tasks: 1. Register issuers of securities 2. Act as a central depositary for the securities. 3. Audit the information entered in the accounts of investors at securities companies which are members in the securities exchange, ensure correctness of information, and enter any additional personal details in the records of the owners of the securities at the Centre. 4. Provide the services of clearance and settlement for the securities exchange and its members. 5. Handle the documentation related to transfer of securities' ownership 6. Register collateral interests in securities, pledges, court orders attaching the security, redemption of the collateral. 7. Monitor the limits on the ownership of securities set by listed companies according to their by-laws or pursuant to the prospectus. 8. Provide, on a regular basis, the issuers of securities with updates concerning the changes reflected in their records. 9. Execute the instruction of the Authority and the securities exchange concerning the shares of the board of directors of listed companies and execute the instructions of listed companies concerning distribution of dividends . . . '
158. These byelaws comprise 54 Articles and address questions such as operating and monitoring securities trading, determining where the headquarters of the exchange should be, management of the exchange, delineating the powers of the board of directors, etc.
159. These comprise 74 Articles.
160. These comprise 70 Articles.
161. These comprise 154 Articles.
162. See Art. 9(2) of *Law No. (12) for the year 2004.*
163. These are known as *Dispute Resolution Regulations*, which became effective on 15 July 2005.

Capital Market Authority (CMA).[164] As a result, the CMA was launched on 11 August 2005 enjoying an independent legal personality.

3.2.5. Sudan

The same, though to a lesser extent, applies to the Khartoum Stock Exchange – whose primary and secondary markets were set up in 1994 and 1995, respectively. For its part, while at the end of March 2004 the Khartoum Stock Exchange boasted of forty-seven listed companies (with a total market capitalisation of USD 755.6 million),[165] listed companies at the end of June 2006 numbered fifty-two and the total market capitalisation was a healthy improvement of USD 3.563 billion.[166] Indeed, the number of listed companies by the end of September 2007 did not decline and remained steady at fifty-two. Nor did it change by June 2010, equally totalling fifty-two listed companies. However, it must be stated here that the Central Bank of Sudan considers the number of listed companies on the Khartoum Stock Exchange to be fifty-three listed companies for 2007, 2008 and 2009 respectively.

For its part, the volume of trading at the end of 2006 increased by 92.1% to reach USD 969 million, when compared with 2005 which was only USD 504 million. However, the most impressive growth that occurred vis-à-vis the KSE was the number of traded shares, which witnessed an increase of over 438% at the end of 2006 when compared to the figures of 2005 – reaching 7.583 billion traded shares, as opposed to 1.731 billion traded shares in 2005.[167] As to average daily trading volume for the Khartoum Stock Exchange in more recent years, it reached USD 3.7 million for the second quarter of 2010.[168] As general macroeconomic indicators, the IMF positively reported that Sudan was tightening its fiscal stance by 1 percentage point of non-oil GDP in 2010.[169]

However, following the referendum of January 2011 which led to the splitting of the country, the Sudanese Pound (SDG) fell nearly 16% against the US dollar, inflation rose to 13.8%. This was of course followed by the emergence of the internationally recognised State of South Sudan, with its official capital in Juba – which gained its official independence on 9 July 2011. The full implications of the division of the country between north and south on the national economy as a

---

164. Article (2) *Law No. (13) for the year 2004* states: 'In accordance with this law, an Authority called (The Capital Market Authority) shall be formed, and shall be an autonomous body. It shall enjoy financial and administrative independence, and legal capacity to manage all its business. It shall carry out its function including the possession of movables and immovables necessary to conduct its business and exercise its activities, and act in accordance with the provisions of the law. 2. The head office of the Authority shall be located in Jerusalem with branches in the other districts. 3. The Authority shall enjoy all the exemptions provided to the ministries and government agencies.'
165. See *Quarterly Bulletin*, Arab Monetary Fund, No. 37, (1st Quarter, 2004), p. 68.
166. See *Quarterly Bulletin*, Arab Monetary Fund, No. 46, (2nd Quarter, 2006), p. 81.
167. See *Quarterly Bulletin*, Arab Monetary Fund, No. 48, (4th Quarter, 2006), pp. 67, 69.
168. See *Quarterly Bulletin*, Arab Monetary Fund, No. 61, (1st & 2nd Quarter, 2010), p. 111.
169. See IMF, *World Economic and Financial Surveys: Regional Economic Outlook, Middle East and Central Asia, International Monetary Fund*, Washington DC, (October 2010), p. 19.

whole and the Khartoum Stock Exchange are still not clear – though a switch to electronic trading in the Khartoum Stock Exchange was expected in the second half of 2011, raising hopes of boosting trading volumes and wider international reach.[170]

3.2.6. Syria

Since the early 1990s, Syria has been adopting more liberal economic policies that aim at encouraging private investment. In this context, *Law No. 10 for the year 1991*, which was in effect for nearly fifteen years and was seen as revolutionary when first enacted, granted productive investments (owned by Syrians or non-Syrians) tax exemptions and regulatory privileges. These 'productive investments' were however expected to create employment, promote exports, and lead to transfer of technology and managerial expertise. *Law No. 10 for the year 1991* was amended (in late 1999), notably by increasing the ceiling of foreign ownership in designated Syrian projects to a maximum of 49%.

This law has now been replaced by *Presidential Decree No. 8 for the year 2007*, which builds on the facilities offered in the previous law and adding significant ones. Most important of which is Article 7, which gives the right of arbitration in case there is a dispute between foreign investors and any private or public bodies. It also provides better protection for foreign investors against public requisitioning of their assets, increases the sectors in which they may invest and lessens the bureaucratic constrains foreign investors are likely to face.

Indeed, economic liberalisation has also gained added momentum since Syria's President approved in August 2000 the establishment of private banks in Syria's free trade zones to finance companies established there. On 2 December 2000, Syria's Regional Command Council of the ruling Ba'ath Party approved the creation of private banks and a stock market. It equally approved the adoption of a banking privacy law, and the amendment of currency laws in a manner that allowed floating the Syrian Lira. In a radical development, two private banks were set up (January 2004). Indeed, the first private bank in Syria (Banque de Syrie et d'Outre-Mer) was officially opened on 7 January 2004. Thus, ending State monopoly over the banking sector that existed for almost forty years. This trend of openness continued with the setting up of the France Bank/Syria in April 2007. However, by the end of August 2007, Syria had unprecedented seven private banks and two further banks were being set up – The Syrian-Jordanian Bank and Transbank.

Syria has also given positive signals that it is keen on reforming its corporate legislation in terms of diversifying the types of its companies.[171] In a similar vein, Syria is also updating its banking and securities laws, enacting for example, *Anti-Money*

---

170. Information provided by the Khartoum Stock Exchange in June 2011.
171. In late 1997, for example, draft Art. 337 of the Syrian Commerce Code was debated in order to introduce holding companies on *par* with Arts 232–236 of the Jordanian Companies Law 1989 or the Lebanese Legislative Degree No. 45 of 24 of June 1983 on holding companies.

Laundering Law No. 33 for the year 2005. As an indication of the increasing availability of shares that would at some stage be traded on the secondary markets, one here mentions that in early February 2007, Syria underwent the then largest ever public offering of shares by a single company – entailing the offering of 5.1 million shares of the Syrian International Islamic Bank.[172] However, it must be emphasised here that the offering of such shares was informal through local banks in various Syrian cities.

Syria equally demonstrated a serious interest in setting up a formal stock exchange and took substantial steps to bring it into fruition. Indeed on 10 October 2006 the President of Syria issued a presidential decree formally to set the Damascus Securities Market – effectively ratifying Law No. 55 which constituted the legal basis for establishing the Damascus Stock Exchange. This, however, had been preceded by *Law No. 22 of 2005*, setting up the regulatory agency. On 10 March 2009, Syria officially launched the Damascus Stock Exchange, with six listed companies at an initial capitalisation of nearly USD 400 million – comprising less than 1% of its GDP.[173] However, (as seen above) the capitalisation of the Damascus Stock Exchange increased from such initial level to reach USD 1.844 billion in June 2010. As to the number of companies listed, they were fourteen in May 2010 capitalised at nearly USD 1.2 billion, reaching eighteen by November 2010.[174] Moreover, sources inside the Damascus Stock Exchange intimated in October 2010 that by the end of the year the number of listed companies would reach twenty – equally expecting listed companies to reach thirty-five by the end of 2011.

One must state that the political unrest that swept much of Syria during May and June 2011 appeared not to have impacted in a fundamental manner on the functioning of the Damascus Stock Exchange. This is due to the fact that much of the unrest took place on the fringes of Syria – particularly initially in its southern boarders with Jordan in the city of Dar'a. For example, the Damascus Stock Exchange continued with business as usual even making announcements on 14 June 2011 regarding modifying the price of the shares of the International Bank for Trade and Finance (IBTF).[175] Additionally, despite its plummeting by nearly 34% due to regional and domestic disturbances, the Damascus Stock Exchange was still sanguine in June 2011 announcing that six more companies were expected to be listed by the end of 2011.[176]

---

172. The total value of shares was 2.55 billion Syrian Lira (USD 51 million).
173. See *Economist Intelligence Unit*, 'Syria Finance: Trading Starts on Damascus Securities Exchange', *The Economist*, 26 March 2009.
174. Information provided by the Damascus Stock Exchange.
175. Indeed, the Damascus Stock Exchange announced on 14 June 2011: 'The Damascus Securities Exchange would like to inform that the trading in the shares of the International Bank for Trade and Finance (IBTF) would be suspended on the 15th and the 16th of June 2011 (Wednesday and Thursday) based upon article 9 of the Stock Split Guide of Listed Companies on the Damascus Securities Exchange. We would also want to inform that the reference price of the shares of the International Bank for Trade and Finance (IBTF) would be modified starting from Sunday the 19th of June 2011, the new reference price would be (204.8) Syrian Pounds.' Information provided by the Damascus Securities Exchange on 14 June 2011.
176. See *The Daily Star*, 20 June 2011.

Nevertheless, the situation in Syria became more acute by September 2011. With anti-government demonstrations spreading, the national economy continued to suffer. Furthermore, in September 2011 the EU banned all imports of Syrian oil in response to the regime's violent suppression of anti-government protests. In this respect it is estimated that Syria produces around 400,000 barrels of oil a day, exporting about 150,000 barrels a day – 95% of it to Europe, where Austria was the most reliant on Syrian oil, importing about 8% of its total needs, while Italy and Germany imported about 3% of their total crude. The oil revenue provides about 25% of the Syria's income.[177]

Additionally, Syria's economy had already been hit hard by other sanctions accentuated by growing isolation. Sectors particularly deeply hit were tourism, manufacturing and foreign investment. For its part, the DSE index fell by nearly half between January 2011 and September 2011, with its Central Bank limiting withdrawals of foreign currency.[178] Nevertheless, the situation in Syria remained highly volatile following the just suspension of its regime by the Arab League in November 2011. With popular resistance intensifying, and given the brutal response by the Assad regime, the author strongly believed that it was only a matter of time before Assad joined fallen Arab dictators of Tunisia, Egypt and Libya.

3.2.7. Yemen

For its part, although it does not yet have a formal stock exchange, Yemen has taken considerable steps to reform its investment legislation. These reforms largely aim at reducing bureaucratic barriers and widening the areas in which foreigners can invest. Considerable changes took place in late 1999 on Yemen's Foreign Investments Law. In this context, Yemen attracted an estimated YER 6.4 billion in 1999 in foreign investment, compared to YER 4.8 billion in 1998. (1 USD = YER 0.0063)[179]

Ditching what appeared to be long-term held anti-foreign economic sentiments, Yemen continues to bolster its appreciation of the role of foreign investment in its domestic economy. It for example, hosted a high profile official conference in April 2007, offering no less than 100 investment opportunities to foreign investors.[180] April 2007 also witnessed another high profile conference that took place in the Yemeni capital in which the Yemeni President himself advocated abolishing restrictions facing foreign investors and opening new sectors for their investments. Such unprecedented call included opening sectors such as agriculture, electricity, industry, tourism, communication, fishing, desalination, etc.[181]

177. See *The New York Times*, 2 September 2011.
178. *Ibid.*
179. See *Al-Sharq Al-Awsat* (London) 5/2/2000.
180. This conference was held in Beirut on 22/23 April 2007 under the patronage of the Yemeni Deputy Prime Minister, Abed El-Karim Al-Arhabi, Yemeni Finance Minister, No'man Al-Suhaibi and senior officials from the Gulf Cooperation Council, GCC.
181. This conference took place on 22 April 2007.

For its part, the IMF also reported positively in 2010 that under its new IMF-supported programme, Yemen's implementation of a general sales tax, along with measures aimed at reducing oil subsidies would account for an adjustment of more than 2 percentage points of non-oil GDP in 2010 – thus widening the base for trade and income taxes as well as increasing the scope for social and capital spending.[182] In this respect, Yemen benefited immensely from the surge of oil prices in 2005 and 2006. For example, while oil revenue was reported to have been USD 1.925 billion in 2005, it reached nearly USD 3.00 billion in 2006.[183] However, while oil revenue had reached giddying heights in 2008 approaching almost USD 4.4 billion, they were nevertheless adversely affected by the downward trend that hit global markets in 2009, amounting only to USD 2.6 billion.[184] As far as 2010 was concerned, Yemen's oil revenue nearly doubled in the first seven months, reaching USD 1.47 billion – from USD 803 million during the same period the previous year.[185]

Before the serious political unrest that swept the country throughout much of 2011, Yemen had been contemplating establishing an official securities market.[186] Indeed, the momentum for setting up a formal capital market had been accelerating significantly in recent years. It is true that Yemeni officials had been expressing their desires to open a securities market for a number of years. But in 2010 concrete steps were taken to implement this and make it a reality. In this respect, on 7 September 2010 a draft Republican Decree establishing a National Stock Exchange Board was ratified by the Yemeni Council of Ministers. The Board had been entrusted to prepare an appropriate investment climate commensurate with the modern requisites of setting up a successful capital market – as well as finalising legal and organisational procedures.

In a similar vein, on 28 August 2010, the *Supreme Committee to Establish the Stock Exchange Market* approved a proposal for forming a board of directors for the Securities Authority, consisting of a chairman and four full-time members. The Committee, chaired by the Finance Minister, also approved referring the final draft decision on the establishment of the Securities Authority to the Council of Ministers for discussion and approval. However, this has now been halted as the country is deeply mired by divisions and violent political struggle that continued throughout much of 2011 – resulting even with a serious assassination attempt against the Yemeni President, Ali Abdullah Saleh, in June 2011 and his immediate hospitalisation abroad.

Indeed, it must be cautioned that in light of such serious political unrest, the Yemeni national economy deteriorated markedly in 2011. This was mainly due to

---

182. See IMF, *World Economic and Financial Surveys: Regional Economic Outlook, Middle East and Central Asia*, International Monetary Fund, Washington DC, (October 2010), p. 19.
183. See *Al-Sharq Al-Awsat* (London) 2/10/2006.
184. Information provided by the Central Bank of Yemen.
185. See *The Yemen Observer*, 11 October 2010.
186. This had come amidst a wider drive by the Yemeni President to reform the economy. Indeed, the dismissal of Prime Minster Abdul-Karim Al-Iryani by President Saleh on 31 March 2001 (after nearly three years in office) was widely seen due to Al-Iryani's inability to accomplish much of Yemen's economic reforms – launched in 1995 with help from the IMF and the World Bank. Yemen's per capita income is still less than YR 50,000 (USD 300) a year.

steep depreciation in its local currency (Riyal) as well as its loss of more than USD 1.00 billion due to sabotaging its oil pipelines, resulting in severely disrupting its export of nearly 120,000 barrels a day. Since the beginning of 2011 the country has also experienced severe depreciation in its living standards, outward capital flights as well as halting many multi-million projects in which local, Arab and foreign investors were involved.

3.3. Stock Exchanges in Oil-Producing Arab Countries

The third group consists of Bahrain, Kuwait, Oman, Qatar, Saudi Arabia and United Arab Emirates, collectively referred to as the Gulf Co-operation Council (GCC). These *capital-surplus* Arab countries enjoy operational securities markets, relatively stable economies and freely convertible currencies.

3.3.1. Bahrain

The Bahrain Stock Exchange was established in 1987 by *Amiri Decree 4/1987*. The Internal Regulations of the BSE are addressed by Ministerial *Resolution No. 13/1988* – which was amended on a number of occasions including amendments by *Resolution No. 8/1993*, *Resolution No. 1/1999*, *Resolution No. 2/1999*, *Resolution No. 4/1999*, *Resolution No. 2/2000*, *Resolution No. 4/2000*, etc. The exchange itself was set up and started operation on 17 June 1989 with, twenty-nine listed companies. At the end of 2006, the number of listed companies was fifty, up from forty-seven listed companies during 2005.[187] The capitalisation of the Bahrain Stock Exchange at the end of December 2006 was USD 21.112 billion, constituting an increase of 21.6% of market capitalisation during 2005 which was USD 17.364 billion.[188] Market capitalisation of the BSE increased further in the following year, reaching by the end of September 2007 USD 24.28 billion.[189] As seen above, by June 2011, it was capitalised at USD 19.06 billion.

For its part, the BSE is supervised and regulated by an independent Board of Directors, chaired by the Minister of Commerce. The Board of Directors has issued a number of important regulations regarding listing, most prominent of which are – *Board of Directors' Resolution No. (6) for the year 1996* regarding listing local and foreign bonds on the BSE;[190] *Board of Directors' Resolution No. (6) for the year 1996* concerning listing foreign companies' securities on the BSE;[191] *Board of Directors' Resolution No. (1) for the year 1993* regarding registration of closed Bahraini shareholding companies on the BSE;[192] *Board of Directors' Resolution No. (4) for the year 1992* concerning the issuance of securities by shareholding companies.[193]

187. See *Quarterly Bulletin*, Arab Monetary Fund, No. 48, (4th Quarter, 2006), p. 19.
188. *Ibid.*, p. 17.
189. See *Quarterly Bulletin*, Arab Monetary Fund, No. 51, (3rd Quarter, 2007), pp. 77–78.
190. Issued on 26 June1996.
191. Issued on 26 June 1996.
192. Issued on 29 March 1993.
193. Issued on 13 January 1993.

The government of Bahrain has also issued a ministerial order to prevent money laundering on the exchange, known as *Ministerial Order No. (1) for the year 2004 to Prevent and Prohibit Money Laundering on the Bahrain Stock Exchange.*[194] Bahrain also paid attention to regulating insider trading as far back as 1990, when it issued *Resolution No. (3) for the year 1990.*[195] More recently, the Bahrain Monetary Agency issued extensive guidelines, on insider dealing known as *Guidelines on Insiders* – October 2004. These contain a detailed commentary on sixty-one articles that deal with various issues such as relevant definitions, the concept of material information, prohibition against abuse of inside information, confidentiality, restriction on insider trading, defences, etc.[196]

Finally, it must be stated here that the impact of the political unrest that swept Bahrain in the early months of 2011 caused serious economic ramifications – with estimates by the Bahrain Chamber of Commerce and Industry putting total financial losses to the national economy at nearly USD 2.00 Billion. Bahrain's creditworthiness also suffered significantly as it was downgraded from (A-) to (BBB-), with its borrowing costs hitting a new high in March 2011, where yield on its nine-year international bond reached 6.84% – rising 2.1 percentage points since November 2010. However, it must be stated that the BSE was not affected significantly – it, for example, was closed only briefly in mid-March 2011 and its relative decline was considerably less than regional markets.

3.3.2. Kuwait

It must be clearly stated that up until very recently, not much regulatory attention has generally been paid in Arab Gulf countries. For, surplus wealth often resulted in equity markets being considered as speculative mediums, rather than engines for economic growth. In order to demonstrate this, one needs to pay more attention when examining the Kuwaiti Stock Exchange (KSE), as it represents the clearest historical example of Arab securities markets being used as mere speculative tools during the 1970s and 1980s. Indeed, the then Kuwaiti regulatory approach typified the state of play in the overwhelming majority of Arab countries, where lack of interest in proper securities regulation was the order of the day. However, one points out that this state of affairs was not too dissimilar to the highly under-regulated era in the USA during the late 1920s –in which margin trading and excessive speculation ultimately led to the crash of 24 October 1929.

One can trace the beginning of equity trading in Kuwait to the 1950s,[197] although the overwhelming majority of Kuwaitis then invested their wealth in real estate as

194. Issued on 31 December 2003.
195. Issued on 22 May 1990.
196. See The Bahrain Monetary Agency, *Guidelines on Insiders*, Capital Markets Supervision Directorate, October 2004.
197. During this period a number of Kuwaiti companies were established. These included: the National Bank of Kuwait (Kuwait's first shareholding company, 1952); the Kuwait National Cinema Company (1954); the Kuwait National Airways (1956); and the Kuwait Oil Tankers Company (1960).

shares were limited in volume and covered a narrow base. The period 1960–1962 witnessed a staggering rise in domestic equity trading, as thirteen public shareholding companies were listed.[198] During 1963–1970, enthusiasm for equity trading abated. This resulted in the listing of only eight new public shareholding companies.[199]

Yet, with the exception of a very few ad hoc bylaws, Kuwaiti share trading lacked (up to the mid-1970s) a regulatory framework. It is no exaggeration to add that early trading was completely unregulated. For example, the Commercial Code 1960 contained negligible references to the regulation of securities markets.[200] However, lack of governmental regulation of many aspects of Kuwaiti commercial activities, especially forward cheques, undermined equity trading in the mid-1970s. Spiralling levels of speculation and excessive forward transactions ultimately led to the first market collapse in early 1977, when on average share value dropped by nearly 20%.[201] Due to the magnitude of this collapse,[202] the Kuwaiti financial authorities responded with a number of regulatory measures expediting the establishment of a limited securities commission.[203]

As the collapse was largely a result of speculation and weak corporate governance, the Ministry of Trade and Industry introduced measures to suspend registering new public shareholding companies. It also prohibited any increase in company capital except as had already been agreed. This suspension was accompanied by banning new public issues. Thus, unwittingly making the official market thin and without sufficient depth to cater for the high demands of speculative equity investors.[204] Ironically though, due to the aforementioned restrictive measures[205] the public circumvented compliance by setting up (Gulf) non-local shareholding companies,[206] trading their equity on an ad hoc non-official, non-regulated local Kuwaiti market known as *Souk Al Manakh*.[207] Indeed, this euphoric rise in

198. Of particular importance was the Kuwait Investment Company (incorporated in 1961) which had equity holdings in projects it supported and occasionally even underwrote entire issues. Private Kuwaiti families later held 50% of this initially publicly held company. See R Wilson, *Banking and Finance in the Arab Middle East*, Macmillan Publishers Ltd. (1983), p. 102.
199. The promulgation of the Commercial Companies Law 1960 had a significant impact on the proliferation of Kuwaiti public shareholding companies. See, for example, M Al-Yahya *Kuwait: Fall and Rebirth*, Kegan Paul International (London), 1993, pp. 20–21.
200. Chapter 6, for example, only briefly touched upon the concepts of brokerages and stock exchanges, explaining in very general terms the nature of brokerage contracts (see Art. 306), and laying down general rules on exchanges' juristic personalities. In this context, Art. 323 stipulates that the Stock Exchange is a legal person with a capacity to litigate and dispose/manage its property.
201. See Al-Yahya, *supra* note 199, pp. 19–20.
202. The government also even instructed the Kuwait Foreign Trading Contracting and Investing Company (KFTCIC) to intervene to maintain share prices.
203. See generally *Ministry of Commerce and Industry Resolution No. 61 of November 1976.*
204. This ban remained in force until mid-1979.
205. Together with tighter corporate rules for registering Kuwaiti companies.
206. These companies where mostly registered in Bahrain and the United Arab Emirates.
207. During the boom years, which extended into the early 1980s, Kuwaiti financial policy encouraged borrowing (e.g., through the subsidised funds provided by the Industrial Bank and the Real Estate Bank) and injected huge sums of governmental funds into the local economy, capping interest rate while not imposing any income tax whatsoever.

companies, non-regulated trading and huge increase in traded shares was reminiscent of the pre-collapse days of the New York Stock Exchange during the late 1920s, when between March and September 1929 nearly sixty new companies were listed offering around 100 million new shares.

Limited avenues for domestic investment meant that Kuwaiti citizens could only invest their capital either in real estate or on under-regulated stock markets. Huge surplus in petrodollars, coupled with virtually non-existent securities regulation led to equity trading again becoming a highly speculative tool, where share value never reflected underlying corporate assets or commercial potential. Legal loopholes that permitted forward equity trading paid by post-dated cheques further fuelled the intensity of share speculation. This was also compounded by lack of listing rules for Gulf shareholding companies, on *par* with Kuwaiti ones. All this predictably resulted in a dramatic market crash in 1982 with aggregate bad debt amounting to USD 7.7 billion.[208]

However, the bulk of the regulatory response came in the form of an *Amiri* (or Royal) Decree issued in 1983 – which was not too dissimilar in many respects to a securities law.[209] This *Amiri* Decree sought fundamentally to restructure Kuwaiti equity markets by re-establishing the exchange as an autonomous (juristic person),[210] and equally bringing more clarity into Kuwaiti securities regulation.[211] It also laid the ground for more effective management of the exchange,[212] prescribing that such exchange should have arbitration[213] and disciplinary[214] committees.[215] It equally established a Securities Market Commission (SMC) to issue all the necessary regulations to regulate the exchange.[216]

208. See J Seznec, *The Financial Markets of the Arabian Gulf*, Croom Helm (London) 1987, p. 61.
209. *Amiri Decree Regulating the Stock Exchange for the year 1983*. Promulgated in *Official Gazette* No. 1492, dated 14 August 1983.
210. Article 1. *Ibid.*
211. Article 2 defines stocks as shares and debentures of Kuwaiti joint-stock companies and/or debentures issued by the government or public bodies. *Ibid.* However, Art. 31 of the *Ministerial Resolution No. 35 of 1983* excepts from the definition 'inheritance, wills or such other cases as are approved by the market'.
212. Articles (5–8) of *Amiri Decree Regulating the Stock Exchange for the year 1983* state that it should be managed by a market committee under the chairmanship of the Minister of Trade and Industry.
213. Article 13. *Ibid.*
214. Article 14. *Ibid.*
215. See *Ministerial Regulation No. 35 of 1983, Pertaining to Enactment of the Bylaws of the Stock Exchange*. Promulgated in *Official Gazette* No. 1505, dated 13 November 1983 – subdivided into: Ch.1 (Objective of the Market); Ch.2 (Registration and Acceptance of Securities); Ch.3 (Market Membership); Ch.4 (Negotiation of Securities); Ch.5 (Market Management); Ch.6 (Budget and Accounts of the Market); Ch.7 (Disputes and Arbitration); Ch.8 (Disciplinary Action); and Ch.9 (General & Transitory Provisions). This Decree was followed by the *1983 Ministerial Regulation Enacting the Bylaws of the Stock Exchange* – an extensive piece of legislation addressing important areas like registration of securities, market membership, negotiation of securities, etc.
216. This Committee includes the Minister of Commerce and Industry as Chairman, the Director General of the Stock Exchange as Vice-President, together with other members from the Central Bank of Kuwait and the private sectors.

The trend of enacting more laws to regulate Kuwaiti capital markets continued long after the collapse of 1982. Subsequent regulatory developments included numerous orders regulating share dealing by the SMC in 1984–1985,[217] establishing arbitration[218] and disciplinary[219] commissions. Brokers[220] were not also neglected as the SMC issued orders regulating listing[221] and the work of jobbers[222] on the exchange. For its part, the KSE now boasts as being the third largest Arab equity market with total capitalisation reaching USD 105.950 billion at the end of December 2006, with 180 listed companies.[223] Indeed, the KSE had consistently remained as the second largest in the Arab world, with its capitalisation by the end of September 2007 estimated at USD 138.24 billion.[224] It also must be mentioned here that as far back as 1996, the KSE had the first equity futures market in the Arab world.[225]

Kuwait's interest in regulating its capital markets and allowing equity foreign investment continues, particularly in recent years. For example, in May 2000 Kuwait officially allowed foreigners to invest on its equity markets. The SMC has also been particularity active in revamping many aspects of equity trading on the KSE. In this context, one must point out that in 2005 the SMC issued a number of important regulations pertaining to financial statements by brokerage firms,[226] forming a committee of six members to look into disputes and violations on the stock market,[227] forming a five-member arbitration committee,[228] setting up a seven-member appeals

---

217. See *Stock Exchange Order No. 1 for the year 1984, Pertaining to Rules and Regulations of Dealing in Shares on the Market*. Promulgated in *Official Gazette* No. 1567, dated 8 July 1984.
218. See *Stock Exchange Order No. 2 for the year 1984, Pertaining to the Formation of an Arbitration Commission and Procedures before it*. Promulgated in *Official Gazette* No. 1583, dated 21 October 1984.
219. See *Stock Exchange Order No. 3 for the year 1984, Pertaining to the Formation of a Disciplinary Commission and Procedures before it*. Promulgated in *Official Gazette* No. 1583, dated 21 October 1984. Also, *Stock Exchange Order No. 1 for the year 1985, Pertaining to the Formation of a Disciplinary Commission*. Promulgated in *Official Gazette* No. 1595, dated 13 January 1985.
220. See *Amiri Decree Concerning Listing of Brokers and their Assistants on the Stock Exchange 1984*. Promulgated in *Official Gazette* No. 1574, dated 19 August 1984.
221. See *Stock Exchange Order No. 4 for the year 1985 Pertaining to the Rules for Listing and Dealing in Securities on the Stock Exchange*. Promulgated in *Official Gazette* No. 1600, dated 17 February 1985.
222. See *Stock Exchange Order No. 16 for the year 1985. The Conditions for Listing and Regulation of the Work of Jobbers of the Stock Exchange*. Promulgated in *Official Gazette* No. 1688, dated 12 October 1986.
223. See *Quarterly Bulletin*, Arab Monetary Fund, No. 48, (4th Quarter, 2006), p. 37.
224. See *Quarterly Bulletin*, Arab Monetary Fund, No. 51, (3rd Quarter, 2007), pp. 77–78.
225. Futures contracts generally mature in three, six, nine or twelve months. The market is called El-Wa'ad Financial Investment Service, covering a limited number of stocks on the KSE.
226. *Securities Market Committee's Resolution No. (1) for the year 2005 Concerning Financial Statements of Brokerage Companies and Membership in their Boards of Directors.*
227. *Securities Market Committee's Resolution No. (2) for year 2005 Concerning Forming a Committee to Look into Violations.*
228. *Securities Market Committee's Resolution No. (3) for year 2005 Concerning Forming an Arbitration Committee.*

committee,[229] control and surveillance over managed portfolios,[230] and organisation of deposits and central depositary system.[231]

In 2007 the SMC equally issued important regulations dealing with listing on the official[232] and parallel[233] Kuwaiti stock markets. Among the more recent decisions are the 2009 *Decision* regarding forward dealing and future trading[234] as well as its 2009 *Decision* regarding dealing in the market 'under extraordinary conditions'.[235] The latter simply refers to the SMC's right to suspend trading in the market in case 'market administration fails to perform its role in organising and protecting securities trading transactions especially in extra ordinary and emergency circumstances such as "force majeure" that disrupts security and public order'.[236]

3.3.3. Qatar

For its part, Qatar is considered one of the Gulf Arab countries that instituted an official capital market at a later stage in its economic development. For, only in 1995 did it promulgate a law establishing the Doha Securities Market (DSM), which started operating two years later in May 1997. For its part, *Law No. 33 for the year 2005* (as amended by *Decree No. 14 of the year 2007*) set up the CMA and the securities exchange as a private company. Towards the end of December 2006 the total capitalisation of the DSE reached USD 60.905 billion, with thirty-six listed companies.[237] The capitalisation of the DSE increased further the following year, reaching by the end of September 2007 USD 76.11 billion.[238] As mentioned above, by June 2011, the Qatar Exchange (as it later become known) was the second largest Arab stock exchange, capitalising at USD 122.22 billion.

Qatar also set up a designated regulatory authority, known as the Qatar Financial Market Authority (QFMA), which took over regulatory and supervisory roles on 1 April 2007. The regulation of listing is embodied in the *Internal Regulations of the Doha Securities Market*, which were last amended on 9 April 2007. Qatar has

229. *Securities Market Committee's Resolution No. (4) for the year 2005 Concerning Forming a Council of Appeal against Decisions Issued by the Committee of Violations.*
230. *Securities Market Committee's Resolution No. (5) for the year 2005 Concerning Control and Surveillance over Managed Portfolios.*
231. *Securities Market Committee's Resolution No. (6) for the year 2005 Concerning Organising Deposits and Central Depository.*
232. *Securities Market Committee's Resolution No. (1) for the year 2007 Concerning the Rules and Conditions for Listing Shareholding Companies on the Official Market.*
233. *Securities Market Committee's Resolution No. (2) for the year 2007 Concerning the Rules and Conditions for Listing Shareholding Companies on the Parallel Market.*
234. *Securities Market Committee's Resolution No. (1) for the year 2009 Concerning Organising Forward Dealing and Future Trading.*
235. *Securities Market Committee's Resolution No. (2) for the year 2009 Concerning organising Dealing in the Market in Extraordinary Conditions.*
236. See Art. (1). *Ibid.*
237. See *Quarterly Bulletin*, Arab Monetary Fund, No. 48, (4th Quarter, 2006), p. 63.
238. See *Quarterly Bulletin*, Arab Monetary Fund, No. 51, (3rd Quarter, 2007), pp. 77–78.

also issued regulations prohibiting money laundering, known as the *Doha's Securities Market Decision No. (3/16) for the year 2005, on the Prohibition and Combating of Money Laundering and Financing Terrorism*. These contain sixteen articles and deal with relevant issues such as definitions, reporting suspect transactions, keeping documents, requirements for identity, etc.

Another significant development in Qatar is the establishment of the Qatar Financial Centre (QFC) in March 2005, which is a business and financial centre. It is run by the QFC Authority and the QFC Regulatory Authority. The main legal framework comes from *Law No. 7 of 2005* as amended by *Law No. 2 of 2009*. This is known as the QFC Law, providing the basic legal framework for the QFC. It equally establishes the QFC Authority and the QFC Regulatory Authority. The QFC Law also sets up the QFC Civil and Commercial Court and the QFC Regulatory Tribunal. The former, the President of which is Lord Woolf of Barnes, provides mechanisms for resolving disputes involving QFC firms as well as arbitration and/or formal resolution of civil disputes – established by Article 8(3) of *Law No. 7 of 2005* as amended by *Law No. 2 of 2009*.[239] The latter, the Chairman of which is Sir William Blair QC, hears appeals by entities, individuals and corporate bodies against the decisions of the QFC Regulatory Authority – established by Article 8(2) of *Law No. 7 of 2005* as amended by *Law No. 2 of 2009*.[240]

---

239. Article 8(3) of *Law No. 7 of 2005*, as amended by *Law No. 2 of 2009* states: 'Pursuant to this law, a court called "The Civil and Commercial Court of The Qatar Financial Centre" is hereby established as set out in the following: (a) the Civil and Commercial Court shall be composed of one or more first instance circuit, and an appellate circuit, each circuit shall consist of three Judges. The circuits shall exercise their jurisdiction as set out in the provisions of Schedule (6) added by Article (5) of this Law; (b) the headquarter of The Civil and Commercial Court shall be in The QFC, and it may, whenever necessary, conduct its proceedings in any other place in the state; (c) the first instance circuit of the court shall have the jurisdiction to hear the following disputes: 1- Civil and commercial disputes arising from transactions, contracts, arrangements or incidences taking place in or from the QFC between the entities established therein; 2- Civil and commercial disputes arising between the QFC authorities or institutions and the entities established therein; 3- Civil and commercial disputes arising between entities established in the QFC and contractors therewith and employees thereof, unless the parties agree otherwise; 4- Civil and commercial disputes arising from transactions, contracts or arrangements taking place between entities established within The QFC and residents of the state, or entities established in the state but outside the QFC, unless the parties agree otherwise; (d) the Appellate Circuit of The Civil and Commercial Court shall have the jurisdiction to hear appeals against decisions of The First Instance Circuit, as well as appeals against decisions of the Regulatory Tribunal. A member shall not sit in the Appeals Circuit to look over an appealed judgement if such member was a member of the circuit that originally issued the judgement.'
240. Article 8(2) states: 'Pursuant to this law, a tribunal called "the Qatar Financial Centre Regulatory Tribunal" is hereby established as set out in the following: (a) the Regulatory Tribunal shall consist of one or more circuits, each circuit shall be formed of three judges. The Tribunal shall exercise its jurisdiction as set out in the provisions of Schedule (5) replaced pursuant to Article (4) of this Law; (b) the headquarter of the regulatory tribunal shall be in the QFC, and it may, whenever necessary, conduct its proceedings in any other place in The State; and (c) the Regulatory Tribunal shall have the jurisdiction to hear appeals raised by individuals and corporate bodies against decisions of the QFC Authority, The Regulatory Authority, and other QFC institutions.' *Ibid.*

3.3.4. Saudi Arabia

The largest amongst these markets (and indeed the largest in the Arab world) is the Saudi equity market. For example, while its capitalisation reached USD 185.176 billion by the end of March 2004, it reached USD 326.852 billion at the end of December 2006 – constituting almost 46% and 36.8% of the total capitalisation of Arab equity markets, respectively.[241] Statistics for the end of September 2007 still placed Saudi Arabia as the largest Arab securities markets, with market capitalisation estimated at USD 355.41 billion.[242] The Saudi Market's status as being the largest in the Arab world (as seen above) did not change much by September 2011.

However, despite its traditionally sizable capitalisation, the Saudi market remained informal, until the early-mid-1980s. In 1984, a ministerial committee consisting of the Ministry of Finance and National Economy, Ministry of Commerce and the Saudi Arabian Monetary Agency (SAMA) was formed to regulate and develop the market.[243] SAMA was additionally charged with the day-to-day regulation of the market. In this context, in 1984, the Saudi Share Registration Company was set up by commercial banks, providing central registration facilities for joint-stock companies – equally settling and clearing.

Saudi Arabia has recently taken serious steps towards regulating its capital markets. In this context, the Saudi Arabian Capital Markets Law was officially approved in 2003. The law, for the very first time, sets up a new regulatory authority to regulate Saudi capital markets – the CMA. The new regulatory agency has the power to license non-bank financial intermediaries and authorise public offers. A securities' depository centre will also be established.

For its part, the CMA was set up by a Royal Decree on 2 July 2004 comprising of a chairman, vice-chairman and three commissioners. It has so far issued a number of important regulations. These include: the *2008 Anti-Money Laundering and Counter-Terrorist Financing Rules*;[244] the *2007 Mergers and Acquisition Regulations*;[245] the *Investment Funds Regulations*;[246] the *2006 Real Estate Investment*

241. See *Quarterly Bulletin*, Arab Monetary Fund, No. 37, (1st Quarter, 2004), p. 22, No. 37, (4th Quarter, 2006), p. 25.
242. See *Quarterly Bulletin*, Arab Monetary Fund, No. 51, (3rd Quarter, 2007), pp. 77–78.
243. The Saudi Arabian Monetary Agency (SAMA), or the central bank of Saudi Arabia, was established in 1952. It aims at achieving the following: (1) issuing the national currency; (2) acting as a banker to the government; (3) supervising commercial banks; (4) managing Saudi foreign exchange reserves; (5) conducting monetary policy for promoting price and exchange rate stability; and (6) promoting the growth and ensuring the soundness of the Saudi financial system.
244. Pursuant to CMA Resolution Number 1-39-2008, dated 1 December 2008. These *Rules* comprise 27 Articles.
245. Pursuant to CMA Resolution Number 1-50-2007, dated 3 October 2007. These *Regulations* comprise 38 Articles.
246. Pursuant to CMA Resolution Number 1–219 –2006, dated 24 December 2006. These *Regulations* comprise 52 Articles.

Funds Regulations in the Kingdom of Saudi Arabia;[247] the *2006 Corporate Governance Regulations in the Kingdom of Saudi Arabia*;[248] the *2005 Authorised Persons Regulations*;[249] the *2005 Securities Business Regulations*;[250] the *2004 Kingdom of Saudi Arabia Market Conduct Regulations*;[251] the *2004 Listing Rules*;[252] and the *2004 Kingdom of Saudi Arabia Offers of Securities Regulations*.[253]

3.3.5. United Arab Emirates

For its part, the United Arab Emirates (UAE) was particularly praised by the IMF in 2005 for an 'outward-oriented' development strategy, sound macroeconomic management, and a friendly business environment that contributed to 'impressive' growth rates.[254] The landmark securities legislation in the UAE was *Federal Law No. (4) for year 2000*, which was amended by *Federal Law No. (10) for the year 2003* and *Federal Law No. (25) for the year 2006*. This federal law (and its amendments) laid the ground for setting up two formal exchanges in Abu Dhabi and Dubai. *Local Law No. (3) for the year 2000* set up the Abu Dhabi Securities Exchange (ADX), which was inaugurated on 15 November 2000. Total market capitalisation for ADX by the end of December of 2006 reached USD 80.745 billion, with listed companies totalling sixty companies.[255] Its capitalisation increased further the following year reaching 95.68 billion.[256] However, the capitalisation of the ADX dropped sharply by June 2010, reaching USD 73.828 billion, with sixty-six listed companies – representing a loss of USD 10.559 billion since March 2010.[257]

For its part, *Local Law No. (14) for the year 2000* laid the ground for setting up the Dubai Financial Market, which was inaugurated on 26 March 2000. Its total market capitalisation by the end of December 2006 reached USD 86.895 billion, with listed companies totalling forty-six companies.[258] Its capitalisation saw a further increase the following year reaching a healthy USD 100.65 billion by

247. Pursuant to CMA Resolution Number 1-193-2006, dated 15 July 2006. These *Regulations* comprise 27 Articles.
248. Pursuant to CMA Resolution Number. 1-212-2006, dated 12 November 2006. These *Regulations* comprise 19 Articles.
249. Pursuant to CMA Resolution Number 1-83-2005, dated 28 June 2005. These *Regulations* comprise 99 Articles.
250. Pursuant to CMA Resolution Number 2-83-2005, dated 28 June 2005. These *Regulations* comprise 21 Articles.
251. Pursuant to CMA Resolution Number 1-11-2004, dated 4 October 2004. These *Regulations* comprise 21 Articles.
252. Pursuant to CMA Resolution Number 3-11-2004, dated 4 October 2004. These *Regulations* comprise 40 Articles.
253. Pursuant to CMA Resolution Number 2-11-2004, dated 4 October 2004. These *Regulations* comprise 19 Articles.
254. See *IMF Survey*, International Monetary Fund, Vo. 34 No. 16, (25 August 2005), p. 253.
255. See *Quarterly Bulletin*, Arab Monetary Fund, No. 48, (4th Quarter, 2006), p. 54.
256. See *Quarterly Bulletin*, Arab Monetary Fund, No. 51, (3rd Quarter, 2007), pp. 77–78.
257. See *Quarterly Bulletin*, Arab Monetary Fund, No. 61, (1st & 2nd Quarter, 2010), p. 75.
258. See *Quarterly Bulletin*, Arab Monetary Fund, No. 48, (4th Quarter, 2006), p. 54.

the end of September 2007.[259] From such level, capitalisation dropped in June 2010 reaching USD 52.259 billion, with listed companies totalling sixty-six.[260]

Federal Law No. (4) for the year 2000 (and its amendments) also laid the ground for setting up a regulatory agency, known as the Securities and Commodities Authority (SCA). In this respect, the SCA has issued a number of important regulations and amended a number of regulations issued by the Council of Ministers.[261] For their part, the current listing regulations in the UAE are found in *Ministerial Regulations No. (12) for the year 2000*, which were amended by *SCA Decision No. (5) for the year 2002*, *SCA Decision No. (16) 2004*, and *SCA Decision No. (7) for the year 2006*.

Having discussed the above two formal exchanges in Dubai and Abu Dubai, one must here mention the development in the UAE where a 'financial free zone' has been established. The legal framework for this innovative regional phenomenon was embedded in *Federal Law No. (8) for the year 2004 Regarding the Financial Free Zone*. Article (1) states that a financial free zone shall be established in any part of the federation of the UAE, where financial activities can be carried out, such as banking, insurance, financial markets, etc.[262] Article (2) states that the zone shall have a body corporate and shall be represented by the president of its board.[263] The financial free zone shall be subject to *Federal Law (4) for the year 2002 Regarding Criminalisation of Money Laundering* and equally all federal laws, except Federal civil and commercial laws.[264] However, it shall not do anything which may contravene the international commitments of the federal state.[265]

The above was then followed by *Federal Law No. (35) for the year 2004*, which stated that the financial free zone should be established in Dubai – known now as the Dubai International Financial Centre (DIFC). In this context, *Dubai*

---

259. See *Quarterly Bulletin*, Arab Monetary Fund, No. 51, (3rd Quarter, 2007), pp. 77–78.
260. See *Quarterly Bulletin*, Arab Monetary Fund, No. 61, (1st & 2nd Quarter, 2010), pp. 79–80.
261. For example, the SCA issued disclosure regulations under *Decision No. (3) for the year 2000*, as amended by *SCA Decision No. (75) for year 2004*, *SCA Decision No. (63) for the year 2005* and SCA *Decision No. (155) for the year 2005*.
262. Article 1 of *Federal Law No. 8 for the year 2004* defines the financial free zone as 'The Free Zone established in any of the Emirates of the State in which financial activities are carried on.' Art. 1 also defines financial activities as: 'Financial and banking activities and services, insurance and re-insurance, financial markets and supporting activities licensed to be carried out in the Financial Free Zone.'
263. Article 2 of *Federal Law No. 8 for the year 2004* states: 'A Financial Free Zone shall be established pursuant to a Federal decree. It shall have a juristic personality and the chairman of its board of directors shall be its lawful representative. It shall be solely responsible for the obligations arising from the conduct of its activity. The Cabinet shall define its location and area.'
264. Article 3 of *Federal Law No. (8) for the year 2004* states: '(1) Financial Free Zones, and all the activities therein, are subject to the provisions of *Federal Law No. (4) of 2002 Concerning the Criminalization of Money Laundering*. (2) Further, these zones and financial activities are subject to all provisions of Federal law with the exception of the Federal civil and commercial laws.'
265. Article 5 of *Federal Law No. (8) for the year 2004* states: 'The Financial Free Zones must not perform any activity that results in the breach of an international treaty to which the State has adhered or will adhere.'

Law No. 9 for the year 2004 established the DIFC and the various bodies required to enable it to run its affairs. The DIFC started operations in September 2004, with the Dubai International Financial Exchange (DIFX) starting operations a year later in September 2005. The DIFX is regulated and supervised by the Dubai Financial Services Authority (DFSA). The DIFX issued a number of important regulations, most prominent of which are the *Listing Rules* on 25 September 2005, and the *Business Rules* on 11 February 2007.

As the DIFC enjoys judicial independence, the above was beefed up by *Dubai Law No. (12) for the year 2004*, which tackled the judicial independence of the DIFC. In this context, courts within the DIFC are independent, with their judges appointed by the ruler of Dubai and their decisions are issued in his name.[266] The jurisdiction of the courts of first instance is exclusive to the disputes that arise from DIFC activities.[267] However, parties to the dispute have a qualified right to submit to the jurisdiction of other courts,[268] or opt for a different choice of law altogether.[269] However, the decision of the courts of first instance can be appealed before a court of appeal.[270]

---

266. Article 3 of *Dubai Law No. (12) for the year 2004, inter alia*, states: '(1) The Courts of the Centre are hereby established and shall carry out their functions in an independent manner, in accordance with the provisions of this Law and the provisions of other Centre's Laws and Regulations. The Courts shall be of two ranks; The Court of First Instance and the Court of Appeal. (4) The judges, including the Chief Justice, shall be appointed by a decree issued by the Ruler. (5) Judgements of the Courts shall be issued in the name of the Ruler.'
267. Article 5(a) of *Dubai Law No. (12) for the year 2004, inter alia*, states: '(1) . . . The Court of First Instance shall have the exclusive jurisdiction over: (a) civil or commercial cases and disputes involving the Centre or any of the Centre's bodies or any of the Centre's establishments; (b) civil or commercial cases and disputes arising from or related to a contract that has been fulfilled or a transaction that has been carried out, in whole or in part, in the Centre or an incident that has occurred in the Centre; (c) objections filed against decisions made by the Centre's bodies, which are subject to objection in accordance with the Centre's Laws and Regulations; and (d) any application over which the Courts have jurisdiction in accordance with the Centre's Laws and Regulations.'
268. Article 5(a) of *Dubai Law No. (12) for the year 2004, inter alia*, states: '(2) Parties may agree to submit to the jurisdiction of any other court in respect of the matters listed under paragraphs (a), (b) and (d) of this Article. (See above.)'
269. Article 6 of *Dubai Law No. (12) for the year 2004* states: 'The Courts shall apply the Centre's Laws and Regulations, except where parties to the dispute have explicitly agreed that another law shall govern such dispute, provided that such law does not conflict with the public policy and public morals.'
270. Article 5(b) of *Dubai Law No. (12) for the year 2004* states: '(1) the Court of Appeal shall have the exclusive jurisdiction over: (a) appeals filed against judgments and awards made by the Court of First Instance; (b) interpretation of any article of the Centre's Laws based upon the request of the Courts in a claim that the Courts adjudicate or the request of any of the Centre's bodies or the request of any of the Centre establishments provided that the establishment obtains the leave of the Chief Justice in this regard. Such interpretation shall have the power of law; and (2) judgements issued by the Court of Appeal shall be final.'

3.4. Stock Exchanges in Non-Oil-Producing Arab Countries

The fourth group consists of Egypt, Jordan, Lebanon, Morocco and Tunisia. These *capital-deficit* Arab countries now boast relatively well-regulated Arab capital markets.

3.4.1. Egypt

As far as Egypt is concerned, one says that the Alexandra Stock Exchange and the Cairo Stock Exchange were initiated in the late 1800s. Particularly in the early 1900s, they were amongst the 5th most active exchanges worldwide. However, the advent of the Nasser era, which brought with it the centralised economy and the demise of the private sector through massive nationalisation, dealt a significant blow to Egypt's capital markets – particularly after July 1961. Something from which Egypt's equity markets were not able fully to recover before the early 1990s. Indeed, they were only rejuvenated after a serious Egyptian drive to revamp its capital markets as evidenced by the enactment of the *Capital Market Law No. 95* for 1992. By the end of March 2004, Egypt's equity markets were capitalised at USD 28 billion, boasting 863 listed companies.[271]

Indeed, although the number of listed companies has somewhat decreased in recent years, the capitalisation of Egypt's stock exchanges continues to increase at a healthy rate. For example, while the number of listed companies by the end of December 2006 was 603 (nearly 37% of the total Arab listed companies), total market capitalisation reached USD 93.5 billion.[272] Market capitalisation increased during 2007 to reach by the end of September USD 115.546 billion.[273] However, (as seen above) the capitalisation of the Egyptian Exchange (as it is now known) depreciated by June 2010 as it was USD 74,780 billion, with 215 listed companies.[274]

Given the political unrest in Egypt in early 2011 that ultimately led to the downfall of the Mubarak regime in February 2011, the Egyptian Stock Exchange suffered nearly 18% drop between January and March 2011 – having also to close down for extended periods during that time. The economy had also suffered significantly, with Egypt having even-faced the risk of default. However, following improvement in the political conditions therein, this risk gradually abated. In this respect, after the new government approved constitutional reforms in March 2011, the cost of protecting Egyptian bonds against default for five years fell nineteen basis points to 352.5.

One must also mention here that a number of measures were implemented by the new government to address a deteriorating stock market. Such measures included a shorter trading day for the first week when the market reopened in March 2011. Additionally, automatic trading was to be suspended if the market

---

271. See *Quarterly Bulletin*, Arab Monetary Fund, No. 37, (1st Quarter, 2004), p. 42.
272. See *Quarterly Bulletin*, Arab Monetary Fund, No. 48, (4th Quarter, 2006), p. 43.
273. See *Quarterly Bulletin*, Arab Monetary Fund, No. 51, (3rd Quarter, 2007), pp. 77–78.
274. See *Quarterly Bulletin*, Arab Monetary Fund, No. 61, (1st & 2nd Quarter, 2010), p. 109.

suffered sharp falls and if it was necessary a 250 million Egyptian pound (EGP)[275] government fund was to be invested in the market immediately to support prices.

3.4.2. Jordan

The Jordanian case shall be considered fully in the course of this book. However, one briefly mentions here that issuance of shares to the public in Jordan dates back to the 1930s and 1940s. The first public shareholding company to be established in Jordan (1930) was the Arab Bank. This was followed by the Jordan Tobacco and Cigarettes Company in 1931, Jordan Electric Power Company in 1938, and Jordan Cement Factories in 1951. The structure of regulating the stock exchange changed dramatically after the enactment of the Provisional Securities Act 1997, which was subsequently amended by the Securities Act 2002.

The Amman Bourse was first set up by the Provisional Securities Act 1997 and took over trading from the former Amman Financial Market on 11 March 1999. This provisional Act equally set up a new regulatory body and a depositary centre. The capitalisation of the Amman Bourse by the end of December 2006 was USD 29.729 billion, with 227 listed companies.[276] Market capitalisation increased during 2007 to reach by the end of September USD 31.514 billion.[277] However, as seen above, the capitalisation of the Amman Stock Exchange depreciated by June 2010 reaching USD 29.361 billion, with a very healthy 275 listed companies.[278]

3.4.3. Lebanon

The Beirut Stock Exchange (BSE) was established in July 1920, though was affected severely by the civil war during the 1970s and early 1980s. It was closed down in 1983 and resumed trading in 1996. By the end of March 2004, the BSE boasted fifteen listed companies and a market capitalisation in excess of USD 1.5 billion.[279] However, the BSE continues to exhibit remarkable resilience in the face of regional and domestic upheaval, particularly during the summer of 2006. The resilience of Lebanese capital markets in the face of such adversity was particularly acknowledged by the IMF in its regional outlook of September 2006.[280]

Indeed, when compared to the previous year, the BSE's capitalisation increased by a staggering 68.9% in 2006 – while capital market capitalisation at

275. This was then equivalent to USD 42 million.
276. See *Quarterly Bulletin*, Arab Monetary Fund, No. 48 (4th Quarter, 2006), p. 14.
277. See *Quarterly Bulletin*, Arab Monetary Fund, No. 51 (3rd Quarter, 2007), pp. 77–78.
278. See *Quarterly Bulletin*, Arab Monetary Fund, No. 61 (1st & 2nd Quarter, 2010), p. 109.
279. See *Quarterly Bulletin*, Arab Monetary Fund, No. 37 (1st Quarter, 2004), p. 37.
280. 'The conflict [Lebanese-Israeli conflict during the summer of 2006] has had devastating economic consequences for Lebanon. Initial estimates put the damage to infrastructure at about USD 3.50 billion, including the international airport and major roads and bridges . . . ' *World Economic and Financial Surveys, Regional Economic Outlook: Middle East and Central Asia*, IMF, September 2006, p. 14.

the end 2005 was USD 4.917, it at the end of December 2006, reached USD 8.304 billion.[281] Market capitalisation increased during 2007 to reach by the end of September USD 9.266 billion.[282] As mentioned above, the capitalisation of the Beirut Stock Exchange in June 2010 was USD 12.501 billion – with the number of listed companies reaching ten.[283] The BSE has Bylaws (Decree No. 7667), which became effective on 21 December 1995.[284]

3.4.4. Morocco

In Morocco, the Casablanca Stock Exchange (*Bourse des Valeurs Mobilières de Casablanca*) was established in 1929 when the first trading session was held on 7 November 1929. In 1948, it acquired legal personality. In 1967, a legal and technical reorganisation (including a change in legal status to that of a public entity) took place. In 1993 (supplemented in 1996 and 2004), a number of regulatory and technical rules were introduced. By the end of March 2004, it was capitalised at USD 14.559 billion, with fifty-two listed companies.[285]

However, the Casablanca Stock Exchange saw excellent appreciation in 2006, when compared to 2005. For example, total market capitalisation by the end of December 2006 reached USD 49.415 billion, which constituted a staggering appreciation of 81.2% when compared to USD 27.274 billion in the previous year. However, market capitalisation of the Casablanca Stock Exchange witnessed a healthy increase the following year – reaching a staggering USD 72.429 billion by the end of September 2007.[286] As seen above, the capitalisation of the Casablanca Stock Exchange depreciated by June 2010, reaching USD 63,571 billion, with seventy-four listed companies,[287] though this capitalisation appreciated to USD 67.14 billion by June 2011.

3.4.5. Tunisia

Trading in shares in Tunis can be traced to the late 1960s, when trading on informal exchanges took place. However, as a precursor, one can state that the Tunisian Stock Market started operating in 1989. Nevertheless, not too much earnest attention was given to regulatory aspects until the mid-1990s – when capital market reform began in 1994 with the promulgation of *Law No. 94-117* of 14 November 1994. The Capital Market Council (CMF), a supervisory agency, became

281. See *Quarterly Bulletin*, Arab Monetary Fund, No. 48, (4th Quarter, 2006), p. 21.
282. See *Quarterly Bulletin*, Arab Monetary Fund, No. 51, (3rd Quarter, 2007), pp. 77–78.
283. See *Quarterly Bulletin*, Arab Monetary Fund, No. 61, (1st & 2nd Quarter, 2010), p. 109.
284. These were preceded by Decree No. 120 dated 16 September 1983 (Regulations of the Beirut Stock Exchange) as amended by virtue of legislative Decree No. 30, dated 23 March 1985, and Decree No. 418 dated 15 May 1995. Equally, Decree No. 4808 dated 29 January 1982 (Bylaws of the Beirut Stock Exchange) as amended by virtue of Decree No. 4729, dated 30 March 1988.
285. *Ibid.*, p. 50.
286. See *Quarterly Bulletin*, Arab Monetary Fund, No. 51, (3rd Quarter, 2007), pp. 77–78.
287. See *Quarterly Bulletin*, Arab Monetary Fund, No. 61, (1st & 2nd Quarter, 2010), p. 109.

operational at the beginning of 1996. The Tunis Stock Exchange (*Bourse des Valeurs Mobilières de Tunis, BVMT*) officially began activity in its new form as a private, broker-owned company also in 1996.

The present capitalisation of the Tunis Stock Exchange is still relatively small, with the total value at the end of December 2006 reaching USD 4.222 billion, with listed companies totalling forty-eight.[288] Market capitalisation increased during 2007 to reach by the end of September USD 4.903 billion.[289] As mentioned above, the capitalisation of the Tunis Stock Exchange in June 2010 was USD 9,464 billion. Moreover, the number of listed companies in June 2010 was fifty-two.[290] This however increased in June 2011 to USD 9.674 billion and fifty-seven listed companies.[291] In this respect, it must be stated here that Tunisia and the performance of its capital market in particular were singled out for praise by the IMF in 2010. Indeed, the IMF particularly reported that Tunisia's Stock Exchange was in 'record' territory, 'bucking' the global downturn trend. This the IMF attributed to efforts to diversify the financial sector as well as providing 'abundant' liquidity in the economy.[292]

However, it must be stated here that the Tunisian economy suffered considerably as a result of the revolution that ultimately led to the downfall of the Ben Ali regime in January 2011. Particularly hit was Tunisia's tourist industry which is a major employer traditionally accounting for (6%–7%) of the country's GDP, employing around 400,000 people – with projected 41% drop in tourists and a 48% decline in revenues in 2011 alone. In this respect, direct foreign investment, a key driver for job growth in Tunisia, crashed 25% over the first four months of 2011 compared to the same period in 2010. Moreover, unemployment, which ultimately drove the unrest against the old regime, could reach 20% of the workforce by the end of 2011, up from 13% in 2010. For its part, Tunisia's Stock Exchange had to close twice in January and March 2011, with Tunisia's benchmark index plunging more than 20%.

Nevertheless, despite the downturn in economic activities in Tunisia during the first half of 2011, the overall picture remains promising. For, within days of the fall of the Ben Ali regime, it was reported that French businessmen, for example, who had been operating in the country returned – with the added bonus of upbeat sentiments resulting from an economic system that was considerably less corrupt.[293] In a similar upbeat assessment, Moody's also predicted that if Tunisia continued its transitioning towards democracy and stability, the country was projected to grow 5% a year from 2013 onward.

---

288. See *Quarterly Bulletin*, Arab Monetary Fund, No. 48 (4th Quarter, 2006), p. 21.
289. See *Quarterly Bulletin*, Arab Monetary Fund, No. 51 (3rd Quarter, 2007), pp. 77–78.
290. See *Quarterly Bulletin*, Arab Monetary Fund, No. 61 (1st & 2nd Quarter, 2010), p. 109.
291. See *Quarterly Bulletin*, Arab Monetary Fund, No. 65 (2nd Quarter, 2011), p. 109.
292. See IMF, *World Economic and Financial Surveys: Regional Economic Outlook, Middle East and Central Asia*, International Monetary Fund, Washington DC, (October 2010), p. 15.
293. Such sentiments also confirmed by Habib Gaida, President of the Franco-Tunisia Chamber of Commerce.

4. CONCLUSION

Arab capital markets vary considerably in terms of their capitalisation, legal infrastructure and socio-economic matrix. They are on the whole a recent phenomenon as most of them have been set up in the past few years. Their role as genuine engines for economic growth differs among Arab countries *inter se*. However, from looking at the role such markets play in domestic economies one finds that, up until very recently, their economic role was more nuanced in countries like Jordan, Lebanon, Morocco and Egypt.

For its part, the Kuwaiti Stock Exchange typified the then general picture across many Arab countries in terms of Arab capital markets being speculative tools, as opposed to being economic engines for growth. Indeed, this misconceived perception of the role of securities markets largely accounts for the evident lack of Arab attention to regulating Arab securities markets – that would have paid attention to addressing all the complex areas involved, something which was indeed indicative of general Arab attitude vis-à-vis this area.

Yet, as the region went through the rapid phase of opening up to the role of securities markets in their respective domestic economies, this attention to the subtlety of regulation became more prominent. Indeed, in the overwhelming majority of such securities markets, the increasing attention to securities regulation is quite evident – with many Arab securities markets being fortified with legal structures that separate between, the regulatory and management aspects.

Having explained the term 'Arab securities markets', the next chapter shall therefore address the general macroeconomic conditions underlying Arab stock exchanges. It shall also explain the reasons for recent Arab interest in regulating its securities markets.

Chapter 3

Recent Arab Interest in Regulating Its Domestic Securities Markets

INTRODUCTION

This chapter looks at the recent phenomenon of Arab interest in regulating its domestic securities markets. This interest can broadly be attributed to a number of factors most important of which is a belated awareness of the role of stock exchanges as economic engines for growth. Additionally, such interest can be attributed to exhortations by the IMF and the World Bank – to set up domestic capital markets and undergo structural macroeconomic adjustment programmes, together with a consistent regional drive at privatisation. The discussion below shall elaborate on the above mentioned factors.

1. BELATED AWARENESS OF THE ROLE OF STOCK EXCHANGES AS ECONOMIC ENGINES FOR GROWTH

From a historical viewpoint, interest in gilt securities markets preceded Arab interest in domestic equity markets. The reason for this is the fiscal and budgetary benefits reaped. For, debt instruments generally provide non-inflationary financing mechanisms for governments relieving budgetary and fiscal pressures. Thus, contributing favourably to the overall stability of the macroeconomic conditions underlying the financial system.[294]

In this context, using debt markets to finance public deficits was less common in capital-surplus GCC Arab countries. However, the spiralling costs of the

---

294. See R Sylla, 'The Rise of Securities Markets: What Can Governments Do?', The World Bank, Policy Research Working Paper No. 1539, (November 1995), p. 2.

Iran-Iraq war and the 1991 Gulf War, coupled with dwindling oil revenues forced many of such countries to offset budget deficits by raising funds through issuing domestic debt securities.[295]

Having said the above, one stresses that the presence of modern Arab economies that enjoy relatively stable macroeconomic conditions should not be taken for granted. Particularly in 1980–2000, the Middle East and North Africa (MENA) region was characterised by weak economic growth, when compared to East Asia and all other developing countries. Reasons for this weak growth have generally been attributed to lack of macroeconomic and trade reforms.[296] Equally, unproductive public services, lack of private investment coupled with excessive interventionist and protectionist policies were among the reasons for such weakness.[297]

Other studies have attributed such weak growth in the region to five key structural factors, which included some of the above-mentioned factors: weak institutions, dominance of the public sector, underdeveloped financial markets, highly restrictive trade regimes, and inappropriate exchange rate regimes.[298] Additional reasons for this also related to the often non-clarity of demarcation between public and private sectors in many MENA countries. This in turn induced conflict of interest, rent seeking through policy makers acting for purely private gain and widespread corruption.[299] Studies that conducted empirical research into explaining the above, attribute weak growth in the Arab region mainly to lack of diversification, large governments and stifling the role of private investment.[300]

For their part, Arab stock exchanges were historically seen as speculative tools for quick enrichment, as opposed to being economic engines for growth and sources for alternative funding. This led to noticeable official neglect in regulating the overwhelming majority of Arab stock exchanges – also accentuated by the fact that Arab countries are bank-based. Indeed, as seen from the above discussion concerning the historical Kuwaiti regulatory experience (which then typified the general approach of Arab regulators), little attention used to be paid to regulatory aspects of Arab equity markets. It is therefore important to attain a general

295. Even the most conservative of all GCC countries, Saudi Arabia, raised its domestic public debt (in the form of debt securities) between 1996 and 1999 from 50% of GDP to over 100% – reaching in the late 1990s a staggering figure of around USD 145 billion. See J Ramanov, 'Saudi Arabia and Kuwait: Closed-Economy Cousins', *Euromoney* (May 1999), p. 62.

296. See generally Dasgupta, Dipak, Jennifer Keller & TG Srinivasan, 2002, 'Reform and Elusive Growth in the Middle East—What Has Happened in the 1990s?' World Bank Working Paper No. 25 (Washington: World Bank).

297. See generally Sala-i-Martin, Xavier & Elsa V. Artadi, 2002, 'Economic Growth and Investment in the Arab World', Columbia University Department of Economics Discussion Paper No. 0203–08 (New York: Columbia University).

298. See generally G Abed, George T, 'Unfulfilled Promise: Why the Middle East and North Africa Region Has Lagged in Growth and Globalization', *Finance & Development*, Vol. 40 (March 2003), pp. 10–14.

299. G Abed et al., *Challenges of Growth and Globalization in the Middle East and North Africa*, IMF (2003), p. 12.

300. See D Hakura 'Growth in the Middle East and North Africa', Research Department, IMF, WP/04/56 (April 2004), p. 5.

appreciation of the reasons that account for the unprecedented recent Arab interest in regulating domestic securities markets.[301]

Indeed, one such reason relates to belated awareness by the majority of Arab countries of the role of domestic stock exchanges as major economic engines for growth. This realisation was particularly poignant when many Arab countries during the early 1990s faced low commodity prices (particularly oil) coupled with sharp decline in foreign aid. Added to this, was the fact that many countries in the region struggled to find external means of financing. Therefore, the exhortations of the World Bank and the IMF on the need to enhance domestic financing and undergo structural reform played an important role in galvanising many Arab countries to re-evaluate their economic policies. As shall be seen below, many of such countries were accordingly engaged in structural programmes that aimed at improving underlying macroeconomic conditions and enhancing the role of their capital markets.

Conducive macroeconomic conditions are important requisites for the well-functioning of securities markets.[302] For, ensuring long-term yield of securities requires a number of essential elements that include non-stagnant economies, convertibility of local currencies, low inflation, reasonable interest rates, non-discriminatory tax policies, etc.[303] For example, there would be little incentive to trade on securities markets where local currencies are not convertible, or where hyper inflation undermines underlying corporate assets and/or drastically diminishes the value of local currency.[304]

2. MACROECONOMIC ADJUSTMENT POLICIES AND UNDERGOING STRUCTURAL ADJUSTMENT PROGRAMMES

Macroeconomic adjustment policies aim at bringing domestic expenditure on *par* with resource availability – thus necessitating sound fiscal, monetary, exchange rate and trade policies in order to ensure that aggregate demand conforms to the pattern of supply.[305] They also aim at improving efficiency in resource use by, *inter alia*, reducing price distortions and dismantling administrative controls.[306]

---

301. See generally, L Al-Rimawi, 'Middle East Report: Why Arab Interest Has Turned to Its Securities Markets?', *European Financial Services Law*, Vol. IV, No. 3, (March 1997), pp. 106–107.
302. See W Wasserfallen, 'Macroeconomic News and the Stock Market', *Journal of Banking and Finance*, Vol. 13, No. 4, (1989), pp. 613–26; M Asprem, 'Stock Prices, Asset Portfolio and Macroeconomic Variables in Ten European Countries', *Journal of Banking and Finance*, Vol. 13, No. 4, pp. 589–612.
303. See Agtmael, *supra* note 6, pp. 43–49.
304. See generally, *International Capital Markets: Developments, Prospects, and Key Policy Issues*, World Economic and Financial Surveys, IMF, Washington, September 1999. [Hereinafter IMF: *International Capital Markets*.]
305. See IMF: *International Capital Markets*, *ibid.*, p. 5.
306. *Ibid.*

Indeed, there is general agreement that macroeconomic stability is essential for the growth of financial sector services.

Countries should accordingly adopt appropriate macroeconomic policies that encourage competition in the financial sector, within an institutional framework that is transparent – coupled with strong creditor rights, and contract enforcement mechanisms.[307] Such an institutional framework should be buttressed by prudential regulations and strong supervision.[308] For, due to informational asymmetries and concomitant (potential) market failures inherent in financial sector transactions, appropriate regulation and supervision are important constituents of financial development.[309]

One must here state that the region has normally been praised by the IMF for its prudential policies. Indeed, in 2010, the IMF stated that the region already made some success in implementing macro-prudential policies – singling out Saudi Arabia for praise regarding its experience with countercyclical provisioning during the boom years.[310] Furthermore, the region has made substantial progress that would have been unimaginable only a decade ago. Nevertheless, although MENA countries have generally been praised for their strong prudential regulations, they still lag behind in providing proper institutional environment and still need to do more to promote non-bank sector development:

> [MENA countries] need to do significantly more to reinforce the institutional environment and promote non-bank sector development. Compared to most other developing country regions, the MENA region performs well, but it ranks far behind the industrialized countries and East Asia.[311]

The theoretical argument for linking financial sector development to growth is that a well-developed financial system performs important roles to enhance the efficiency of intermediation by lessening information, transaction and monitoring costs.[312] However, the question of whether real sector adjustment should be achieved before starting financial sector reforms has not been answered conclusively. Advocates for a slower pace of financial sector reform over real sector reform state that lifting capital accounts restrictions should be preceded by

---

307. See S Creane et al., 'Financial Sector Development in the Middle East and North Africa', Middle East and Central Asia Department, WP/04/201, (October 2005), p. 4.
308. *Ibid.*
309. *Ibid.*, p. 9.
310. See IMF, *World Economic and Financial Surveys: Regional Economic Outlook, Middle East and Central Asia, International Monetary Fund*, Washington DC, (October 2010), p. 22.
311. *Ibid.*, pp. 3–4.
312. Indeed: 'A modern financial system promotes investment by identifying and funding good business opportunities, mobilises savings, monitors the performance of managers, enables the trading, hedging, and diversification of risk, and facilitates the exchange of goods and services.' These functions are seen to result in a more efficient allocation of resources, and equally lead to more rapid accumulation of physical and human capital – as well as faster technological progress, which in turn feed economic growth. See Creane *supra* note 307.

dismantling distortions in industrial sectors.[313] On the other hand, procrastination in reforming the financial sector is likely to undermine macroeconomic stabilisation and limit countries' ability to respond to unexpected shocks.[314]

2.1. IMF's Instrumental Role in Arab Structural Reform Programmes

It is true that adjustment programmes may not have had a direct impact on Arab equity markets per se. Nevertheless, the IMF supported many early initiatives to set up some of these markets. Indeed, the World Bank, through its International Finance Corporation (IFC) and the IMF were also involved (formally or informally) with advising on relevant legal infrastructure for establishing Arab equity markets – as shall be seen later when discussing the case study, Jordan's experience in this area points to these efforts. Moreover, IMF conditionality made Arab countries become more aware of the need to improve the overall economic and legal environs necessary to attract foreign investment (whether direct or portfolio).

In its *1999 World Economic Outlook*, the IMF particularly highlighted the need to continue regional structural programmes.[315] This need for continued structural reform was again highlighted by the IMF in its report, *2004 World Economic Outlook: Advancing Structural Reforms*, where structural reform was particularly seen as a 'crucial' requisite to achieving medium-term growth prospects.[316] In its report of September 2006, the IMF was, however, considerably less critical, commending the various steps taken generally by countries in the region to effect structural reform and address long-standing fiscal imbalances.[317] Indeed, the IMF further suggested that prudent fiscal policy and declining public debt deserve

313. For example, 'overshooting' of prices in financial markets can be due to differential speed of adjustment of goods and capital markets and large capital inflows leading to appreciation in real exchange rate. See M Guitian, 'The Role of Financial Sector Reform in Macroeconomic and Structural Adjustment', in S El-Naggar, *supra* note 126, pp. 7–8.

314. *Ibid.*, p. 8.

315. Areas highlighted were: (1) improvements in commodity prices particularly oil; (2) continuing pressures for structural reforms; and (3) improvements in trade and political cooperation. See *World Economic Outlook: International Financial Contagion*, World Economic and Financial Surveys, IMF, Washington, (October 1999), p. 23. [Hereinafter IMF: *World Economic Outlook.*]

316. However, the IMF equally highlighted that unemployment rates across the [Middle Eastern] region remain high, adding that '[i]n some countries, fiscal imbalances are still large or are likely to reemerge as oil revenues decline. Thus, medium-term growth prospects depend crucially on structural reforms and, in some countries, fiscal consolidation to address vulnerabilities.' See *World Economic Outlook: Advancing Structural Reforms*, World Economic and Financial Surveys, IMF, Washington, (April 2004), p. 44.

317. See *World Economic Outlook: Financial Systems and Economic Cycles*, World Economic and Financial Surveys, IMF, (September 2006), pp. 71–2.

particular credit for maintaining macroeconomic stability in the Middle East and North Africa region. This is especially as according to the IMF a sound fiscal position constitutes a necessary condition for macroeconomic stability:

> Hence, fiscal policy and public debt deserve particular attention for maintaining macroeconomic stability, by and large consistent with Fund policy advice to MENA countries.[318]

IMF's favourable assessment of the region's prospects also continued in its report of April 2007, where it praised continued regional growth and noticeable fiscal balances.[319]

The theme of the need for continued structural reform in Arab countries was also revisited by the IMF in its *2010 World Economic and Financial Surveys, Regional Economic Outlook: Middle East and Central Asia.* In this respect, the IMF stated that the region would also need to focus more on advancing structural reforms as well as bringing a more business friendly regulatory environment.[320] This it added was needed with some 'urgency', given Middle Eastern countries' objective to maintain high growth and reduce unemployment.[321] Indeed, in this 2010 report, the IMF added that further opening of the financial sector and efforts to develop local capital markets would support this process and attract investment.[322]

Accordingly, both fiscal and monetary reforms were initiated by the overwhelming majority of Arab countries. Fiscal reforms included introducing value added tax (VAT), lessening the reliance on public subsidies and better management of public expenditure. Indirect monetary policy instruments were introduced such as allowing foreign direct investment as well as foreign equity investment, with liberalising exchange rates and trade regimes.[323] It however must be cautioned here that despite reasonable Arab achievements in addressing imbalances in their underlying macroeconomic conditions the impact of recent oil price increases should not be discounted – that is, when looking at the factors that have contributed to regional macroeconomic stability.

For their part, many Arab countries have complied with IMF structural adjustment programmes and took substantial measures to foster privatisation and reduce public expenditure. Arab countries in which the World Bank has had various ongoing operations over different periods include – Algeria, Egypt, Jordan,

318. See D Fanizza et al., 'Fiscal Determinants of Inflation: A Primer for the Middle East and North Africa', Middle East and Central Asia Department, IMF, WP/06/216, (October 2006), pp. 1, 3–4.
319. See *World Economic Outlook: Spillovers and Cycles in the Global Economy*, World Economic and Financial Surveys, IMF, (April 2007), pp. 77–8.
320. See IMF, *World Economic and Financial Surveys: Regional Economic Outlook, Middle East and Central Asia*, International Monetary Fund, Washington DC (October 2010), p. 15.
321. *Ibid.*
322. *Ibid.*
323. See, G Abed et al., *supra*, note 299, pp. 2–3.

Lebanon, Morocco, Tunisia, the Palestinian entity and Yemen.[324] Arab countries' attempts at stabilising their economies can be traced back to the mid-1980s. For example, Jordan, Morocco and Tunisia have been engaged in macroeconomic stabilisation and structural reform programmes since the mid-1980s. In 1994, Algeria followed similar programmes.

As mentioned above, commodity price stability has often had a significant part to play in buttressing the fundamentals of underlying macroeconomic conditions in many Arab countries. But to various degrees, because of the positive impact of structural reform programmes, inflation and budget deficits have equally (generally) been dropping steadily in most Arab countries – while GDP figures (real or nominal) have (generally) been on the increase. This shall become more evident in the discussion below.

2.2. Improved Prospects of Growth in GDP: Real and Nominal

Middle East and North Africa[325] has seen encouraging real GDP percentage annual growth over the years. Between 1992–2001 it was a respectable 3.4%. It reached 5.3% in 2005, 5.8% in 2006, 6.0% in 2007, and 5.0% in 2008.[326] However, with the onset of the severe credit crunch real GDP percentage annual growth registered 2.0% in 2009. Nevertheless, the region's collective real GDP figures continue to mend. This is especially as IMF projections (in October 2010) for 2010, 2011 and 2015 were, 4.1%, 5.1% and 4.9%, respectively.[327]

Indeed, when one looks at the GDP figurers in selected Arab countries, one finds an encouraging narrative. For example, Algeria's real GDP annual percentage growth in 1992–2001 was 2.0%, reaching 5.1% in 2005, 2.0% in 2006 and 3.3% in 2010. IMF projections for 2011 and 2012 were, 2.9% and 3.3%, respectively.[328]

Jordan, Morocco and Iraq are also examples of Arab countries that have seen encouraging levels of annual percentage growth in their real GDP. For example, Jordan's average real GDP annual percentage growth in 2000–2005 was 6%, reaching 8.1% in 2006 and 8.2% in 2007. It was 7.2%, 5.5% and 2.3% in 2008, 2009 and 2010, respectively. IMF projections for 2011 and 2012 were, 2.5% and 2.9%, respectively.[329] Its average nominal GDP in 2000–2005 was USD 10.2 billion, increasing to USD 15.1 billion in 2006 and USD 17.1 billion

324. See generally: *The World Bank Annual Report: Middle East & North Africa.* The World Bank, (1998).
325. This refers to Algeria, Bahrain, Djibouti, Egypt, Iran, Iraq, Jordan, Kuwait, Lebanon, Libya, Mauritania, Morocco, Oman, Qatar, Saudi Arabia, Syria, Tunisia, United Arab Emirates and Yemen.
326. See *World Economic Outlook: Recovery, Risk and Rebalancing*, World Economic and Financial Surveys, IMF (October 2010), p. 183.
327. *Ibid.*
328. See IMF, *World Economic and Financial Surveys: Regional Economic Outlook, Middle East and Central Asia*, International Monetary Fund, Washington DC, (October 2011), p. 82.
329. *Ibid.*

in 2007. It reached USD 22.0 billion, USD 23.8 billion and USD 26.4 billion in 2008, 2009 and 2010, respectively. It was projected to reach USD 28.4 billion and USD 30.9 billion in 2011 and 2012, respectively.[330]

For its part, Morocco's average real GDP annual percentage growth in 2000–2005 was 4.4%, reaching 7.8% in 2006. It was 2.7%, 5.6%, 4.9% and 3.7% in 2007, 2008, 2009 and 2010, respectively. IMF projections for 2011 and 2012 were, 4.6% and again 4.6%, respectively.[331] As far as Iraq is concerned, IMF projections for its annual percentage growth remained bullish – putting it at 0.8%, 9.6% and 12.6% for 2010, 2011 and 2012, respectively.[332] Its nominal GDP in 2006 was USD 45.1 billion and USD 57.0 billion in 2007. It reached USD 86.5 billion, USD 64.2 billion and USD 81.1 billion in 2008, 2009 and 2010, respectively. It was projected to reach USD 108.6 billion and USD 118.7 billion in 2011 and 2012, respectively.[333]

One must also mention Qatar in terms of its impressive GDP growth which was rarely matched by any other Arab country. Indeed, its average real GDP annual percentage growth in 2000–2005 was 8.7%, reaching 26.2%, 18.0%, 17.7% and 12.0% in 2006, 2007, 2008 and 2009, respectively. IMF projections for 2011 and 2012 were 18.7% and 6.0%, respectively.[334] Its average nominal GDP in 2000–2005 was USD 25.7 billion, increasing to USD 60.8 billion in 2006 and USD 79.5 billion in 2007. It reached USD 115.0 billion, USD 97.6 billion and USD 127.3 billion in 2008, 2009 and 2010, respectively. It was projected to reach USD 173.2 billion and USD 180.7 billion in 2011 and 2012, respectively.[335]

Indeed, as seen above, the Arab region's growth rate has been moving in the right direction. Even the IMF in 2010 commented that the Arab region 'stood out' by how 'well' activity managed to weather the global recession. While singling out only Mauritania (for having experienced negative growth in 2009) the IMF added that by the end of 2010 most countries in the region already 'largely' closed any remaining gap between actual and potential output.[336] Nevertheless, one must however caution in this subsection that despite the strides the overwhelming majority of Arab countries made in this area, Arab growth rate remains below the average for Emerging Markets – still far short from enabling the region to address many of its chronic problems, not least unemployment.

2.3. Fiscal Consolidation

Arab countries have, for a number of years, been engaged in fiscal consolidation programmes. Indeed, the region as a whole came in for praise by the IMF in 2010

330. *Ibid*, p. 83.
331. *Ibid*, p. 82.
332. *Ibid.*
333. *Ibid*, p. 83.
334. *Ibid*, p. 82.
335. *Ibid*, p. 83.
336. See IMF, *World Economic and Financial Surveys: Regional Economic Outlook, Middle East and Central Asia,* International Monetary Fund, Washington DC, (October 2010), p.29.

for its fiscal consolidation drive which it anticipated would lead to reduction in government deficits by 2011 in all countries apart from Lebanon.[337] Among the efforts undertaken by some Arab countries to consolidate their fiscal stance, one mentions those of Egypt, Jordan, Mauritania, Syria and Tunisia.[338]

In 2010 Egypt resumed its medium-term fiscal consolidation strategy – in the hope of reducing its budget deficit by 0.5% in 2011 and a further 3.5% by 2014/2015. This it aims to achieve through, *inter alia*, through strengthening tax enforcement, raising sales taxes and rationalising food and energy subsidies. Jordan was also intent on reducing its deficit by 1% of GDP in 2011 – through elimination on VAT exemptions, a freeze on civil service hiring (except for the health and education sectors), lowering subsidies, as well as reduced spending on goods and services. Mauritania equally wanted to trim its public deficit by nearly 4.5% of GDP in 2010 – with additional savings expected in 2011. This it intended to achieve through an increase in VAT, undergoing administrative reforms and reduction in discretionary spending.

For its part, Syria plans in 2011 to introduce VAT and continue its moderate programme of fiscal tightening – through restraining current spending and rationalising capital outlays. Tunisia equally intends to impose a nominal cap on transfers and subsidies, as well as attempting more active debt management. In order to bring its deficit down for 2010, 2011 and beyond, it also intends to lower interest payments, control wages and conduct a major anticipated reform of its pension system.

The IMF equally praised the sizable and 'rapid' fiscal policy response in many Arab countries, particularly in oil exporting economies. In its *2010 World Economic Outlook: Recovery, Risk and Rebalancing*, the IMF added that such response played a substantial role in supporting non-oil sectors.[339] However, it must also be cautioned here that the IMF equally saw a 'significant' downside risk to Arab oil-importing countries due to 'heightened' economic turbulence in Europe – as it accounts for nearly half of their total exports.[340]

2.4. Reducing External Government Debt

One must caution here that Arab countries' public debt percentage of GDP remains high when compared to other emerging economies. This was highlighted in 2010 by the IMF particularly *vis-à-vis* most MENAP oil-importing countries – whose public debt remains higher than Emerging Markets' average.[341] Indeed, in 2007 the IMF argued that in 2003, nearly half of regional countries had a debt level above Emerging Markets mean of about 60% of GDP. Furthermore, more than two-thirds

337. *Ibid.*, p.30.
338. *Ibid.*, pp..30-1.
339. See *World Economic Outlook: Recovery, Risk and Rebalancing*, World Economic and Financial Surveys, IMF (October 2010), p.85.
340. *Ibid.*, p.86.
341. See IMF, *World Economic and Financial Surveys: Regional Economic Outlook, Middle East and Central Asia*, International Monetary Fund, Washington DC, (October 2010), p.30.

of such countries were above 50% – corresponding to the median debt level of vulnerable Emerging Market economies.[342] In this respect, a number of short term factors have been advanced to account for averting a major debt crisis in the future. These included the ability of some countries to convert natural resources into liquid assets relatively quickly; the need for some regional countries to hold assets that match or exceed their debt liabilities; and the need to remedy the absence of large amounts of marketable debt in the region.[343]

Nevertheless, despite persistent difficulties in this area, Arab countries have achieved reasonable progress in reducing the percentage of their total gross external debt when measured by their GDP. A number of selected Arab countries shall demonstrate this as shall be seen below.

For example, while Oman's average total gross external debt percentage of its GDP in 2000–2005 was 23.3% it decreased to 15.5% in 2006. This further reached 17.2%, 15.1% and 18.6% in 2007, 2008 and 2009, respectively. While it registered 11.9% in 2010, it was however projected to decrease to 9.6% and 8.3% in 2011 and 2012, respectively.[344] Algeria equally made similar progress. For, while its average total gross external debt percentage of its GDP in 2000–2005 was 34.1%, it decreased to 5.0% in 2006. This further deceased to 4.2% and 3.5% in 2007 and 2008, respectively. While it reached 2.8% in 2010, it was nevertheless projected to decrease to 2.0% in 2011 and 1.7% in 2012.[345]

Djibouti, Jordan, Lebanon, Mauritania, Morocco and Tunisia have all been making steady progress. Indeed, although these countries have been tackling this at varying degrees, some countries have made better headway than others. This can particularly be seen in Syria's and Egypt's efforts in this area.

For example, while Syria's average total gross external debt percentage of its GDP in 2000–2005 was 92.9%, it impressively decreased to 24.5% in 2006. This further steadily deceased to 20.6%, 15.6%, 15.4% and 15.1% in 2007, 2008, 2009 and 2010, respectively. It was projected to reach 15.3% and 16.4% in 2011 and 2012, respectively.[346]

2.5. Steady Increase in Official Arab Reserves

Other healthy indicators can also be seen through general increases in gross official reserves. Indeed, the region as a whole continues to make satisfactory progress in this are. For example, MENAP (oil exporters) average gross official reserve in 2000–2005 was USD 191.5 billion. This increased to USD 504.3 billion in 2006 and USD 734.8 billion in 2007. It reached USD 887.7 billion, USD 864.8 billion

342. M Fouad *et. al.*, 'Public Debt and Fiscal Vulnerability in the Middle East', IMF, WP/07/12 (January 2007), p.4.
343. *Ibid.*, pp.15-7.
344. See IMF, *World Economic and Financial Surveys: Regional Economic Outlook, Middle East and Central Asia*, International Monetary Fund, Washington DC, (October 2011), p. 101.
345. *Ibid.*
346. *Ibid.*

and USD 948.4 billion for 2008, 2009 and 2010, respectively. It was projected to reach USD 1,004.4 billion and USD 1,160.9 billion in 2011 and 2012, respectively.[347]

Admittedly to a lesser extent, MENAP (oil importers) have nevertheless achieved progress. Their average gross official reserve in 2000–2005 was USD 59.6 billion, increasing to USD 97.7 billion in 2006 and USD 114.0 billion in 2007. It reached USD 122.4 billion, USD 135.2 billion and USD 147.7 billion for 2008, 2009 and 2010, respectively. It was projected to reach USD 138.6 billion and USD 130.6 billion in 2011 and 2012, respectively.[348]

Individual Arab countries have also made similar commendable strides in this area. For example, average gross official reserve for Oman in 2000–2005 was USD 3.3 billion, increasing to USD 5.0 billion in 2006 and USD 9.5 billion in 2007. It reached USD 11.4 billion, USD 12.2 billion and USD 13.1 billion for 2008, 2009 and 2010, respectively. It was projected to reach USD 13.9 billion and USD 15.1 billion in 2011 and 2012, respectively.[349]

Qatar and Saudi Arabia have equally performed reasonably well. For, while Saudi average gross official reserve in 2000–2005 was USD 73.4 billion, it increased to USD 225.2 billion in 2006. It further increased to USD 305.3 billion in 2007, USD 441.9 billion in 2008, USD 408.6 billion in 2009 and USD 443.7 billion in 2010. It was projected to reach USD 538.8 billion and USD 607.9 billion in 2011 and 2012, respectively.[350] Qatar's average gross official reserve in 2000–2005 was USD 2.5 billion. This increased to USD 5.4 billion in 2006, further increasing to USD 9.8 billion in 2007. Though it remained steady at USD 9.8 billion in 2008, it nevertheless reached USD 18.8 billion in 2009 and USD 31.1 billion in 2010. It was projected to reach USD 17.8 billion and USD 21.4 billion in 2011 and 2012, respectively.[351]

Other Arab countries have also made good progress in this area. These include Egypt, Jordan, Lebanon, Morocco, Syria and Tunisia. Jordan's average gross official reserve in 2000–2005 was USD 3.8 billion. It increased to USD 6.2 billion in 2006 and USD 6.9 billion in 2007. It further increased to USD 7.7 billion in 2008, to USD 11.1 billion in 2009 and to USD 12.4 billion in 2010. Gross official reserves were projected to reach USD 11.7 billion and USD 11.2 billion in 2011 and 2012, respectively.[352] Lebanon's average gross official reserve in 2000–2005 was USD 7.5 billion. It increased to USD 11.4 billion in 2006 and USD 11.5 billion in 2007 – further increasing to USD 18.8 billion in 2008, USD 27.4 billion in 2009 and USD 30.2 billion in 2010. It was projected to reach USD 30.5 billion and USD 33.4 billion in 2011 and 2012, respectively.[353]

347. *Ibid.*, p. 100.
348. *Ibid.*
349. *Ibid.*
350. *Ibid.*
351. *Ibid.*
352. *Ibid.*
353. *Ibid.*

2.6. Taming Inflation

As mentioned above, many Arab countries have achieved reasonable success in controlling inflation. The region's success in confronting inflation has indeed been praised by the IMF on many occasions. This state of reasonably controlled inflation has given much hope of solidifying the macroeconomic fundamentals of the region as a whole. Indeed, when one glances at the inflation figures for the region in the past few years one finds that the overwhelming majority of Arab countries have maintained commendable single-digit figures. This has especially been the case as the illustration below shall demonstrate.

One of the most impressive performances by an Arab country in tackling its inflation is surprisingly Iraq. For example, its annual consumer price inflation in 2006 and 2007 was 53.2% and 30.8%, respectively. It impressively decreased to 2.7% in 2008, registering even (-2.2) % in 2009. Although Iraq's inflation is expected to increase over the coming years, the Iraqi economy is nevertheless not expected to revert to the former situation of hyperinflation. Indeed, its projected annual consumer price inflation for 2011 and 2012 was 5.0% and again 5.0%, respectively.[354] For their part, Oman, Bahrain, Algeria, Kuwait, Jordan, Morocco, Tunisia and Libya are among Arab countries that have, on the whole, managed to keep their inflation within single digits over the past 10 years.

For example, Oman's average annual consumer price inflation percentage in 2000–2005 was 0.1%. Its inflation in 2006 and 2007 was 3.4% and 5.9% respectively. It however spiked to 12.6% in 2008 before receding back to 3.5% in 2009. Oman's inflation was projected to reach 3.8% in 2011 and 3.3% in 2012.[355] Morocco's inflation figures are equally encouraging. For example, its average annual consumer price inflation in 2000–2005 was 1.5%, reaching 3.3%, 2.0%, 3.9%, 1.0% and again 1.0% for 2006, 2007, 2008, 2009 and 2010, respectively. Its annual consumer price inflation was projected to reach 1.5% and 2.7% in 2011 and 2012, respectively.[356]

Algeria has also had reasonable success in confronting inflation. Its average annual consumer price inflation in 2000–2005 was 2.3%. It was again 2.3%, 3.6%, 4.9%, 5.7% and 3.9 in 2006, 2007, 2008, 2009 and 2010, respectively. Its annual consumer price inflation was projected to reach 3.9% and 4.3% in 2011 and 2012, respectively.[357]

3. CONSISTENT REGIONAL DRIVE AT PRIVATISATION

Privatisation has provided opportunities for investors to own shares in formerly off-limits, state-owned corporations in the majority of Arab countries. Not only has it increased the volume of shares owned by private and institutional investors.

354. *Ibid.*, p.86.
355. *Ibid.*
356. *Ibid.*
357. *Ibid.*

It has also augmented the number of listed companies especially utility, transport and telecommunications – thus deepening Arab stock exchanges.

However, the presence of private sector role in the Arab region should not be taken for granted, as it was often anathematised, with some Arab commentators viewing privatisation as vestiges of colonialism.[358] Indeed, many Arab countries were even ideologically opposed to handing their publicly held companies to the private sector or foreign investors – often engaged in nationalisation rather than privatisation. For example, during the Nasser era almost 95% of foreign and Egyptian corporations were nationalised.[359]

Nevertheless, one can date attempts at privatisation in the majority of Arab countries to the early 1990s, when privatisation programmes were introduced in a number of Arab countries. Indeed, Egypt is one of the Arab countries that has been repeatedly praised by the IMF for its privatisation drive.[360] Morocco too had a sophisticated privatisation programme that resulted in restructuring large sectors of its economy to accommodate this process of privatisation – which it dates back to the 1980s.

When it came to privatisation, Tunisia was equally never left behind. For, as early as July 1985 the Tunisian government passed a law limiting direct governmental control to 164 parent companies and in 1986 a *National Commission for the Rationalisation and Restructuring of the Public Enterprise Sector* was formed to assess which companies should be privatised, liquidated or nationalised.[361]

Privatisation of formerly owned public companies has not however been restricted to non-GCC countries. Even conservative countries like Saudi Arabia have been engaged in extensive privatisation programmes, which have eventually led to the Saudi Stock Exchange becoming consistently the largest Arab capital market – that is, in terms of capitalisation as seen above. Indeed, when implementing privatisation programmes, Arab countries have on many occasions relied on local equity markets. For example, the Kuwait Investment Authority (KIA) sold off more than USD 2 billion worth of government assets relying almost exclusively on the KSE.[362] As shall be seen later, Jordan too has equally relied on its domestic equity markets when implementing some aspects of its privatisation programme.

358. See generally, A Abu Isma'eel et al., 'Arab Future Seminar Concerning the Call to Move from Public Ownership to Private Ownership in the Arab World', *Majallat El-Mustqbal Al-Arabi*, Vol. 126, Cairo (1989), pp. 134–160.
359. See S Ibrahim, *Egypt, Islam and Democracy, Twelve Critical Essays*, 1996, p. 137.
360. See 'Keeping the Ball Rolling', *Euromoney*, (May 1997), p. 112; I Abdel-Rahman & M Abu Ali, 'The Role of the Public and Private Sectors with Special Reference to Privatisation: The Case of Egypt', in S El-Naggar, *supra* note 126, pp. 141–181; S El-Naggar 'Prospects and Problems of Privatisation: The Case of Egypt', paper presented to the Thirteenth Annual Symposium, Centre for Contemporary Arab Studies, Georgetown University, April 1988.
361. See P Heller et al., 'The Fiscal Impact of Privatisation, with Some Examples from Arab Countries', in El-Naggar, *supra* note 126, p. 107.
362. See L Namethy, 'KIA's Privatisation: A Pioneering Experience', paper presented in a seminar entitled 'Privatisation Programme: Review and Prospects', Kuwaiti Investment Authority. (17 December 1996), p. 108.

Indeed, Arab countries have now progressed far in their collective drive for privatisation and appreciation of the role their domestic capital markets play. This is even in Arab countries that have traditionally been ideologically hostile to Western style economic models – with their 'reprehensible' paraphernalia of capital markets and economic liberalisation. For example, prior to fall of the former Gaddafi regime, Libya in late 2010 was contemplating selling 40% of each of its two mobile-phone operators on the stock market. The former Libyan government had been expected to offer 5% of the State-owned '*Libyana*' and '*Al-Madar*' in 2011 in an initial public offering (IPO). This however came after Libya had sold two smaller instalments in these two companies valued at a total of USD 400 million. Indeed, the new sale had been expected to more than triple the market value of listed companies traded on the exchange to more than USD 7.8 billion.[363] However, it remains to be seen how matters shall unfold in Libya – though there is no indication whatsoever that any post-Gaddafi regime would not be a pro-market regime and even go deeper in its capital market reform and privatisation drive.

Indeed, as privatisation has become more pervasive in the region, many Arab countries now boast of equity markets that list almost all major companies in national economies. This has been reflected in an increasingly larger number of listed companies. For example, in 1996–2010 the number of listed companies on Arab equity markets increased from 1,194 at the end of 1996 to reach 1,414 listed companies by June 2010. (See Table 3.1 – it excludes the number of companies listed on the capital markets in Iraq, Syria and Libya.)

Moreover, hostile notions regarding allowing foreign ownership of local companies, in terms of foreign direct investment (FDI) have been changing since the early 1990s. In this context, Arab countries now allow foreigners to own stakes in domestic economic activities at levels never seen in the history of the region. The Middle East and North Africa economic summits, various Euro-Mediterranean agreements, coupled with Arab countries' desire to join multinational treaties like the WTO, have added impetus to the momentum of opening up to foreign investors.

For example, Bahrain allowed foreign ownership to increase from 49% to 100% of businesses in all but a few strategic sectors such as oil and aluminium industries. Kuwait now allows foreigners to own 100% of most Kuwaiti companies. Oman equally permits 100% foreign ownership of companies in most sectors. For its part, Qatar allows 100% foreign ownership in agriculture, industry, health, education, and tourism sectors, etc. Saudi Arabia permits 100% foreign ownership in most sectors such as gas, power generation, water desalination, petrochemicals,

363. Moreover, sources in the Libyan Stock Market confirmed that that was just the first phase and that total privatisation of these two companies could reach 30% or 40% in the future. Moreover, Libya had also been contemplating to list twenty new companies on the Libyan Stock Market by 2011 – including listing at least 10% of the State-owned Libyan Iron and Steel Company. See Reuters (Africa), 'Libya Mobile IPOs to be Early 2011 – Bourse', 25 October 2010.

Table 3.1 Arab Companies on Selected Arab Equity Markets from the Fourth Quarter of 1996 to June 2010[364]

Year	1996 4th	1997 4th	1998 4th	1999 2nd	2000 4th	2001 4th	2002 4th	2003 4th	2004 4th	2005 4th	2006 4th	2007 4th	2008 4th	2009 4th	2010 Sep
Listed companies	1194*	1184*	1446*	1549*	1665*	1687*	1826**	1723***	1597***	1665***	1623***	1550***	1542***	1495***	1414***

Source: The Arab Monetary Fund. Information collated from a collection of quarterly bulletins: (1st Quarter, Year 2001), (4th Quarter, Year 2002), (4th Quarter, Year 2003), (4th Quarter, Year 2005), (4th Quarter, Year 2006), (4th Quarter, Year 2007), (4th Quarter, Year 2008), (4th Quarter, Year 2009), (2nd Quarter, Year 2010).
* Based on equity markets in *Jordan*, *Bahrain*, *Tunisia*, *Saudi Arabia*, *Oman*, *Kuwait*, *Lebanon*, *Egypt* and *Morocco*.
** Taking into account the above countries plus the newly set up Abu Dhabi Stock Exchange (from 1st quarter in 2002 having initially sixteen listed companies), Dubai Stock Exchange (from 1st quarter in 2002 having initially twelve listed companies) and Doha Stock Exchange (from 1st quarter in 2002 having initially twenty-four listed companies).
*** Taking into account all the above plus the Khartoum Stock Exchange (from 1st quarter in 2003 having initially forty-seven listed companies) and Algiers Stock Exchange (from 1st quarter in 2003 having initially three listed companies).

364. Excluding the number of listed companies on the capital markets in Iraq, Syria and Libya.

etc.[365] As mentioned above, the UAE and Qatar have taken a radical approach in order to become regional financial centres, particularly with the setting up of the financial free zone and the QFC, respectively.

Equally, rigid Arab attitudes regarding foreign portfolio investments have been changing. Arab countries now allow foreign equity ownership either directly or through buying units in investment funds. Egypt, Tunisia, Jordan, Lebanon, Morocco and Oman were among the first Arab countries that adjusted their regulations to allow foreign corporate ownership.[366] However, it must be stated here that Arab countries vary in the level of their tolerance of foreign corporate ownership. As opposed to offering *some* access to foreigners to invest on their equity markets (as is the case in most Arab countries), Egypt and Morocco for example offer *unfettered* access to investors regardless of nationality.[367]

Indeed, even traditionally hostile Arab countries vis-à-vis foreign ownership in their domestic economies are amongst the latest to permit foreign equity ownership. For example, in Libya, *Decree No. 14* (issued in June 2009) allowed foreigners (non-residents) to own up to 5% of a Libyan listed company. Syria under *Regulation No.538* (issued on 29 October 2009) allowed foreign investment on the Damascus Securities Exchange and provided for the protection of foreign investors thereon. As shall be seen, Jordan equally took serious steps that have resulted in increasing the foreign portfolio of its equity markets.

All the above reforms have now led to opening the region in an unprecedented manner to foreign investors. These, at various stages of entry and exit, included investors such as Flemings Securities, Barings Securities, Foreign and Colonial, Merrill Lynch and JP Morgan, etc., some of which even set up specialised Middle Eastern mutual funds.[368] Such specialised funds included Arab Countries Fund (Fleming), Emerging Middle East Fund (Foreign and Colonial), Atlas Maroc (Financiers Atlas/France), Maghreb Fund (Framlington), Maroc Privatisation Fund (GP Banque/France), etc.

Indeed as a (direct or indirect) result of the above developments, the capitalisation of Arab securities markets has generally been increasing. For example, while in the fourth quarter of 1996, capitalisation of Arab equity markets was USD 108.251 billion, it reached USD 869.872 billion in June 2010 (see Table 3.2 – it excludes the number of companies listed on the capital markets in Iraq, Syria and Libya.)

---

365. See U Fasano et al., *GCC Countries: From Oil Dependence to Diversification*, International Monetary Fund, 2003, p. 13.
366. Bahrain, Djibouti, Kuwait, Morocco, Egypt, Qatar, Tunisia and United Arab Emirates are all members of the WTO. They joined in January 1995, May 1995, January 1995, January 1995, June 1995, January 1996, March 1995 and April 1996, respectively.
367. Concerning the GCC countries, restrictions on local corporate ownership were abolished vis-à-vis Gulf citizens after December 1994.
368. American funds that invest on Middle Eastern and North Africa equity markets included the First Fund for Partners in Peace (Bonil), the US Overseas Private Investment Corporation, the US Salomon Brothers Asset Management and Morocco Omnium North Africa, etc.

Table 3.2 Total Capitalisation of Selected Arab Equity Markets from the Last Quarter of 1996 to June 2010[369] *(in Billion US Dollars)*

Year	1996 4th	1997 4th	1998 4th	1999 2nd	2000 4th	2001 4th	2002 4th	2003 4th	2004 March	2005 4th	2006 4th	2007 4th	2008 4th	2009 4th	2010 June
Capitali-sation	108.251*	145.562*	122.9*	127*	148.158*	152.230*	208.858**	361.824***	407.056***	1,290.938***	888.121***	1046.794***	769.589***	903.427***	869.872***

Source: The Arab Monetary Fund. Information collated from a collection of quarterly bulletins (issues No. 8-18 & (1st Quarter, Year 2001), (4th Quarter, Year 2002), (4th Quarter, Year 2003), (1st Quarter, Year 2004), (4th Quarter, Year 2006), (4th Quarter, Year 2007), (4th Quarter, Year 2008), (4th Quarter, Year 2009) and (2nd Quarter, Year 2010)).
* Based on equity markets in *Jordan*, *Bahrain*, *Tunisia*, *Saudi Arabia*, *Oman*, *Kuwait*, *Lebanon*, *Egypt* and *Morocco*.
** Taking into account the above countries plus the newly set up Abu Dhabi Stock Exchange (from 1st quarter in 2002 with an initial capitalisation of USD 6,278.6m), Dubai Stock Exchange (from 1st quarter in 2002 with an initial capitalisation of USD 8,224.87 million) and Doha Stock Exchange (from 1st quarter in 2002 with an initial capitalisation of USD 7,327.09 million).
*** Taking into account all the above plus the Khartoum Stock Exchange (from 1st quarter in 2003 with an initial capitalisation of USD 607.83 million) and Algiers Stock Exchange (from 1st quarter in 2003 with an initial capitalisation of USD 143.67 million).

369. Excluding the number of listed companies on the capital markets in Iraq, Syria and Libya.

Needless to say, more shares are being traded than ever before – thus enabling wider sectors of Arab populations and foreign investors to have a stake in Arab national economies. Indeed, it is not difficult not to observe the increasing daily traded volumes, as well as number and value of annually traded shares on Arab securities markets. For example, the number of annually traded shares in 2003 was 63.388 billion shares.[370] This number increased to 110.847 billion shares in 2005 and to 168.582 billion shares in 2006.[371] Moreover, the number of annually traded shares increased to 303.996 billion by the end of December 2008,[372] further increasing to 364.338 billion by the end of December 2009.[373]

However, although the annual value of traded shares on Arab securities markets has also seen steady increases over the years, it nevertheless offers a mixed picture. For example, the annual value of traded shares in 2003 hit USD 230.417 billion.[374] This increased to USD 1,435.412 billion and to USD 1,684.998 billion in 2005 and 2006, respectively.[375] However, this annual value of traded shares on Arab securities markets declined in 2007 reaching USD 1.108,070 billion, further declining to USD 997.874 billion in 2008.[376] Due to the global crisis that hit global equity markets, by the end of December 2009, this annual value of traded shares understandably dropped further to USD 653.458 billion.[377]

In contrast, the average number of daily traded shares on Arab equity markets has been on the increase. While it was 255.655 million shares in 2003,[378] it increased to 414.000 million shares in 2005 and to 649.000 million shares in 2006.[379] This average number of daily traded shares on Arab securities markets reached 1.233 billion in 2008,[380] increasing to 1.460 billion in December 2009.[381] By June 2011 it was 1.481 billion.

4. CONCLUSION

Unlike anything seen before, Arab countries now demonstrate highly nuanced keenness in regulating and integrating their capital markets. This has spurred an unprecedented interest in many important legal aspects of securities trading. Indeed, as opposed to what was seen in the previous chapter (when Arab stock exchanges were historically no more than speculative tools), they are now being viewed as engines for economic growth.

370. See *Quarterly Bulletin*, Arab Monetary Fund, No. 40 (4th Quarter, 2004), p. 73.
371. See *Quarterly Bulletin*, Arab Monetary Fund, No. 48 (4th Quarter, 2006), p. 87.
372. See *Quarterly Bulletin*, Arab Monetary Fund, No. 56 (4th Quarter, 2008), p. 86.
373. See *Quarterly Bulletin*, Arab Monetary Fund, No. 60 (4th Quarter, 2009), p. 94.
374. See *Quarterly Bulletin*, Arab Monetary Fund, No. 40 (4th Quarter, 2004), p. 72.
375. See *Quarterly Bulletin*, Arab Monetary Fund, No. 48 (4th Quarter, 2006), p. 88.
376. See *Quarterly Bulletin*, Arab Monetary Fund, No. 56 (4th Quarter, 2008), p. 85.
377. See *Quarterly Bulletin*, Arab Monetary Fund, No. 60 (4th Quarter, 2009), p. 93.
378. See *Quarterly Bulletin*, Arab Monetary Fund, No. 40 (4th Quarter, 2004), p. 73.
379. See *Quarterly Bulletin*, Arab Monetary Fund, No. 48 (4th Quarter, 2006), p. 88.
380. See *Quarterly Bulletin*, Arab Monetary Fund, No. 56 (4th Quarter, 2008), p. 86.
381. See *Quarterly Bulletin*, Arab Monetary Fund, No. 60 (4th Quarter, 2009), p. 94.

As the success of securities markets cannot be achieved through advances in their microstructure alone, Arab countries have on the whole been making satisfactory strides in revamping their macroeconomic underlaying conditions. This has, *inter alia*, been translated into controlling inflation, lessening public deficit, encouraging growth, increasing official reserves, etc.

Additionally, under the exhortations of the World Bank and the IMF, currency exchange regimes have been significantly liberalised, rigid controls on capital entry and exit requirements have now been loosened and severe restrictions against foreign portfolio ownership are now being replaced with a welcoming attitude. Needless to say, the drive for privatisation has also been prevalent in the overwhelming majority of Arab countries, with significant headways made by many Arab countries in this area.

Indeed, the processes of domestic economic reform and the desire to set up modern capital markets are now intertwined in many Arab countries, particularly as these countries are keen to bring equity foreign investors – whether individual or institutional. Accordingly, international regulatory standards are now relevant more than ever to Arab securities markets. For, given the observations made in this chapter, as such Arab countries continue to revamp their underlying macroeconomic conditions in their attempts at attracting foreign capital, they become increasingly keen to achieve regulatory edge – that complies with minimum international standards. Moreover, as there is no evidence that Arab countries are attempting to cocoon their financial institutions from current global regulatory developments, international regulatory standards become ever more relevant.

Having discussed recent Arab interest in regulating its securities markets and the role structural reform programmes played, one shall consider the relevance of international regulatory standards. However, before doing so one must briefly explain the relevance of the notion of investor protection to securities regulation. The next chapter shall therefore explain this relevance and the tools deployed to achieve this, mainly through the concept of mandatory disclosure.

Chapter 4

Securities Regulation, Investor Protection and Disclosure When Offering Shares to the Public

INTRODUCTION

This chapter first discusses the relationship between securities regulation and investor protection, before assessing disclosure as the main tool for investor protection when offering shares to the public.

1. SECURITIES REGULATION AND INVESTOR PROTECTION

This subsection looks at the relationship between securities regulation and investor protection. It briefly looks at what is meant by securities regulation before looking at 'investor protection' as being its dominant theme. This subsection then looks at securities regulation prudential orientation before addressing the notion that securities regulation is not an all-inclusive panacea.

1.1. What Is Securities Regulation?

In its basic form, securities regulation refers to sets of rules that address aspects related to supervising, monitoring and regulating both primary and secondary trading activities.[382] Its objectives lie in the protection of the interests of investors and suppliers of financial services (micro level), as well as the maintenance of

382. See M Chuppe et al., 'Regulation of Securities Markets', World Bank, WPS/829, (January 1992).

systemic stability of the financial system (macro level). However, it is not always feasible to separate the rules designed for maintaining securities markets at the operational level from the rules devised to protect those who invest in such markets.[383]

As opposed to banking regulation, which primarily aims at maintaining systemic stability, securities regulation's primary objective is investor protection in the sense of providing a system of adequate protection that maintains investors' confidence in the integrity of securities markets. Hence, securities regulation's less prudential orientation.[384] Securities regulation also attempts at achieving allocative efficiency.[385] This is done through maintaining the integrity of the payment system and imposing minimum standards. Equally through enhancing market rules on supplying and evaluating information, promoting the safety and soundness of financial institutions and devising extra measures to control risks undertaken by financial institutions.[386] Indeed, many empirical studies have even pointed to the correlation between investor protection and strong securities markets as a whole.[387]

1.2. Securities Regulation and the Theme of Investor Protection

Investor protection, as the main rationale for securities regulation, is particularly important in the EU regulatory context:

> The aim of this Directive [2003/71/EC] and its implementing measures is to ensure investor protection and market efficiency, in accordance with high regulatory standards adopted in the relevant international fora.[388]

383. See D Llewellyn, 'Consumer Protection in Retail Investment Services: Protection against What?', *Journal of Financial Regulation and Compliance*, Vol. III, No. 1, p. 43, (1995), p. 45. [Hereinafter referred to as 'Llewellyn, 1995'.]
384. See Norton et al., *supra* note 3, p. 338.
385. Efficient markets are those 'where there are large numbers of rational, profit maximisers actively competing, with each other to predict future market values of securities, and where important current information is almost freely available to all participants'. See E Fama, 'Random Walks in Stock Market Prices', *Analyst Journal*, pp. 55–99 (September–October 1965), in R Posner et al., *Economics of Corporation Law and Securities Regulation* (Little, Brown and Company – Boston and Toronto), 1980, p. 157.
386. See D Vittas, 'Policy Issues in Financial Regulation', Country Economics Department, World Bank, WPS 910, (May 1992), p. 5. See also Llewellyn, *supra* note 383, pp. 44–45; Page et al., *Investor Protection*, Weidenfield & Nicolson (London), 1992, pp. 35–39; D Llewellyn, 'Reflections on Recent Experience of Regulation in the UK', *Butterworth Journal of International Banking and Financial Law*, p. 367, September (1993), pp. 375–376. [Hereinafter referred to as 'Llewellyn September (1993)'.]
387. These have been particularly pointed out in B Black, 'The Core Institutions that Support Strong Securities Markets', Stanford Law School, John M. Olin Programme in Law and Economics, Working Paper No. 200 June 2000, pp. 1–2.
388. Paragraph 10 of the Preamble to EU Directive No. 2003/71/EC.

Indeed, the theme of providing investor protection is not exclusive to the regulatory discourses on emerging markets. Regulators in advanced markets specifically consider the twin provision of 'investor protection' and 'market confidence' as the *raison d'être* of regulation. Such *raison d'être* is seen as never changed by innovation of trading systems or delivery mechanisms.[389] In this context, the theme of investor protection was specifically highlighted in the influential 1995 Securities and Investment Board's (SIB) report, *Regulation of the United Kingdom Equity Markets*.[390]

The report stated that in order to achieve and retain investor confidence, a regulatory system must achieve equitable treatment, confidence in the integrity of the market and confidence that all steps would be taken to safeguard against market abuse. Here, market users must be confident that they are treated equitably in the sense that no one group of market participants should use the market to the disadvantage of another. Additionally, regardless of the method by which market users choose to deal, they must be able to do so in the confidence that quoted prices, so far as practicable, reflect the full extent of market activity at the time of the transaction.[391]

1.3. Securities Regulation Prudential Orientation

One can broadly speak of two types of financial regulation: *prudential* regulation (safety and soundness of financial institutions, solvency, etc.), and *conduct of business* regulation (the manner in which financial firms conduct business with their customers).[392] Providing protection to investors is not restricted to state or public law. Investor protection is principally found in specialised statutes regulating investment relations. Provisions that bear upon it are also found in 'private legal systems' and equally in codes of conduct issued by private self-regulatory bodies. For its part, the increased legal awareness of investor protection is largely attributable to the decrease of *immediate* ownership and the growth of *intermediated* credit and property relations, which are characterised by lack of direct personal control.[393]

---

389. See H Davies, former Chairman, FSA, 'Global Markets, Global Regulation', IOSCO Annual Conference Sydney, 17 May 2000.
390. See 'Regulation of the United Kingdom Equity Markets: Report by the Securities and Investment Board', SIB, June 1995, London.
391. For a follow-up report, see also 'Regulation of the United Kingdom Equity Markets, Market Views: A Digest of Responses to SIB's Discussion Paper', SIB, June 1995 London.
392. See A Page et al., *supra* note 386, p. 10. However, the economic rational for financial regulation is occasionally treated with scepticism. See, for example, G Benston, 'Regulating Financial Markets: A Critique and Some Proposals', Hobart Paper No. 135, London, London Institute of Economic Affairs, 1998; G Benston & G Kaufman, 'The Appropriate Role of Bank Regulation', *Economic Journal* (May 1996), pp. 688–697; K Dowd, 'The Case for Financial *laissez-faire*', *Economic Journal* (May 1996), pp. 679–687 and E Kane, 'Foundations of Financial Regulation', *Mimeo*, Boston College (January 1997).
393. See Page et al., *supra* note 386, pp. 8–10.

In its attempts at protecting the investor, securities regulation should provide an appropriate balance between 'fairness' among market participants as well as at the same time promote the 'efficiency'[394] of securities markets.[395] However, the concept of 'fairness' in securities regulation is not conclusive. For, it could refer to various meanings that include creating a level playing field, protecting investors from abusive market practices and resolving potential conflict of interest between market participants.[396] Securities regulation cannot therefore be isolated from wider legal questions pertaining to transfer of property rights, corporate and civil liabilities, contractual relations, etc.[397]

For their part, customers' need for protection varies, depending on whether they are retail or institutional investors. An important argument for according added statutory protection to retail investors is justified by what is termed as the absence of 'repeat orders' in the sense of not making frequent investment contracts.[398] This is seen as limiting retail investors' learning experience when compared to the experience gained by institutional investors. Disadvantages of asymmetric information also have a greater adverse impact on (less experienced) retail consumers, as opposed to institutional ones who are generally better adept at utilising it.

Other grounds for protecting lay investors include lack of ability to monitor suppliers of financial services and limited skill and knowledge to enter into complex financial contracts. Additionally, the balance of power between retail and institutional investors vis-à-vis suppliers of financial products tilts heavily towards the latter.[399] The various requirements for investor protection, depending on differing levels of investor expertise, are particularly acknowledged by the EU regulatory regime which accepts that:

> One of the objectives of this Directive [2003/71/EC] is to protect investors. It is therefore appropriate to take account of the different requirements for protection of the various categories of investor level of expertise.[400]

The specific need for protecting the consumer has also been justified on the grounds of 'catastrophe', 'information' and the 'fiduciary role of institutions'.[401] For, ordinary investors need extra regulatory protection in light of the likely

394. See S Keane, *Stock Market Efficiency: Theory, Evidence and Implications*, Philip Allan (Oxford) 1983; W Baumol, *The Stock Market and Economic Efficiency*, Fordham University Press (New York) 1965; M Firth, *Share Price and Mergers: A Study of Stock Market Efficiency*, Saxon House, 1976; I Asimakopoulos et al., 'Stock Prices, Exchange Rate and Market Efficiency', Research Paper No. 97/4, Institute of European Finance, University of Wales, 1997.
395. See Dattels, *supra* note 4, pp. 27–28.
396. See M Long et al., 'Financial Regulation: Changing the Rules of the Game', Country Economic Department, World Bank, WPS 803 (November 1991), p. 13.
397. See Blommestein, *supra* note 24, p. 23; Pardy, *supra* note 33, pp. 2–3.
398. See Llewellyn September (1993), *supra* note 386, p. 367; D Llewellyn, 'The Economic Rationale for Financial Regulation', FSA, Occasional Papers, No. 1 (April 1999), pp. 41–42. [Hereinafter referred as 'Llewellyn April (1999)'.]
399. *Ibid.*
400. Paragraph 16 of the Preamble to EU Directive No. 2003/71/EC.
401. See Llewellyn September (1993), *supra* note 386, p. 375.

significant financial consequences suffered should consumers' investments founder. Thus causing a catastrophe to them. Lay consumers also often have limited access to information concerning the nature and costs of contracts and are generally unable to assess the sophisticated risks that they undertake. Because of this, statutory intervention is needed not only to compel disclosure of information, but also to ensure that such disclosure is clear and unambiguous. The fiduciary role of financial institutions is seen in the sense of consumers not buying financial products for immediate consumption and that, more often than not, they entrust others to handle them on their behalf.[402] This necessitates that lay consumers are safeguarded from the manipulation and fraudulent activities of such institutions through conduct of business rules that ensure investors' protection.

1.4. Securities Regulation Is Not an All-Inclusive Panacea

Having said the above, one must clearly state that securities regulation should not be viewed as purely *paternalistic* – in terms of attempting to protect investors from *all* conceivable risks. Neither does it aim at providing a risk-free regulatory system. When pondering the question of 'against what exactly is the consumer protected?' the answer has typically been that protection should be granted against *market imperfections*.[403] In this sense, the parameters of remedying market imperfections are confined to avoiding dishonesty, market fraud, manipulation, misrepresentation, potential conflict of interest and abuse arising from agent-principal relations, inadequate (or asymmetrical) information, etc.[404]

The yardstick in applying all the above is granting *reasonable* protection to investors. For, there is no regulatory system that can safeguard against all conceivable investment risks. In this context, Llewellyn has presented a succinct projection of customers' 'reasonable' demands from a regulatory system. These are: (1) provision of relevant information before a contract is entered into; (2) presumption of integrity by supplier of a contract; (3) assurance of contracts and ability to fulfil liability at all time; (4) a reasonable degree of competence in the supplier of contract; (5) good products at reasonable and fair prices; (6) good advice when advice is sought; (7) agents serve customers' interests not merely their own; and (8) some measure of compensation should the contract founder.[405]

However, although Llewellyn enumerates the bulk of consumers' 'reasonable' expectations, he appears to overlook paying due emphasis on their need for adequate legal protection. For, contract assurance in terms of capital and solvency requirements that ensures ability to 'fulfil liability at all times' is not synonymous with a legal system that ensures adequate remedies (i.e., civil, criminal and

402. See generally Llewellyn September (1993), *supra* note 386, Llewellyn April (1999), *supra* note 398.
403. See Llewellyn September (1993), *supra* note 386, pp. 379–380.
404. Some writers refer to market imperfections as 'market failure'. Broadly speaking, market failure occurs when markets are not efficient. See Page et al., *supra* note 386, p. 35.
405. See Llewellyn September (1993), *supra* note 386, p. 379.

administrative). This is especially as the general law often provides inadequate remedies in this area. Llewellyn equally appears to ignore foreign consumers' need for a flexible legal system that is also accessible. This is particularly important for non-local investors, where the need for an accessible legal system is as important as the ability of such a system to address their needs substantively.

Additionally, the requirement of 'some measures of compensation should the contract founder', may not always be sufficient to protect investors' interests. For, there will be occasions when investors require adequate legal remedies for actions that would have taken place at a pre-contractual stage. This is especially regarding liability for inaccurate or misleading statements that induce a contract – something that shall be examined in detail when this book looks at the case study in the Jordanian context in Chapters 10 and 11.

2. DISCLOSURE AS THE MAIN TOOL FOR INVESTOR PROTECTION WHEN OFFERING SECURITIES TO THE PUBLIC

This subsection looks at disclosure as the main tool of investor protection. In addressing this, it points out that disclosure is not the only such tool before addressing the question of whether disclosure should be mandatory.

2.1. Disclosure Is Not the Only Tool for Achieving Investor Protection

One, at the beginning, must emphasise that disclosure is only one of the many regulatory tools deployed to achieve investor protection. For example, disclosure is contrasted to trusteeship or merit regulation, under which:

> Most major jurisdictions maintain at least vestigial traces of the trusteeship strategy in the form of substantive review by securities officials or stock exchanges. In the vernacular of US securities law, this form of trusteeship strategy is termed 'merit regulation'.[406]

Yet, although merit regulation remains important,[407] over-reliance on it will be even more costly than mandatory disclosure and is likely to bar risky firms from entering securities markets.[408]

406. G Hertig et al., 'Issuers and Investor Protection', in R Kraakman et al., *The Anatomy of Corporate Law: A Comparative and Functional Approach*, Oxford University Press, Oxford, (2004), p. 207.

407. These tools include some listing rules, ombudsman service, compensation schemes, market monitoring, registration, authorisation, supervision of firms, etc. See 'Financial Services Authority: A New Regulator for the New Millennium', FSA, (January 2000), pp. 5–9, 25–30.

408. See Hertig et al., *supra* note 406, p. 208. Indeed, it is no coincidence therefore that mandatory disclosure (as a regulatory device) has aided the enforcement of laws, discouraged acts

It however must be noted here that the discussion in the literature has never been on whether or not information per se is useful to investors. For, no writer has ever contended against better-informed investors. The contention is on whether its provision should be *mandated* by positive law or be *voluntarily* left to market forces. The discussion next shall therefore project the arguments for and against mandatory disclosure.

2.2. Should Disclosure Be Mandatory?

This subsection looks at the question of whether or not disclosure should be mandatory. It very briefly tackles this by looking at arguments based on economic hypotheses, models and theorems (i.e., ECMH, no-trade theorem, portfolio theory, reputational or self-interest model, etc.). This subsection also argues that mere reliance on anti-fraud disclosure provisions will not suffice to compel disclosure. It equally looks at other arguments in favour of mandatory disclosure such as accuracy and efficiency enhancement arguments and goods-like characteristic of information.

2.2.1. Arguments Based on Economic Hypotheses, Models and Theorems

One starts by mentioning the Efficient Capital Market Hypothesis (ECMH). In its strong form, the ECMH roughly argues that since (historical, public and non-public) information is impounded in the price of securities, then mandatory disclosure is superfluous and costly.[409] However, criticism of the ECMH has often been premised on a number of empirical grounds such as that tests on market efficiency seem to support the 'weak' form only and the 'temporal lag' between the production of information and its relay.[410] Here, the temporal lag grants

---

disproved by the lager public and has had an inherent informative value. See generally, Note 'Disclosure as a Legislative Device', 76 *Harvard Law Review*, 1273 (1962–1963).

409. ECMH postulates three forms of capital markets. In the 'weak' form only historical (or past) price information is included in securities' price. In 'semi-strong' markets, securities' price includes not only past information but also all publicly available one, while in the 'strong' form, not only historical and all available public information is included in securities' price, but also non-publicly available information as well as market forecasts. See generally, E Fama, 'Efficient Capital Markets: A Review of Theory and Empirical Work', 25 *Journal of Finance* (1970) 383; Brealy & Myers *Principles of Corporate Finance*, 2nd edn, Ch. 13 (1984); Downes & Dyckman 'The Efficient Market Reconsidered', 4 *Journal of Portfolio Management*, (1977) 4.

410. For its part, it is argued that the ECMH has been challenged on empirical grounds. Also on the ground that the ECMH model does not address the question of the mechanism through which prices adjust to information in the sense that it only provides a description of the type of information and that 'In the end, prices can convey to market participants, under the assumption that investors observe and use prices to form their economic decisions. Besides that, the relationship between the market for information and the capital market, which is relevant to

insiders and other privileged parties a better chance of utilising information before it reaches the market, which means that (mandatory) interference to make transmission mechanisms more efficient becomes justified. It has also been argued that while the ECMH may hold true in some situations where certain 'well-known' stocks traded on major exchanges are closely monitored by analysts, the market will not be efficient[411] vis-à-vis less well-known stocks. Thus, presenting opportunities for trading on information not yet impounded in the price.[412]

The so-called noise and chaos theories attempted to address some of the criticism levelled at the ECMH, particularly its postulate that securities have intrinsic values in terms of their worth being defined by market prices.[413] While the ECMH deems capital markets linear, noise theory argues they are essentially non-linear systems (i.e., actions and reactions are not necessarily proportional), in which individuals overreact to information. From this angle, noise theory argues that mandatory disclosure is useless and unhelpful to investors as information disclosed will not remedy underlying irrational trading by individuals. However, the ECMH and noise theory's rejection of mandatory disclosure has been discounted on the grounds that they are founded on the precarious referents of 'relative efficiency' and 'relative rationality', from which chaos theory breaks away.[414]

---

define a concept of efficiency, is not modelled.' See S Barsellah 'Mandatory Disclosure Regulation, Insider Trading and the Economics of Information', MPhil thesis, York University 1989, pp. 6, 102–158. See, Kripke in which he refers to P Samuelson's work stating that 'tests made mostly on stocks traded on the New York Stock Exchange, seem conclusively to show that the semi-strong hypothesis of market efficiency is correct'. See H Kripke, *The SEC and Corporate Disclosure: Regulation in Search for Purpose* (New York: Law and Business Inc.), Harcourt Brace Jovanovich Publishers, 1979, p. 85.

411. It is however argued that the term 'efficient' markets in this respect may not represent an accurate usage of the term as it misleadingly may carry normative or value-laden connotations. This is especially the case as the term market efficiency refers here to 'a relationship between stock prices and some defined information set. It is not to be confused with other uses of the term, efficiency, such as those which refer to how resources are allocated in the economy.' See W Beaver Report of the Advisory Committee on Corporate Disclosure to the SEC, 95th Cong., 1st Sess. 618–656 (House Comm. Print 95–29, 1977), in Posner et al., *supra* note 385, pp. 328–329.

412. See Kripke, *supra* note 410, p. 85.

413. Noise theory has introduced a behavioural and psychological element to the ECMH in the sense of attributing an (irrational) human element that over-reacts to the flow of information causing the excess volatility and breakdowns from which capital markets occasionally suffer. In this context, it has concurred with the ECMH in that information is digested rapidly and rendered useless once traded upon, but attributes 'pricing bias' to some imperfections in the digested information leading prices to depart from their fundamental values. But, while chaos theory agrees with the ECMH and noise theory that information is digested rapidly, it disagrees with the proposition that information is rendered useless once traded upon contending that empirical studies show that information remains useful for some time. See L Cunningham, 'Capital Market Theory, Mandatory Disclosure and Price Discovery', 51 *Washington & Lee Law Review* (1994), 843, pp. 843–44, 855.

414. Chaos theory generally argues that public market phenomena that seem random (efficient) are in fact non-random and internally dependent. 'It also suggests that behaviour or action that may appear to be irrational (noisy) may well be rational because it occurs in a system that is inherently nonlinear.' It is equally argued that noise theory is a 'crude' account of more subtle and complex systematic process and its non-linear perspective shows that 'linear perspectives

But while chaos theory agrees with the ECMH and noise theory that information is digested rapidly, it disagrees with the proposition that information is rendered useless once traded upon, contending that empirical studies show that information remains useful for some time.[415] As it emphasises the importance of market microstructure in achieving accurate price discovery, chaos theory is less dismissal of mandatory disclosure.[416]

Another argument against mandatory disclosure has been premised on the 'no-trade theorem'. According to the 'no-trade theorem', in a pure exchange setting, public information is valueless to individuals as it does not change the trading decisions of agents – as opposed to private information which, given the possibility of its exploitation on the market, is always valuable to any individual.[417] It has been argued that the change of investors' endowment allocation depends more on the strength of their income and substitution effects produced by the change in subjective probabilities, rather than exclusively on the arrival of additional information. However, this theorem has been criticised on empirical grounds as well as that it is impossible, *a priori*, to state the effect induced by the new public information.[418]

One also briefly mentions portfolio theory which roughly argues that due to diversifying portfolios in terms of the simultaneous holding of different securities by investors, any general overpricing of securities prices (due for example to lack of disclosing firm-specific information) is likely to be offset when assessing the portfolio as an overall unit – not merely looking at it in terms of its single components of individual securities in isolation from each other.[419] However, this may

---

underlying the ECMH . . . are inadequate bases to test the responsiveness of price information flows'. *Ibid.*, pp. 856–58.

415. Chaos theory further argues that information still has value even after it has been traded upon, relying on studies that have indicated that public capital markets have average cycle length of up to four years.

416. Viewing capital markets as non-linear systems gives overall importance to both discrete bits of fundamental information on securities per se and extraneous informational variables (e.g., the industry in which a firm operates, macroeconomic conditions, etc). See Cunningham, *supra* note 413, pp. 857–73.

417. See Barsellah, *supra* note 410, pp. 7–8, 11. The 'no trade theorem' is mainly based on Hirshleifer, who has argued that the introduction of public information, in a pure exchange economy, is 'useless' and under particular conditions can be harmful. See generally, J Hirshleifer, 'The Private and Social Value of Information and the Reward of Incentive Activity', 61 *American Economic Review*, (1971), 561.

418. For a detailed empirical refutation of this theorem see Barsellah, *supra* note 410, pp. 11–98.

419. Portfolio theory characterises investment decisions as a trade off between expected return and risk. Thus having two immediate implications for disclosure: (1) not evaluating individual securities with isolation from the whole portfolio, which consists of other securities; and (2) investors are concerned with both risk and return in terms of minimising the former and maximising the latter. From this angle the role of disclosure to investors is important as it is concerned with both a better assessment of risk and performance of securities – though the theory distinguishes between two types of risks. The unsystematic or diversifiable risk, which can be eliminated by diversification, and the non-diversifiable, which cannot be eliminated by diversification. See W Beaver Report of the Advisory Committee on Corporate Disclosure to the SEC, 95th Cong., in Posner et al., *supra* note 385, pp. 326–328.

not always be the case as investors may not choose to diversify despite having the capacity to do so. Additionally, the general problem of resource misallocation shall persist due to no (or little) disclosure if portfolio theory is narrowly interpreted.[420]

Nevertheless, the above arguments are contended on a number of grounds which point out to the benefits of mandatory disclosure. Indeed, mandatory disclosure here is seen as a remedy to some of the shortcomings associated with voluntary disclosure, largely premised on the economic theories of the firm.[421] Roughly speaking, voluntary disclosure is based on market forces of supply of information by corporate managers who want to achieve the best prices for their issued securities. Self-interest in the sense of reputational incentives leads corporate mangers to disclose all material information. Additionally, the same reputational self-interest also propels underwriters and accountants to verify the information supplied by firms and issuers of securities with highest degrees of accuracy.[422]

However, among the main criticisms adduced against the self-interest model is the conflict of interest between management and shareholders. This is especially given management's propensity to either release adverse information to fight off a hostile take-over or undervalue the company in a bid for a leveraged buyout.[423] Agency problems between shareholders and corporate insiders are likely to appear. For, on the whole, 'bad news' threatens managers' compensation packages and their job security.[424] The same model has also been criticised on the grounds that management may refrain from disclosing information harmful to firms' competitiveness in the market – though it has been equally argued that investors' expectations of the worse-yet-to-come will 'force' the disclosure of all material information including bad one. Here, corporate managers risk that investors may become sceptical about all information disseminated by firms, viewing silence as hiding of non-favourable information.[425] Yet, one hastens to add that such a proposition remains a mere hypothetical assertion. For, it has not been empirically proven (beyond doubt) that investors will always associate management's non-disclosure of unfavourable information with hiding something that is even worse.

---

420. This is in addition to problems associated with unequal access to disclosure by all investors as well as management's ability to use non-disclosure to negotiate for greater compensation. *Ibid.*, p. 328.
421. Economic theories of the firm are largely based on the works of Jensen & Meckling, 'Theory of the Firm: Managerial Behaviour, Agency Costs and Ownership Structure', 3 *Journal of Finance and Economics* (1976), 305, and S Ross, 'Disclosure Regulation in Financial Markets: Implications of Modern Finance Theory', in *Issues in Financial Regulation* (F Edwards ed. 1979), p. 177.
422. See Easterbrook & Fischel, *Economic Structure of Corporate Law*, Harvard University Press, Cambridge (1991), pp. 276–314.
423. See J Coffee, 'Market Failure and the Economic Case for Mandatory Disclosure System', 70 *Virginia Law Review* (1984), 717, pp. 740–743.
424. See Hertig et al., *supra* note 406, p. 204.
425. See Easterbrook & Fischel, *supra* note 422, pp. 290–93.

2.2.2. Mere Reliance on Anti-Fraud Disclosure Provisions Will Not Suffice

Mandatory disclosure also remedies problems such as unequal access to information attained by 'outsiders' and 'insiders', which may arise under a system of voluntary disclosure.[426] Additionally, mere reliance on anti-fraud disclosure provisions (such as in the case of insider dealing) gives rise only to causes of action in certain circumstances of fraud. This, on its own, cannot deter underlying misbehaviour or 'activate' the market for corporate control by ensuring sufficient dissemination of information.[427] Indeed, even those who advocate a voluntary system of disclosure acknowledge that under anti-fraud disclosure provisions firms can remain reticent and still enjoy impunity under the general law.

In a world with an anti-fraud rule but no mandatory disclosure, firms could remain silent with impunity. Firms that disclosed could do so in any way they wished, provided they did not lie.[428]

2.2.3. Accuracy and Efficiency Enhancement Arguments

As opposed to fairness-based justifications for its imposition (such as enhancing investor confidence, investor protection and deterring fraud),[429] mandatory disclosure when offering shares to the public has also been justified on efficiency-based arguments. It is therefore argued that mandatory disclosure enhances the accuracy and widens the dissemination of (accurate) information on issued securities.[430] Here, mandating the provision of certain information improves the overall veracity of information offered on issued securities.[431] It has also been argued that wide availability of accurate information on the market is not only conducive to better pricing of securities and financial assets, enhancing allocative efficiency and indirectly reducing price volatility. It also contributes to avoiding

---

426. 'The only regulatory objective is that access to material information be enjoyed equally, but this objective requires nothing more than the disclosure of basic facts so that outsiders may draw upon their own evaluative expertise in reaching their own investment decision with knowledge equal to that of the insiders.' See *SEC v. Texas Gulf Sulphur Co.*, 401. 2d 833, 848 (2d Cir.) 394 US 976 (1968).
427. See Coffee, *supra* note 423, pp. 740–743.
428. See Esterbrook & Fischel, *supra* note 422, p. 286.
429. See 'much quoted' US Congress passage: 'No investor, no speculator, can safely buy and sell securities upon the exchanges without having an intelligent basis for forming his judgement as to the value of the securities he buys or sells. The idea of a free and open public market is built upon the theory that competing judgements of buyers and sellers as to the fair price of a security brings about a situation where the market price reflects as nearly as possible a just price . . . ', US H.R. REP. No. 1383, 73d Cong. 2d Sess. at 11 (1934) quoted in E Kitch, 'The Theory and Practice of Securities Disclosure', 61 *Brooklyn Law Review* (1995), 763, p.765.
430. Scepticism over mandatory disclosure in achieving accuracy enhancement revolves mainly around the heavy liabilities for misstatements. *Ibid.*, pp. 770–772.
431. C.f.: Easterbrook & Fischel, *supra* note 422, pp. 298–300.

misallocation of resources by reducing the costs associated with acquiring and verifying information.[432] Indeed:

> The compliance effort is rationalized [*sic*], to a significant degree, by one empirical goal of securities laws: to create stock markets in which the market price of a stock corresponds to its fundamental value.[433]

However, although its 'accuracy enhancement' role in improving informational accuracy per se, has not been doubted as such, some have nevertheless contended that the efficiency justification for mandatory disclosure lies in its reduction of agency costs – that is, by addressing certain agency problems arising between corporate promoters and investors on the one hand and between corporate managers and shareholders on the other.[434]

Yet, it must be stated that it is sometimes difficult to separate fully between justifying disclosure on 'enhancing market efficiency' grounds or 'maintaining market integrity' arguments. In this context, the purported role of mandatory disclosure in enhancing accurate pricing also equally enhances investors' confidence in the market and its integrity. For, given their knowledge of all material information affecting the security, the price they pay becomes a 'fair' or a 'just' return – as they would have not been overcharged due to lack of knowledge of undisclosed information that may depreciate securities' true value.

2.2.4. Goods-Like Characteristic of Information

Among other cogent arguments in support of mandatory disclosure is the public goods-like characteristic of information – rendering it as both non-excludable (no one can be excluded from utilising it even if they have not paid for it) and equally indivisible (its utilisation by one investor does not diminish its value).[435] Given that information has public-goods-like characteristic, this gives rise to the 'free

---

432. Coffee has argued the decline of variance in debt securities returns after the implementation of the Securities Act 1934. See Coffee, *supra* note 423, p. 720. See also P Mahoney, 'Mandatory Disclosure as a Solution to Agency Problems', 62 *University of Chicago Law Review* (1995) 1047, p. 1047 note 1, where he cites those for and against the theoretical argument on efficiency of mandatory disclosure.
433. M Kahan, 'Securities Laws and the Social Costs of "insurance" Stock Prices', 41 *Duke Law Journal* (1992), p. 979.
434. The so-called agency cost model, which argues that mandatory disclosure in the US was an 'incremental' change emanated from a set of judicial doctrines designed to overcome a 'specific' agency problem identified as the promoter problem. See Mahoney, *supra* note 432, pp. 1048, 1111–12.
435. See generally A De Jasay, *Social Contract, Free Ride: A Study of the Public Goods Problem* (Oxford Press), 1989; D Schmidtz, *The Limits of Government: An Essay on the Public Goods Argument* (Boulder, London, Westview), 1990; R Mendez, 'The Provision and Financing of Universal Public Goods', London School of Economics. Centre for the Study of Global Governance (Discussion paper No. 7), 1993; R Hjerppe, 'Provision of Public and Merit Goods: Towards an Optimal Policy Mix?' Helsinki: United Nations University, World Institute for Development Economics Research, (Research in progress 10), 1997.

rider' problem in the sense that the use of public information cannot be only restricted to those who pay for acquiring it. This argument has sometimes been viewed in the sense that corporate disclosure induces 'externalities' resulting from the public-goods-like nature of information.[436]

In this context, a number of additional issues have been introduced when considering the public-goods-like approach to securities disclosure.[437] But the main 'externality' resulting from such an approach has been seen in the diminution of the reward for exclusive exploitation of information, which would also equally be utilised by free riders. Thus, inducing under-provision of information – mainly research by securities analysts. This in turn leads to both lack of optimal verification of information provided by corporate issuers and also a reduction of efforts to ferret out information from non-corporate issuer sources.[438] It has therefore been argued that mandatory disclosure eliminates the 'repetitive cost' of individual acquisition of information by securities analysts as well as wasteful duplication.[439] Needless to say, mandatory disclosure equally 'relieves' lay investors from either conducting 'expensive' search for such information or risk potentially making a 'disastrous' choice without it.[440]

Additionally, as compensation for information is on an *ex post facto* basis, another problem arises from the public-goods-like characteristic of securities research in terms of the difficulty in having to contract for it, especially by lay investors.[441] In this context, 'standardisation' of mandated information also relieves lay investors from having to negotiate the disclosure of each individual issue. For, without it disclosure would have been driven solely by market forces in which some firms may offer higher investment returns in exchange for less disclosure.[442] Indeed, the standardisation of disclosed information has often

---

436. For example, externalities in the sense that 'the actions of one party have effects on other parties, who are not charged (or compensated) *via* the price mechanism. . . . However, without some form of collective action, the party undertaking the action has no incentive to internalise the effects on third parties, and it may lead to inefficiency'. See W Beaver Report of the Advisory Committee on Corporate Disclosure to the SEC, 95th Cong., in Posner et al., *supra* note 385, pp. 317–322.
437. These generally relate to, *inter alia*: (1) little empirical evidence assessing the importance of potential externalities; (2) the costs of compelling disclosure and regulations; (3) regulatory behaviour and its incentives; and (4) the question of alternative to governmental regulation – i.e., private sector collective agreements. See Posner, *supra* note 385, pp. 321–322.
438. Securities analysts enjoy 'significant' economies of scale. The basic functions of securities analysts are: (1) searching for exogenous information to which issuers have no special knowledge and have significant bearing on securities' prices; and (2) preventing 'deliberate' fraud and 'unconscious' bias when verifying, testing and comparing issuers' disclosure. See Coffee, *supra* note 423, pp. 722–333.
439. *Ibid.*, pp. 725–733.
440. See Page et al., *supra* note 386, pp. 8–10, 37.
441. See Coffee, *supra* note 423, pp. 725–33. However, this is further complicated by the fact that payment is often not made by cash (i.e., requesting brokerage firms to continue/discontinue using the services of particular analysts), tipping the balance in favour of institutional investors.
442. See E Ferran, *Company Law and Corporate Finance*, Oxford University Press, Oxford, 1999, p. 569.

been seen as one of the important functional benefits of mandatory disclosure. This is especially as it enables lay investors to compare and contrast between firms of similar sectors through the standardisation of released information. In this sense, standardisation increases the value of information to investors through improving the comprehensibility and comparability of disclosed information:

> Standardization [*sic*] improves comprehensibility and comparability, thus increasing the value of information to investors. . . . A regime of mandatory disclosure permits immediate standardization without waiting for it to evolve through private ordering.[443]

After having discussed the fundamental role that mandatory disclosure plays as the main tool for investor protection when offering securities to the public, one, in the next chapter, looks at the relevance of international standards to Arab securities markets.[444]

3. CONCLUSION

Unlike banking regulation, which primarily focuses on prudential aspects and systemic risks, securities regulation is more concerned with investor protection. However, it does not aim at protecting investors from all conceivable risks, as it

---

443. See Hertig et al., *supra* note 406, p. 206.

444. However, mandatory disclosure has also been criticised that it too may lead to underproduction of information as it assigns property rights on market information, lessening market players' chances of enjoying the 'full economic value' of their endeavours. See J Hirshleifer & Riley, 'The Analytics of Uncertainty and Information', 17 *Journal of Economic Literature* (1979), 1375. Hence, eliminating some of the entrepreneurial incentives for conducting costly information research and acquisition. Kitch has particularly argued that mandatory disclosure, through prescribing heavy liabilities for misstatements (e.g., ss 11 & 12 of the US Securities Act 1933), induces underproduction of information as issuers and underwriters try to limit their liabilities which may arise from the information that they release. See Kitch, *supra* note 422, pp. 770–772. C.f. with studies that pointed to limited impact of liability on disclosure. For example, when an empirical study examined ninety-three IPOs from 1969 to 1990 in order to test the 'Lawsuit Avoidance Hypothesis', it found that they had average initial returns not too dissimilar to control firms that did not get sued. See P Drake & M Vetsuypens, 'IPO Underpricing and Insurance against Legal Liability', *Financial Management* (Spring 1993), pp. 64–73. Another study pointed out to the huge legal costs that deter small investors from suing, thus minimising the legal liability risk. See J Cooper Alexander, 'Do the Merits Matter? A Study of Settlements in Securities Class Actions', *Stanford Law Review* 43, (1991), pp. 497–597. Also, R Ibbotson, 'The Market's Problem with the Pricing of Initial Public Offerings', *Journal of Applied Corporate Finance*, Vol. 7 (1994), 67, p. 71. Additionally, mandatory disclosure equally suffers from compliance costs incurred by its enforcement. But as Coffee has argued, gains from mandatory disclosure should not be discounted notwithstanding compliance costs. Indeed, benefits of mandatory disclosure should be considered when looking at the tradeoffs between its cost and increased overall allocative efficiency, particularly as the collectivisation of information produces more information, not constituting trading gains per se in the sense of generating a zero-sum outcome between investors and analysts. See Coffee, *supra* note 423, pp. 736–737.

merely fulfils customers' expectations of 'reasonable' statutory protection. In this sense, securities regulation is not paternalistic and rather aims at remedying market imperfections, particularly correcting informational distortions caused by asymmetrical distribution of information. Here, the need for timely and adequate information accounts for disclosure being a main tool of securities regulation.

Yet, although no writer on the subject matter has ever disputed the value of better-informed investors, debate in the literature has been on whether disclosure should be *mandatory* or *voluntary*. However, the overwhelming majority of the literature accepts that when offering securities to the public, mandatory disclosure is by far the primary remedy to many of the shortcomings associated with voluntary disclosure.

These include unequal access to information between 'outsiders' and 'insiders'. Mandatory disclosure equally enhances price accuracy as it widens the dissemination of (accurate) information. Thus, reducing price volatility and contributing to avoiding misallocation of resources by reducing the costs associated with acquiring and verifying information. It also eliminates the 'repetitive cost' of individual acquisition of information by securities analysts and wasteful duplication. 'Standardisation' of mandated information also relieves lay investors from having to negotiate the disclosure of each individual issue, risking making a disastrous choice without it.

Having addressed the basic question of what securities regulation is, explaining its prudential approach in terms of overriding emphasis on investor protection (with mandatory disclosure as its main regulatory tool), the next chapter contextualises its Arab relevance. In addressing this, it attempts to answer the question of why international regulatory standards in securities regulation are relevant to Arab securities regulation.

The above is especially important as Arab interest in regulating its securities markets is a recent phenomenon as has been seen so far. The next chapter shall therefore specifically address the question of the relevance of international regulatory standards to Arab securities markets.

Chapter 5

Relevance of International Regulatory Standards to Arab Securities Markets

INTRODUCTION

This chapter briefly looks at the relevance of international regulatory standards to Arab securities markets. It first briefly explains that from a historical viewpoint, securities regulation was often a response to domestic and institutional factors. It then briefly mentions the recent phenomenon of coordinated global responses to issues related to global financial stability, before addressing the fact that Arab policy makers are embracing globalisation and international regulatory standards.

1. SECURITIES REGULATION WAS HISTORICALLY A RESPONSE TO DOMESTIC AND INSTITUTIONAL FACTORS

When discussing contemporary regulatory trends driving the momentum towards the 'internationalisation' of capital markets, one cautions that securities regulation was on many historical occasions a response to pure domestic factors – particularly financial scandals.[445] Securities regulation can also equally depend on the peculiarity of the historical relationship between the central government and the financial sector, as witnessed in the self-regulatory system of the City of London before

445. For example, the *1697 Act to Restrain the Numbers and Practices of Brokers and Stock Jobbers* – passed after the damning report of the Royal Commission of Trade in England. Also the 1720 Bubble Act enacted after the collapse of the share price of the South Sea Company.

the Big Bang.[446] Here the unique importance of the City as a financial centre, that had even occasionally financed expensive Crown activities, resulted in regulatory autonomy favouring the City and its operators.[447]

However, different institutional structures, varying scales of economic development and political ideology, all inevitably lead to different methods of regulating securities industries.[448] Nevertheless, underlying macroeconomic and institutional differences between developed and emerging economies should not undermine the intrinsic value of comparative legal studies in securities regulation. For, although a choice between Civil or Common Law may justifiably present itself in choosing between 'basic' commercial and contract law models, more sophisticated legal areas such as banking and securities laws do not necessarily lend themselves exclusively to the Civil or Common Law models.[449]

Yet, in the specific context of much of the literature on Emerging Markets' securities regulation, it is accepted that there is no 'unique blueprint' that can be transplanted from advanced economies into emerging markets' regulatory systems.[450] It is true that comparative law has, over the years, been used as a tool for bringing about institutional and regulatory change. Nevertheless, it must be cautioned that it is inconceivable empirically to tailor a regime of securities regulation that would address *all* regulatory requirements in *all* countries.[451]

2. COORDINATED GLOBAL RESPONSES TO ISSUES RELATED TO GLOBAL FINANCIAL STABILITY

Coordinated global responses to issues related to global financial stability are increasingly resulting in setting up multinational forums, which are bringing about more globally coordinated approaches. An example in mind is the setting up of the Financial Stability Forum, which came to light in the context of the

446. The financial self-regulatory system of the City of London is often attributed historically to decentralisation and lack of strong State interference. In more recent times, however, the lobbying efforts of City professionals, its developed internal structures, which were averse to public models in regulations, together with its unique links with the Treasury and the Bank of England, have all helped maintain the City's regulatory independence. See G Gilligan, 'The Origins of UK Financial Services Regulation', *The Company Lawyer*, Vol. 18, No. 6, 1997, pp. 167–74; C Goodheart, 'Structural Changes in the British Capital Markets', in C Goodheart et al., *The Operation and Regulation of Financial Markets*, Macmillan (London), 1987, pp. 32–36.

447. See Gilligan, *ibid*., p. 169.

448. See generally, M Moran, *The Politics of the Financial Services Revolution: The USA, UK and Japan*, Macmillan 9 (London), 1990. However, the role of the legal elite in transplanting entire foreign legal systems, on few occasions, proved influential. An example was Turkey's adoption of the Swiss Civil Code, largely due to its Minister of Justice having studied law in Switzerland. See A Watson, *Legal Transplants: An Approach to Comparative Law*, University of Georgia Press, London, 1993, pp. 115–16.

449. See Norton et al., *supra* note 3, p. 440.

450. See Blommestein, *supra* note 24, p. 3; Norton et al., *supra* note 3, p. 351.

451. See Norton et al., *supra* note 3, pp. 339–41.

discussions of the IMF in the Autumn of 1998. This Forum was set up following the Asian crises of 1997 and 1998, and has two prime objectives. The *first* is to achieve an understanding of current global trends concerning stability of the global financial system and develop early warning mechanisms through shared experiences of Member States. The *second* is to identify gaps in the global financial system.

For its part, academic literature is awash with studies that have addressed various aspects of the globalisation of securities markets and its impact.[452] In this respect, different reasons have been advanced to account for the globalisation of securities markets. These include removal of currency restrictions, financial innovations, cross-jurisdictional share portfolios, securitisation (particularly cross-jurisdictional), growth of universal banking, etc.[453] The ever-increasing palpable impact of such factors is leading academics to speculate on the significant changes that are likely to take place in securities markets in a manner that irrevocably transcends their national orientation.[454]

Indeed, among the likely emergent forms, are 'truly' international markets that will comprise of two or three global exchanges – that is, the New York Stock Exchange, the Tokyo Stock Exchange, etc. Another likely emergent form is alliance of stock exchanges on regional basis – that is, Nordic, European, American, Asian, Middle Eastern, etc. The trend of national exchanges linking international issuers with international investors and cross-jurisdictional listing of securities is also likely to intensify.

Admittedly, the internationalisation of securities markets brought with it the associated problems of 'regulatory arbitrage' in the sense that investors may seek out less regulated markets. But there is no empirical evidence that conclusively suggests that less regulated stock exchanges are more popular with investors (individual or institutional), whether foreign or domestic. If anything, internationalisation has led to increased cooperation between international enforcement agencies, especially when confronting cross-boarder market manipulation.[455] Moreover, trans-national trading in securities has (since the mid-1980s) resulted in the development of international regulatory agencies working at achieving common standards.[456]

The subsection below shall therefore briefly discuss the most important international self-regulatory bodies.

---

452. That is, whether on domestic financial services industries, direct investment or on multi-jurisdictional questions specifically related to emerging capital markets. See, for example, O Ajayi, 'Regulatory Techniques in Internationalisation and Emerging Capital Markets', Ph.D. thesis, Cambridge University, 1990; E Carazzai, 'The Internationalisation of the Financial Market and its Impact on Direct and Indirect Investment on Brazil', M.Phil. thesis, Manchester University, 1990; J Ross, 'The Globalisation of Financial Markets and its Impact on the Financial Services Industry', MSc thesis, Heriot Watt University, 1995.
453. See S El-Najjar, *Financial Policies and Capital Markets in Arab Countries*, IMF, Washington DC (1994), pp. vii–viii.
454. See N Jul Clausen, 'Securities Market Co-operation: A New Regulatory Standard in the Next Millennium', *The Company Lawyer*, Vol. XXI, No. 2, p. 43.
455. See *Securities Markets in OECD Countries: Organisation and Regulation*, OECD Documents (1995), p. 15.
456. Particularly in areas such as international equity offerings and international capital adequacy.

3. INTERNATIONAL SELF-REGULATORY BODIES CEMENTING THE GLOBALISED ASPECTS OF SECURITIES REGULATION

The work of the International Organisation of Securities Commissions (IOSCO) has been influential in cementing the globalised aspects of securities regulation in terms of its international standardisation. The IOSCO also strives to enhance the international integration (and harmonisation) of domestic securities markets. IOSCO first came to being in 1983 "flourishing now" into a truly international cooperative body.[457] Indeed, the Organisation's wide membership regulates more than 95% of the world's securities markets and IOSCO is the world's most important international cooperative forum for securities regulatory agencies. In this respect, up until November 2011, IOSCO membership included 115 jurisdictions.

In September 1998, IOSCO adopted a comprehensive set of thirty *Objectives and Principles of Securities Regulation* (IOSCO Principles), recognised as the international regulatory benchmarks for all securities markets. These thirty principles act as a framework for addressing the fundamental aspects of securities regulation.

The Principles were updated as of May 2003 to cross-reference additional IOSCO resolutions and reports to each Principle. These are:

(1) Principles Relating to the Regulator.
(2) Principles for Self-Regulation.
(3) Principles for the Enforcement of Securities Regulation.
(4) Principles for Cooperation in Regulation.
(5) Principles for Issuers.
(6) Principles for Auditors, Credit Ratings Agencies, and other information service providers.
(7) Principles for Collective Investment Schemes.
(8) Principles for Market Intermediaries.
(9) Principles for Secondary Markets.

It, however, must be stated that in June 2010, eight new principles were added to the existing thirty. The new principles cover specific policy areas such as hedge funds, credit rating agencies and auditor independence and oversight. They equally address broader areas that relate to:

(1) monitoring, mitigating and managing systemic risk;
(2) regularly reviewing the perimeter of regulation; and
(3) requiring that conflicts of interest and misalignment of incentives are avoided, eliminated, disclosed or otherwise managed.

---

457. Eleven securities regulatory agencies from North and South America gathered in Quito, Ecuador in April 1983 to take that important decision.

For their part, the IOSCO thirty-eight Principles are one of twelve standards and codes highlighted by the Financial Stability Forum as key to sound financial systems and deserving priority implementation.[458] They are designed to give effect to three key objectives deemed the essence of securities regulation:

(a) the promotion of investor protection;
(b) ensuring that markets are fair, efficient and transparent; and
(c) reducing systemic risk.

---

458. These principles relate to: A. Principles Relating to the Regulator: (1) The responsibilities of the Regulator should be clear and objectively stated; (2) The Regulator should be operationally independent and accountable in the exercise of its functions and powers; (3) The Regulator should have adequate powers, proper resources and the capacity to perform its functions and exercise its powers; (4) The Regulator should adopt clear and consistent regulatory processes; (5) The staff of the Regulator should observe the highest professional standards, including appropriate standards of confidentiality; (6) The Regulator should have or contribute to a process to monitor, mitigate and manage systemic risk, appropriate to its mandate; (7) The Regulator should have or contribute to a process to review the perimeter of regulation regularly; (8) The Regulator should seek to ensure that conflicts of interest and misalignment of incentives are avoided, eliminated, disclosed or otherwise managed. B. Principles for Self-Regulation: (9) Where the regulatory system makes use of Self-Regulatory Organizations (SROs) that exercise some direct oversight responsibility for their respective areas of competence, such SROs should be subject to the oversight of the Regulator and should observe standards of fairness and confidentiality when exercising powers and delegated responsibilities. C. Principles for the Enforcement of Securities Regulation: (10) The Regulator should have comprehensive inspection, investigation and surveillance powers; (11) The Regulator should have comprehensive enforcement powers; (12) The regulatory system should ensure an effective and credible use of inspection, investigation, surveillance and enforcement powers and implementation of an effective compliance programme. D. Principles for Cooperation in Regulation: (13) The Regulator should have authority to share both public and non-public information with domestic and foreign counterparts; (14) Regulators should establish information sharing mechanisms that set out when and how they will share both public and non-public information with their domestic and foreign counterparts; (15) The regulatory system should allow for assistance to be provided to foreign Regulators who need to make inquiries in the discharge of their functions and exercise of their powers. E. Principles for Issuers: (16) There should be full, accurate and timely disclosure of financial results, risk and other information which is material to investors' decisions; (17) Holders of securities in a company should be treated in a fair and equitable manner; (18) Accounting standards used by issuers to prepare financial statements should be of a high and internationally acceptable quality. F. Principles for Auditors, Credit Ratings Agencies, and other information service providers: (19) Auditors should be subject to adequate levels of oversight; (20) Auditors should be independent of the issuing entity that they audit; (21) Audit standards should be of a high and internationally acceptable quality; (22) Credit rating agencies should be subject to adequate levels of oversight. The regulatory system should ensure that credit rating agencies whose ratings are used for regulatory purposes are subject to registration and on-going supervision; (23) Other entities that offer investors analytical or evaluative services should be subject to oversight and regulation appropriate to the impact their activities have on the market or the degree to which the regulatory system relies on them. G. Principles for Collective Investment Schemes: (24) The regulatory system should set standards for the eligibility, governance, organisation and operational conduct of those who wish to market or operate a collective investment scheme; (25) The regulatory system should provide for rules governing the legal form and structure of collective investment schemes and the segregation and

Under the umbrella of the IOSCO principles, the IOSCO MMoU (Multilateral Memoranda of Understanding) together with its *Appendix A* is a crucial instrument through which member signatories demonstrate their regulatory commitment – that is, to provide each other with mutual assistance and exchange information to deter cross-border fraud and other securities violations.[459] Adopted in 2002, the MMoU compliance assessment centres on key issues and questions specifically affecting the implementation of IOSCO principles 11, 12 and 13 concerning cooperation in regulation. These namely are Principle (11): The Regulator should have the authority to share both public and non-public information with domestic and foreign counterparts; Principle (12): Regulators should establish information sharing mechanisms that set out when and how they will share both public and non-public information with their domestic and foreign counterparts; and Principle (13): The regulatory system should allow for assistance to be provided to foreign regulators who need to make inquiries in the discharge of their functions and exercise of their powers.

Additionally, the IOSCO endorsed in October 2003 a comprehensive methodology (IOSCO Principles Assessment Methodology) that enables an objective

---

protection of client assets; (26) Regulation should require disclosure, as set forth under the principles for issuers, which is necessary to evaluate the suitability of a collective investment scheme for a particular investor and the value of the investor's interest in the scheme; (27) Regulation should ensure that there is a proper and disclosed basis for asset valuation and the pricing and the redemption of units in a collective investment scheme; (28) Regulation should ensure that hedge funds and/or hedge funds managers/advisers are subject to appropriate oversight. H. Principles for Market Intermediaries: (29) Regulation should provide for minimum entry standards for market intermediaries; (30) There should be initial and on-going capital and other prudential requirements for market intermediaries that reflect the risks that the intermediaries undertake; (31) Market intermediaries should be required to establish an internal function that delivers compliance with standards for internal organisation and operational conduct, with the aim of protecting the interests of clients and their assets and ensuring proper management of risk, through which management of the intermediary accepts primary responsibility for these matters; (32) There should be procedures for dealing with the failure of a market intermediary in order to minimize damage and loss to investors and to contain systemic risk. I. Principles for Secondary Markets: (33) The establishment of trading systems including securities exchanges should be subject to regulatory authorisation and oversight; (34) There should be on-going regulatory supervision of exchanges and trading systems which should aim to ensure that the integrity of trading is maintained through fair and equitable rules that strike an appropriate balance between the demands of different market participants; (35) Regulation should promote transparency of trading; (36) Regulation should be designed to detect and deter manipulation and other unfair trading practices; (37) Regulation should aim to ensure the proper management of large exposures, default risk and market disruption; (38) Securities settlement systems and central counterparties should be subject to regulatory and supervisory requirements that are designed to ensure that they are fair, effective and efficient and that they reduce systemic risk. See generally, 'Objectives and Principles of Securities Regulation.' International Organization of Securities Commissions (June 2010). *The above Principles are reproduced with kind permission from the IOSCO following formal communications between the author and the relevant IOSCO department.*

459. Multilateral Memorandum of Understanding Concerning Consultation and Cooperation and the Exchange of Information.

assessment of the level of implementation of the IOSCO Principles in the jurisdictions of its members and the development of practical action plans to correct deficiencies.[460] It however must be stated that the MMoU application, screening and signature process is neither intended to create legally binding obligations nor to override domestic laws. Rather, it encourages securities regulatory agencies to identify and tackle the legislative, regulatory and institutional obstacles that could curtail their ability to cooperate with foreign regulators and to share information during cross-border investigations on possible securities violations.[461]

As an example of its proactive approach, in light of the global crisis that hit equity markets, the Technical Committee of IOSCO published a *Consultation Paper* in March 2009 entitled 'Regulation of short selling'. This culminated in final report issued in June 2009 in which IOSCO's Technical Committee recommended that effective regulation of short selling should comprise the following four principles:

(1) short selling should be subject to appropriate controls to reduce or minimise the potential risks that could affect the orderly and efficient functioning and stability of financial markets;
(2) short selling should be subject to a reporting regime that provides timely information to the market or to market authorities;
(3) short selling should be subject to an effective compliance and enforcement system; and
(4) short selling regulation should allow appropriate exceptions for certain types of transactions for efficient market functioning and development.

For its part, the global self-regulatory organisation, the International Securities Market Association (ISMA) has also been instrumental in developing many regulations – particularly settlement on over-the-counter international trading in securities. This is a far cry from its humble origins when, in 1969, a group of senior bond dealers representing banks and securities houses set up the Association of International Bond Dealers (AIBD) – especially as AIBD oversaw the formation of a series of rules and recommendations governing trading and settlement in this market. This later changed from AIBD to ISMA, which over the past fifteen years has enjoyed a membership of more than 700 organisations – focusing as mentioned above mainly on addressing the various problems associated with settlement on securities markets.

As far as the EU regulatory context is concerned, one can easily, for example, discern the regulatory response of the EU to the internationalisation of securities markets, which was primarily focused on prospectus and disclosure

460. See generally, IOSCO 'Methodology for Assessing Implementation of the IOSCO Objectives and Principles of Securities Regulation.' International Organisation of Securities Commissions (October, 2003).
461. See EASRA, Advice on achieving compliance with IOSCO MMoU, Summary Project Completion Report, The East African Securities Regulatory Authorities (February 2007).

requirements.[462] Most recently, however, following the conclusions of the report of the *High Level Group on Financial Supervision in the EU* (the de Larosiere group), the EU Commission put forward concrete legislative proposals on 23 September 2009 in order to establish a European System of Financial Supervisors (ESFS). This comprised a network of national financial supervisors working in tandem with new European Supervisory Authorities (ESAs).

Indeed, from January 2011, the regulation of financial services across Europe was being undertaken by three ESAs. These work with the newly established European Systemic Risk Board (ESRB) in order to maintain financial stability, strengthening and enhancing the EU supervisory framework. The ESAs will improve coordination between national supervisory authorities, thus raising standards of national supervision across the EU.

The ESAs are: the European Securities and Markets Agency (ESMA), the European Banking Agency (EBA) and the European Insurance and Occupational Pensions Authority (EIOPA). They replace the level 3 (otherwise known as Lamfalussy) committees: Committee of European Banking Supervisors (CEBS), Committee of European Securities Regulators (CESR) and Committee of European Insurance and Occupational Pensions Supervisors (CEIOPS). However, in order to provide a clearer discussion, one shall summarise below the aims and objectives of such ESAs.[463]

To begin with one says that the ESAs aim is to create a single EU rule book. Additionally, should the ESAs feel that a national supervisory authority is not applying EU law, or breaching it, they have investigatory powers to delve into such perceived breaches, misapplications or non-application of EU law. In this respect, the ESAs can temporarily ban certain financial activities. The parameters in terms of setting out what they can ban and under what circumstances shall be determined later by subsequent legislation. Where an emergency has been called by the EU Council, they have wide-ranging powers to ban financial activities. In a crisis, the ESAs will be able to provide EU-wide coordination. If an emergency is declared, and subject to certain conditions and compliance with EU law, the ESAs may even make decisions that are binding on national supervisors and firms.

The ESAs will also play a mediatory role in certain situations where national supervisory authorities disagree – even rendering binding decisions to ensure compliance with EU law. The ESAs shall also have a role in EU supervisory bodies to ensure that they function efficiently and that consistent approaches and practices are followed. In order to improve the consistency of supervision across the EU, they will also be able to conduct regular peer reviews of national supervisory authorities. In the fulfilment of their roles, the ESAs will be able to collect information from national supervisors.[464] Additionally, they also will have a remit to consider consumer protection issues, while ESMA shall have direct supervisory responsibility for credit rating agencies.

462. See Jul Clausen, *supra* note 454, p. 43.
463. Information provided by the FSA on 22 June 2011.
464. This information will be used for analysing market developments, coordinating EU-wide stress tests and the macro prudential analysis undertaken by the ESRB.

4. ARAB POLICY MAKERS EMBRACING GLOBALISATION AND INTERNATIONAL REGULATORY STANDARDS

Here one explores the fact that Arab policy makers have not been indifferent to global regulatory trends. Equally, recent Arab engagement in cross-listing, linkage with technologically advanced markets as well as unprecedented openness to international regulatory standards.

4.1. Arab Policy Makers Not Indifferent to Global Regulatory Trends

Arab policy makers have not been immune from much of the above-mentioned global factors that are creating global regulatory trends. For their part, international regulatory standards are relevant to Arab countries for at least *two* reasons.

The *first* relates to Arab countries' desire to upgrade their regulatory standards in the hope of attracting foreign investment. Indeed, as seen earlier in Chapters 2 and 3, Arab countries are actively revamping their economic systems in order to attract foreign investors to relieve budgetary pressures and compensate for increasingly unavailable external funding. For, many Arab countries are rapidly awakening to the importance of foreign portfolio investment in their domestic markets, whether individual or institutional. The World Bank, too, is actively prescribing that Arab countries strengthen their capital markets and equally link them with international capital markets in order to better attract foreign investors.[465] The *second* reason relates to the contemporary phenomenon of the globalisation of securities markets, which is forcing local regulators to take cognisance of new international regulatory standards.

Additionally, recent flows of funds from industrial countries have also inadvertently created a 'worldwide allocation of savings', which makes financial regulators more receptive to developing international supervisory standards that would promote the 'robustness' of financial systems in industrial and Emerging Economies alike.[466] One must here mention that the recent tendency to internationalise emerging securities markets can achieve many benefits. *First*, it reduces the cost of unfavourable international price developments by enhancing Emerging Markets' ability to utilise market-based risk management techniques. *Second*, it brings about external improvements resulting from the involvement of sophisticated institutional investors from developed countries in emerging securities markets, manifesting in a better financial intermediation process and transfer of

465. See, for example, 'Egypt in the Global Economy, Strategic Choices for Savings, Investments, and Long Term Growth', World Bank, Middle East and North Africa Economic Studies, Research Paper No. 19 (1998).
466. See J Heimann, 'Global Institutions, National Supervisions and Systemic Risk', *Financial Stability Review*, No. 3 (Autumn 1997), pp. 82–91.

expertise and technology. *Third*, greater integration with international markets can result in enhancing policy credibility of emerging economies and provide an indirect effective disciplinary policymaking instrument.[467]

Indeed, there is no evidence whatsoever to suggest that Arab countries are deliberately pursuing an insular stance vis-à-vis regulating their financial institutions that cocoons them from current global regulatory developments.[468] It is more likely than not that Arab openness and interest in catching up with international capital markets will increase their keenness on more sophisticated regulations in the future.

Indeed, Arab regulators have been demonstrating more willingness to buttress local securities regulation by adopting internationally accepted norms in securities regulation – that is, for example by becoming signatories to the aforementioned IOSCO MMoU, a process that is rigorous and can take place only upon verifying potential compliance with many important international regulatory standards. Among Arab regulatory agencies that were signatories to the IOSCO MMoU (by 31 October 2010) are: DFSA, Dubai; Central Bank of Bahrain, Kingdom of Bahrain; Jordan Securities Commission (JSC), Jordan; CDVM, Morocco; The CMA, Saudi Arabia; The Syrian Commission on Financial Markets and Securities (SCFMS), Syrian Arab Republic; and CMF, Tunisia.

4.2. Active Engagement in Cross-Listing, Linkage and Unprecedented Openness to International Regulatory Standards

The above factors, in various degrees, are also applicable to Arab securities markets, as Arab countries have not been immune from current global trends.[469] The internationalisation of Arab capital markets is taking place through cross-regional listing arrangements, listings of American Depository Receipts (ADRs) and Global Depository Receipts (GDRs), etc. Thus, giving foreign investors and fund managers substantially freer access to domestic securities markets.[470]

Additionally, although the impact of globalisation on Arab capital markets has not been equivalent to its impact on advanced counterparts or Emerging Markets, it is nevertheless increasingly becoming a factor that cannot be discounted. One cites here the unprecedented intention to link some Arab capital markets with technologically advanced electronic markets. The discussions of July 2000, which were held in New York between NASDAQ officials and representatives of capital

467. Kumar et al., *supra* note 50, p. 14.
468. See generally T Shoker, 'The Internationalisation of the Arab Gulf Banks', PhD thesis, University of Wales, Bangor, 1989.
469. For a critique of selected Arab regulatory issues see generally, L Al-Rimawi, 'Emerging Financial Markets in the Middle East: A Critique of Selected Issues in Arab Securities Regulation', *Journal of Financial Regulation and Compliance*, Vol. VII, No. 2, June 1999, pp. 149–76.
470. See generally P Alonso-Gamo, 'Globalisation and Growth Prospects in Arab Countries', Middle Eastern Department, IMF, WP/97/125, (September 1997).

markets of Egypt, Jordan, Bahrain, Kuwait, Dubai and the Palestinian entity were indicative of Arab countries attempts at catching up with the globalisation of securities markets.

In this respect, in June 2009, the Dow Jones Indexes and the Federation of Euro-Asian Stock Exchanges (FEAS) launched the Dow Jones FEAS Indexes. This was done in order to create a measurement of the performance of companies across the Euro-Asian region. The three indexes that have been launched are a composite, and two regional sub-indexes. Dow Jones FEAS Composite Index currently includes component stocks of ten of the thirty-two Member States of the Federation of Euro-Asian Stock Exchanges. The exchanges included are Abu Dhabi (UAE), Amman (Jordan), Bahrain (Kingdom of Bahrain), Belgrade (Serbia), Bulgaria (Bulgaria), Istanbul (Turkey), Karachi (Pakistan), Macedonia (Republic of Macedonia), Muscat (Oman) and Zagreb (Croatia). The Dow Jones FEAS Middle East/Caucasus Index currently includes stocks from the following four FEAS member exchanges: Abu Dhabi, Amman, Bahrain and Muscat.[471]

Arab regulators and capital markets officials are confident enough in their internationalist orientation and ability to compete globally that they are even calling for the establishment of Middle Eastern and regional equity markets – in order to compete with European and North Atlantic markets. For example, in 2002 Jordan signed the Cooperation Protocol between Tunisia, Malta, Cairo and Alexandra stock exchanges to set up a Mediterranean stock exchange – the BorzaMed. Indeed, as early as a decade ago, Arab empirical studies even suggested that there were no fundamental problems regarding cross-listing between Arab and EU stock markets – taking into account, *inter alia*, the price earning ratios as well as performance growth in index shares of listed companies.[472]

There are equally calls for cross-listing agreements between Arab securities markets *inter se* to deepen them. For example, Jordan and Kuwait signed in May 1999 a cross-listing memorandum enabling local companies to list on the Amman Bourse and the Kuwaiti Stock Exchange. In the mid-1990s, the Bahrain Stock Exchange signed a number of cross-listing agreements with the Muscat Securities Market, the Amman Bourse and the Egypt Capital Market Authority. It also signed a tripartite agreement for cross-listing with the Kuwait and Muscat stock exchanges.

More recent intra-Arab cross-listing agreements included one signed in November 2006 between Abu Dhabi Securities Market and Jordan. Companies will be able to cross-list their shares on Abu Dhabi Securities Market and Amman Stock Exchange. The Arab Bank was the first Jordanian company expected to list on Abu Dhabi Securities Market. In a similar vein, in December 2006 the Abu Dhabi Securities Market, Muscat Securities Market and the Muscat Depository and Securities Registration Company also signed a cross-listing agreement. Oman and

471. See 'Dow Jones Indexes and the Federation of Euro-Asian Stock Exchanges to Design Regional Indexes'. Dow Jones Indexes Press Room, 3 June 2009.

472. See generally, Sabri N, 'Cross-Listing of Stocks among European-Arab (Mediterranean) Markets', *Finance India*. Vol. XVI, No. 1, March 2002. pp. 205–27.

Emirates Company[473] would be the first Omani company to list on Abu Dhabi Securities Market.

There are even tentative regional aspirations to set up a single Arab capital market in an attempt to harness Arab listed companies (over 1,458 listed companies in September 2011) and the overall capitalisation of Arab securities markets (over USD 871.521 billion in September 2011). Indeed, in their 25th meeting, which took place in Kuwait in December 2003, the Union of Arab Stock Exchanges, spent considerable energies discussing the establishment of a unified Arab stock exchange. The success of such projects undoubtedly requires Arab adoption of high regulatory standards in order to compete regionally and internationally.[474] It also requires adopting contemporary international trends. Indeed, in its desire to remodel itself, the Union of Arab Stock Exchanges was restructured into three separate boards: The Board of Stock Exchanges; the Board of Supervisory Commissions (Arab Union Regulatory Commissions) and the Board of Clearance and Depository Centres. The meeting that took place in Abu Dhabi in January 2007 (in order formally to launch the Union of Arab Securities Commissions) was an indication of the progress that Arab regulators achieved in this area.

The call for further sophistication in regulating Arab securities markets has also been gathering momentum in order for them genuinely to integrate in international capital markets. Indeed, Arab capital market officials are now commendably displaying high nuanced keenness on placing Arab stock markets on the map of international investment opportunities – through becoming part and parcel of Emerging Markets. Indeed, in late 2010 calls were made to upgrade more of Arab stock markets by international institutions from frontier to Emerging Markets. In this respect the success achieved by the financial markets in the UAE through the upgrade from frontier to secondary Emerging Market by FTSE is a milestone. Officials in the UAE stock markets even expect a similar upgrade by MSCI – which was expected to result in the flow of about USD 40.0 billion of foreign investments to the country.[475]

Moreover, Arab officials are under no illusion that achieving such upgrade represents a major challenge for all Arab markets. This is especially as it requires adherence to international norms and standards of efficiency, settlement, clearance, custody and depository requirements. This is in addition to the need for

473. This company was established in 1993.

474. As opposed to Arab securities markets being mere speculative tools with poignant lack of structured regulation, the sophistication of regulation in many Arab countries is now increasingly reaching basic international levels – that even justify comparative studies with advanced Regulatory Regimes. See for example, L Al-Rimawi, 'Jordanian, Kuwaiti and Omani Securities Regulation: Can They Be the Subject-Matter of a Viable Comparative Study with EU Securities regulation?', *Journal of Financial Regulation and Compliance*, (Part One) in Vol. VIII, No. 4, November 2000, pp. 349–457 & (Part two) in Vol. IX, No. 3, August 2001, pp. 253–73; and same author 'Jordan's Financial Laws: An Introduction to an Arab Model in Securities Regulation', *Yearbook of Islamic and Middle Eastern Law*, Vol. IV, 1998, pp. 73–98.

475. See interview with Rashed Al Baloushi, ADX's Deputy Chief Executive, in an article entitled: 'Abu Dhabi Securities Exchange Projects Growth of Foreign Investments after Upgrading UAE to Emerging Market.' 25 October 2010. <www.ameinfo.com/246792.html>.

enhancing the elements of transparency and governance to generate confidence among foreign investors – needless to say this gives prominence to listed Arab companies that would achieve international exposure. For its part, in catching up with the above, for example, the ADX was expected to introduce Extensible Business Reporting Language (XBRL) as a standard for disclosure – in addition to providing new investment vehicles and financial products resulting in further diversification and market depth.[476]

Indeed, among the strong indications of the earnest desire to set regional stock exchanges that match the highest international standards in terms of regulation, trading systems and financial products, one mentions here NASDAQ Dubai – formerly known as the DIFX, having opened in Dubai on 26 September 2005. From the outset, its declared objective was to become the leading stock exchange between Western Europe and East Asia. On 19 November 2008 it even launched an equity derivatives platform – consisted of futures on the FTSE NASDAQ Dubai UAE 21 index and on twenty individual UAE stocks listed on NASDAQ Dubai, the Dubai Financial Market and the Abu Dhabi Securities Market.

Moreover, while it has now become an acclaimed major (regional) platform for *Sukuk* (Islamic debt instruments), with twenty listed *Sukuks*, NASDAQ Dubai in April 2009 even introduced a UAE equity options service. For a breakdown of the total capitalisation of NASDAQ Dubai, see Table 5.1.

Table 5.1 Capitalisation of NASDAQ Dubai by 31 August 2010

Class of securities	*USD*
Ordinary shares	13,934,423,886
DGR's and ADS's	12,313,279,314
Bonds	6,129,925,000
Sukuks	16,246,226,157

Source: NASDAQ Dubai, *Market Capitalisation Report* (31 August 2010).

Finally, as another strong indication of some Arab countries' earnest desire to be part and parcel of this unprecedented globalised trend that is sweeping regional financial services, one mentions here their interest in laying the foundations for truly cutting-edge legal systems – thus enhancing the international reputation of their respective jurisdictions in terms of their ability to deal efficiently and fairly with highly complex financial disputes with integrity and competence. As discussed in Chapter 4, securities regulation's overriding thrust is to provide adequate investor protection. Indeed, that chapter argued that one measure of ensuring investor protection for local and international investors was to ensure open accessibility to a highly competent local legal system.

476. *Ibid.*

For, as was argued in Chapter 4, the requirement of 'some measures of compensation should the contract founder', may not always be sufficient to protect investors' interests. This is especially as there will be occasions when investors require adequate legal remedies for actions that would have taken place at a pre-contractual stage. In order to address much of the above concerns, countries like Qatar, for example, has revolutionised important aspects of its judicial system. For, as mentioned in Chapter 2, in order to keep abreast with, *inter alia*, disputes arising from financial activities in its financial centre (QFC) it has now set up a commensurate world-class legal infrastructure, manifesting itself in the form of the QFC Civil and Commercial Court and the QFC Regulatory Tribunal – complete with judges of the highest international calibre in terms of expertise, integrity and competence.

5. CONCLUSION

The picture vis-à-vis regulating Arab capital markets could not have been more different from only a decade ago. For, while (as seen in Chapter 2) securities markets were largely viewed as speculative tools considerably lacking in regulation, their regulation is now seen as a national priority. For, after having awakened, to the potential of securities markets as genuine engine for growth, Arab countries are keen to develop their regulatory standards.

Indeed, more than ever before, international regulatory standards are now relevant to Arab securities markets, as such countries continue to revamp their underlying macroeconomic conditions in their attempts at attracting foreign capital. Moreover, as there is no evidence that Arab countries are attempting to cocoon their financial institutions from current global regulatory developments, international regulatory standards become ever more relevant.

As Arab countries seek to cross-list their securities, link with technologically advanced markets and aspire to establish regional markets that compete internationally, Arab regulars become ever more assiduous in their drive to catch up with international standards. This is especially being evidenced by an increasing number of Arab regulators becoming signatories to the IOSCO MMoUs.

However, the question of securities regulation cannot be addressed in isolation from examining the local legal environment. This is especially as there are no ready-made, regulatory blueprints that can be transplanted from advanced regulatory regimes to emerging markets. A preliminary investigation is therefore needed here in order to assess the general law's consistency with modern notions of capital markets regulation.

Part of this investigation is also to examine the general law's receptiveness to securities regulation in terms of whether or not it contains any inherent juridical risks that may result in jeopardising the legal certitude of the regulatory regime. One shall accordingly look in the next chapter at the juridical risks posed by the general law in selected Arab jurisdictions, with particular reference to *Shari'a* or Islamic law.

Chapter 6

Shari'a's Juridical Risks in the Context of Arab Securities Regulation

Given the recent significant interest in Islamic finance and Islamic financial products, a discussion of Arab securities markets would be truncated without tackling some aspects pertaining to Islamic financial law. In particular, there is an ever growing importance to explain the position of *Shari'a* within Arab legal framework as both a constitutional source as well as being a legal source for commercial legislation in a majority of Arab countries.

As mentioned in Chapter 4, there are no ready-made models of securities regulation that can be transplanted cross-jurisdictionally in all countries. It is therefore important to attain a deeper understanding of certain dynamics of the general law inasmuch as it impacts upon securities regulation. This chapter therefore particularly investigates the question of juridical risks that may be inherent in Arab general law and potential constraining impact on relevant commercial legislation.

As shall be seen below, *Shari'a* (or Islamic law) affects the general law in the majority of Arab countries. This chapter therefore looks at the specific juridical risks posed by *Shari'a*,[477] seen through the concepts of *riba*[478] and *gharar*.[479] For, despite Islam's active encouragement of partnership and equity holdings, *riba* and *gharar* are constraints that limit the *modus operandi* of equity markets and the choice of securities.

Accordingly, this chapter first examines the contemporary juridical importance of *Shari'a* and answers the question of why, if at all, it is essential to address concepts that exclusively belong to *Shari'a*. It then considers the sources of *Shari'a*

477. Referred to here as Islamic law. See subsection dealing with *Shari'a* and its legal sources.

478. Referred to here as interest on loans. See subsection dealing with *riba*.

479. Referred to here as *jahel* (want of knowledge) of, *inter alia*, contractual aspects relating to consideration, delivery, subject matter, etc. It also refers to uncertainty, speculation or excessive risk. See subsection dealing with *gharar*.

in order to shed light on the reasons for the diversity in ascertaining the juridical meaning of *riba* and *gharar*. The chapter equally examines the juridical concepts of *riba* and *gharar*, before addressing their impact on relevant commercial legislation. It concludes by examining the effect of such juridical concepts on capital markets.

1. THE IMPORTANCE OF EXAMINING *SHARI'A* JURIDICALLY[480]

A question that has legitimately been asked from a Western perspective is why, if at all, *Shari'a* is still relevant in the modern legal context of Arab countries, particularly in commercial aspects? Additionally, how does this relevance manifest itself in a legalistic manner? Indeed, given apparent secularisation of many aspects of Arab countries, particularly in their legal systems (in terms of seemingly pro-Western substantive rules and legal procedures), it is surprising that one should contemplate the legal relevance of *Shari'a* in areas outside personal status and family law.

The above observation, though somewhat true, does not address the structural legal relevance of *Shari'a* – which at least in terms of the letter of the law certainly goes beyond paying lip-service to Islamist Arab movements and their populist demands. For, as shall be observed from the discussion below, the designation of *Shari'a* as a legal source to many Arab constitutions has often been a response calculated to assuage populace demands – that is, in terms of giving the impression that Islam remains pervasive at a State level particularly as the official religion. However, although this methodology may have served political expediency by appearing to give more prominence to *Shari'a* than was actually intended, it is not necessarily without potentially serious legal ramifications – as at least was the case in Egypt in the 1980s as shall be seen below. This subsection therefore attempts to explain the modern dynamics of this relevance.

Indeed, in the contemporary Arab and Islamic worlds of today, *Shari'a* remains influential and cannot be ignored, especially when examining questions of socio-juridical nature. For, due to the belief that the principal source of its moral-juridical precepts is revelation rather than reason, much of *Shari'a's* fundamental legal principles have remained impervious to change.[481] Additionally, unlike Western legal systems, which long separated cannon and secular laws, *Shari'a* principles still continue to constitute an important source of

480. This subsection was an article by the author first published by Sweet & Maxwell and is reproduced by agreement and kind permission by them. See L Al-Rimawi, 'Relevance of *Shari'a* as a Legislative Source in Modern Arab Legal Context: A Brief Constitutional Synopsis with Emphasis on Selected Commercial Aspects.' *The Company Lawyer*, Vol. XXXII, No. 2, January 2011, pp. 57–64.

481. See N Comair-Obied, *The Law of Business Contracts in the Arab Middle East: A Theoretical and Practical Comparative Analysis with Particular Reference to Modern Legislation*, Kluwer Law International, London, 1996, p. 12.

legislation in the majority of Arab countries. This subsection accordingly examines the nature of the juridical importance of *Shari'a*, arguing that it can at least be attributed to its role as a constitutional source as well as *Shari'a's* ever-enduring societal relevance.

1.1. *Shari'a* as a Constitutional Source

The position of Arab countries on the role of *Shari'a* in their respective constitutions has varied considerably. While some Arab constitutions still hold *Shari'a* to be *the* principal source of law, others have held it as *a* principal source of legislation. Other Arab constitutions have attempted to limit the role of Islam to being the religion of the State, without making any reference to *Shari'a* being a legislative source. The remainder of Arab constitutions as shall be seen below simply referred to 'freedom of conscience' designating 'the nation' as the source of all powers – even stating that 'temporal' laws should carry the expression of the will of the people.

1.1.1. Different Levels to *Shari'a* Being a Constitutional Source

Indeed, in order to try to structure the modern position of *Shari'a* as a constitutional source one can speak of five clear categories – albeit not mutually exclusive:

(1) *Shari'a* is an overall constitutional source and the apparent embodiment of the State;
(2) *Shari'a* does not necessarily represent the embodiment of the State, though it constitutes *the* principal source of legislation;
(3) strong degree of commitment to *Shari'a* as *a* legislative source in Arab constitutions;
(4) marginal role for *Shari'a*. Here, although some Arab constitutions hold Islam to be 'the religion of the state', they nevertheless equally hold 'the nation' or 'the people' as the source of 'all power'; and
(5) *Shari'a* plays no role as a constitutional source in some Arab countries.

The discussion below shall therefore elaborate on the above categories regarding the importance of *Shari'a* in Arab constitutions as a legislative source – which as mentioned above are not necessarily mutually exclusive. In doing so, the discussion shall look at the wording of selected Arab constitutions in order to ferret out *Shari'a's* place as a constitutional source.

1.1.1.1. Shari'a as an Overall Constitutional Source as the Apparent Embodiment of the State

Nowhere can the role of *Shari'a* be more prominent than in the constitution of Saudi Arabia. In this respect, Article (1) of the 1992 Saudi Constitution takes a strong view on the position of *Shari'a* and the role of the *Koran* and the Prophet's sayings as an overall source of the Constitution itself. Article (1) of the 1992 Saudi Constitution states:

> The Kingdom of Saudi Arabia is a sovereign Arab Islamic state with Islam as its religion; God's Book and the *Sunnah* of His Prophet, God's prayers and peace be upon him, are its constitution. Arabic is its language and Riyadh is its capital.

Moreover, Article (23) of the 1992 Saudi Constitution prescribes that the Saudi State must implement *Shari'a*. Article (23) of the 1992 Saudi Constitution states:

> The state protects Islam; it implements its *Shari'a*; it orders people to do right and shun evil; it fulfils the duty regarding God's call.

It is clear from the above constitutional provisions that the Saudi constitution does not simply pay lip-service to *Shari'a* as a constitutional source, as it represents the embodiment of the State. In this respect, its commitment to *Shari'a*, as a legislative source, is quite evident. This commitment can be contrasted to much watered-down or non-commitment to *Shari'a* as a legislative source by other Arab constitutions as shall be seen from the discussion below.

1.1.1.2. Shari'a *as the Principal Source of Legislation*

Having *Shari'a* constitutionally as representing the embodiment of the State is exclusive to Saudi Arabia as seen above. However, other Arab countries' constitutions, although do not go as far as the above, they nevertheless give strong commitment to *Shari'a* constitutionally. Such Arab countries designate *Shari'a* as *the* main source of legislation. In this respect, Egypt (under its new 1971 Constitution and subsequent amendments) and Oman belong to this category, as the discussion below shall reveal:

(1) Egypt is an Arab country where the constitution designates *Shari'a* as *the* principal source of legislation. Article (1) of the 1971 Egyptian Constitution states that Egypt is a 'democratic' and 'socialist' state: *The Arab Republic of Egypt is a democratic, socialist State based on the alliance of the working forces of the people . . .* For its part, Article (2) which was amended on 22 May 1980 further strengthened the role of *Shari'a* stating that Islam is *the* religion of the State and Islamic jurisprudence is *the* principal source of legislation: *Islam is* the *religion of the State and Arabic its official language. Islamic jurisprudence is* the *principal source of legislation.*

However, it must be stated that Egypt's 1971 Constitution and its subsequent amendments was not immune from the ebb and flow that underlined the dynamics of Egyptian politics. For, it was promulgated in the early days of President Sadat who had wanted to adopt a less confrontational relationship with popular Islam (as represented by the Muslim Brotherhood). This was especially as his predecessor's term in office had been marked by huge confrontations with the Islamic group.

For, unlike President Nasser, President Sadat attempted a more accommodating approach with Islamist trends.[482] Indeed, as shall be seen below (in the discussion on the legal implications of *Shari'a* being designated the legislative source) the amendment of the Egyptian constitution caused legal upheaval.

(2) For its part, Oman has equally adopted a strong view on the legislative role of *Shari'a* in its constitution. Article (2) of the 1996 Omani Basic Law declares that Islam is *the* religion of the State and *Shari'a* is *the* basis of legislation. *Royal Decree No. 102/1996* which promulgated Oman's first Basic Law states in Article (2): *The religion of the State is Islam and the Islamic Shari'a is* the *basis of legislation.* Indeed, it is clear that while *Shari'a* doesn't represent the embodiment of the State, as is the case in Saudi Arabia above, Oman nevertheless represents strong commitment to *Shari'a* as it designates it as the main legislative source.

(3) Yemen also belongs to this category as enunciated under its May 1991 Constitution – which was amended in September 1994 and in February 2001. Article (1) for example states that the Republic of Yemen is an Arab, Islamic and independent sovereign State whose integrity is inviolable, and no part of which may be ceded. It equally adds that the people of Yemen are part of the Arab and Islamic nations. Article (2) states that Islam is the religion of the State, and Arabic is its official language. For its part, Article (3) states that *Shari'a* is *the* source of all legislation. However, given the violent political turmoil that Yemen has been experiencing throughout 2011, it is still early to project a definitive landscape of the likely resultant political and legal system.

1.1.1.3. Strong Degree of Commitment to Shari'a *as a Legislative Source in Arab Constitutions*

This category includes a number of Arab countries that have designated *Shari'a* as *a* main source of legislation. This category includes Bahrain, Kuwait, Qatar and Syria. In this sense such Arab countries have committed themselves to accepting *Shari'a* as *a* source of law, though to a lesser degree than that witnessed in, for example, Saudi Arabia, Egypt and Oman. The discussion below elaborates on such category of Arab countries:

(1) In Bahrain, *Shari'a* is *a* main source of legislation, as enunciated by Article (2) of the new 2002 Constitution. Article (2) of the 2002 Bahraini Constitution states: *The religion of the State is Islam. The Islamic Shari'a is a principal source for legislation. The official language is Arabic.* This was also the position under the previous 1973 Constitution. In this respect one sees that the Kingdom of Bahrain has consistently maintained *Shari'a*

---

482. For an interesting account of Islamist impact on Egypt's legal system see generally: Tamir Moustafa 'The Islamist Trend in Egyptian Law', Simon Papers on Security and Development, Simon Fraser University, No. 2/2010, May 2010.

as *a* source of legislation without having to upgrade or downgrade this steady level of commitment.

(2) Another clear example is Kuwait. For example, Article (2) of the 1962 Kuwaiti Constitution states that *Shari'a* constitutes *a* principal source of law as opposed to *the* principal source of law. It however must be stated here that given the vibrancy of Kuwaiti politics (particularly in the wake of the Iraqi invasion), the question of the position of *Shari'a* as a constitutional source came to the fore – due to Islamist pressure as shall be seen in the discussion of the practical implications below.

(3) The position is similar in Qatar, where under its new Constitution of 2003, *Shari'a* is *a* main source of legislation. Article (1) of the 2003 Qatari Constitution states that: *Qatar is an independent sovereign Arab State. Its religion is Islam and Shari'a law shall be a main source of its legislations. Its political system is democratic. The Arabic language shall be its official language. The people of Qatar are part of the Arab nation.* Article (150) repeals the 1972 Constitution. Here, similar to countries included in this category, Qatar makes it clear that its legal system is quite committed to *Shari'a*, notwithstanding it is not as strong as seen in the previous two categories.

(4) Given its political (socialist) orientation it may come as a surprise to see Syria included in this category. For, its State ideology has consistently propagated secular Arab nationalism with a twist of socialism. Nonetheless, Syria also holds a similar position adopted in this category where Article (3)(2) of the 1973 Syrian Constitution states that *Shari'a* is *a* source of legalisation. In this respect, Article (3)(2) of the 1973 Syrian Constitution states that *Islamic jurisprudence is a main source of legislation.* Here, like all the countries in this category, Syria, too, commits itself to upholding *Shari'a* as a legislative source.

(5) Iraq has also joined this category following its 2005 constitution, which was ratified on 15 October 2005 – after having been subjected to a national referendum. It, however, must be stated that although it refers to *Shari'a* in Article (2) as *a* fundamental source of legislation, the 2005 Iraqi Constitution adopts a more pro-*Shari'a* stance by equally declaring that no subsequent law should contradict the established provisions of *Shari'a*:

> Islam is the official religion of the State and it is *a fundamental source of legislation*:
>
> A. No law that contradicts the established provisions of Islam may be established.
> B. No law that contradicts the principles of democracy may be established.
> C. No law that contradicts the rights and basic freedoms stipulated in this constitution may be established. [Italics added.]

However, it is clear that the above may be a recipe for future controversy. This is especially as the 2005 Iraqi Constitution equally states that no law shall contract the principles of democracy. For, such terminology is evidently vague and may, on certain occasions, conflict with the first *caveat* that no law shall contradict the established position of *Shari'a*. Needless to say, it is often difficult even to ascertain *Shari'a's* established provisions due to intricate jurisprudence and its *sui generis* legal make-up.

(6) A curious country that can be added to this category due to the fact that it has shown strong commitment to implementing *Shari'a* is Sudan under its 1998 Constitution. It under Article (65) specifically referred to Islamic law (together with the consensus of the nation through referendum, Constitution and custom) as the *sources* of legislation, adding that no legislation in contravention with these fundamentals shall be made. However, after the Interim Constitution of 2005 (which paved the way to the secession of the south), the remit of *Shari'a* was limited to the north of the country. In this respect, clearly excluding the south of the country, Article 5 (1) of the 2005 Interim Constitution states that only legislation enacted for the north of Sudan shall have *Shari'a* as a source:

> 5 (1) Nationally enacted legislation having effect only in respect of the Northern states of the Sudan shall have as its sources of legislation Islamic *Shari'a* and the consensus of the people.

However, following the internationally recognised independence of the State of South Sudan in 2011, it is only a matter of time before the Republic of Sudan consolidates its constitutional provisions *vis-à-vis* the legislative role of *Shari'a* – most likely in a manner that should not be too dissimilar to the original position under Article (65) of the 1998 Constitution as mentioned above.

1.1.1.4. Marginal Role for Shari'a *in Arab Constitutions*

This category of Arab countries appears to attempt to impose a more pronounced separation between cannon and secular law. For, while accepting that the religion of the State is Islam, such category equally states unequivocally that 'the people' or 'the nation' is the source of all powers – and equally that 'temporal law' is the expression of the will of the people. In this sense what such Arab constitutions are implying is respect for Islam as a religion, but following a semi-secular legal path. Among these countries are Algeria, Jordan, Morocco and Tunisia. The discussion below shall elaborate on the position of the constitutions of this Arab category:

(1) Algeria holds Islam as the religion of the State without any further implication to its role as a legislative source. For example, Article (2) of the 1976 Constitution (amended in 1996) states merely that Islam is the religion of the State. In this context, Article (2) of the 1976 Algerian Constitution states: *Islam is the religion of the State.* Here, as seen above, Algeria's stance is not much different from other Arab countries that belong to this category – that is, in the sense that it too has paid lip service to considering Islam as providing the general orientation of the State, without stating in substantive terms that *Shari'a* has any constitutional role to play.

(2) For its part, the 1952 Jordanian Constitution adopted a similar position to Arab countries included in this category – declaring in Article (2) that Islam is the 'religion of the State', while stating in Article (24)(1) that the nation is *the source of all powers*. In this context, Article (2) of the 1952 Jordanian Constitution states: *Islam is the religion of the State and Arabic is its official language*. The Jordanian Constitution does not state clearly that *Shari'a* is a source of legislation. Neither however does it state emphatically (as shall be seen below in some Arab countries) that temporal law is the source of legislation. Thus, walking a tight political rope between secularism and Islamism.

It is worth mentioning here that Jordan was undergoing important constitutional changes during 2011. However, these changes do not impact on the position of *Shari'a* in terms of whether it should form a constitutional source – as such constitutional amendments largely aimed at making Jordanian ministers more accountable, setting up a Jordanian constitutional court as well as limiting the interference of the executive authority.

(3) Morocco under Article (6) of the 1996 Moroccan Constitution states that Islam is the religion of the State. Article (6) of the 1996 Moroccan Constitution states: *Islam shall be the State religion. The State shall guarantee freedom of worship for all.* Yet Article (4) makes it clear that temporal law (not *Shari'a*) shall be the supreme expression of the will of the people. Article (4) of the 1996 Moroccan Constitution states: *The law shall be the supreme expression of the will of the Nation. All shall abide by it. The law shall have no retroactive effect.*

Here it is clear that the role of *Shari'a* is confined to the generic question of the identity of the State in terms of its overall public orientation as opposed to it playing a substantive constitutional role. However, similar to Jordan above, Morocco was also undergoing important changes in 2011 regarding its political system that aim at delineating the power structure in favour of openness and accountability – though, such liberal changes are not likely to impact on the position of *Shari'a*.

(4) Under its constitution adopted on 1 June 1959 the Tunisian Constitution states that Islam is the religion of the State. In this respect, Article (1) states that: *Tunisia is a free, independent and sovereign State. Its religion is Islam, its language is Arabic and its type of government is the Republic.* Article (3) further elaborates that sovereignty belongs to the people: *Sovereignty belongs to the Tunisian people, who exercise it in accordance with the Constitution.* Here, it is clear that *Shari'a's* role as a constitutional or legislative source, contrary to what was seen in other Arab countries, is virtually non-existent. In this respect, Tunisia has plainly adopted a heavy secular approach placing sovereignty in the hands of the people.

However, with the general elections held in October 2011, following the collapse of the Ben-Ali regime, Islamists gained 41.5% of the votes, winning 90 out of the 217 member assembly seats that will rewrite the constitution, appoint a president and form a caretaker government – something which will undoubtedly impact on the constitutional role of *Shari'a*.

1.1.1.5. Shari'a *Plays No Role as a Constitutional Source*

If Saudi Arabia represented the highest degree of constitutional commitment to *Shari'a* seeing it as the embodiment of the State, this final category represents the extreme opposite where *Shari'a* doesn't feature or hold any legislative prominence. This position is found in Arab countries that have attempted completely secularising their respective societies, without leaving any illusion that *Shari'a* has any constitutional role to play. Examples of Arab countries in this category include Lebanon and Libya (under the former Gaddafi regime) as shall be seen below:

(1) Lebanon is among Arab countries the constitution of which does not designate *Shari'a* as a source of legislation. Article 1(4) of the 23 May 1926 Lebanese Constitution states that *The people are the source of authority and sovereignty.* Furthermore, the constitution refers to safeguarding the freedom of 'conscience' as opposed to referring to a particular monolithic religion. In this respect, Article (9) of the 1926 Lebanese Constitution states: *There shall be absolute freedom of conscience. The State . . . shall respect all religions and creeds and guarantees, under its protection, the free exercise of all religious rites provided that public order is not disturbed. It also guarantees that the personal status and religious interests of the population, to whatever religious sect they belong, is respected.*

From the above extensive emphasis that the people are the source of authority and sovereignty, the Lebanese Constitution has clearly distanced itself from nominating *Shari'a* as the religion of the State, choosing instead to guarantee freedom of conscience. Here, as is clearly seen there is no reference to Islam or *Shari'a*. But rather respect to all religions and to the wishes of the people in terms of choosing to apply their religious rules to their respective communities – in terms of, for example, inheritance, personal status law, etc.

(2) The role of *Shari'a* as a legislative source was equally non-prominent in Libya under the Gaddafi regime. Although Article (2) of the Constitution of December 1969[483] stated that Islam is the religion of the State, Article (6) for example proclaimed that the aim of the State is to achieve socialism. In a diluted reference to Islam, it also added that the State is 'inspired' by its Arabic and Islamic heritage, humanitarian values, etc. In this respect, Article (2) of the 1969 Libyan Constitution stated that: *Islam is the religion of the State and Arabic is its official language. The State protects religious freedom in accordance with established customs.* Article (6) of the 1969 Libyan Constitution stated that: *The aim of the State is the realisation of socialism through the application of social justice which forbids any form of exploitation . . . . . . Its inspiration is its Arabic and Islamic heritage, humanitarian values and the specific conditions of the Libyan society.*

483. Article (33) of the 1969 Libyan Constitution repeals the previous Constitution of 1951.

However, the Libyan constitution under the Gaddafi regime specifically referred to *Shari'a* as a source of law of inheritance. Article (8) of the 1969 Libyan Constitution stated that:

> Public ownership is the basis of the development of society, of its growth and of self-sufficiency in production. Private ownership, if it is non-exploitative, is protected. Expropriation will take place only in accordance with the law. Inheritance is a right which will be governed by the Islamic *Shari'a*.

However, following the collapse of the Gaddafi regime in August 2011, the Libyan National Transitional Council (NTC) has now proposed a new constitution that is likely to place much more emphasis on *Shari'a* –in terms of accentuating its overall role in the Libyan society. The Libyan draft constitution proposed by the NTC states that *Shari'a* is *the* principal source of legislation. Article (1) of the new draft constitution states:

> Libya is an independent democratic state wherein the people are the source of authorities. The city of Tripoli shall be the capital of the State. *Islam is the religion of the State and the principal source of legislation is Islamic jurisprudence (Shari'a).* Arabic is its official language while preserving the linguistic and cultural rights of all components of the Libyan society. The State shall guarantee non-Muslims the freedom of practising religious rites and shall guarantee respect for their system of personal status. [Italics added]

It is abundantly clear from the above that once implemented, the new Libyan Constitution will place Libya in the aforementioned second category, where *Shari'a* plays a significant role as *the* principal legal/constitutional source.

1.1.2. Practical Implications to the Imposition of Interest, Particularly in Egypt and Kuwait

The above gradation of the constitutional relevance of *Shari'a* is not merely academic or pedantic. For, depending on the ebb and flow of underlying Islamist dynamics such gradation can, on some occasions, have quite serious ramifications. Indeed, it must be stated that the role of *Shari'a* as a legislative source in Arab constitutions is not static. Such a role has on occasions brought intense domestic debate into the supremacy of *Shari'a* as an overall legislative yardstick as shall be seen below.

No more can the socio-politico-legal dynamics be seen more than in Egypt – that is, in terms of their legislative impact in the Arab world. As mentioned above, Article (2) of the 1971 Egyptian Constitution (under considerable Islamist pressure) was amended in May 1980 to make *Shari'a* as *the* principal source of law.[484] Such amendment was also followed by Islamist demands to annul 'unconstitutional' provisions of the Egyptian Civil Code (ECC) that permit interest – mainly referring to Article (226) of the 1948 ECC. Indeed, it is a well-known

484. Article 2 had previously stated that *Shari'a* is *a* principal source of law.

fact that in the first ten years of its existence (established in 1979) the Supreme Constitutional Court (SCC) received 215 constitutional challenges invoking Article 2.[485]

The first of such attempts at challenging interest payments (as stipulated under Article (226) of the ECC) dates back to 1980. This was barely a year after setting up the SCC, with two more similar challenges within a month of the first case. While the first case (*Case 31, Judicial Year 2*) did not proceed due to the plaintiff withdrawing his request for constitutional review, the two others (*Cases 21 and 72, Judicial Year 6*) were dismissed on technical grounds. Nevertheless with fifty-three similar cases challenging interest on similar constitutional grounds, the SCC had in the end to tackle this matter once and for all.[486]

This was a landmark case as it brought to the fore the apparent conflict between Article (2) of the Egyptian 1971 Constitution and its subsequent amendments and the imposition of interest. The case itself was brought by *Sheikh al-Azhar*, Abd al-Halim Mahmud, against the offices of the President of the Republic, the Prime Minister, and the President of the Legislative Committee of the Peoples' Assembly, in addition to Fuad Gudah, who had a concrete, personal interest in the case.[487] Here, *Sheikh al-Azhar* was objecting to the payment of 4% interest ordered by an administrative court regarding an overdue payment for equipment that did not exceed 600 Egyptian pounds.

However, the Egyptian Supreme Constitutional Court dismissed such demands in its decision rendered on 4 May 1985.[488] In Case No. 20/1985 the SCC argued that the change brought about by amending the Constitution was not retroactive. But merely futuristic in terms of making *Shari'a* the main source of 'future legislative enactments'. It also further added that the Constitution as amended did not 'automatically' make *Shari'a* an all-inclusive temporal law that replaced the ECC.[489] This rejection of the retroactive impact of Article (2) of the Egyptian Constitution provided a basis for rejecting many subsequent cases relating to different aspects including personal status cases as well as criminal ones. Moreover, this decision was equally criticised on the grounds that it did not cease the opportunity to resolve once and for all the controversy surrounding *Shari'a's* constitutional role. Equally, on technical grounds as the case was not a dispute about charging interest per se as it related to a contractual breach. Rather it related to a pecuniary penalty that would have been allowed under *Shari'a* rules – especially as it resulted from an overdue contractual payment as mentioned above.

Even after the promulgation of many Egyptian laws post-1980, under the pretext of stability, the SCC was still very reluctant to accept that Article (2)

485. See Tamir Moustafa, *supra* note 482, p. 14.
486. *Ibid.*
487. *Ibid.*
488. See Case No. 20 of the Judicial Year No. 1.
489. See S Habachy, 'Commentary on the Decision of the Supreme Court of Egypt Given on 4 May 1985 Concerning the Legitimacy of Interest and the Constitutionality of Article 226 of the new Egyptian Civil Code of 1948', *Arab Law Quarterly* [*ALQ*], Vol. 1, No. 2 (1986), p. 240.

had changed the fundamentals of Egyptian law – notwithstanding that the SCC was more prepared to delve into *Shari'a* reasoning and objectives when enunciating some of its decisions.[490] However, this is not to say that the constitutional changes as embodied under Article 2 making *Shari'a* as *the* main source of legislation were completely without any impact. This was manifest in an unusual case that was not relevant to commercial aspects of Egyptian law. For, in the 1990s, the Cairo Court of Appeals,[491] stated that the apparent anti-Islamic work of Nasr Hamid Abu Zayd, a professor of Islamic and Arabic Studies at Cairo University, was blasphemous and in violation of Article (2) of the constitution. This decision, which was later upheld by the Court of Cassation, led to Abu Zayd being declared an apostate – thus allowing his marriage from a Muslim woman to be annulled by order of the court on public interest grounds without the request of his wife.[492]

However, *Shari'a's* constitutional relevance vis-à-vis the question of interest in terms of its judicial implications is not only exclusive to Egypt. For, this, *inter alia*, has equally been observed in Kuwait, the UAE and Pakistan. Indeed, the ebb and flow of domestic political dynamics in terms of their impact on constitutionalist Islamic demands can also be seen in Kuwait. This was largely due to the incessant efforts of the Kuwait's Islamic Constitutional Movement (ICM), which was set up in 1991. In this respect, it has been rightly commented that although it is seen as a relatively new comer, the ICM nevertheless boasts of being one of the most experienced in parliamentary and electoral politics.[493] Nevertheless, despite its parliamentary experience and repeated attempts, it has so far failed to succeed in amending Article (2) of the Kuwaiti Constitution to make *Shari'a* as *the* main source of legislation as opposed to being *a* main source of legislation as mentioned above. Indeed, subsequent attempts at challenging Articles (110) and (113) of the Kuwaiti Commercial Code (on the grounds that they contradict Article (2) of the Kuwaiti Constitution as they permit interest) were rejected by the Kuwait Constitutional Court – particularly under Court Decision of 28 November 1992.

The above stance in allowing interest to be charged in commercial transactions had been previously adopted by other Arab Gulf countries particularly in the UAE under the UAE Supreme Federal Court Decision of 6 June 1983.

As seen above, from a contemporary legal viewpoint, the imposition of *Shari'a* as a constitutional source may present an unquantifiable juridical risk – that is, in the sense that all commercial laws and regulations contrary to *Shari'a* remain subject to future annulment. However, this remains a remote possibility, and with the

490. See for example *Case 8 Judicial Year 17*. The SCC did not uphold the plaintiff's request to allow his daughter to wear the *niqab* (full Islamic facial veil) instead of school uniform as there was no evidence that wearing *niqab* was mandated by *Shari'a*. The inference here was that the SCC may have reached a different verdict had *niqab* been indeed mandated by *Shari'a*.
491. Cairo Courts of Appeals Case No. 287, for the year 1995.
492. Indeed, by then Professor Abu Zayd and his wife had already left Egypt to live in Holland in anticipation of such a decision which they were determined not to accept.
493. See generally Nathan J Brown 'Pushing Toward Party Politics: Kuwait's Islamic Constitutional Movement', Democracy and Rule of Law Programme, Paper No. 79. Carnegie Endowment for International Peace (January 2007).

exclusion of the examples above, does not seem to have surfaced in a serious manner to threaten the validity of various pieces of Arab legislation that do not adhere strictly to *Shari'a*. Nevertheless, this does not mean that should Islamists gain more foothold in Arab countries (depending on future political dynamics) more serious challenges cannot be disregarded: Libya and Tunisia revolutions of 2011 are examples in mind.

1.2. GAP-FILLING ROLE: *SHARI'A*'S RELEVANCE TO MODERN COMMERCIAL TRANSACTIONS

Historically, many Arab countries, at one stage or another, relied on Ottoman civil laws largely embodied in *Majallat el-Ahkam el-Adliyya* or *Majallat*, which was promulgated in the late Nineteenth Century and was heavily influenced by *Shari'a*.[494] The *Majallat* was relied upon by Egyptian judges and is still a source of civil law in many Arab countries including Jordan and Iraq.[495] For its part, the ECC 1948 has influenced many Arab civil codes, especially in the Arab Gulf. Because of the almost identical historical-juridical sources, most Arab civil codes of today have much in common as they were promulgated in the latter half of the Twentieth Century. Arab codes in mind are those of Syria,[496] Iraq,[497] Jordan,[498] Kuwait[499] and the United Arab Emirates.[500]

Indeed, *Shari'a* is still an important contemporary legal source to Arab civil codes and, to a lesser extent, commercial codes. It contains the general principles that apply in circumstances where there are no provisions to the contrary. For example, the Jordanian and Kuwaiti civil codes now both hold Islamic jurisprudence to be their first source of law in the absence of legislation. This is evidenced in Article (1)(2) and Article (3) of the Jordanian Civil Code (JCC), together with the amended Article (1)(2) of the Kuwaiti Civil Code (KCC).[501] This fact is especially important as, from a *Shari'a* standpoint, the presence of *riba* or *gharar* renders contractual obligations *fasid/batil* or null and void.[502] For, *gharar* is a

494. The Ottoman Empire did not rely exclusively on *Shari'a* to govern all its commercial transactions. French models influenced the Ottoman Trade Law 1850 and the Commercial Code Procedures 1861.
495. Note that Egypt used to have its own Civil Code of 1875 which is often seen as a hybrid of *Shari'a* and Western laws.
496. In 1949.
497. In 1951.
498. In 1976.
499. In 1980.
500. In 1985.
501. *Royal Decree No. 67 of 1980, Pertaining to Enacting the Civil Code*. Promulgated in *Official Gazette* No. 1335, dated 5 January 1981. However, Kuwait made *Shari'a* as the first source to the KCC by Law No. 15/1996, which replaced custom – as it was then the first source of law to the KCC.
502. See subsection on the effects of *riba* and *gharar*, which considers the juristic meaning of the terms *fasid* and *batil*.

concept that was developed under *Shari'a* in order to protect the weaker party in Islamic contractual obligations from *ghubn* (or injury) due to *jahel* (want of knowledge)[503] and was subsequently adopted by the overwhelming majority of modern Arab civil codes.

Indeed, even when examining purely commercial concepts that may be subject to special Arab legislation, developing an understanding of *Shari'a's* juridical stance remains necessary. For, although the conceptual risk of annulling pieces of legislation that contravene *Shari'a* varies in Arab countries, such a risk nonetheless cannot be discounted. *Shari'a's* gap-filling role in terms of providing the general principles for much of Arab legislation, together with its being an ever-present force that influences people's decisions, also buttresses its contemporary relevance. However, the above factors remain unquantifiable, collectively underpinning the socio-juridical importance of *Shari'a* in the present Arab legal context.

1.3. Ever-Enduring Societal Relevance of *Shari'a*

The relevance of *Shari'a* does not arise mainly from its importance as a constitutional source as seen above. Or indeed from its role in gap-filling vis-à-vis commercial statutory provisions in the Arab world. For, this ignores taking account of the overall importance of *Shari'a* in the wider aspects of Arab Islamic society. With the rising and ebbing of underlying populist adherence to Islam, the impact of *Shari'a* can equally gain or lose noticeable momentum.[504] Many learned writers acknowledge this fluid state of affairs and the potential of Islamising many pieces of financial legislation.[505]

In this context, a wave of 'modernising' Islamic legal revivalism has taken it upon itself to re-examine Islam's position vis-à-vis modern commercial issues, paving the way to recent detailed studies on Islamic insurance,[506] Islamic

503. Want of knowledge of, *inter alia*, aspects relating to consideration, date and place of delivery, existence of subject matter, etc.

504. See generally J Bill, 'Resurgent Islam in the Persian Gulf', *Foreign Affairs* (Fall 1984); W Ballantyne, 'The Second Coulson Memorial Lecture: Back to the Shari'a?', *ALQ*, Vol. 3, No. 4 (November 1988), pp. 317–28; M Al-Moqatei, 'Introducing Islamic Law in the Arab Gulf States: A Case Study of Kuwait', *ALQ*, Vol. 4 No. 2, (May 1989), pp. 138–48; R Peters, 'Divine Law or Man-Made Law? Egypt and the Application of the Shari'a', *ALQ*, Vol. 3, No. 3, (August 1988), pp. 229–30.

505. See, for example, M Khan, 'Islamic Interest-Free Banking: A Theoretical Analysis', in M Khan et al., *Theoretical Studies in Islamic Banking and Finance*, IRIS Books, (USA), 1987, p. 15.

506. See generally, F Moghaizel, 'Insurance in the Light of Islamic Legal Principles', Ph.D. thesis, London University, 1991; M Al-Zarqa, *Nazam Al-Ta'min*, Beirut, 1984; M Muslehuddin, *Insurance and Islamic Law*, New Delhi, 1982; M Siddiqi, *Insurance in an Islamic Economy*, The Islamic Foundation, 1985; M Billah, 'A Model of Life Insurance in the Contemporary Islamic Economy', *ALQ*, Vol. 12, No. 3 (September 1997), pp. 287–306; S Mankabady, 'Insurance and Islamic Law: The Islamic Insurance Company', *ALQ*, Vol. 4, No. 3 (August 1989), pp. 199–205.

commercial litigation,[507] Islamic banking,[508] Islamic contract law,[509] Islamic contractual and non-contractual liability,[510] Islamic intellectual property,[511] Islamic maritime law,[512] Islamic taxation,[513] Islamic arbitration,[514] etc.

Furthermore, *Shari'a's* restrictions on securities markets resulting from *riba* and *gharar* cannot be ignored, as they have largely been responsible for creating an overall reluctance among the wider (pious) Islamic public to invest substantial sums of its funds in equity markets. For, while this problem was tackled in the context of secular banking resulting in workable modalities of Islamic banking, no such advancement was historically achieved vis-à-vis the question of Islamic financial markets – notwithstanding *Shari'a's* amenability through its active encouragement of equity financing.

Indeed, it is worth mentioning here that in the securities markets of the Middle East and North Africa in 1997 alone, only 3%–4% of all Islamic assets were invested in equities.[515] It is true that different historical factors account for this lack of Arab interest in domestic equity markets. Such historical factors, *inter alia*, include: thin

---

507. See, for example, I Ghanem, 'The Role of Islamic Law in Commercial Litigation in North Yemen', Ph.D. thesis, University of London, 1987; Z Jaffar, 'The Concept and Application of Daman in Islamic Commercial Law', Ph.D. thesis, Edinburgh University, 1994.
508. See, for example, E Ahmed, 'Islamic Banking: Distribution of Profit', Ph.D. thesis, Hull University, 1990; Y Tobbal, 'Islamic Banks and Investment Depositors: Their Relationship and Accounting Implications under the Profit and Loss Sharing *Mudaraba*', Ph.D. thesis, Kent University, 1988; T Khan, 'An Analysis of Risk Sharing in Islamic Finance with Reference to Pakistan', Ph.D. thesis Loughborough University, 1996; F Idris, 'Islamic Banks' Financial Reporting and its Usefulness to Investors: A Case Study of Bank Islam Malaysia Behrad, Malaysia', Ph.D. thesis, Cardiff University, 1995; M Abdel-Haq, 'The Relationship between Islamic Banking Theory and Practice', Ph.D. thesis, Oxford Brookes University, 1993; B El-Sharif, 'Law and Practice of Profit-Sharing in Islamic Banking with Particular Reference to *Mudarabah* and *Murabaha*', Ph.D. thesis, Exeter University, 1990.
509. See, for example, M Napiah, 'The Theory of the Contract of Agency (*al wakilah*) in Islamic Law', Ph.D. thesis, Glasgow Caledonian, 1995; A Baloglu, 'Law of Sales in the Works of Marwazi, Quduri and Sarkhasi', Ph.D. thesis, Manchester University, 1991; S Al-Kuhaimi, 'Contract Law and the Judicial System in Saudi Arabia', Ph.D. thesis, London University, 1982; M Hamid, 'The Role of Consent in Formation of Contracts: A Comparative Study in English and Islamic law', Ph.D. thesis, London University, 1971; I Edge, 'Comparative Commercial Law of Egypt and the Arabian Gulf', *Cleveland State Law Review*, Vol. 34, 1985–1986.
510. See, for example, G Mosmar, 'Civil Liability in the Jordanian Civil Code: A Comparative Study with the Shari'a', Ph.D. thesis, London University, 1998; A Mohamad, 'The Islamic Law of Tort', Ph.D. thesis, Edinburgh University, 1997.
511. See, for example, M Azmi, 'Intellectual Property Laws and Islam in Malaysia', Ph.D. thesis, London University, 1995.
512. See, for example, D Rice-Noble, 'The Principles of Islamic Maritime Law', Ph.D. thesis, London University, 1988; M El-Ghirani, 'The Law of Charterparty with Particular Reference to Islamic Law', Ph.D. thesis, Glasgow College of Technology, 1990.
513. See, for example, N Kahveci, 'Modes of Taxation in Islamic Laws as Reflected in the Jurisprudence of Zain al-Din Ibin Nujaim al-Midsri', Ph.D. thesis, Manchester University, 1990; I Al-Barrak, 'Application of Islamic Law to Taxation in Saudi Arabia', Ph.D. thesis, Exeter University, 1981.
514. See, for example, A Al-Sharif, 'Euro-Arab Arbitration Systems and Islamic Shari'a Law', M.Phil. thesis, Salford University, 1990.
515. See P Moore, *Islamic Finance: A Partnership for Growth*, Euromoney Publications (1997), p. 75.

equity markets; limited numbers of listed companies; weak corporate governance; lack of cohesive regulation; weak market microstructure; stronger Arab interest in real estate investments; lack of institutional investors and unit trust funds, etc. But one cannot discount the fact that lack of developing Islamic financial products that comply with *Shari'a* was also one of these important factors.

2. SOURCES OF ISLAMIC LAW UNDER *SHARI'A*

This subsection introduces *Shari'a*'s *sui generis* juridical nature. It also introduces the unique juridical sources of *Shari'a* in order to explain why there has been so much juristic controversy surrounding *riba* and *gharar*.

The term *Shari'a* refers generically to Muslim law. This Muslim law is not unified in one single code and there can be quite noticeable differences in its application depending on sectarian divisions and geo-political Islamic variations. It is also unrealistic to speak of a uniform Islamic legal system on a practical level that encompasses identical procedural and substantive legal rules all over the Islamic world.[516] This is important when addressing the solutions to many Islamic legal questions, as legal answers depend largely on the schools of law to which a given Islamic country belongs. Moreover, the diversity of Muslim jurists' legal opinions is compounded by the fact that considerable difficulties still exist in finding comprehensive English sources on Islamic law:

> Although there are a number of important seminal works in English on aspects of Islamic law generally, there is still no completely comprehensive guide to the history of Islamic law together with a description of the legal principles underlying it. Of course the fragmentation of Islamic law into a number of different expressions according to the various schools of law hinders the production of a single comprehensive text which encompasses all this material. However, such a text is not available for any of the schools – not even for that of the Sunni Hanafi school which was considered the orthodox school of the Ottomans and which was adopted in British India.[517]

For their part, Muslims are broadly divided into *Sunni* and *Shi'ite* sects. These two sects are in turn subdivided into sub-sects, each often adhering to distinct interpretations of Islamic law. It is therefore not unusual to observe that, in light of diverse readings as to what constitutes *halal* (legal), *makruh* (legally acceptable but religiously reprehensible) and *haram* (illegal), different sects reach irreconcilable juridical solutions.[518] *Sunnis* can broadly be subdivided into four schools: the *Hanafi, Maliki*, *Shafi'i* and the *Hanbali*. These four juristic schools are based on

516. See W El-Malik, *Mineral Investment under the Shari'a Law*, Graham & Trotman (1993), p. 4.
517. See I Edge, *Islamic Law and Legal Theory* (Dartmouth Publishing Company Ltd), 1996, p. xxi.
518. The clearest example is *Sunni* and *Shi'ite* diametrically opposed views on the legality of temporary marriage, which is predetermined from the outset to last for a specific time. While *Sunnis* condemn it as illegal bordering on prostitution, *Shi'ites* on the other hand accept it as legitimate.

the interpretations of *Shari'a* by the four prominent *Sunni* jurists: Abu Hanifa;[519] Malik Ibn Anas;[520] Idris El-Shafi'i;[521] and Ahmad Ibn Hanbal,[522] respectively. The overwhelming majority of Arab countries are *Sunnis*, and the majority of *Sunnis* belong to the *Hanafi* School. *Shi'ites* are subdivided into three major schools: the *Athna-Asharias*, *Ismailyas* and the *Zaidyas*.[523]

Sources of law under *Shari'a* are divided into revealed and non-revealed. The revealed comprises the Qur'an and *Sunna* or *Hadith* (referring to the Prophet's deeds and proven Citations).[524] The non-revealed or *Ijtihad*,[525] consists of *Ijma'* (the consensus of the community of scholars),[526] *Qiyas* (reasoned analogy by Islamic jurists deducing what the aforementioned three sources would have said in a similar question)[527] and *Istihsan* (seeking the most equitable solution according to Islamic jurists).[528] Added to the non-revealed sources of *Shari'a* are also *Istislah* (seeking the best solution for the general interest according to Islamic jurists or public interest),[529] and *Taqlid* (precedents).[530]

3. THE NATURE OF *SHARI'A'S* JURIDICAL RISKS

The occasional tension between temporal law in Arab countries and specific provisions of *Shari'a* often stems from the dichotomy of ideological difference. This

519. (AD 699–767).
520. (AD 712–795).
521. (AD 767–820).
522. (AD 780–855).
523. See M Mannan, *Mulla's Principles of Mahomedian Law* (Pakistan Edition), P.L.D. Publications, Lahore, 1991, pp. 30–33.
524. See M Kamali, 'Methodological Issues in Islamic Jurisprudence', *ALQ*, Vol. II, No. 1, 1996, p. 3. For other interesting works on Islamic legal theories see generally W Hallaq, *A History of Islamic Legal Theories: An Introduction to Sunni Usul Al-Fiqh*, Cambridge University Press, Cambridge, 1997; A Ibrahim *Sources and Development of Muslim Law*, Malayan Law Journal Ltd Singapore, 1965; A Rahim *Muhammadan Jurisprudence*, Lahore, 1970; J Schacht, *The Origins of Muhammadan Jurisprudence*, Clarendon Press, Oxford, 1979; N Coulson, *Conflicts and Tensions in Islamic Jurisprudence*, University of Chicago Press, Chicago, 1969.
525. *Ijtihad* literally means scholarly endeavour or deduction.
526. See N Ray, *Arab Islamic Banking and the Renewal of Islamic Law*, Graham & Trotman, London, 1995, p. 27. *Ijma'* means the consensus of the Islamic nation, though some argue that *ijma'* refers to the concurrence of the Prophet's companions on a solution to a particular question that was not addressed in revealed sources. See M & A Hidayatullah, *Mulla's Principles of Mahomedan Law*, N M Tripathi Private Ltd, Bombay, 1990, s. 33.
527. Hidayatullah define *Hadith* as: 'Precepts, actions and sayings of the Prophet Mahomed [*sic*], not written down during his lifetime, but preserved by tradition and handed down by authorized [*sic*] persons.' *Ibid.*
528. See D Dwyer, *Law and Islam in the Middle East*, Bergin & Garvey Publications, New York, 1990, p. 2.
529. *Ibid.* Dwyer, however, defines *Sunna* as 'the model behavior [*sic*] of the Prophet' and *Qiyas* as 'analogic reasoning'. *Ibid.*
530. *Taqlid* literally translates to 'imitation'. See R Sharma & N Maheshwari, *Key to Islamic Law*, Baroda Law House, India, 1988, p. 1.

however is not a new phenomenon. It is deeply rooted in a number of Arab civil codes. The reason for this is that on many occasions some Arab civil codes profess to be Islamic in their spirit and yet temporal in their orientation. Nevertheless, it must be stated here that this is not a problem created by Arab civil codes per se. Rather, it is an inherited one as it finds its roots in the Ottoman *Majallah* – which in many respects ambivalently sought to formulate itself on Islamic principles while attempting at the same time to model many of its provisions on Western civil codes – particularly the Swiss and the French ones. Indeed, as seen from the discussion above, notwithstanding the many opportunities to do so, Arab judicial authorities never addressed this dichotomy in a structured and comprehensive manner.

It is because of the above that in some respects *Shari'a* can pose a juridical risk. For example, both of the *Shari'a* concepts of *riba* and *gharar* pose a conceptual juridical risk that can potentially result in annulling offending contemporary Arab commercial legislation. The concepts of *riba* and *gharar* are not straightforward. Ascertaining them has engendered much controversy among Islamic jurists. This diversity in legal opinion can largely be attributed to the inherent structure of the sources of *Shari'a*. For, when interpreting matters relating to the non-revealed, the main Islamic juridical schools through the process of *ijtihad* often started from different premises and reached different conclusions. Moreover, this diversity of Islamic legal opinion is further compounded by the fact that the Qur'an and many Prophet Citations prohibiting *riba* and *gharar* were not precise and rather generic. This subsection, therefore, examines the juridical nature of these two concepts and explains why there has been so much controversy in determining their exact connotations.

3.1. *Riba*

The term *riba* generically refers to an increase, augmentation, gain and accretion.[531] Religiously, *riba* refers to charging interest (whether exorbitant or otherwise), as *Shari'a* prohibits levying interest on loans. In this sense, Islam is not unique. Ancient Egyptian, Babylonian, Greek and Roman legislations, together with Christianity, Judaism (at varying historical periods) and materialistic ideologies like Marxism have all condemned charging interest.[532] Prohibiting *riba* is evidenced by many Qur'anic verses, all of which concur in outlawing the pre-Islamic Arab practice of charging an excess amount of money on loans made for specific periods.[533] The main authority is the famous Citation by the Prophet:

> Gold for gold, silver for silver, wheat for wheat, barley for barley, dates for dates, and salt for salt. Like for like, exchanged equal for equal, measure for

531. See W Ballantyne, *Commercial Law in the Arab Middle East: The Gulf States*, Lloyd's of London, London, 1986, p. 122; Comair-Obied, *supra* note 481, p. 43.
532. See P Ireland, 'Company Law and the Myth of Shareholder Ownership', *The Modern Law Review*, Vol. 62, No. 1, January 1999, p. 37.
533. Main Qur'anic Versus are found in *Suret Ar Rum*, *Suret An Nissa'*, *Suret Al Imran*, *Suret Al-Baqara*.

measure, and hand-to-hand [on the spot]. If anyone gives more or asks for more they have dealt in *riba*. The receiver and the giver are equally guilty.[534]

It is unclear from Islamic jurists why one entrant into a barter exchange would want to spend time and energy exchanging an item for another identical one. But it is thought that the Citation may have intended to encourage using money in the early Islamic economy. It is moreover argued that it sought to protect the weaker party from deferred deliveries that involved exploiting an immediate need for a commodity by stipulating doubling or tripling its future in-kind repayment.[535] Yet, although this Citation talks about a barter economy, most of the Islamic legal schools have extended its application beyond its literal meaning through *qiyas* or reasoned analogy.

However, differences between the various Islamic schools occurred when determining the *illa* [the efficient cause that jointly governs the *anaw'* (species) and *jins* (the class of articles) mentioned in the Citation].[536] Moreover, when extending *qiyas* beyond the articles mentioned in the Citation, Islamic schools differed further in determining the *anaw'* and *jins* over which *qiyas* can be extended. For example, in regard to *illa*, *Hanafis* looked at whether exchanged articles belonged to the same *jins* and the fact that they were amenable to measurement and weight. *Shafis* considered that the *illa* for silver and gold was their amenability to being currency and the *illa* for wheat, barley, dates and salt was their liability to being foodstuff consumed by humans or animals. For the purposes of this book, it is sufficient to say that the Islamic juridical terminology *riba* is subdivided into two main broad types. These take place when there is an exchange of two countervalues governed by the same *illa* and belong to the same *jins* or *anaw'*.[537]

The first is *riba al-fadl*,[538] in which an excess amount accrues in one of the countervalues. For example, lending 1 kilogram of sugar and stipulating that it should be returned as 1.250 kilogram. Items sharing the same *illa* and belong to the same *jins* or *anwa'* must not be exchanged with any disparity in the countervalues. Furthermore, ownership must be transferred immediately.[539] The second is *riba al-nasi'a*,[540] which refers to delaying (or deferring) the delivery of one of the countervalues, with or without excess.[541] Islamic schools have differed in their analysis of *riba al-nasi'a*. According to the *Hanafis* and *Hanbalis*, it takes place when deferment in delivery happens either: (i) when countervalues (whether or not

534. See S Madi, 'The Concept of Unlawful Gain and Legitimate Profit in Islamic Law', Ph.D. thesis, London University, 1989, p. 96.
535. See A Saeed, *Islamic Banking and Interest: A Study of the Prohibition of Riba and its Contemporary Interpretation*, E.J. Brill, (New York), 1996, p. 34.
536. See N Saleh, *Unlawful Gain and Legitimate Profit in Islamic Law: Riba, Gharar and Islamic Banking*, Graham & Trotman, London, Boston, 1992, p. 16.
537. See Ray, *supra* note 526, p. 29.
538. *Fadl* in Arabic literally means excess.
539. See Ballantyne, *supra* note 531, p. 124.
540. *Nasi'a* in Arabic literally means to postpone.
541. See Saleh, *supra* note 536, pp. 16–17.

of the same *jins* or *anwa'*) are measurable or weighable; or (ii) when countervalues (whether or not measurable or weighable) are of the same *jins* or *anwa'*.[542] For the *Shafi's*, *riba al-nasi'a* takes place when the countervalues (whether or not of the same *jins* or *anwa'*) are items of food or precious metal.[543]

A number of Islamic modernisers like Fazlur Rahman, Muhammad Asad, Said al-Najjar and Abdel al-Mun'im al-Namir have argued that the *raison d'être* for the Islamic prohibition of *riba* was confronting exploitation and protecting the weaker party.[544] They point to an economic rational in prohibiting *riba* in that it encourages idle money and deprives the wider society from prospects of growth associated with employment and engagement in risk-sharing enterprises. In a similar vein, other contemporary Islamic jurists attribute the rational behind prohibiting *riba* to an Islamic legal maxim which states that 'Financial gain must be earned against taking risk'.[545] Hence, the advocacy by many such writers for a modern Islamic interpretation of *riba* that draws a distinction between interest and usury, seeing the former as a reward for taking risk.[546]

However, unlike historical developments that refined the linguistic nuances of the opprobrious English term 'usury' distinguishing it from 'interest', much of Islamic theological opinion has remained consistent in not differentiating between both terms.[547] Additionally, modernist views did not register much success due to the emergence of neo-revivalist views on *riba*, which continue successfully to reassert the rigid but prevalent traditional view.[548] For their part, orthodox Muslim legal scholars have traditionally concurred in that *riba* refers to charging interest (whether usurious or not) on loans granted for specific periods.[549]

Furthermore, this unified approach is supported by many Qur'anic verses that prohibit levying fixed interest when lending money.[550] It has also been argued that the early unanimous juristic interpretation of *Sunna* and Qur'an prohibition of *riba*

---

542. See Ballantyne, *supra* note 531, p. 124.
543. *Ibid.*
544. See Saeed, *supra* note 535, pp. 41–49.
545. See S Amin, *Islamic Banking and Finance: The Experience of Iran*, Vahid Publications, Iran, 1986, p. 25.
546. *Ibid.*
547. See Moore, *supra* note 515, p. 17.
548. See Saeed, *supra* note 535, p. 49.
549. See generally C Mallat, 'The Renaissance of Islamic Law: Constitution, Economics and Banking in the Thoughts of Muhammad Baqer As-Sadr', Ph.D. thesis, London University, 1990; N Thani, 'Legal Aspects of the Regulatory Framework of the Malaysian Financial System', Ph.D. thesis, London University, 1993, pp. 278–320; Saleh, *supra* note 536, pp. 11–43; A Kharrufa *Al-Riba Wa'l-Fa'ida*, Baghdad, 1962; A Qureshi, *Islam and the Theory of Interest*, Lahore, 1974; Saeed, *supra* note 535, pp. 17–49. Comair-Obied, *supra* note 481, pp. 171–72. For articles, see: A Mayer, 'The Regulation of Interest Charges and Risk Contracts: Some Problems of Recent Libyan Legislation', *International and Comparative Law Quarterly*, Vol. 28, No. 4, (October 1979), pp. 541–53; N Cagatay, 'Riba and Interest Concepts and Banking in the Ottoman Empire', *Studia Islamica*, Vol. 32 (1970); R Wilson 'The Issue of Interest and the Islamic Financing Alternative', *Journal of International Banking*, Issue 1 (1998), pp. 23–25.
550. Found in *Suret Ar Rum*, *Suret An Nissa'*, *Suret Al Imran*, *Suret Al-Baqara*.

(to include lending money with interest), has over the centuries constituted *ijma'* (or consensus) which on its own right is a binding legal source of *Shari'a*. Such *ijma'* can only lose its legal efficacy if there was another counter-*ijma'* to the contrary.[551]

However, one stresses that the inflexibility of Islam vis-à-vis its prohibition of *riba* arises from the fact that it is not primarily premised on protecting the weaker party as such. Neither is it predicated on economic or utilitarian interpretations of the role of risk in galvanising economic activity and increasing employment. Rather, on following the letter of the Qur'an and the fact that the concept of *riba* has been extended by *qiyas* to encompass currency exchanges. Thus, fulfilling *qiyas's* juristic requirements through profiting when exchanging countervalues which share the same *illa, jins* or *anaw'*. This, for example, relates to exchanging money for money or, for that matter, exchanging money for any other currency with a pecuniary gain. Islamic writers who have pointed to the conspicuous lack of *hikma* (or underlying rationale) on the part of Islamic jurists when addressing the question of *riba* support this view.[552]

3.2. *Gharar*

In its ordinary linguistic meaning, *gharar* connotes deception or cheating. In a broad lexicon sense, *gharar* can refer to danger, peril, jeopardy, hazard or risk.[553] Like *riba*, the prohibition of *gharar* is evidenced by a number of Qur'anic verses and Prophet Citations.[554] However, if the interpretation of *riba* proved to be difficult and controversial among Muslim jurists, delimiting the conceptual and juridical parameters of *gharar* has traditionally even proved to be much harder. For example, in its Qur'anic and *Hadith* connotations, the word *gharar* was used more than fifty times (and in many variations), denoting anything from deception to danger.[555]

Moreover, a considerable difficulty in pinning down *gharar* juridically is attributed to the fact that it is an inherently vague term that arises in the context of Islamic contractual obligations. It is even often argued that the overwhelming majority of cases involving *gharar* that confronted early Muslim jurists were drawn from contracts of sale, whether real or hypothetical.[556] The rationale behind prohibiting *gharar* can, ironically, be seen as a rather cumbersome form of protection designed to safeguard the weaker party in a transaction. Such protection is through stipulating that contracts should not contain uncertainty or *jahel* (lack of

---

551. See Saleh, *supra* note 536, p. 15.
552. See Saeed, *supra* note 535, pp. 35–36.
553. See A Buang, 'The Prohibition of Gharar in the Islamic Law of Contracts: A Conceptual Analysis with Special Reference to the Practice of Islamic Commercial Contracts in Malaysia', Ph.D. thesis, London University, 1995, p. 131.
554. For an account of such Qur'anic Versus and Prophet Citations see *ibid.*, pp. 129–65.
555. *Ibid.*, pp. 132–34.
556. See Saleh, *supra* note 536, p. 63.

knowledge) by ensuring that the weaker party has considerable knowledge of contractual aspects mainly relating to the subject matter.[557]

The fact that *gharar* was not a strictly sacrosanct Islamic concept but rather a means to protect the weaker party from *ghubn* (injury) resulting from uncertainty or *jahel* in contractual relations, enabled many early Islamic jurists to widen its scope. To give a general idea of the width of such scope, one can only point to the many early Islamic jurists who examined *gharar* and expanded its meaning.[558] From the various works which expounded the concept of *gharar*, one observes that in a contract of sale it refers to a number of things. These include uncertainty, excessive risk, chance, speculation and lack of control over the subject matter. The term *gharar* also refers to *jahel* (or want of knowledge) concerning consideration, the existence and identification of the subject matter or the time of delivery.[559] It has accordingly been argued that elimination of want of knowledge regarding the characteristics, identification, existence, date of future performance will all generally avoid vitiating contracts of sale on grounds of *gharar*.[560] So will exercising control over the subject matter.[561]

4. *SHARI'A'S* JURIDICAL IMPACT ON JORDANIAN CIVIL AND COMMERCIAL CODES

In order to pin down the interaction between *Shari'a* and Arab civil and commercial laws, it is important that an in-depth vertical study be undertaken as opposed to a fleeting horizontal one that will focus on generalities. This subsection shall accordingly first outline the relationship between *Shari'a* and the JCC, before proceeding to examine *Shari'a's* impact on the (civil and commercial) codes of Jordan.

4.1. *Shari'a* and the Jordanian Civil Code (JCC)

The relationship between *Shari'a* and the JCC is organic and cannot be ignored. For, *Shari'a* is a source to many JCC's provisions. Earlier drafts of the JCC of 1954

557. Here, the subject matter must be licit or *mashru'*, fulfilling four conditions: (1) its existence when contracting; (2) the possibility of its delivery; (3) be legitimate, not contravening public order and moral; and (4) its genus, specie, value and quality must be determined. See, for example, N Comair-Obeid 'Particularity of the Contract's Subject-Matter in the Laws of the Arab Middle East', *ALQ*, 1994, p. 335.
558. For example, Al-Awzani, Abu Hanifia, Ibn Abi Laylia, Malik, Abu Yusuf, Shaybani, Al-Shafi'i, Muzani, Sahnun, Ali ibn Zayed, Saghadi, Sarakhsi, Samarqandi, Ibn Humam, Ayni, Karlani, Afghani, Manfufi, Adwani al-Sa'idi, Khalil ibn Ishaq, Muwaq, Dardir, Abi, Ibn Rushd, Qarafi, Sawi, Shirazi, Nawawi, Ibn Hajar, Shirbini Al-Khatib, Bajuri, Ibn Qudama, Ibn Taymiyya, Ibn Al-Qayyim, Ibn Hazm, etc. See Madi, *supra* note 534, pp. 173–214.
559. See, for example, Buang, *supra* note 553, pp. 219–55; Ray, *supra* note 526, pp. 30–31; Saleh, *supra* note 536, p. 64; Comair-Obied, *supra* note 481, pp. 57–66.
560. See Saleh, *supra* note 536, p. 66.
561. *Ibid.*

and 1964 were even rejected by the Jordanian Upper House of Parliament because they were incompatible with *Shari'a*.[562] Indeed, this stalemate prompted the Late King Hussein specifically to write to the Speaker of the Upper House of Parliament stating that:

> A number of scientists, scholars and jurists have appealed to us to ensure that our Hashemite Kingdom *abides by a Civil Code based on Shari'a principles*. We therefore desire the formation of a commission that includes leading scholars and jurists to reconsider the proposed draft of the Civil Code. [Italics added.] [563]

Accordingly, a new Committee was appointed.[564] The new Committee however adopted the view that only drafting a completely new version (that adheres more closely to *Shari'a's* teachings) would achieve the objectives set by the Royal letter. But the Six Day War of 1967 interrupted the completion of the new draft, delaying the final delivery day to January 1976. It came into effect on 1 January 1977 and was not debated in Parliament due to marshal law, which was in place following the Six Day War. Neither was the JCC debated when Parliament was re-instituted in 1993. This was for fear that the Islamically tilted Lower House might even reject the already heavily Islamised JCC on the grounds that it did not go far enough in enshrining *Shari'a* teachings. However, both Houses of Parliament eventually ratified the JCC in 1996 – though without any substantive debate.[565]

4.2. Impact of *Riba* and *Gharar*

This subsection examines the impact of *riba* and *gharar* generally, before looking at their impact on Jordanian civil and commercial codes.

4.2.1. Generally

To begin with, one says that the presence of *riba* and *gharar* can potentially nullify Islamic contracts and render contractual obligations either *fasid*[566] or *batil*.[567] Broadly speaking, contracts according to *Shari'a* are *sahih* (valid), *makruh* (juristically and legally acceptable, yet contain an element which is religiously reprehensible), *fasid* (voidable) or *batil* (void or without legal effect).[568]

---

562. See the *Explanatory Memorandum of the Jordanian Civil Code*, Vol. I, pp. 20–22.
563. *Ibid.*
564. These included the Chief of Religious Justice, the Head of the Religious Affairs Department in the Jordanian Radio Broadcasting, the President of the Institute of Islamic Studies.
565. *Official Gazette* No. 4106, 16 March 1996.
566. *Fasid* means rancid, rotten, or out of date. Food can be *fasid* if it is off.
567. *Batil* means without legal effect.
568. See S Rayner, *The Theory of Contracts in Islamic Law: A Comparative Analysis with Particular Reference to the Modern Legislation in Kuwait, Bahrain and the United Arab Emirates*, Graham & Trotman (1991), p. 148.

There have, however, been juristic differences in determining the legal meaning of the term *fasid*. For, it is the *Hanafi* School that recognised the difference between *batil* and *fasid* contracts, elaborating that a *fasid* contract is valid except for the illegal contractual term or offending clause (which in itself is not enforceable).[569] The remainder of Islamic juristic schools did not draw such a distinction between *fasid* and *batil*, as they used these terms interchangeably denoting that such contracts are null and without any legal effect. The vitiating effect of *riba* and *gharar* does not depend upon proof of financial damage. For, the parties have no liberty to validate contracts that stipulate *riba* or contain elements of *gharar*. Moreover, because of the element of uncertainty inherent in the concept of *gharar*, consequential damages in rescinded contracts are not recognised due to the 'uncertainty' of calculating anticipated profit.[570]

Vitiating contractual obligations on the grounds of *gharar* can, on many occasions, be quite overreaching due to the vagueness and pervasiveness of such concept. However, after the seminal work of Islamic legal scholars like Ibn Qayyim and Sanhuri, future contracts were validated with the *caveat* that they do not involve *material* elements of uncertainty, risk or speculation. One adds that clarifying the confusion between the non-existence of the subject matter of the contract of sale and the uncertainty of its future existence is largely credited to Ibn Qayyim.[571]

Most Arab civil codes of today adopt Ibn Qayyim's distinction between material and non-material *gharar*, permitting parties to contract on non-existent subject matters that will exist in the future.[572] Examples in mind are Iraq (Article 129/1 of the Iraqi Civil Code), Qatar (Article 33 of the Qatari Civil Code),[573] the United Arab Emirates (Article 202/1 of the UAE Civil Code) and Egypt (Article 131 of the Egyptian Civil Code).

4.2.2. Impact on Jordanian Civil and Commercial Codes

This subsection first looks at the impact of *riba* before looking at the impact of *gharar* on Jordanian civil and commercial codes.

4.2.2.1. Impact of Riba

As Jordan relied historically on the *Majallat* (which adopted the *Hanafi* School), it treats *riba* as a *fasid* condition, the elimination of which validates contractual

569. Sanhuri's *Masadir al-Haq*, Vol. IV (1957), pp. 135–36.
570. See N Coulson, *Commercial Law in the Gulf States: The Islamic Legal Tradition*, Graham & Trotman, (1984), p. 84; P Sloane, 'The Status of Islamic Law in the Commercial World', *International Lawyer* (Fall, 1988), Vol. 22, No. 3, p. 747; Rayner, *supra* note 568, p. 170.
571. See N Saleh, 'Financial Transactions and the Islamic Theory of Obligations and Contracts', in C Mallat's *Islamic Law and Finance*, Graham & Trotman Ltd, London, 1988, p. 26.
572. Most Arab civil codes associate material *gharar* with an accident of chance. See, for example, Art. 168 of the KCC.
573. See Qatari Law No. 16 of 1971, embodying the Civil and Commercial Code.

obligations. The JCC nullifies stipulations that impose interest per se, rather than invalidating the whole loan agreement. It stipulates that any excess benefit in a civil loan beyond securing the lender's right shall be null and void, without voiding the whole contract of loan:

> If a benefit in excess of securing the lender's right is stipulated in a loan contract, such stipulation shall be void without invalidating the whole contract. [574]

Article (636) further prohibits charging interest on money loans or fungibles stating that loaned objects must be returned (without interest or benefit) and in a manner equivalent in 'amount, type and description' to that which has been loaned:[575]

> The loan . . . upon maturity must be paid back to the lender . . . equivalent in amount, type and description.[576]

However, the Jordanian Commercial Act (JCA)[577] allows charging interest on commercial loans. Technically, commercial codes in Arab countries are treated as 'special' legislation that takes precedence over civil codes. For example, Article (1448) of the JCC states quite clearly that special laws take priority over its provisions:

> When applying the provisions of this Code, priority shall be given to special laws.[578]

As mentioned above, the origins of the above legal device, whereby special laws take precedence over general ones in order to circumvent applying interest, stem from legal practices under the Ottoman era – dating back to 1800s. For, while the *Majallat* prohibited charging interest, special laws were then enacted to circumvent applying interest in areas such as commercial transactions.[579] For its part, the JCA[580] treats charging interest as a legitimate *de facto* reality exercised in various aspects of commercial activities. This can be evident in dealings between agent and principal in a commercial agency (Article 84),[581] brokerage (Article 110),[582]

574. Article 640 of the JCC.
575. Once the loan has been settled, it is acceptable under *Shari'a* for the borrower to give the lender a 'gift' providing it is voluntary.
576. Article 636 of the JCC.
577. Law No. 12 of 1966.
578. Article 1448(2) of the JCC.
579. See *Nitham Al-Murabaha Al-Uthmani* 1887.
580. Articles 2, 4 and 5 of the JCA state that sources of commercial legislation in Jordan include the JCA, the JCC and trade custom. Art. 2(1) states that, if there is no adequate legislation available, then the rules of the JCC should be applied.
581. Article 84 reads: 'The agent shall pay interest on the principal's money from the day which they ought to have delivered or deposited the money in compliance with the principal's instructions.' *Ibid.*
582. Article 110, *inter alia*, reads: 'If not determined by agreement or custom, all payments that generate interest for the benefit of the depositor must be paid . . . according to the legal rate.' *Ibid.*

banking (Articles 115/3[583] & 121/2),[584] bills of exchange (Articles 128,[585] 186/b[586] & 187/b),[587] promissory notes (Article 225),[588] cheques (Articles 263/b[589] and 264/b),[590] etc.

In a radical move, contractual rates of interest (regardless of the limit) are now valid in Jordan, providing that such rate does not contradict those set by the Central Bank of Jordan (CBJ). It is pertinent here to mention the amendment of Article (43) of the 1971 Central Bank of Jordan Law in 1989, which was followed by CBJ Memo No. 11/90 floating interest rates.[591] Interest rate on deposits and loans in Jordan could even reach 17%. For its part, the Jordanian Court of Cassation has, in numerous cases, ruled that charging interest in Jordan is legitimate, once it complies with relevant domestic regulations.[592]

However, the unquantifiable juridical risks of annulling offending commercial legislation that does not comply with the provisions of the JCC remain real. This was precisely the case when a challenge was launched against the legality of charging interest before the Amman's Court of First Instance, claiming that laws permitting interest were contrary to the JCC. Yet, although this was a golden opportunity for the Jordanian Court of Cassation to settle the question of juridical risks once and for all, its ruling was devoid of legal depth. For, it merely restated that permitting interest in Jordan was legitimate as it was conforming with special laws. Indeed, without concerning itself with re-examining the very foundations of

583. Article 115(3), *inter alia*, reads: 'Interest shall accrue where necessary from the date pursuant to placing every deposit . . . unless otherwise agreed.' *Ibid.*
584. Article 121(2), *inter alia*, reads: 'The bank may recover all amounts paid or expenses incurred in the course of executing its function with agreed interest or legal interest . . . .' *Ibid.*
585. Article 128 reads: 'A drawer of a bill of exchange on sight or after a certain period may stipulate that interest be added to the amount of the bill.' *Ibid.*
586. Article 186, *inter alia*, reads: 'A holder [of a bill of exchange] may claim the following from any person against whom he has a right of recourse: . . . (b) Interest calculated at the legal rate from the date of maturity vis-à-vis bills drawn and payable in the territories of the Hashemite Kingdom of Jordan . . . ' *Ibid.*
587. Article 187, *inter alia*, reads: 'A person discharging a bill may demand the following from its guarantors: . . . (b) Interest on the sum paid, calculated at the legal rate from the date of payment vis-à-vis bills drawn and payable in the Hashemite Kingdom of Jordan.' *Ibid.*
588. Article 225, *inter alia*, reads: 'The provisions pertaining to bills of exchange . . . . as well as demands for paying interest, . . . shall be applicable to promissory notes.' *Ibid.*
589. Article 263, *inter alia*, reads: 'The holder of a cheque may claim the following from any person against whom he has a right of recourse: . . . (b) Interest calculated from the date of presentation at the legal rate for cheques drawn and payable in the Hashemite Kingdom of Jordan . . . ' *Ibid.*
590. Article 264, *inter alia*, reads: 'A person discharging a cheque may claim the following from its guarantors: . . . . (b) Interest calculated at the legal rate for cheques drawn and payable in the Hashemite Kingdom of Jordan . . . ' *Ibid.*
591. See *Law No. 37 of 1989 Amending Central Bank of Jordan Law No. 23 of 1971*, together with CBJ Memo No. 11/90 (16 January 1990).
592. See Court of Cassation Decision [CCD] No. 346/84, *Law Society Journal* [*LSJ*] (1985), p. 860; CCD No. 625/84, *LSJ* (1985), p. 410; CCD No. 176/85, *LSJ* (1985), p. 1442.

the legal fiction that allows special laws to contravene the general law, the Court of Cassation merely stated:

> The Ottoman Regulations governing interest . . . are in fact special laws and are not regulations. As such they must be upheld in pursuance with Art. (1448)(2) [which states that when applying the JCC special laws must be observed].[593]

4.2.2.2. Impact of Gharar

Jordan has shied away from strict adherence to *gharar*. The JCC explicitly sanctions contracts, which contain elements of *gharar* that would have otherwise been banned. It has a specific chapter entitled '*Gharar* Contracts', which sanctions salaries for life under Articles (916–919) (otherwise would have been void due to *gharar* arising from the uncertainty of the length of life). The chapter also sanctions insurance contracts under Articles (920–949) (otherwise would have been void due to *gharar* arising from the unknowability of the materialisation of the events against which one has insured). The JCC also accepts the distinction between material and non-material *gharar*:

> A future contract may in the absence of material *gharar* be the subject matter of financial compensatory transaction.[594]

However, the JCC takes a more traditional stance by specifically stating that contractual obligations shall be void if the subject matter was impossible at the time of contracting:

> If the subject matter was impossible when the contract takes place, the resulting contract is null and void.[595]

The JCC further stipulates that the subject matter of a contractual obligation should be specifically determined in order to avoid material *gharar*:

> (1) It is a condition . . . that the subject matter be determined in a manner that avoids gross *jahel* through pointing to it or its place if it was present when transacting, or pointing to its distinctive features . . . or other indications that negate gross *jahel*.
> (2) If the parties knew the subject matter, then there is no need to identify or describe it.
> (3) If the subject matter was not identified as mentioned above, then the contract is null and void.[596]

593. CCD No. 288/81 *LSJ* (1981), p. 2053.
594. Article 160(1) of the JCC.
595. Article 159. *Ibid.*
596. Article 161(1), (2) and (3). *Ibid.*

Finally, the JCC allows the buyer to sell their property before receiving delivery. Thus accepting Ibn Qayyim's clarifications mentioned above between the non-existence of the subject matter and the uncertainty of its future existence:

> It is permissible for the buyer to sell or dispose of the subject matter before delivery.[597]

5. *SHARI'A'S* JURIDICAL IMPACT ON SECURITIES MARKETS

What makes Islamic economy distinct is its value system, which has significantly shaped its saving, investment, consumption and production decisions.[598] Acquiring an equity holding per se (to be distinguished from equity trading which often involves speculating) is not illegal under *Shari'a*. Equity holdings have therefore not traditionally engendered the same theologian legal concerns that have long accompanied the topic of modern banking. While modern banking (with its reliance on interest) comes into direct conflict with *Shari'a* rules prohibiting *riba*, Islam's economic theory has actively encouraged equity holdings through partnerships by taking risk and sharing profit. Such Islamic approach is not too dissimilar to early Western legal understandings of what constitutes loans and partnerships. In *Grace v. Smith* Blackstone J, for example, said that profit in a partnership (as opposed to a loan) is achieved through monies that are not 'certain' and 'defined', but rather 'casual', 'indefinite' and dependent on the 'accidents' of trade.[599]

Key features of the Islamic economic system are its respect for private property, encouragement and reward for work (private and public), aversion towards hoarding/monopoly, social solidarity through its tax system (or *zakat*) and the prohibition of *riba*.[600] Islamic writers have suggested two further broad objectives for Islamic development, namely narrowing the distributional gap in the state and maximising the utilisation of economic resources.[601] It is, however, this emphasis on the utilisation of economic resources that gives equity financing a distinguished place in Islamic economic and social justice theories.

Indeed it has even been argued that the Islamic financial system, while averse to debt financing, actually encourages equity financing in a manner that likens it to a 'purely equity-based financial system' that, in addition to equity securities, boasts many more financing techniques.[602] In this sense, Islamic banking can itself be broadly seen as an equity-based system in which depositors are treated as

597. Article 535. *Ibid.*
598. See generally M Arif, *Monetary and Fiscal Economics of Islam*, King Abdulaziz University Press, Saudi Arabia, 1982, pp. 2–7.
599. (1775) 2 Wm BI 997.
600. See M Zineldin, *The Economics of Money and Banking: A Theoretical and Empirical Study of Islamic Interest-Free Banking*, Almqvist & Wiksell International (Stockholm), 1990, pp. 43–51.
601. See A El-Ashker, *The Islamic Business Enterprise*, Croom Helm, London, 1987, p. 60.
602. See Moore, *supra* note 515, pp. 15, 69.

shareholders, where Islamic commercial banks are largely similar to mutual funds or investment trusts.[603]

As a corollary to the aforementioned prohibition of charging interest or holding/trading in interest-bearing instruments in favour of equity holdings, traditional Islamic jurists developed a number of alternative financing techniques since the early days of Islam nearly fourteen hundred years ago.[604] The constant evolution of these Islamic financing techniques (which are deeply rooted in Islamic practice and legal jurisprudence) has enabled contemporary Islamic jurists to develop alternative models of modern Islamic banking that avoid charging interest. These are mainly, *murabaha*[605] (or cost plus financing), *musharaka*[606] (or venture capital) and *mudaraba*[607] (or trust financing).[608]

However, *Shari'a's* juridical impact on securities markets can largely be seen in its influencing either the *modus operandi* or the choice of securities. In regard to the former, unlike its rejection of *riba*, *Shari'a* does not espouse such antipathy vis-à-vis securities markets per se. Moreover, it was seen that *Shari'a* even actively encourages equity holdings, partnerships and trading through buying/selling. Yet, due to the concept of *gharar* the *modus operandi* of trading on equity markets will be affected through vitiating transactions that contain elements of speculation, chance or excessive risk.

---

603. See M Khan, 'The Financial System and Monetary Policy in an Islamic Economy', in Khan et al., *supra* note 505, pp. 163–64.
604. See M Chapra, 'Money and Banking in an Islamic Economy', in Arif, *supra* note 598, p. 152.
605. Involves a deferred sale in which a bank purchases the goods and sells them to the customer for a pre-arranged price. *Murabaha* is suitable for financing real estate investments and forms an important component of project financing. See C Price et al., 'Legal Aspects of Islamic Banking and Finance' in Moore, *supra* note 515, p. 113.
606. Entails a partnership whereby the parties put capital or labour, sharing profit and loss according to a pre-agreed ratio. See generally S Al-Harran, 'Introduction: Cases in Islamic Finance', *ALQ*, Vol. 14, No. 3, 1999, pp. 193–202; M Usmani, 'The Concept of *Musharakah* and Its Application as an Islamic Method of Financing', *ALQ*, Vol. 14, No. 3, 1999, pp. 203–20. In Islamic banking, equity participation is referred to as 'permanent *musharakah*', entailing three modes of equity participation. First, direct equity participation for the purpose of financing enterprises that yield short- or medium-term returns. Second, participation in the equity capital of a given project in order to enhance its equity base. Third, lines of equity for the purpose of a development finance institution (fund) in order to finance small entrepreneurs. See, for example, A Bananga et al., *External Audit and Corporate Governance in Islamic Banks*, Athenaeum Press Ltd (UK), 1994, pp. 15–16.
607. A partnership in which the owner of the capital (*rab el mal*) invests with a partner (*el mudarib*) who manages the investment, providing expertise as his/her share in the project. *Mudaraba* is an arrangement between one or more investors (*rab el mal*) with an agent-manager (*el mudarib*) with whom they entrust their capital. The agent-manager trades with the capital, returning the principal and a pre-determined share of the profit. See, for example, El-Ashker, *supra* note 601, p. 75.
608. It is argued that these techniques comprise most methods used for Islamic financing, with *murabaha* occupying 70%, *musharaka* and *mudaraba* occupying 20% and 10% respectively. See Ray, *supra* note 526, p. 37. Other financing techniques include *al-qard el-hassan* (benevolent loan), which is either paid back at the end of the loan period without any increment, or converted into an equity share in the project and *ujra* (leasing), which is not different from leasing for a consideration.

Transactions in which there is considerable lack of knowledge about the subject matter or the place or time of delivery, will also be unacceptable. So will transactions in which the consideration is unspecified or the determination of which is left to chance or fortuitous events. The concept of *gharar* also vitiates transactions in which there is lack of control over the subject matter. Transactions that are optional or conditional on chance, uncertain or impossible events will also be vitiated by *gharar*. Additionally, under *Shari'a* securities must not be issued or underwritten by financial intermediaries that deal in *riba* or *gharar*, including the ones leveraged at interest, wholly or partially.[609]

Islamically acceptable securities per se must not contain any element of *riba* or *gharar*. This excludes all interest-bearing and derivatives/hedging instruments, excepting only few instruments such as equities and certificates of participation in profit-sharing arrangement.[610] It has also been argued that a number of Islamic financing instruments, such as *murabaha*, *musharakah* and *mudarabah* should be included in the definition of modern securities.[611]

However, it must be reminded that under *riba al-nasi'a* (*riba* by delaying delivery of the countervalues) some futures trading can be deemed Islamically unacceptable. Such unacceptability is attributable to the fact that it often involves exchanging money for money (or any other type of currency) at a future date, but with disparity in the original value. Such futures trading would be forbidden under the four Islamic *Sunni* Schools (i.e., *Hanbali*, *Shafi'i*, *Hanafi* and *Maliki*).[612] Neither is it Islamically acceptable to acquire shares in companies that deal (directly or indirectly) in alcohol, tobacco, pornography, pork, gambling, prostitution, etc. One also adds that according to the prevalent orthodox Islamic view, shares in companies that pay (fixed interest) dividends, issue corporate bonds/convertibles or deal in derivatives and hedging instruments may be off limits.[613]

---

609. Some writers argue that up to 10% leverage is Islamically acceptable. See, for example, 'Islamic Equity Investment', *The Arab Banker*, Vol. IV, No. 4, 1997, London, pp. 26–30 and 'Legal Structure of Islamic Finance and Privatisation', *Yearbook of Islamic and Middle Eastern Law*, Vol. II, 1996, Kluwer, London, pp. 32–50.
610. See L Errico et al.,'Islamic Banking: Issues in Prudential Regulations and Supervision', Monetary and Exchange Affairs Department, IMF (March 1998), p. 24.
611. See Z Iqbal, 'Islamic Banking Gaining Momentum, Expands Markets and Competes with Conventional Banking in the Arab States', *Middle East Executive Reports* 9–19; A Zohny, 'The Suitability of US Security Laws and Regulations to Serve as a Model Law for Egyptian Financial Markets', *ALQ*, Vol. XV, No. 1 (2000) 5, p. 26.
612. See Ray, *supra* note 526, p. 30.
613. However, the need to develop financial instruments is not purely academic: 'A major breakthrough was IFC's creation of an Islamic financial instrument, a redeemable income note that will enable the IFC to syndicate significant funds from financial institutions in the Gulf Cooperation Council countries for the benefit of *modaraba* leasing companies in Pakistan . . . . This instrument opens the way to deploy Islamic funds into long-term industrial and financial service projects to supplement IFC funding, and will have significant ramifications for project financing in the region.' See Central Asia, Middle East and North Africa. IFC *Annual Report 1995* (Washington), 1995.

6. *SHARI'A'S* JURIDICAL IMPACT ON JORDANIAN SECURITIES REGULATION

Article (5)[614] of the JCA states that, *inter alia*, financial markets should be governed by special rules and regulations. Article (59)(2)[615] of the JCA further elaborates by stating that stock exchange transactions are governed by the special regulations of the stock exchange.

For their part, securities markets laws of Jordan do not follow the limitations posed by strict adherence to *riba* and *gharar*. They do not prohibit speculative trading on equity markets on the grounds of *gharar*. Nor do they prohibit trading in companies that are considered Islamically unacceptable such as the ones that deal in alcohol or tobacco. Jordanian securities laws equally do not prohibit trading in companies that are leveraged, issue bond instruments or pay dividends.

Furthermore, Jordanian securities laws have historically adopted all-inclusive definitions of 'securities' that clearly depart from *Shari'a's* strict limitations. For example, Article (2) of the Amman Financial Market Law of the year 1976 did not take cognisance of inherent *Shari'a* limitations as enshrined in the JCC. It defined 'securities' as shares, bonds, debentures or any negotiable financial paper.[616] Neither does Article (3) of the new Securities Act 2002 (SA 2002) reconcile the Islamic understanding of the term 'securities' with modern definitions. It simply states that:

(a) The term 'securities' shall mean any ownership, rights or any evidence (local or foreign) that are commonly recognised as securities and considered as such by the [Jordanian Securities Commission] Board.
(b) In particular, the term 'securities' shall include the following:
  (i) transferable and tradable companies' shares;
  (ii) bonds issued by companies;
  (iii) securities issued by the Government, official public institutions, public institutions, or municipalities;
  (iv) securities depository receipts;
  (v) shares and investment units of mutual funds;
  (vi) equity option bonds;
  (vii) spot contracts and forward contracts;
  (viii) put and call option contracts; and
  (ix) any right to acquire any of the aforementioned in subparagraphs (1)–(8) of this Paragraph, subject to Board approval.

---

614. Article (5) of the JCA, *inter alia*, reads: 'Financial markets . . . shall be governed . . . by special rules and regulations.'

615. Article (59)(2), *inter alia*, reads: 'Stock exchange transactions, . . . shall be governed by the special regulations of the stock exchange.' *Ibid.*

616. Article (2) of the former *Rules Covering Trading in Financial Papers on the Amman Financial Markets* also repeated the same definition. So did the former *Internal Regulations of the Amman Financial Market 1980* and the *Amman Financial Market Law No. 31 of the year 1992.*

The above Jordanian definition under the SA 2002, which is also almost a replica of Article 3 of the Securities Act 1997 (SA 1997) can equally be criticised on the grounds that large sections of it are vague and do not reflect domestic practice.[617] For example, the concept of 'equity option bonds' referred to in Article 3 is not adequately defined nor developed in Jordanian company law. Additionally, Article 3 says that any other 'international' security will be acceptable as a Jordanian security, without any regard to the aforementioned juridical constraints under the general law.

Here, relying on 'international' interpretations to determine what may retrospectively constitute a Jordanian security can be impractical. For, highly complex financial instruments are evolving in a constant manner that often eludes definition even in advanced economies. Indeed, an 'international security' may in itself, be subject to controversy abroad.

Even among Anglo-American jurisdictions *inter se*, there has been noticeable difference in judicial leeway in interpreting the term 'securities'. For example, while there has been inchoate British judicial contribution in delineating the boundaries of the term 'securities', US jurisprudence has centred around the notion of 'investment contracts'. Additionally, given the different legal framework between common-law countries and civil-code ones, problems may arise when assessing the cross-jurisdictional admissibility of evidence of 'international securities'.

Needless to say, Jordanian judges still considerably lack the necessary expertise to interpret the term 'international securities'. In this context, one only needs to look at the extensive and complex work done by US judges to define the term 'securities'. Indeed, the occasional generic definition of US securities, coupled with an apparent inability to keep up with market innovation has often spurred US courts to develop an elaborate system of jurisprudence in order to deal with evolving definitional challenges. This has enabled US courts to add their interpretations, deploying a variety of tests in order to determine whether a transaction involves a security.[618]

7. CONCLUSION

Any analysis that aims at examining comparative aspects of securities regulation in Arab countries would be incomplete if it does not take cognisance of the juridical

617. For a critique of the definition of Jordanian 'securities' under the SA 1997, see, for example, L Al-Rimawi, 'The Jordanian Definition of "Financial Security" in Light of British and American Definitions', *European Financial Services Law*, Vol. V, Nos 5 & 6 (May/June 1998), pp. 127–30.

618. See, for example, *SEC v. Joiner Leasing Corporation* (1943) [the first definition of 'security' by the US Supreme Court]; *SEC v. Howey & Co.* (1946) [on the 'investment contract' concept and the economic reality test]; *United Housing Foundation v. Forman* (1975) [on real estate and 'stock']; *Landerth Timber Co. v. Landerth* (1985) [on the sale of part of a business], etc. [(1943) 320 US 344, (1946) 328 US 293, (1975) 421 US 837, (1985) 471 US 681, respectively.] See L Loss, *Fundamentals of Securities Regulation*, Little Brown & Company (Canada) (1988), pp. 165–202.

risks posed by the general law therein. For its part, *Shari'a* produces unquantifiable juridical risks that at best render 'offending' modern Arab commercial legislation precarious, and at worst may result in annulling it. *Shari'a's* socio-legal influence therefore must not be discounted when examining Arab commercial legislation. These risks are particularly important in the context of securities markets regulation. For, juridical concepts such as *riba* and *gharar* limit the *modus operandi* of securities markets and negate many aspects of the very definition of what constitutes a 'security'.

However, the legal fiction of designating commercial legislation as a special legal stratum (which is permitted to deviate from *Shari'a*) is devoid of legal underpinnings. This is especially as the problematic and often mutually exclusive relationship between *Shari'a* and 'offending' modern commercial laws, remains unresolved by such legal fiction. For their part, judicial authorities in Jordan fail to resolve this legal contradiction and merely behave in a manner that is oblivious to it – repeating the legally devoid mantra of 'special legislation can contradict general legislation', without examining the larger legal implications for this evident legal contradiction.

Remedying this legal contradiction is beyond the scope of this book, as it requires political will to reconstruct the Jordanian constitution and the Jordanian Civil Code. Nevertheless (such reconstruction, which may be perceived as de-Islamising its legal orientation) will undoubtedly encounter populous misgivings. For, it is a question that touches upon the very fabric that makes the threads of contemporary Jordanian society in terms of its modernist legal choices and socio-politico-religious system. Needless to say, this legal fiction that tinkers around notions of 'general' and 'special' law is not exclusive to Jordan. For, this legal dichotomy exists in virtually all Arab civil and commercial legislation – representing a phenomenon that has seeped deeply into regional jurisdictions.

However, as far as Arab countries (including Jordan) maintain this incongruous dichotomy between general principles of law enshrined in *Shari'a* and particular secular laws, juridical risks will always jeopardise the certitude of modern commercial legislation.[619] Indeed, as shall be seen in the context of this book, this is not a problem that merely impacts upon the *modus operandi* of securities markets or the definition of securities. For, this theme will re-emerge in Chapter 10 when one looks at remedies under the Jordanian general law for inaccurate or misleading statements in the prospectus.

Having said the above, one adds that the discussion vis-à-vis the question of disclosure and the general law under *Shari'a* will not be complete without reaching an understanding of what a securities disclosure under *Shari'a* would look like. The next chapter shall therefore attempt to construct a *Shari'a* (securities) disclosure model to see if such a model withstands modernist scrutiny.

---

619. The juridical risks of *Shari'a* cannot also be ignored in non-Arab Islamic countries as well.

Chapter 7

Securities Disclosure under *Shari'a*: Selected Comparative Aspects with the UK General Law, Particularly under the Principle of *Caveat Emptor*

INTRODUCTION

Chapter 7 now constructs a securities disclosure model under *Shari'a's* general juridical principles. However, a problem here is that there is no general Islamic theory of securities disclosure (on *par* for example with Islamic theory on Islamic banking) that would inform about the content of such a regime. Moreover, no writer has even ever attempted to analyse what such a regime would look like. Yet, this should not stultify investigating *Shari'a's* juridical position on securities disclosure.

The chapter therefore adopts the methodology of investigating *Shari'a's* disclosure requirements generally in terms of whether or not they would differ from those of the Common Law under the doctrine of *caveat emptor*. In the process it discusses *Shari'a's* strong exhortations on the importance of transacting on the marketplace. Chapter 7 equally examines *Shari'a's* disclosure requirements under contracts of sale vis-à-vis the question of 'defects'. It concludes by assessing the implications for a disclosure regime premised on *Shari'a's* general principles and whether or not such a regime would withstand the scrutiny of contemporary arguments in favour of mandatory disclosure.

1. SHARI'A'S JURIDICAL STANCE VIS-À-VIS THE PRINCIPLE OF *CAVEAT EMPTOR*

The Common Law principle of *caveat emptor* is generally based on the notion that, barring any fiduciary relationship or fraud, sellers are not under a direct duty to disclose defects in goods sold. Instead, they merely allow buyers the right to inspect the goods for themselves, though they must not wilfully conceal defects.[620] Under the Common Law, the failure to disclose material facts does not give rise to rescinding the contract – even if it might influence the mind of a prudent party to a contract.[621] In this sense, although the duty to disclose is applicable in *uberrimae fidei* contracts, it is nevertheless considered to apply outside the realm of contracts of sale. For example, Lord Atkin observed that:

> The failure to disclose a material fact which might influence the mind of a prudent contractor does not give the right to avoid the contract. The principle of *caveat emptor* applies outside the contract of sale.[622]

However, it must be stated here that the influence of *laissez-faire* economics and Ricardian notions of individualism, which historically resulted in added demands for freedom and sanctity of contracts (which courts were expected to foster and vindicate),[623] did not per se mean that there was judicial antipathy towards protecting buyers as such. The invocation of the 'less extensive' duty of disclosure was substituted by both the techniques of statutory and judicial implied terms in the English contract of sale. This can (depending on the circumstances) be treated as promissory conditions, mere warranties or representations.[624] Indeed, market practice (that considered certain implicit terms to apply in a contract of sale) led to the modification of the original maxim of *caveat emptor*, with English courts accommodating these modifications during the first half of the nineteenth century.[625]

From a Common Law viewpoint, it is this notion embodied in the principle of *caveat emptor* that requires positive legal interference when using the law to compel the disclosure of information when offering securities. However, the conceptual difficulty to justify mandatory dissemination of information (over and above the principle of *caveat emptor*) is experienced much less under *Shari'a*. For, one can argue that mandatory disclosure on securities markets would be viewed favourably by *Shari'a*.

Here, the need for the provision of full information to parties engaged in commercial transactions (particularly relating to defects under contracts of sale) is an important feature that distinguishes *Shari'a* from the Common Law. In regard to the question of disclosure per se, *Shari'a's* juridical starting point of analysis is

---

620. The doctrine of *caveat emptor* developed following the early seventeenth century case of *Chandler v. Lupos*, in which the defendant (selling his store) was held not liable for the defect, when the plaintiff (buyer of the defective store) was at liberty to inspect it. See P Atiyah, *The Rise and Fall of Freedom of Contract*, Clarendon Press, Oxford, 1979, pp. 179, 466. However, current English contract law has not been immune from EU social trends. See, for example, T Wilhelmsson, *Social Contract Law and European Integration* (Aldershot, Dartmouth) 1994, pp. 28–29.
621. See, for example, *Smith v. Hughes* (1871) LR 6 Q.B. 597.
622. *Bell v. Lever Bros Ltd* [1932] AC 161, at p. 227.
623. See *Cheshire, Fifoot & Furmston's Law of Contract* (Butterworths) 1991, pp. 19–20.
624. Warranties give rise to damages, promissory conditions give rise to rescission and conditions precedent give rise to releasing parties from all obligations. See, for example, P Atiyah, *An Introduction to the Law of Contract*, Clarendon Press, Oxford, 1981, pp. 218–20.
625. See *Cheshire, Fifoot & Furmston's Law of Contract*, *supra* note 623, pp. 136–37.

different from that of the Common Law. This is especially as there is a marked jurisprudential difference between Islamic principles of disclosure in commercial transactions from that of the Common Law. For example, one can make the prima facie argument that the notion of mandatory disclosure is in tandem with *Shari'a* principles. Indeed, *in abstracto*, the concept of mandatory disclosure (in the sense of a positive prescriptive duty to disclose certain sets of information) is a fundamental *Shari'a* principle. The importance of the pervasive role of disclosure under *Shari'a* can be attributed to at least two main reasons.

The *first* is due to the Islamic concept of *gharar*, which, as seen in Chapter 6, is a very wide juridical rubric that embodies a broad range of contractual situations. Indeed, when it comes to discussing disclosure under *Shari'a*, *gharar* is a particularly important juridical concept. This is due to its pervasiveness in regulating Islamic contractual obligations through not only proscribing aleatory elements such as risk, uncertainty, speculation or chance. It also equally eliminates *jahel* (lack of knowledge) concerning the subject matter, price, value, delivery, date of future performance, etc. In fact, given that it developed largely through Islamic contracts of sale, *gharar* itself can be seen as a juridical tool, the purpose of which is the protection of the weaker party to a transaction who is at risk of being outdone by experienced parties.

The *second* reason relates to the fact that *Shari'a* does not espouse the principle of *caveat emptor* and instead places the seller under a general obligation to be fully honest and not abstain from disclosing to the buyer defects in the goods that they know exist. This point shall be clearer when one discusses below *Shari'a's* strong exhortations that transactions take place on the marketplace due to maximum availability of information.

2. *SHARI'A'S* STRONG EXHORTATIONS ON TRANSACTING ON THE MARKETPLACE

It is true that *Shari'a* may be viewed as somewhat paternalistic in its overprotection of weaker parties to transactions. Nevertheless, it is rather distinct in its desire to ensure that, as far as possible, parties transact on the marketplace, under which there is ample provision of information. Indeed, this subtle attention to the need for optimal information can have great bearing on the discussion of *Shari'a's* approach vis-à-vis mandatory disclosure on securities markets, particularly when offering shares to the public. Additionally, *Shari'a's* exhortations on transacting under circumstances most congenial to optimal availability of information goes in tandem with many arguments justifying mandatory disclosure. In this context, *Shari'a's* concern for the protection of the weaker party goes well beyond obligating the seller to disclose all 'material' information relating to defects in contracts of sale.

Indeed, in a manner that would be difficult to justify under the Common Law (which advocates minimal interference in contractual relations), *Shari'a* requests certain 'procedural' requirements for some sale transactions. It, for example, requires that transactions are executed on the marketplace where there is the best chance for full access to information about price, quality, supply, demand, etc., where parties would be better able to assess the risks they are taking. The Prophet Muhammad is reported to have said:

> Let no one among you sell in order to take the place of his brother who is already in the market. *Do not go to meet the merchandise, but wait for it to be unloaded off the marketplace.*[626] [Italics added.]

Here, it is presumed that overall circumstances when transacting outside the marketplace make it easier for one party to take advantage of the other party's *jahel* (ignorance) of information affecting the transaction. This is particularly the case if, for example, one party suffers from socioeconomic disadvantages that render them unable to assimilate such 'material' information. It is therefore reported that the Prophet Muhammad prohibited townsmen (known then for their commercial acumen) to go to the desert to sell their merchandise to Bedouins (known then for their commercial naivety), lest they be taken advantage of. Instead, both parties were asked to exchange their goods on the marketplace, where Bedouins would have a real chance of becoming better informed about both price and quality of products.

For the same reason, Muslims were equally required to abstain from accosting strangers (caravans) coming from faraway towns with the intent to sell merchandise. They were instead requested by the Prophet Muhammad to buy goods from them on the marketplace, lest such strangers be taken advantage of due to presumed lack of information about ongoing prices in different localities. Indeed, all four *Sunni* juridical schools justify Islam's requirement that both parties to commercial transactions be in circumstances most conducive to ensuring optimal supply of 'material' information.

However, although the above discussion explains *Shari'a's* starting point and its active encouragement of parties to contract under circumstances most congenial to providing maximum flow of information, it does not explain what is meant by *Shari'a's* 'material' information. Accordingly, a deeper analysis to clarify this point shall be attempted through visiting *Shari'a's* mandatory disclosure requirements under contracts of sale, where sellers are expected fully to disclose all material information relating to defects. By looking at the different juridical interpretations of 'defect',[627] one can extend the analogy to situations where non-disclosure also results in the depreciation of securities' monetary values. The subsection next develops this argument further.

3. *SHARI'A'S* DISCLOSURE OF ALL MATERIAL INFORMATION REGARDING DEFECTS UNDER CONTRACTS OF SALE

To pick up from the above discussion, one here attempts to look at what kind of information would be deemed as 'material' in the context of a *Shari'a* mandatory

626. Quoted in *Sahih El-Bukhari*, Vol. II.
627. Particularly in terms of viewing 'defect' as a diminution in goods' monetary value.

disclosure regime. *Shari'a* principles dictate that sellers disclose all material information about defects, regardless of whether or not buyers have asked for such disclosure.[628] Sellers cannot simply be silent whether they have concealed defects or not. But how is this discussion going to explain *Shari'a's* approach to mandatory disclosure on securities markets when offering shares to the public?

To answer, one says that the analogy with *Shari'a's* requirement for the disclosure of all material information concerning defects in contracts of sale, serves as the closest tool to explaining what is meant by 'material' disclosure. For, as shall be seen below, Islamic jurists have not been unanimous in determining what constitutes a 'defect', with some viewing it as anything that results in depreciating the financial value of the merchandise. Indeed, it is this liberal interpretation of defect (seeing it as any diminution in goods' monetary value) that is relevant to the question of disclosing information when offering shares to the public.

For, one can use this analogy to argue that if depreciation of goods' value amounts to a 'defect', then the same can theoretically be applied to the need for disclosing all material information that may affect the price of offered shares, lest they be considered 'defective'. This argument is highly relevant in the context of contemporary debates over the role of mandatory disclosure when offering securities to the public as shall be explained below. This however necessitates an examination of *Shari'a's* juridical rules on the need to disclose all information relating to defects under contracts of sale.

For his part, the Prophet Muhammad declared it 'illegal for sellers to sell merchandise if they know it has a defect, unless they inform buyers of that defect'.[629] He also warned that *if anyone sells a defective article without drawing attention to the defect, he will remain under God's anger, or the angels will continue to curse him.*[630] Equally, *if both parties speak the truth and describe the defects and quantities (of the goods), then they will be blessed in their transaction. If they tell lies or conceal anything, then the blessing on their transaction will be blotted out.*[631]

It is true that the Prophet Muhammad did not himself formulate *Shari'a's* juridical approach to defects in contracts of sale per se. However, the above admonitions against selling defective goods without full disclosure subsequently led Muslim jurists to rule that merchandise sold under Islamic contracts should always be free from defect. They further agree that the presence of defect entitles the buyer to rescind the contract under the option of 'defective goods', known under *Shari'a* as *khiyar al-ayib*.[632] Yet although the four *Sunni* schools agree that buyers are entitled to rescind contracts of sale on the grounds of 'defect', they

---

628. C.f., M Billah, '*Caveat Emptor* versus *Khiyar al-aib*: A Dichotomy', *ALQ*, Vol. 13, Pt. 3, (1998), p. 287, arguing that *Shari'a's* demands for full disclosure extend to all contracts of sale, regarding all aspects.
629. Narrated by Uqba bin Amir and quoted in *Sahih al-Bukhari*, Vol. II.
630. Reported by Ibn Majah *Mishkatul Masabih*, Vol. I.
631. Quoted in *Sahih Muslim*, Vol. III.
632. *Khyiar* literally means option, while *ayib* means defect. Regarding the implicit Islamic legal warranty that merchandise sold must be free from defects, see the Ottoman civil code, the

nevertheless differ in considering what constitutes a 'defect'. Comair-Obeid has succinctly summarised their approaches:[633]

(1) The *Hanifites* consider 'defect' as a diminution (whether major or minimal) in the commercial value of the goods. For them, buyers can rescind the contract of sale if the defect reduces the value of the subject matter, whether or not such a defect affects the intended purpose. So, the buyer according to the *Hanifites* is entitled to rescind the contract regardless of the amount of the depreciation of the commercial value of the items.
(2) The *Shafi'ites* on the other hand consider 'defect' as damage that prevents the goods from being used for their legitimate purpose. They accordingly grant the buyer the right to rescind only if the defect frustrates the intended purpose, otherwise only to be compensated financially in a manner commensurate with the defect.
(3) When determining what constitutes a 'defect', the *Malikites* draw a distinction between 'major' and 'minor' damage to the goods. They however combine a number of factors to determine defect, considering it resulting from both reduction in its commercial value and suitability for its intended purpose. While major defects entitle the buyer to rescind the contract, minor ones make them eligible for a proportionate compensation only.
(4) The *Hanbalites* rely on regional custom in determining what constitutes a 'defect' in order to enable the purchaser to rescind the contract. Accordingly, the standard of damage considered as the threshold for determining whether or not goods are defective may vary from one region to another. The *Hanbalites* deem the buyer entitled to compensation commensurate with the difference in the value of defective merchandise even if they choose to affirm the contract.

Having shed light on the general understanding of the question of 'defect', one shall next assess the implications for *Shari'a's* securities disclosure regime.

4. IMPLICATIONS FOR A *SHARI'A* SECURITIES DISCLOSURE REGIME

One argues that the *Hanifites* interpretation of defect[634] is the one which bears most on the question of what constitutes material information of *Shari'a's* disclosure when offering shares – that is, in terms of disclosing all aspects that may affect the accuracy of the price of issued securities. The *Hanifites* interpretation is highly

---

Majallat, Art. 336. Also Art. 193 of the JCC. Other 'options' include the 'option of stipulation' or *khiyar ash-shart*, the 'option of designation' or *khiyar at-ta'yin*, and also the 'option of inspection' or *khiyar ar-ru'yat*. Indeed, given the intertwining relationship between *Shari'a* and Arab civil codes, these options are not juridical relics. See Arts 323–328 of the KCC and Arts 177–198 of the JCC.

633. See Comair-Obeid, *supra* note 557, pp. 80–82, 84–86.

634. Viewing it as synonymous with monetary deprecation in goods' value.

relevant, not least due to the fact that the JCC dwells heavily on the *Hanifite* School teachings. For, this argument if applied results in Islamic disclosure being mandated in order to ensure the dissemination of all material information that impacts upon achieving accurate pricing of securities – something which incidentally coincides with efficiency justifications for mandatory disclosure as seen in Chapter 4.

However, one must hasten to add that the above analogy has its limits, as the role of *Shari'a's* mandatory disclosure will only contribute to 'partial' accurate pricing – in terms of ensuring that securities offered to the public will not be overpriced while may be underpriced. For, if one follows the *Hanifites* interpretation of the concept of defect to its logical conclusion and applies it when offering shares, one finds that it only refers to any depreciation of securities' prices that induces a loss to investors. It therefore has no qualms if the same investors buy an undervalued security from which they stand to profit. Indeed, an underpriced security from buyers' perspective is not a 'defective' one, but rather an investment opportunity that must be seized. From this angle, the objective of achieving price accuracy will not be guaranteed under Islamic disclosure on securities markets.

Additionally, it would be conceptually very difficult to broaden the *Hanifites* interpretation of what constitutes a 'defect' into a public policy objective that aims at correcting securities' price distortions. However, the *Hanbalites* interpretation of 'defect', as anything that diminishes the value of merchandise according to regional customs, may be of interest here. For, 'regional custom' can be loosely stretched to be the modern equivalent of market value in the place where shares are offered. But in deeper analysis one finds that the *Hanbalites* proposition suffers from at least three fundamental problems when applied to offering securities to the public.

First, on occasions it may prove difficult to estimate a 'market value' of securities. This is especially if they are issued for the first time to the public and there is no past experience of the performance of the issuer. *Second*, determining the price of a security by looking at its 'equivalent market value' may also be difficult to apply in practical terms. For, securities prices are generally more volatile than conventional merchandise and their prices may even vary considerably between one minute and another. *Third*, with the advent of multi-listing where shares can be offered simultaneously across many jurisdictions, the 'regional' denominator adopted in the *Hanbalites'* understanding of 'defects' loses its significance.

In a similar vein, the *Malikites* interpretation is also unhelpful to identifying 'defective' securities offered to the public. Such interpretation further complicates the matter when viewing defect as resulting from any 'major' diminution in the value of goods. It also poses subjective questions. For, what is a 'minor' or 'major' diminution in the value of securities? Is it, one-fifth, one-tenth, one-twentieth? In addition, as mentioned earlier, in order for goods to be classified as 'defective', *Malikites* demand that they are rendered 'unsuitable' for the purpose for which they were bought. This requisite is of no relevance to notional goods such as securities. For, fitness for purpose does not come into consideration, unless of course it is the generic objective of making profit. This problem also appears under *Shafi'ites'* interpretation, which also considers 'defect' as damage that prevents goods from being used for their legitimate purpose.

5. THE NEED FOR THE POSITIVE LAW TO COMPEL DISCLOSURE UNDER *SHARI'A*

From the above discussion one argues that the need for the law to intervene to compel disclosure when offering securities under a *Shari'a* disclosure regime can be justified on at least three grounds.

First, the limitation of the analogy with non-notional goods. *Second*, the problem of achieving standardisation of issuer-specific information under a *Shari'a* disclosure regime. *Third*, information disclosed under a *Shari'a* disclosure regime would not guarantee price accuracy of offered securities. The discussion next shall elaborate.

5.1. The Limitation of the Analogy with Non-notional Goods

Over-reliance on the analogy of defective goods would be impractical, as securities remain 'notional' financial instruments not amenable to physical inspection, as is the case under goods. The limitation of the analogy with non-notional goods is not however exclusive to *Shari'a's* disclosure regime. For example, consumers of merchandise goods in the UK are protected by general contractual and tortious remedies.[635] Yet, purchasers of financial products, more often than not, find it difficult to recourse to such remedies mainly because financial products are 'intricate' merchandise.[636]

As 'experience goods' (which differ from 'search goods' such as clothing), information in an investment context cannot generally be evaluated in advance by lay investors. Thus, rendering them particularly vulnerable to the skill and probity of financial advisors.[637] The general problem arising from the different nature of securities in terms of repeat experience and verification (justifying the law's interference to protect investors) has particularly been elaborated by Easterbrook and Fischel – where it was highlighted that the problem is more serious for securities when compared to most physical goods due to the difficulty of verification, especially as misstatement will affect the probability of repeat purchases. So it was argued that the seller has little incentive to misrepresent. This is especially as many sellers have competitors keen to expose misstatements, which is seen as effective in tempering the release of misinformation regardless of what the law does about fraud:

> But because each security is an interest in a unique project, neither competitors' statements nor the prospect of repeat purchases will impose constraints, and it is very hard for a buyer to verify statements before the sale.[638]

---

635. Together with statutory provisions which make correspondence with description, merchantability, fitness for a particular purpose, etc., implied terms of the contract of sale. See, for example, UK's Sale of Goods Act 1979, especially ss 13(1) & (2), 14(2), 15(2)(c).
636. See Page et al., *supra* note 386, pp. 35–38. Although there is nothing (in theory) that prohibits purchasers of financial products from recoursing to tortious, contractual or statutory remedies.
637. *Ibid.*
638. See, for example, Easterbrook & Fischel, *supra* note 422, p. 281 (note 8 therein).

The above point is equally relevant when theoretically looking at a potential disclosure regime under *Shari'a*. For, it would also bring about the same problems of verification and repeat experience in 'notional' goods. Subsequent inspection of notional goods sold under *Shari'a* contracts would also not be feasible – that is, in a manner that would enable lay investors to verify the information provided by issuers.

Additionally, due to the complexity of financial instruments and issuers' disproportional privileged knowledge, it is most likely that such lay investors would take a longer period to accumulate 'repeat experience' – than in the context of merchandise, risking in the process significant financial losses.

5.2. The Problem of Not Achieving Standardisation of Information under a *Shari'a* Disclosure Regime

Another important critique of any resulting disclosure regime under *Shari'a's* general principles is its lack of horizontal uniformity in terms of achieving standardisation in the format of released information. As seen in Chapter 4, a potent argument in favour of mandatory disclosure is that it achieves standardisation of disclosed information. Thus, enabling investors to compare and contrast the same sets of information provided by different issuers.

Having invested time and energy in familiarising themselves with understanding the significance of the information provided by one issuer, investors can then deploy the same knowledge to interpret other similar sets of information provided by other issuers. In this context, the problem with a disclosure regime based solely on *Shari'a's* general principles is that standardisation of released information will not be achieved.

In the first place, as has earlier been discussed, there are often fundamental differences in the orientation of the four *Sunni* schools when looking at the question of what constitutes a defect. Second, even if one juridical school was adopted across the board, there is nothing in any of such schools that would compel the rigorous disclosure of 'standardised' information by issuers when publicly offering their securities. Hence, the need for the law not only to compel the disclosure of information. But also to ensure horizontal standardisation of such disclosed information.

5.3. Information under *Shari'a* Would Not Guarantee Price Accuracy of Offered Securities

Shari'a's general principles would not be too inconsistent with earlier discussion on mandatory disclosure in Chapter 4, which views it as compelling the dissemination of information that would make investors better able to assess investment risks. Moreover, *Shari'a's* exhortations for parties to transact on the marketplace, where there is ample provision of information, also seem to dovetail with fairness-based arguments. Here, arguments for including information such as past performance of companies (firm-specific information) and fundamental information on securities would be the least controversial under a *Shari'a* securities disclosure regime.

But contemporary justifications of mandatory disclosure are not exclusive to fairness-based arguments. Indeed, as seen in Chapter 4, accuracy enhancement argument remains influential today when justifying mandatory disclosure in terms of its role in improving the accuracy of securities' prices. However, accuracy enhancement does not write off fairness-based arguments as such. It rather gives a functional role to mandatory disclosure, in the sense of mandating the dissemination of information in order to achieve optimal accuracy of securities' pricing.[639]

The above efficiency arguments would not necessarily feature under a *Shari'a* securities disclosure regime. Indeed, any resulting disclosure regime under *Shari'a* is likely to be a limited one, covering at best (under the *Hanifites*) the disclosure of partial information that might ensure that the price of offered securities is not overpriced – though not necessarily underpriced.[640] From this angle alone one can *a priori* argue that information disseminated pursuant to such a disclosure regime would do little to guarantee price accuracy of securities offered to the public.

Shari'a interpretations in terms of viewing information disseminated for the purpose of ensuring that the price of issued securities corresponds to market value (under the *Hanbalites*), would also be equally inadequate to ensure price discovery. For, they would compare the price of offered securities with existing market prices, without necessarily looking at the efficiency of underlying pricing mechanisms used to arrive at such prices. Here, requesting disclosure of information to ensure that offered securities are traded (priced) on *par* with market value of other 'similar' securities, is conceptually and methodologically different from requiring information in order to achieve price discovery and accurate pricing.

Apart from the doctrinal problems with viewing securities as merchandise, there are a number of practical difficulties arising specifically from the aforementioned Islamic interpretations. The operational difficulty of establishing what constitutes equivalent 'market value' for offered securities (under the *Hanbalites*) was evident in earlier discussion. So was viewing defective securities as those whose

---

639. Accuracy enhancement role for mandatory disclosure goes 'deeper' beyond the conventional notion of the 'prudent-investor', which simply means that investors and their agents should be made aware of the risks they take through issuers' provision of credible information. See, for example, Kitch, *supra* note 422, p. 767.

640. However, one hastens to add that underpricing when offering securities to the public may not entirely result from asymmetrical flow of information as such. This is particularly the case in IPOs, where securities may be deliberately underpriced. This deliberate underpricing is attributed to a number of models. These include: the 'Dynamic Information Acquisition' model, under which investment banks deliberately on occasions underprice securities in order to elicit 'real' evaluation from investors; the 'Information Cascade' model, under which investment banks may deliberately underprice offering price in order to induce the first few investors to pre-empt a general public perception of overpricing; and the 'Political Motives' model, under which securities are deliberately underpriced when offered to selected investors as indirect 'kickbacks'. See, for example, R Ibbotson, 'The Market's Problem with the Pricing of Initial Public Offerings', *Journal of Applied Corporate Finance*, Vol. 7, 1994, 67, pp. 70–72.

value have suffered from 'major' depreciation and are equally not 'fit' for their purpose (under the *Malikites* and *Shafi'ites*). Neither do *Shari'a's* general principles explain in a substantive manner what issuer-specific information needs to be disclosed in order to ensure a disclosure regime that achieves the multi-pronged objective of fairness, market integrity, investor protection as well as enhancing price accuracy.

Finally, extraneous information relating to underlying sectoral conditions that may have a bearing upon securities' prices would not also necessarily form part of information disseminated under a *Shari'a* disclosure regime. For, it has no connection to the question of defect in a strict technical sense. It would also be difficult to perceive a system of timely or periodic disclosure regime under *Shari'a's* general rules extrapolated from the above Islamic jurists' interpretation of defects. Needless to say, due to the concept of *gharar* which mainly focuses on disclosing *ex post facto* information it would be difficult to perceive *Shari'a's* conceptual support for disclosing projections or forecasts. However, it must be admitted that intense debate about the usefulness of mandating the disclosure of forward-looking information rose mainly in the US context.[641]

6. CONCLUSION

The informational boundaries of a disclosure regime under *Shari'a's* general principles pose an important question for Arab jurisdictions when considering the question of offering securities to the public. Although Arab countries are increasingly adopting modern disclosure regimes, no juridical analysis in the literature has ever tackled the question of why a disclosure regime based on general law there would not be workable. Yet, when discussing mandatory disclosure on Arab securities markets, one needs to be conceptually clear about two distinct questions.

First, the position of the general law vis-à-vis the question of disclosure in contracts of sale, in order to determine whether the principle of *caveat emptor* applies. Here, there is a marked difference between *Shari'a* and the Common Law. While the latter applies the doctrine of *caveat emptor* generally, the former requires the disclosure of all material information. Second, whether the general rules on their own would give rise to a disclosure regime that stands the scrutiny of modern arguments for mandating securities disclosure. For, although *Shari'a's* general principles would dovetail with fairness-based arguments in support of mandatory disclosure, its general principles would not necessarily give rise to a mandatory disclosure regime that incorporates efficiency arguments. Indeed, the resulting

641. The US 'conventional' role of disclosure has often been criticised for not furnishing investors with forward-looking information. See generally Kripke, *supra* note 410; J Benston, 'The Value of the SEC's Accounting Disclosure Requirements', *Accounting Review* Vol. 44 (1969) 515; Johnson et al., 'The Impact of Securities Litigation Reform on the Disclosure of Forward-Looking Information by High Technology Firms', *Journal of Financial Accounting*, Vol. 39 (2001), p. 297.

disclosure regime would not guarantee nor enhance the accuracy of securities' pricing or price discovery. Neither would it, for example, equally ensure standardisation of disclosure.

However, despite the differences in conceptual orientation concerning the starting point of analysis between *Shari'a* and the Common Law, the general law on its own in both jurisdictions fails to compel securities disclosure. Hence the need for mandatory disclosure to compel securities disclosure under *Shari'a* and the Common Law alike.

Part II

Vertical Case Study in an Arab Jurisdiction: The Case of Jordan

Chapter 8
The Jordanian Regime for Public Offers Before 1997

Jordan has made solid progress in the monetary and financial sectors by implementing a comprehensive economic adjustment and reform program. The reforms have resulted in a well-developed financial sector, placing Jordan among the MENA countries with the highest financial development scores in all areas. . . .[642]

INTRODUCTION

The first part of this book has looked at horizontal aspects in order to contextualise the phenomenon of Arab securities regulation. In order to produce a non-truncated analysis a vertical study is now undertaken, with an Arab jurisdiction as a case study. This is important in order to point out how an Arab regulatory regime has evolved, and how the theory of securities regulation and notions of investor protection dovetail with reality on the ground.

Chapter 8 therefore now vertically looks at the Jordanian regulatory regime to assess its methodology of achieving investor protection and the adequacy of its disclosure regime when offering/listing shares. As Jordan changed its regulatory regime in 1997, this chapter only focuses on the legal structure that existed prior to 1997 – leaving Chapter 9 to look at the post-1997 regulatory regime. Chapter 8 therefore explains the legal framework for regulating public offers/listing before 1997 – assessing in the process whether such a regime provided adequate investor protection.

642. See generally S Creane et al., *Financial Development in the Middle East and North Africa*. International Monetary Fund (2003).

1. THE LEGAL FRAMEWORK FOR PUBLIC OFFERS BEFORE 1997

The regulatory regime for public offers prior to the enactment of the SA 1997 was incremental, passing through many stages: (1) the early stage; (2) under the Companies Law 1964; and (3) under the Companies Law 1989.

1.1. THE EARLY STAGE

The 'early stage' spans from 1927 until 1964. Issuance of shares to the public in Jordan (formerly Transjordan) can be traced back to the 1930s and 1940s.[643] The first public shareholding company to be established in Jordan was the Arab Bank, which was incorporated in 1930. The setting up of the Arab Bank was subsequently followed by the setting up of the Jordan Tobacco and Cigarettes Company in 1931, Jordan Electric Power Company in 1938, and Jordan Cement Factories in 1951. For its part, Jordanian company legislation finds its roots in corporate legislation enacted in neighbouring Arab countries.[644]

Before the enactment of the Companies Law 1964, companies in Jordan were subject to the *Provisional Companies Law No. 33 of 1962*. Before that, they were governed by the Companies Registration Law 1927 and more generally the Ottoman Trade Law of 1850.[645] There were no particular disclosure requirements imposed by the Companies Registration Law 1927 that went over and above the information that had to be disclosed by companies when they first register to start business.

In this context, Article (2) of the Companies Registration Law 1927 mandated that every shareholding company must register within one month from the date of this law's publication.[646] The information which companies had to provide then related to their commercial name, capital, headquarter, nominal value of shares, names and addresses of directors and objective:

> If incorporated in Transjordan, every (shareholding) company must provide . . . the following: the company's commercial name; the company's authorised and paid-up capital; number of shares and their nominal value; company's headquarter and branches; name and addresses of company's directors; and the company's objectives.[647]

---

643. The Emirate of Transjordan gained its independence and became the Kingdom of Jordan in 1946.
644. When dealing with limited liability and foreign companies, the Companies Law 1964, for example, re-enacted earlier Palestinian company legislation. Regarding public shareholding companies it adopted rules from the Syrian Trade Law.
645. Adapted from the French Trade Law of 1807.
646. *Official Gazette* No. 162, dated 11 August 1927.
647. Article 2 of the Companies Registration Law 1927.

1.2. Under the Companies Law 1964

The first proper regulation of public offers in Jordan came in the wake of the Companies Law 1964.[648] This law specifically addressed the question of public offering of equities by public shareholding companies. The conditions for issuing securities were quite simple. Promoters had first to subscribe to *no less* than 10% of the company's authorised capital.[649] The rationale behind this was to protect investors against fraud by ensuring that promoters took a stake in the subscription. The rest of the shares could then be offered to the public by means of a subscription advertisement published in two dailies at least one week before the subscription day.

The information that had to be disclosed was minimal and mainly related to: (1) companies' objectives, capital, number of shares; (2) names of promoters, their nationalities and the amount of their paid up capital; (3) subscription conditions, total value of offered shares and method of payments; and (4) name of the bank to which money was paid.[650]

1.3. Under the Companies Law 1989

The main impetus behind the enactment of this law was to overcome the inadequacy of the Companies Law 1964 in its regulation of public shareholding companies. For, as the Jordanian economy was growing, increasing governmental emphasis was being placed on involving the private sector in driving the economy. In this context, various Jordanian governments pursued a number of long-term economic plans, known as 'Development Plans'. These plans aimed at achieving a number of objectives, most important of which was ensuring the substantial involvement of the private sector in the Jordanian economy. For example, while the (1964–1980) Development Plan envisaged capital expenditure of JOD 260 million, with governmental participation of around 50%, the (1981–1985) Development Plan envisaged capital expenditure of JD 3,300 million, with governmental participation of 61%.[651]

Indeed, in order to better regulate public shareholding companies and enhance public confidence in them, the Companies Law No. 1 for the Year 1989[652] amended some of the requirements needed to offer shares in Jordan. However, these amendments largely aimed at ensuring that the Jordanian public was not duped by unscrupulous promoters, when new public shareholding companies offered their shares. To be able to issue shares publicly, no single promoter was allowed to own more than 10% of a company's authorised capital.[653]

648. Law No. 12 for the year 1964.
649. See Art. 51 of the Companies Law 1964.
650. *Ibid.*
651. See generally the *Social Economic Plan (1981–1985)*, The Jordanian Ministry of Planning, Amman.
652. *Official Gazette* No. 3596, dated 1 January 1989.
653. Unless they were a government entity or a public body. See Art. 102(b) of the Companies Law 1989.

Additionally, prior to issue, promoters were expected to have paid their subscriptions in full, providing such subscriptions constituted *no less* than 20% of the company's authorised capital and *no more* than 50% if the company was a bank, financial or insurance company. Promoters' subscriptions were equally expected to constitute *no more* than 75% of the authorised capital of all other types of companies.[654] It also required public shareholding companies to appoint auditors.[655]

However, the most important change that the Companies Law 1989 introduced was the setting up of the so-called *Issuing Committee*. Its members included the General Secretary of the Ministry of Trade and Industry, the Deputy Chairman of the CBJ, the General Secretary of the Ministry of Finance, the General Manager of the Amman Financial Market (AFM), the Company Comptroller and four members from the private sector. The tasks of the *Issuing Committee* were primarily to approve and supervise securities issues as well as proposing laws and policies to regulate trading on the AFM:

> The *Issuing Committee* is particularly responsible for the following: (a) determining the dates of issuing securities in liaison with the AFM in a manner that maintains the balance of the AFM; (b) approving prospectuses after having studied and examined them and equally ensured the veracity of the data and information in subscription advertisements; and (3) suggesting proper legislation and policies to organise the AFM and presenting recommendations to the Minister [of Trade and Industry] and other relevant entities.[656]

Issuers had to publish a subscription advertisement over three consecutive days (in two local newspapers) one week before the offer date.[657] However, although the content and wording of the subscription advertisement had to be approved and verified by the *Issuing Committee*, the Committee did not play any significant role in verifying the content of prospectuses or subscription advertisements. It rather left it to the AMF to register prospectuses that were accepted by the AFM.

Having discussed the laws and limited disclosure applicable to public offers before 1997, the next subsection looks at the regulation of listing in that period.

2. THE LEGAL FRAMEWORK FOR LISTING BEFORE 1997

Similar to public offers, the regulation of listing in Jordan also passed through a number of regulatory phases. These are: (1) the early stage; (2) under the Amman Financial Market Law 1976; (3) under the *Internal Regulations of the Amman Financial Market 1980*; (4) under the *1990 Amman Financial Market Law as amended by Law No. 31 of the year 1992*; and (5) under the regulations of the Management Committee of the Amman Financial Market.

654. See Arts 102(a)(1)(2) and 135–138. *Ibid.*
655. See Arts 220–231. *Ibid.*
656. See Art. 94. *Ibid.*
657. See Art. 104(b). *Ibid.*

2.1. The Early Stage

As mentioned above, public shareholding companies in Jordan can be traced back to the early 1930s. Trading in the equities of shareholding companies in that period was conducted in an informal manner. This lasted until the setting up of the AFM in 1978, before which the regulation of securities trading was absent and a formal exchange was even non-existent. As was the case in almost all Arab countries, trading in government bonds preceded the establishment of a formal equity market on which shares could be traded. For example, the Jordanian Public Debt Law 1966[658] (which regulated government bond trading in Jordan) preceded by a decade the Amman Financial Market Law 1976, which established the first stock exchange in Jordan.

Up until 1978, the only way to exchange shares in Jordan was informally through estate agents and part-time (unlicensed) brokers whose role was literally to introduce the parties to each other.[659] The actual contract for the sale of shares used to be concluded at the offices of the company whose shares were being traded. Once the contract of sale had been concluded, the company concerned would then grant owners shares certificates.

This non-regulation did not change much even after the promulgation of major company and commercial laws in Jordan. Even after the enactment of the Companies Law 1964, acute under-regulation of securities trading prevailed. Neither did the question of regulating unlicensed brokers, who had for decades been engaged in buying and selling shares, arise under the 1966 JCA. For, although it dealt extensively with brokerage and commercial agency,[660] it never addressed any of the general aspects of share brokerage.[661] This omission is difficult to justify given the fact that, as opposed to the JCC, which was the general legislation regulating civil contracts, the JCA was itself a special legislation.[662]

2.2. Under the Amman Financial Market Law 1976

Due to increased sophistication of the Jordanian economy and the heavy investments it needed in order to mobilise domestic resources, the government's three-year Development Plan (1973–1975) and five-year one (1976–1980) *specifically* called for the setting up of a stock exchange. Added to this was the Jordanian government's desire to finance such development plans through issuing public

658. Law No. 96 for the year 1966 – replaced by Public Debt Law No. 1 as amended by Law No. 59 for the year 1976. *Official Gazette* No. 2658, dated 5 October 1976.
659. Particularly by two Brokerage firms: Suliman Brakat & Brother and Ghazaleh & Judeh.
660. See Pt. IV of the JCA entitled 'Commercial Agency, Commission Agency and Brokerage'.
661. The regulation of securities brokers did not start until almost more than a decade later when the 1976 Amman Financial Markets Law (Provisional Law No. 31) entered into force.
662. According to the JCA, the activities of share brokers were 'commercial' by 'virtue of their nature'. Art. 6 states: '1. The following activities shall be deemed – by virtue of their nature – commercial activities.... (h) Brokerage and intermediation.' However, Art. 105 stated that intermediation and brokerage on stock markets should be governed by special legislation.

debt.[663] As the old informal arrangements were proving highly inadequate, the first attempt at regulating securities trading in Jordan took place with the promulgation of the Amman Financial Market Law 1976 (AFML 1976).[664]

The AFML 1976, which was a special law, was promulgated when the Companies Law 1964 and the Commercial Law 1966 were operative. It became effective on 1 June 1976,[665] and although one acknowledges that it was by no means comprehensive, as it contained only fifty-two Articles,[666] most of which were general, it nevertheless was a watershed. For, it was the first time that a formal securities exchange (within a legal framework) was ever set up in Jordan.[667]

However, contrary to the view held by some commentators, the AFML 1976 itself did not at all address insider dealing or market manipulation.[668] For, such aspects were first addressed (albeit in passing) by the *1980 Internal Regulations of the Amman Financial Market*.[669] The next subsection shall take a closer look at the structure of the AFM.

2.2.1. The Amman Financial Market (AFM)

As mentioned above, despite its limitations, the importance of the AFML 1976 cannot be overstated enough. For, among its prime achievements was that it set up for the first time in Jordan an exchange for '... the sale and purchase of financial papers ... called the Amman Financial Market.'[670] This exchange was designed to be '.... a public institution practising commercial transactions in dealing with others'.[671] For its part, Article 50 of the AFML 1976 authorised the Minister of Finance to fix the date on which dealing on the AFM would commence.[672] Trading on the AFM started on 1 January 1978, with sixty-six companies listed by the end

663. See A Abdel-Hadi, *Stock Markets of the Arab World: Trends, Problems and Prospects for Integration*, Routledge (London), 1988, p. 53.
664. Provisional Law No. 31 for the year 1976.
665. *Official Gazette* No. 2629 dated 1 June 1976.
666. This Law initially comprised fifty-one Articles. See *Amendment Law to the Amman Financial Market Law for the year 1976*, *Official Gazette* No. 2807, dated 1 September 1978.
667. The AFML 1976 comprised eight small chapters addressing questions pertaining to 'Definitions and Basic Provisions' (Ch. I, Arts 1–5); 'Members and Brokers' (Ch. II, Arts 6–14); 'Acceptance of the Financial Papers at the Market' (Ch. III, Arts 15–18); 'Market Finance' (Ch. IV, Arts 19–25); 'Management of the Market' (Ch. V, Arts 26–34); 'Government Supervision' (Ch. VI, Arts 35–38); 'Disciplinary Action'(Ch. VII, Arts 39–43); and 'General Supervisions' Ch. VIII, Arts 44–52).
668. See Abdel-Hadi, *supra* note 663, where he mistakenly quotes A Agtmeal, *Emerging Securities Markets*, Euromoney Publications, (1984): '[the AFML 1976] which provides a basic framework for new issue regulation, disclosure, financial reporting, supervision of the exchange, and monitoring of insider trading and price manipulation,' p. 164.
669. See Art. 65 of the *Internal Regulations of the Amman Financial Markets No. 26 for the year 1980*.
670. See Art. 3 of the AFML 1976.
671. *Ibid.*
672. Art. 50 reads: 'The Minister shall, by a decision, fix the date on which dealing in financial papers shall start on the Market floor, in accordance with the provisions of this Law.' *Ibid.*

of that year.[673] In order to give a more accurate view of its structure (as envisaged by AFML 1976), questions pertaining to membership, brokers, management and government supervision over the AFM, shall all be tackled next.

2.2.1.1. Membership and Brokers

Membership in the AFM included the CBJ, licensed banks, 'specialised credit institutions',[674] public Jordanian shareholding companies whose paid up capital was at least JD 100,000 and brokers approved by the Management Committee[675] of the AFM.[676] Share brokers, who if natural persons,[677] were expected to have been of certain age[678] and good character,[679] providing minimum paid up capital[680] and additional financial guarantees,[681] etc.[682] If legal persons,[683] brokers were expected to have been Jordanian companies, with managers of good character,[684] possessing minimum education[685] or relevant professional experience.[686] Paid up capital was not expected to be less than JD 10,000, providing additional financial guarantees,[687] etc.[688]

A member or a broker of the AFM would have to be disqualified if they lost any of the requirements above or if a decision was taken to that effect by the Management Committee of the AFM.[689] By the end of 1978, the number of brokers totalled eleven with the addition of the Arab Finance Corporation and the Arab Jordan Investment Bank.

2.2.1.2. Management

The AFM was managed by a so-called Management Committee appointed by the Jordanian Council of Ministers upon the recommendation of the Minister of

---

673. Since 1980 the AFM has had a share price index, which in 1992 was revised and updated in cooperation with the IFC. The index currently comprises the sixty top Jordanian companies. This indicator was developed to represent market trends. Companies in the index are based on their market capitalisation, liquidity and price.
674. Art. 2 of the AFML 1976 defines 'specialised credit institutions' as 'every institution or legal entity established in the Kingdom whose main objective is the granting of loans for specialised purposes and which is designated as such by the Council of Ministers . . . '
675. See discussion below on the Management Committee of the AFM.
676. See Art. 6 of the AFML 1976.
677. That is, an individual.
678. No less than 25 years old.
679. Not convicted for misdemeanour or felony, neither declared bankrupt.
680. The minimum paid capital was JOD 10,000.
681. A bank guarantee of no less than JD 10,000.
682. See Art. 9(a)(1-5) of the AFML 1976.
683. That is, a company or partnership.
684. Not convicted of misdemeanour or felony, neither declared bankrupt.
685. At least secondary education.
686. Worked in financial or banking institutions for no less than five years.
687. A bank guarantee of no less than JD 10,000.
688. See Art. 9(b)(1-7) of the AFML 1976.
689. See Arts 10–14. *Ibid.*

Finance.[690] The Committee's duties, *inter alia*, included issuing instructions to regulate market affairs, discipline violators, as well as issuing necessary instructions to control the AFM's accounts, revenues and expenses.[691] However, a curious element in the management of the AFM was the supervisory role of the government over its activities. This was done through a 'government representative' who attended all the meetings of the AFM's Management Committee and took part in its discussions, but with no voting powers.

Government representatives were expected to supervise the 'accuracy of transactions' carried out in the market and especially the implementation of the AFM's laws and regulations.[692] Such representatives could also object at the Committee's decisions, particularly if such decisions had a financial bearing or appeared illegal. For their objection to be effective, they needed the support of two-thirds of attending Management Committee members.[693] Government representatives were also expected to write quarterly to the Minister filing their recommendations on how to improve the AFM.[694] However, the role of these representatives proved either limited or superfluous, largely due to their lack of expertise in handling matters related to securities markets.

2.3. Listing Requirements under the Amman Financial Market Law 1976 (AFML 1976)

One here turns to look at the regulation of listing or the 'acceptance of financial papers' – as the AFML 1976 put it. Despite its importance, the question of listing was addressed in only four brief Articles (15–18). Article 15 stated that it was up to the AFM Management Committee's discretion to 'accept' securities.[695] Article 16 added that bonds issued by the government and debt securities issued by companies were both 'accepted' at the AFM.

However, despite its generality and poor structure, Article 17 was the closest the AFML 1976 got to laying down substantive listing conditions:

> Every Jordanian public shareholding company, whose paid up capital is at least JD 100,000 shall apply for the acceptance of its shares at the AFM. Other shareholding companies have the right to apply for the acceptance of their

690. Members of the Committee were: (1) the AFM's general manager; (2) Companies Comptroller in the Ministry of Industry and Commerce; (3) representative of the Central Bank of Jordan; (4) representative of licensed banks and specialised credit institutions; (5) representative of member shareholding companies; and (6) representative of the Amman Chamber of Industry. While the general manager of the AFM was the chair of the Committee, the rest were members. See Art. 26. *Ibid.*
691. See Art. 32. *Ibid.*
692. See Art. 36. *Ibid.*
693. See Art. 38. *Ibid.*
694. *Ibid.*
695. Article 15 of the AFML 1976 reads: 'Financial papers are accepted at the Market upon a decision by the Committee.'

> shares at the AFM, regardless of their capital volume if they had published their balance sheets for two subsequent fiscal years. In all cases, the Committee [of the AFM] shall have the right to accept or reject the application in light of the regulations and instructions it issues concerning the organisation of the acceptance of financial papers.[696]

From the above, one sees that the criteria for listing or 'accepting' shares into the AFM was minimalist and laden with ambiguity. Neither did Article 17 construct a disclosure regime. It simply mandated that public shareholding companies whose paid up capital was JD 0.1 million or more had to apply for listing their shares – notwithstanding that it omitted stating when exactly such listing should take place.[697] The reason behind this unusual mandatory rule was an attempt to deepen the AFM, by ensuring that shares in all shareholding companies were listed and traded. Indeed, as shall be seen below, the pursuit of this public policy objective (in terms of being conscious of the need to continue deepening Jordanian capital markets) has remained a persistent theme, reinforced even in Jordan's latest securities laws – the Securities Act 2002, which came into effect on 31 December 2002.[698]

Article 17 also suggested that Jordanian shareholding companies, whose paid up capital was less than JD 0.1 million, could be 'accepted' if they had published balance sheets for two subsequent years – without necessarily determining the period these sheets covered in terms of them being recent or not. Additionally, there was no explanation whether or not such sheets needed to be certified by external audits. For its part, Article 18 simply repeated that the 'acceptance' of shares on the AFM would be regulated by further regulations.

2.4. Listing Requirements under the Internal Law of the Amman Financial Market 1980

The *Internal Law of the Amman Financial Market No. 26 for the year 1980* was issued in pursuance to the AFML 1976. As far as listing was concerned, it stated that the Management Committee of the AFM had the right to impose additional listing requirements.[699] It also made it compulsory for every public shareholding company whose paid up capital was at least JD 0.1 million to request the listing of its shares on the AFM, within six months of having been granted the permission to start business.[700] Thus, rectifying the earlier vague request for listing that did not determine the period, during which listing should take place under Article 17 of the AFML 1976.

696. Article 17. *Ibid.*
697. Rectified in subsequent laws as shall be seen below.
698. See discussion in Ch. 9 below.
699. See Art. 3(16) of the *Internal Law of the Amman Financial Market 1980.*
700. See Arts 26(4) & 34. *Ibid.*

The *Internal Law of the Amman Financial Market 1980* also gave the Management Committee of the AFM the right to accept listing from other public shareholding companies whose paid up capital was at least JD 0.06 million.[701] It also added the condition that no single shareholder was allowed to own more than 10% of such companies' capital.[702] It equally gave the Management Committee the right to ask companies to publish additional information in order to assure investors and maintain sound trading.[703] Listed companies were also under an obligation to provide the AFM with any information it might require.[704] The AFM however excluded its responsibility from verifying the accuracy of the information provided.[705]

2.5. Listing Requirements under the 1990 Amman Financial Market Law, As Amended by Law No. 31 of the Year 1992

The Amman Financial Market Law 1990[706] contained almost the same fifty-two Articles included in the AFML 1976, though with minor administrative changes. As far as listing was concerned, it did *not* bring any significant changes into the regulatory structure. The slight difference was however in Article 17, when it required public shareholding companies (whose paid up capital was at least JD 0.1 million) to list their shares on the AFM within three months from having been granted the right to start business. This period was instead of the six months under the *Internal Law of the Amman Financial Market 1980*. The new Article 17 also repeated verbatim that 'acceptance' of shares would be governed by regulations issued by the Management Committee of the AFM, something that shall be elaborated next.

2.6. Listing Requirements under the Various Regulations Issued by the Management Committee of the AFM

Before elaborating on such regulations it must be stated that Jordan initially had one market on which companies could be listed, known as the *Regular Market*. However, in order to make the AFM become inclusive of less established Jordanian shareholding companies, the AFM in 1982 set up another market known as the *Parallel Market*. Trading on the *Parallel Market* started on February 1982, with minimal listing conditions – by the end of the same year (1982), the *Parallel Market* was capitalised at JD 16 million.

---

701. Such companies were only expected to have published two consecutive balance sheets, showing no loss in the two years preceding their listing request. See Art. 27(1) & (2). *Ibid.*
702. This excludes government and public bodies. See Art. 27(3). *Ibid.*
703. See Art. 28. *Ibid.*
704. See Art. 29. *Ibid.*
705. See Art. 35. *Ibid.*
706. As amended by Law No. 31 of the year 1992.

In order to be able to list their shares on the *Parallel Market*, shareholding companies were only required to submit a listing application to the AFM supported by the relevant documents,[707] after having ensured that the value of at least 50% of their share capital was paid.[708] To be listed on the *Regular Market*, shareholding companies had to ensure the payment of at least 50% of their share capital and that a full year must have passed since their registration. Public shareholding companies listed on the *Regular Market* were also expected to publish (twice in two subsequent dailies) their annual reports, showing audited profit and loss accounts for the past year.[709]

These above simple conditions for listing were subsequently amended by a number of listing regulations issued by the Management Committee of the AFM. For example, expanding on the requirements for listing on both markets, the Managing Committee of the AFM issued *Regulations No.51/93* (on 27 July 1993).[710] These *Regulations*, which came into effect on 1 July 1994, *inter alia*, required that in order to be listed on the *Parallel Market*, 50% of the company's share capital must have been first paid,[711] a full year must have passed since registration,[712] and that shareholders equity must have not been less than 25%.[713] Public shareholding companies applying for listing on the *Parallel Market* had also to submit their annual reports which had to show the balance sheet for the first year, together with the final account reports and the audited report.[714]

They also had to undertake to publish the above information at least once in two newspapers[715] and present a summary of their progress as well as their future development,[716] after having submitted a listing application.[717] For listing on the *Regular Market*, public shareholding companies had to be listed for at least one year on the *Parallel Market*.[718] They equally must have actually started operation,[719] with shareholders equity being no less than 75%.[720] They also had

707. These documents included copies of the company's articles of association, registration certificate, list of shareholders and members of the board of directors, sample of authorised signatures and data on the number of shares and subscribers, etc.
708. See *Amman Financial Market Report for the Year 1982*, p. 85.
709. As well as providing the AFM with a listing application containing a copy of the company's articles of association, a list of the shareholders names, a list of the members of the board of directors, three copies of the company's most recent audited final accounts, etc. *Ibid.*, p. 45.
710. These were preceded by the listing regulations issued by the Management Committee of the AFM on 31 March 1991, which only slightly differed from *Regulations No.51/93* issued on 27 July 1993.
711. See Art. 4 of AFM Management Committee *Regulations No.51/93*.
712. See Art. 6. *Ibid.*
713. See Art. 5. *Ibid.*
714. See Art. 7(a). *Ibid.*
715. *Ibid.*
716. See Art. 7(b). *Ibid.*
717. That included the documents required by the above set of regulations. Art. 8. *Ibid.*
718. See Art. 9. *Ibid.*
719. See Art. 10. *Ibid.*
720. See Art. 11. *Ibid.*

to present and publish similar financial information,[721] also ensuring that at least 10% of all subscribed equities have been traded on the *Parallel Market*[722] – submitting upon listing also all documents required by the AFM.[723]

Regulations No.51/93 remained applicable until 30 April 1996 and were later repealed by the *1996 Regulations for Listing and Suspending the Shares of Public Shareholding Companies*. These required that at least 45% of the subscribed capital should have been paid in order for public shareholding companies to be listed on the *Parallel Market* and that shareholders' equity should have been no less than 40%.[724] When listing on the *Regular Market*, public shareholding companies were expected to have at least 100 shareholders,[725] having also achieved pre-tax profit for the year preceding listing application.[726] Equally, shareholders' equity should have been no less than 100%,[727] and 10% of their equities should have traded for at least a year on the *Parallel Market* for no less than thirty days.[728] The *1996 Regulations for Listing and Suspending the Shares of Public Shareholding Companies* came into effect on 1 May 1996 and remained applicable until they were repealed by the *1999 Directives for Listing and Suspension of Shares of Public Shareholding Companies* – which shall be elaborated later when one considers the regulatory regime implemented after the enactment of the Securities Act (SA) 1997.

Having elaborated on the legal framework for public offers and listing before the enactment of the SA 1997, the next subsection shall assess such regulatory regime.

3. ASSESSMENT OF THE REGULATORY REGIME BEFORE 1997

This subsection now assesses the Jordanian regulatory regime before the enactment of the SA 1997 inasmuch as it relates to investor protection when offering/listing equities. The methodology adopted here shall be through identifying and assessing the Jordanian regulatory techniques deployed to ensure investor protection in this period.

3.1. The Jordanian Regulatory Techniques to Ensure Some Standards of Investor Protection

As seen above, the Jordanian regulatory regime was characterised by legal simplicity. Yet, this did not mean that Jordanian policy makers were completely oblivious to the

721. See Art. 12. *Ibid.*
722. See Art. 13. *Ibid.*
723. See Art. 15. *Ibid.*
724. See Arts 4 & 5 of the *1996 Regulations for Listing and Suspending the Shares of Public Shareholding Companies.*
725. See Art. 10. *Ibid.*
726. See Art. 11. *Ibid.*
727. See Art. 12. *Ibid.*
728. See Art. 14. *Ibid.*

notion of investor protection. For, the Jordanian regulatory regime had recourse to a number of measures to achieve some standards of investor protection. These were:

(1) Requiring promoters of public shareholding companies compulsorily to subscribe to a minimum percentage of their companies' shares. In light of lack of regulatory agencies to prescribe, vet and monitor disclosure, this basic statutory requirement aimed at minimising fraud by obliging promoters to take a direct stake in the shares offered. The Companies Law 1964 required promoters to subscribe to no less than 10% of the company's equity before offering shares to the public.[729] The Companies Law 1989 increased this to 20%.[730] However, as the new regulatory regime under the SA 1997 increasingly relied on disclosure, this minimum requirement was no longer required by the Companies Law 1997.

    Promoters were also prohibited from selling their subscribed equity holdings before the passage of at least two years from their companies' registration.[731] This requirement was mandated by the Companies Law 1989[732] and later reinforced by the Companies Law 1997.[733] With few exceptions, both laws considered all transfers of such equities before the passage of the prescribed two years as 'null and void'.[734] Again, this basic regulatory technique aimed at minimising the chances of fraud by obliging promoters to hold onto their shares for a minimum of two years, making it harder for them to flog worthless shares into the marketplace.[735]

(2) Jordanian company legislation also nullified any public offer that did not result in the subscription of a minimum percentage of equities. The rationale behind this was to ensure that the public would not be swindled. If two-thirds of the company's equities were not subscribed to, promoters under the Companies Law 1964 were given the option of extending it for another three months,[736] after which they had either to cancel[737] the proposed company or decrease[738] its capital.[739] Under the Companies Law 1989, if two-thirds of the shares had not been subscribed to, promoters

729. See Art. 51 of the Companies Law 1964.
730. It also prohibited each promoter from owning more than 10% of the company's equity, and also capped the number of shares that could be held by promoters – restricting subscribed equities to 50% and 75%. See Art. 102 of the Companies Law 1989, Art. 99(a) & (b) of the Companies Law 1997.
731. The same also applied if promoters' shares were also in kind, and special procedures were adopted to achieve fair assessment of promoters' contributions. See, for example, Arts 109–11 of the Companies Law 1997.
732. See Art. 103 of the Companies Law 1989.
733. See Art. 100(a) of the Companies Law 1997.
734. Exceptions relate to transfer of equities through inheritance, and from a promoter to another or transfer by a court order, etc. See Art. 103 of the Companies Law 1989 and Art. 100(b) of the Companies Law 1997.
735. Bearing in mind that the nominal value of all issued shares in Jordan is always JD 1.0.
736. See Art. 54(2) of the Companies Law 1964.
737. See Art. 54(3). *Ibid.*
738. *Ibid.*
739. Article 54(4) instructed banks immediately to return funds paid to them during subscription. *Ibid.*

were given an extra thirty days to decide[740] between cancelling[741] the proposed company or buying[742] the remaining shares themselves. The Companies Law 1997 has abolished the two-third minimum as it now differentiates between authorised and paid up capital – allowing initial public offers to go ahead as long as subscribed shares were more than 20% of the authorised capital.[743]

(3) Investors were prohibited from subscribing more than once in any given subscription.[744] Fictitious subscriptions and the usage of false names also resulted in nullifying public offers.[745] There were two main public policy objectives here. The first was to ensure that subscribers did not exceed their allotted quotas when subscription outstripped offered shares. The second was to ensure that public offers were not fronts for fraudsters who wanted to give an impression of exaggerated public interest in the subscription. To ensure that the process was genuine, promoters were equally required to present the Company Comptroller with a declaration containing detailed lists of, *inter alia*, the names, number of subscribed shares, amount of money paid, etc.[746] Moreover, to decrease the possibility that unsuspecting investors would be duped, subscriptions were considered binding and irrevocable.[747] In order to minimise fraud, payments made by investors in the course of public offers were strictly made through banks.[748]

(4) Regulatory techniques were also adopted to ensure achieving some standards of investor protection when companies listed their equities on the AFM. An important measure was the two-tiered listing system which had been applied since February 1982. For, the creation of the *Parallel Market* had been intended to provide the Managing Committee of the AFM with an opportunity to monitor shares for a year before transferring them to the *Regular Market*. Thus, adding a layer of market supervision. However, this Jordanian public policy objective had not necessarily been adopted because of government empirical studies that supported a two-tiered

740. See Art. 109(a) of the Companies Law 1989.
741. See Art. 109(a)(1). *Ibid.*
742. See Arts 105 & 109(a)(2). *Ibid.*
743. Equally if a minimum paid up capital had been paid. See Art. 99(d) and Art. 95(a) of the Companies Law 1997. Promoters also had the right to subscribe to any remaining shares, once three days had passed after the closing date – See Art. 99(c). *Ibid.*
744. See Art. 108(a) of the Companies Law 1989; Art. 102(a) of the Companies Law 1997.
745. *Ibid.*
746. See Art. 57 of the Companies Law 1964; Art. 110 of the Companies Law 1989; Art. 103 of the Companies Law 1997.
747. See Art. 52(2) of the Companies Law 1964. Additionally, subscribers were also expected to pay the full value of their subscribed shares within four years [under Art. 47(8) of the Companies Law 1964/ Art. 100 of the Companies Law 1989] and within three years [under Art. 95(b) of the Companies Law 1997, with the Company Comptroller having full capacity to monitor and enforce this legal requirement].
748. Article 52(1-3) of the Companies Law 1964; Art. 107 of the Companies Law 1989; Art. 105 of the Companies Law 1997 obligate issuers to return any money owed to subscribers within thirty days.

listing system. Rather, it was adopted on the ad hoc perception that both, market depth and the interests of investors would be better served by such a division. Providing market depth through lowering the threshold for listing on the *Parallel Market*, while providing a better opportunity for investors to assess companies' performance before transferring their shares to the *Regular Market*.[749]

(5) Not only shares had to be listed for a year on the *Parallel Market* in order to be transferred to the *Regular Market*. Actual trading in at least 10% of the company's equities (taking place in no less than thirty days of trading) had also been expected.[750] This technique intended to ensure genuine trading in the shares of companies listed on the *Parallel Market*. The condition that companies listed on the *Regular Market* should have at least 100 shareholders,[751] was also designed to minimise conspiracy between fraudsters who may act in concert to create fictitious public shareholding companies. Reliance on a large number of shareholders was seen as a practical means to achieving this public policy objective. Similarly, stipulating a threshold of shareholders net equity that reached 100%[752] when listing on the *Regular Market*, was also another method to protect investors. This rule was devised to ensure that the company was not overburdened with debt that diminished its underlying equities value.

(6) Finally, in order to list on either the *Parallel* or the *Regular Market*, public shareholding companies had also to ensure that at least 50% of their share capital had been paid.[753] Again, just like the rationale explained in the context of requiring promoters to subscribe to at least 20% of the company's share capital, this condition aimed at achieving additional standards of investor protection. For, this meant that the enterprise must have been earnest enough for existing shareholders, that it warranted the payment of half of their total subscriptions.

Simplistic they may have been, but did the above techniques guarantee proper investor protection? The answer shall be tackled in the next subsection.

3.2. Did the Regulatory Regime before 1997 Protect Investors When Offering/Listing Equities?

The answer to the above question is that although such techniques attempted at achieving some standards of investor protection, the regulatory system before the

749. Neither the AFM, nor the Ministry of Trade and Industry had ever published any empirical studies in support of any findings that buttress the two-tiered system.
750. See Art. 14 of the *1996 Regulations for Listing and Suspending the Shares of Public Shareholding Companies*.
751. See Art. 10. *Ibid*.
752. See Art. 12. *Ibid*.
753. See Art. 4 of AFM Managing Committee Regulations No. 51/93.

enactment of the SA 1997 suffered from chronic problems. Such problems can be seen through: (1) incomplete understanding of the role of investor protection in defining some market practices; (2) legal uncertainty; (3) wanting informational content in Jordanian prospectuses; and (4) unreliable company annual reports, together with lack of accountancy/auditing standards and non-existent enforcement mechanisms.

The discussion below shall elaborate on all the above.

3.2.1. Incomplete Understanding of the Role of Investor Protection in Defining Some Market Practices

As to the lack of appreciation of the role of investor protection in the legal understanding of some market practices, one only needs to look at the then statutory understanding of private placements. It is acknowledged that the Companies Law 1989 provided the first-ever Jordanian legal thinking on what constitutes a 'private placement'. However, there is no evidence that Jordan's statutory understanding of private placement was based on harnessing the notion of investor protection – that is, in the sense of excluding investors who do not require statutory protection.

For, rather than protecting the various sections of the Jordanian public (who are not able to look after themselves), private placements were exclusively contingent on the 'typology' of companies involved:

> The *Issuing Committee* may approve that public shareholding companies offer shares by means of a private placement. It also may allow promoters to underwrite the company's shares in full among themselves or together with outsiders without offering the said shares for public subscription if the company is listed under one of the following:
>
> a. Companies formed in the Kingdom in accordance with agreements concluded between the government and another State, and joint Arab companies from the Arab League or the institutions and organisations affiliated therewith;
> b. Holding companies;
> c. Mutual fund companies; and
> d. Other companies to which the *Issuing Committee* decides to apply this provision.[754]

Indeed, from the above legal definition one observes that undue Jordanian regulatory emphasis was placed on the type of companies. This was opposed to adopting criteria that distinguish between those who are capable of looking after themselves and those who are not. For, the main yardstick in determining who is and who is not included in the legal definition of private placements must be the level of financial expertise, something which can be attained by both companies and individuals.

---

754. Article 113 of the Companies Law 1989.

It is therefore difficult to justify why the Jordanian legislature relied exclusively on corporate status vis-à-vis its legal understanding of private placements. Thus, ignoring investor protection in terms of differentiating between individuals who could and who could not look after themselves. This is especially as by 1989 Jordan had an increasingly sophisticated economy, boosted by hundreds of private and public shareholding companies which themselves were underpinned by tens of thousands of investors with substantially varying levels of financial acumen.[755]

3.2.2. Legal Uncertainty

The regulatory regime in place did not aid much in achieving legal certainty, particularly when some bylaws erroneously addressed regulatory aspects outside their ambit. This, as shall be seen below, was largely due to the legal basis of introducing Jordanian prospectuses, which was set on unsound legal grounds. In this context, the *Internal Law of the Amman Financial Market 1980* (a bylaw), did not limit itself to expanding on the areas assigned to it by the AFML 1976 (a primary source). For, Article 34 of the AFML 1976 specifically stated that the internal law of the AFM should regulate matters pertaining to 'the general management of the AFM and the procedure of its work'.[756] Article 34 in fact narrowed the areas, which would be regulated by the internal law to the following:

> (1) The authorities of the AFM Management Committee and its functions; (2) The approval of the AFM members and brokers; (3) The financial affairs of the AFM; (4) Listing and delisting on the AFM; (4) Trading on the AFM; (5) Members' subscriptions, brokers' fees and commission; (6) Disciplinary actions and procedures; and (7) Any other matter necessary to manage the AFM and secure its proper functioning. [757]

From Article 34 above one observes that regulating matters pertaining to public offers and even introducing 'prospectus' requirements would clearly be outside the scope of any future internal law of the AFM. But, paradoxically, that was exactly what the *Internal Law of the Amman Financial Market 1980* erroneously did. Without any legal grounds,[758] it, *inter alia*, addressed the question of public offers – even introducing for the first time in the Jordanian regulatory context the concept of a 'prospectus' or *nashrat el-esdar*.[759] Here, Article 33 stated that public shareholding companies were expected to prepare and submit a 'prospectus' or *nashrat el-esdar* when they offer their securities to the public:

755. Indeed, as mentioned earlier, while the number of shareholders in 1978 reached 181,000 it reached 444,450 in 1991.
756. Must be read in conjunction with Art. 51 of the *1990 Amman Financial Market Law as amended by Law No. 31 for the year 1992.*
757. Article 34 of the AFML 1976.
758. That is, under Art. 34 of the AFML 1976 or Art. 51 of the *1990 Amman Financial Market Law as amended by Law No. 31 for the year 1992.*
759. See discussion below.

> Public shareholding companies must prepare and submit *nashrat el-esdar* [a prospectus] when they offer their financial papers to the public . . .[760]

The above problem of not having a legal basis to regulate prospectuses under the *Internal Law of the Amman Financial Market 1980* was not however rectified by subsequent AFM or company laws. Here, despite this conflict between Jordanian bylaws and primary sources, the *Internal Law of the Amman Financial Market 1980* still constituted the major source of regulating prospectuses until the enactment of the SA 1997. Indeed, all subsequent laws and regulations took for granted the prospectus requirements under the *Internal Law of the Amman Financial Market 1980*. Thus building an entire public offers regime on fundamentally unsound legal grounds. In this context, the legal basis for prospectuses is even often confused by specialised Jordanian literature.[761]

3.2.3. Inadequate Informational Content in Jordanian Prospectuses

As to the problem of inadequate informational content in Jordanian prospectuses or *nasharat el-esdar*, one says that the disclosure regime prior to the enactment of the SA 1997 was, at best, minimal. Mandated disclosure prescribed by various statutory instruments and implementing regulations did not also ensure the disclosure of information that would aid investors accurately to assess investment risks. Neither did it reflect the fundamental values of offered/listed shares.

For, disclosure did not focus its thrust on providing investors with all the necessary information on issuers and their offered equities and was rather diluted by requirements to provide additional information that did not necessarily aid in achieving price accuracy. Here, the disclosure requirements were generic.[762] Indeed, when one scrutinises the informational content of numerous *nasharat el-esdar* as set and approved by the AFM and the *Issuing Committee*, one finds that the bulk of the information disclosed did not provide investors with detailed knowledge of issuers and their securities. In this context, one can categorise the informational content of Jordanian prospectuses then into eleven general sections. These eleven sections were adhered to as the standard format for all prospectuses issued by all various public shareholding companies in Jordan when they offered their securities to the public.

---

760. Article 33 of the *Internal Law of the Amman Financial Markets No. 26 for the Year 1980*.

761. Some writers have erroneously considered that the legal basis for requiring public shareholding companies to issue a prospectus stemmed from the Companies Law 1964. [For example, Y El-Issa 'The usefulness of corporate financial disclosure to investors in the Amman Financial Market', Ph.D. thesis, Lancaster University, 1988, p. 45.] However, although the Companies Law 1964 required companies to publish subscription advertisements, it did not require issuing prospectuses per se.

762. Expected to be included in an advertisement subscription published in two dailies one week before the offer date.

In order to illustrate the above one only needs to look at any of such prospectuses. For example, when one looks at the prospectus[763] of the Jordanian International Trading Centre Company,[764] which typified prospectuses issued and approved by the AFM and the *Issuing Committee* in that period, one finds the following eleven sections: (1) covering sheet of the prospectus;[765] (2) general information on the prospectus;[766] (3) conditions of the subscription; (4) a disclaimer entitled as 'Important Declaration' – which was mainly taken from Article 33 of the *Internal Law of the Amman Financial Market 1980*;[767] (5) name of the company, its registration and commercial objectives; (6) brief description of issued shares; (7) reasons for the offer of shares; (8) description of the company and its commercial activities; (9) brief description of management of the company and its senior staff; (10) description of procedures and methods of the subscription; and (11) signatures of promoters and authorised personnel.

On first glance, the title of the above sections detailing the informational requirements in the prospectus of the Jordanian International Trading Centre Company may come across as adequate. However, when one actually scrutinises it one finds that the information therein is generic and non-specific. It is then not surprising that the above pieces of information did not provide in-depth knowledge of the issuers or their offered shares. Indeed, in many respects the information in Jordanian prospectuses (particularly the sections on issuers and their shares) did not differ considerably from the information already provided in companies' articles of association and was in fact no more than word-for-word repetition of them.

For example, when one looks at section 6 of the prospectus of the Jordanian International Trading Centre Company, entitled 'Description of the Offered Shares', one finds general information on the number of offered shares and the company's authorised capital. One also finds a list of promoters' names, together with the quantities of shares owned by them and their value. After that section 6 repeats word-for-word legal statements concerning shareholders' rights, responsibilities and general rules on transferability of shares.

However, the above generality was not exclusive to the Jordanian International Trading Centre Company. Indeed, one has reached similar findings when one contrasted the content of articles of association with the prospectuses of a number of contemporaneous Jordanian companies. These included the Jordan Petroleum Refinery, Jordanian Cement Factories, the Jordan Phosphate Mines, the Arab Pharmaceutical Manufacturing, Jordan Diary, the Union Tobacco &

763. The subscription concerned was between 2 and 31 January 1983, for the subscription of 2 million ordinary shares.
764. Registered with the Company Comptroller under No. 177 on 14 December 1982.
765. Or the prospectus's table of contents.
766. Very brief summary of the company's name, its authorised capital, method of subscription, etc.
767. Stating in general terms that '... the prospectus should include the important information without omission or concealment that may have a negative implication on investors when they make their decision ... the company bears responsibility for the correctness of information ... Neither the Ministry of Trade and Industry, nor the Amman Financial Market is responsible for the correctness and sufficiency of the information contained in this prospectus ...'

Cigarette Industries, etc. All prospectuses in these companies contained the fundamental eleven sections seen above, with the bulk of the information being almost taken word-for-word from their articles of association.[768]

3.2.4. Lack of Accounting Standards and Non-Existent Enforcement Mechanisms

As to the problem of the unreliability of company annual reports, one says that this resulted from a congregation of factors. These were mainly due to exclusive reliance on internal auditors to the exclusion of external ones, as well as chronic lack of accounting and auditing standards. This contributed significantly to the low level of Jordanian disclosure in terms of not providing Jordanian investors with all the pertinent information they require in order to formulate an informed assessment:

> In Jordan, besides the lack of useful information disclosed in companies annual reports, the information given is often vague, subjective and may sometimes be misleading... [The empirical results] provide additional evidence of the low level of disclosure requirements and practice in Jordan...[769]

Another persistent problem associated with the Jordanian disclosure regime was particularly the lack of statutory attention to setting accounting and auditing standards.[770] This problem was further aggravated by the fact that the Managing Committee of the AFM over-relied on companies' internal auditors to verify the information included in companies' annual reports and balance sheets.[771] The few writers on the subject matter rightly share this concern over the problem of extensive reliance on internal auditors, amidst lack of auditing and accounting standards. Indeed, it was not unusual to hear arguments that although the AFM had guidelines requiring that listed companies should prepare financial reports, there was no mention of any specific disclosure requirements. There were also no standards to which such reports must conform. This was especially as the accounting profession, represented by the Jordanian Association of Certified Public Accountants (JACPA), had not issued any national standards or defined Generally Accepted Accounting Principles (GAAP):

> Nevertheless, in 1989 the JACPA recommended that its members should use international accounting standards (IAS) in auditing corporate reports. However, this recommendation must be considered as optional, as to become mandatory it would need to have been incorporated in the Companies Act 1989 or the AFM Law.[772]

768. Sample surveyed by the present author included fifteen major companies that offered shares to the public *via* a prospectus.
769. El-Issa, *supra* note 761, pp. 144–45.
770. It was not before 1985 when Law No. 32 of the year 1985 established an Auditing Professional Bureau.
771. The Companies Law 1964 made it mandatory for public shareholding companies to appoint internal auditors. See for example Art. 168(1) & (2), and Art. 171.
772. R Buckland et al., 'Companies' Voluntary Disclosure Behaviour and Raising Equity Capital on the Amman Financial Market', *Aberdeen Papers in Accountancy, Finance & Management Working Paper* (1998), p. 6.

Moreover, it was not uncommon to hear learned voices raising the concern that in Jordan the accounting profession was still in its 'infancy' and was not sufficiently developed to be able to set national accounting standards. The government, too, was not expected to be 'unwilling' to take the responsibility for setting accounting standards:

> There is no Jordanian accounting plan . . . . The same can be said about auditing, there being no statement of auditing standards as a guide for auditors such as that issued by AICPA in the USA or the ICAEW in the United Kingdom.[773]

Also, amongst the few studies that looked at the relationship between Jordanian primary market issues and domestic accounting standards was the one conducted in 1999 by the IFC.[774] While this study noted a slight increase in Jordanian primary market issues in 1980–1995,[775] it nevertheless rated the correlation between equity issues relative to GDP percentage when conditional on accounting standards in Jordan as 'average' or 'not good'.[776]

Most crucially, there were also no enforcement mechanisms under the regulatory regime prior to the enactment of the SA 1997. For, neither Jordanian company legislation nor the AFML 1990 and subsequent regulations contained specific sanctions to buttress their requirements. Measures taken by the AFM against companies that delayed the release of their financial statements were also exceptionally uncommon. Predictably, this laxity did not foster a culture of prompt corporate disclosure among Jordanian listed companies. It is therefore not unusual to hear that:

> Listed companies who delay publishing their financial statements are not penalized, suspended or even warned. Some auditors are more concerned with maintaining their business relations with clients rather than protecting the interests of investors . . .[777]

4. CONCLUSION

Although the Jordanian regulatory regime before 1997 was characterised by legal simplicity, policy makers were not completely oblivious to investor protection. Measures to achieve some standards of investor protection included requiring promoters of public shareholding companies compulsorily to subscribe to a minimum percentage of their companies' shares. Promoters were also prohibited

773. See El-Issa, *supra* note 761, pp. 60–61.
774. See A Aylward et al., 'Primary Securities Markets: Cross Country Findings', IFC, Washington D.C., Discussion Paper No. 39, (1999), pp. 10–11.
775. That is, as compared to overall issues by emerging capital markets.
776. 'Good' accounting standards were those internationally acceptable in so far as they adhered to IASC – even though companies may not be legally obliged to comply with them. 'Poor' accounting standards on the other hand were those deemed to be in need of significant reform.
777. H Azzam, *The Emerging Arab Capital Markets: Investment Opportunities in Relatively Underplayed Markets*, Kegan Paul International (London), 1997, p. 225.

from selling their subscribed equity holdings before the passage of a certain period of time from when their companies were first registered.

Jordanian company legislation also nullified any public offer that did not result in the subscription of a minimum percentage of equities. Additionally, investors were prohibited from subscribing more than once in any given subscription, where fictitious subscriptions and the usage of false names also resulted in nullifying public offers. Another important measure was the two-tiered listing system, where shares had first to be listed for a period of time on one exchange before being listed on the main market.

However, although the aforementioned techniques attempted at achieving some standards of investor protection, the regulatory system as a whole then suffered from chronic problems. For example, there was incomplete understanding of the role of investor protection in defining some market practices. In this context, there was no evidence that Jordan's statutory understanding of private placements was based on harnessing the notion of investor protection – that is, in terms of excluding investors who do not require statutory protection. Neither there was a clear legal understanding of what constituted a public offer.

Moreover, the regulatory regime did not aid much in achieving legal certainty, particularly when some bylaws erroneously addressed regulatory aspects outside their remit. This was due to inconsistencies between laws and bylaws that purported to regulate some aspects of equity market trading. As some of the regulations then addressed trading aspects that were clearly outside their scope, this, for example, resulted in building an entire public offers regime on unsound legal grounds.

The Jordanian regulatory regime equally suffered from the problem of inadequate informational content in prospectuses or *nasharat el-esdar*, where disclosure requirements were, at best, minimal. Added to this were unreliable company annual reports, together with lack of accounting/auditing standards.

All the above, for decades, left Jordanian shareholders with inadequate standards of investor protection. Indeed, consecutive Jordanian governments were very slow in reacting to improving the regulatory standards of the domestic equity markets in a manner that better protects investors. However, although there was no evidence of domestic desire substantially to improve the regulatory standards in Jordan vis-à-vis regulating its domestic equity markets, Jordan was nevertheless ultimately galvanised into action – radically reforming its regulatory system.

Chapter 9 next shall therefore explain the reasons for the dramatic regulatory change in Jordan, and whether the new regulatory system achieves better standards of investor protection.

Chapter 9

The Jordanian Regulatory Regime for Public Offers and Equity Listing After the 1997 Regime

INTRODUCTION

Chapter 9 looks at the structure of regulation after the enactment of the Provisional SA 1997. However, this Act has since been replaced by the SA 2002, which incidentally has kept the structure of regulation as first espoused by the SA 1997.[778] Additionally, it is also expected that certain aspects of the SA 2002 shall be amended by a special amendment law – most probably by an 'Amendment Act to the SA 2002'. In order to provide a rounded discussion, whenever relevant, this chapter shall therefore touch on both the Amendment Act to the SA 2002 as well as the SA 1997.

Chapter 9 equally looks at the reasons behind the structural regulatory change in Jordan, as well as addressing the question of why mandatory disclosure is needed in Jordan. It then looks at the substantive disclosure requirements by the new regulatory regime, before assessing its efficacy in ensuring proper investor protection.

1. THE CATALYSTS FOR THE STRUCTURAL CHANGES AND THE IMPACT OF PRIVATISATION

The reason for the radical changes in the Jordanian regulatory regime relates mainly to the structural adjustment programmes that Jordan has had to undergo. For its part, Jordan engaged in adjustment programmes since 1985 to weather

778. See Art. 122 of the SA 2002, abolishing the SA 1997 – effective from 31 December 2002.

mounting budgetary pressures. These pressures resulted from the cumulative impact of diminution in external aid, decrease in money transfers from expatriate labour, shrinking national exports and over-expansion in the Jordanian public sector.[779]

Indeed, the worsening economic situation in Jordan post-1985 could be contrasted to the relatively prosperous years during 1976–1984, when growth rates varied from 7.5% to 25.9%.[780] For example, budget deficit in 1987 reached 13.1% of Jordan's GDP, compared to only 5.8% in 1983.[781] The local adjustment programme, which the Jordanian government then adopted (1986–1990) intended, *inter alia*, to reduce public spending, achieve annual growth rate of 5%, narrow the gap between income and expenditure and create around 100,000 new job opportunities.[782]

However, the above objectives were not met and Jordan's economic situation significantly worsened due to the collapse of the Jordanian Dinar in 1989. Indeed, the exchange rate crisis of 1989, which resulted in a nominal devaluation of nearly 50% against the US dollar, produced an acutely adverse impact on Jordanian living standards. In 1989 alone, real GDP shrunk by 13%, while inflation increased to over 25%.[783] Feeling unable to cope, the Jordanian government asked for technical and financial assistance from the IMF and the World Bank.[784] An added problem was also Jordan's spiralling external debt – from USD 6,446.60 million in 1986 to USD 7,346 million in 1991.[785]

The government in cooperation with the World Bank and the IMF therefore adopted a new comprehensive adjustment programme to address the above macroeconomic imbalances.[786] However, this programme did not succeed and was halted due to the first Gulf War in 1990, after which a new adjustment programme was adopted (1992–1998).

For their part, the IMF and the World Bank, *inter alia*, exhorted that Jordan lessened its reliance on external aid/debt, liberalise its economy and engage in privatisation in order to attract foreign investment. Because of such programmes, Jordan's macroeconomic figures have continued to improve, earning Jordan consistent praise from the World Bank and the IMF.[787] Indeed, as a reflection of the

779. Equally, due to depreciation in aid coming from Arab Gulf countries as oil prices plummeted.
780. Collated from the *Monthly Bulletin*, Central Bank of Jordan (1975–1985).
781. This figure takes into account foreign aid. Collated from the *Monthly Bulletin*, Central Bank of Jordan (1982–1988).
782. See generally, *The Development Plan (1986–1990)*, Ministry of Planning, Jordan, 1986.
783. See 'Jordan: Selected Issues and Statistical Appendix', IMF, IMF Country Report No. 04/121 (May 2004), p. 12.
784. For its part, Jordan joined the International Monetary Fund (IMF) and the International Bank for Reconstruction and Development (IBRD) on 29 August 1952. It joined the International Finance Corporation (IFC) on 20 July 1956 and the International Development Association (IDA) on 4 October 1960.
785. Collated from the *Monthly Bulletin*, Central Bank of Jordan (1985–1992).
786. This adjustment programme was between 1989 and 1993.
787. See, for example, *World Bank News Release No. 2003/246/MNA* (6 March 2003), *IMF Press Release No. 04/136* (6 July 2004), *IMF Press Release No. 04/71* (2 April 2004), *IMF Press Release No. 03/113* (11 July 2003) and *IMF News Brief No. 02/40* (30 April 2002).

positive results that Jordan has been achieving through its structural programmes, the IMF in a recent study noted that the transformation of the Jordanian economy over the past twenty years is largely attributed to the economic reforms implemented by the government with support from the IMF. For their part:

> These reforms have aimed at (i) stabilizing the economy, so as to foster growth; (ii) liberalizing foreign trade and domestic prices; (iii) reducing public debt; and (iv) privatizing state-owned enterprises. These reforms have, in turn, brought about a structural transformation that is just beginning to bear fruit . . . [788]

Because of the IMF and World Bank exhortations that it should open up its economy, Jordan has taken serious steps to integrate itself in the international economy. On 16 November 1997 Jordan signed the Qualifying Industrial Zones Agreement with Israel to help its manufacturing industries.[789] It also signed the Euro-Mediterranean agreement in 1997,[790] and officially joined the WTO on 11 April 2000. Jordan also signed a free trade agreement with the US on 14 October 2000.[791] Indeed, this unprecedented liberalisation of the Jordanian economy gave the right signals to international investors, resulting in significant improvement in foreign capital flows.

For example, while direct foreign investment in the Jordanian economy, which was almost non-existent in the mid-1970s (reaching approximately JD 0.4 million, JD 1.1 million and JD 3.5 million in 1972, 1973, 1974, respectively),[792] it reached JD 91 million in 1999.[793] Indeed, total investments (domestic and foreign) in the Jordanian economy almost doubled in the span of the past decade, from JD 563.2 million in 1989 to JD 1189.5 million in 1999, with the highest ever recorded in 1995 (following the high expectations after Jordan signed a peace treaty with Israel) reaching JD 1554.4 million.[794]

However, material steps to implement privatisation did not take place before the mid-1990s, when the Jordanian government, in cooperation with the World Bank, set up a specialised privatisation unit in the Prime Ministry in 1996. This unit, which reported to the Prime Minister, aimed to select targets for privatisation, value them and choose the best way to dispose of them. Sectors examined by this unit included energy, transport, telecommunication, water, manufacturing, services, etc. However, the Jordanian march towards privatisation suffered from confusion due to the fact that there was no specific legislation that determined

---

788. See 'Jordan: Selected Issues and Statistical Appendix', (May 2004), *supra* note 783, p. 10.
789. The agreement, *inter alia*, enables end-products to enter into the US directly, with 100% Jordanian tax exemption for exporters from such zones.
790. The agreement allows immediate access to Jordanian goods, while giving Jordan twelve years to dismantle its customs over European exports.
791. Giving Jordanian goods further access to the US markets.
792. Collated from the *International Financial Statistics Yearbook*, (1972–1992).
793. Statistics released by the Jordanian Ministry of Trade and Industry, Amman, Jordan (1998–2000).
794. Collated from the *Monthly Bulletin*, Central Bank of Jordan (1989–2000).

how to handle future funds generated from selling government's stake in publicly owned shareholding companies.

In order to address the above, the regulatory structure for privatisation in Jordan was revisited by the *Privatisation Law No. 25 for the Year 2000*, which set up the Higher Council for Privatisation under the chairmanship of the Prime Minister.[795] This Law prescribed that revenues from privatisation should be deposited in a special fund administered by the Higher Council for Privatisation.[796] The same law equally stipulated that revenues should be first dispersed to pay the outstanding liabilities of privatised projects, and after that might contribute towards government debts, be invested, or be used to train employees of restructured companies, etc.[797]

For its part, the stock exchange played an important role in facilitating the Jordanian government's disposal of many of its shares held in various shareholding companies. For example, when it sold its 34.6% stake in the Hemeh Spa, the government disposed of all such stake on the Amman Bourse.[798] The government equally used the stock exchange when it sold its 40% stake in the Jordan Vegetable Oil Company and nineteen other companies in which it owned 5% of the shares or less.[799]

Moreover, the Jordanian government also offered to the public the sale of 15% of its ownership in the Jordan Telecommunication Company in October 2002, offering 37,500,000 shares. A total of 70% of these shares were subscribed to by the public, amounting to 10.5% of the company's capitalisation. Indeed, the privatisation of the Telecommunication Company has now resulted in the listing of all of its shares on the *First Market*, with a total capital of 250 million shares worth (up to January 2004) JD 610 million. Hence, as seen in Chapter 5, it being the second largest listed Jordanian company in terms of market capitalisation.

On occasions, even the mere fact that former public companies were listed on the Amman Bourse, gave added incentives to investors to participate in the privatisation process. For, they knew that they could always consolidate their equity holding through the market. When the Jordanian government sold off 33% of its share in the Jordanian Cement Factories Company to the French company Lafarge in late 1998, Lafarge consolidated its control through buying extra 6.9% of the shares on the Amman Bourse – thus raising its stake to nearly 40%.

However, it must be stated that not all shares of privatised companies were offered to the public. In fact, many of such companies were sold (wholly or

795. In addition to the Prime Minister, membership in the Higher Council for Privatisation also included the Minister of Finance, Minister of Trade and Industry, Minister of Planning, Minister of Justice, Chairman of the Jordan Central Bank, etc.

796. See Art. 13 of the *Privatisation Law No. 25 for the Year 2000*.

797. *Ibid.*

798. See H Hamad, 'Privatisation of the Jordanian Electric Company: A Field Study of its Managers' Attitudes', Master's thesis, Jordan University (1999), p. 54.

799. These companies are included in the portfolio of the Jordanian Corporation for Investment. *Ibid.*

partially) to overseas business concerns. An example in mind is the Jordanian Telecommunication Corporation, which part of its shares was offered to the public in October 2002 as mentioned above. For, in January 2000 the Jordanian government had sold 49% of that company: 40% to France Telecom, 8% to the SSC and 1% to the Jordanian Telecommunication Corporation's staff. Other similar examples include the recent selling of the Duty Free Shops at Jordanian airports to foreign companies, the 80% selling of the Catering Company[800] and the selling of the Training, Simulation and Telecommunications Centre Company.[801] On 16 October 2003 the Jordanian government equally sold 50% of its share in the Arab Potash Company to a Canadian corporation, Potash Corporation of Saskatchewan or PotashCorp (PCS).

2. WHY IS MANDATORY DISCLOSURE NEEDED IN JORDAN?

Disclosure in Jordan remains an important tool to local investors. For example, it has empirically been found that annual reports issued by listed Jordanian companies impacted upon the level of trading in their securities, with price driven upwards or downwards depending on the content of such disclosure.[802] Moreover, a number of empirical studies have supported this view, pointing out to Jordanian investors' reliance on disclosure when making their investment decisions.[803] Such findings add weight to the argument that in order to protect local investors, who clearly depend on disclosure when they make their investment decisions, the Jordanian disclosure regime needs to be accurate and free from misleading information or omissions.

Yet, generally speaking, increased levels of voluntary disclosure take place when companies raise equity capital.[804] But does this apply to Jordan, too? For, if this was the case, then this chapter does not have to be concerned very much with Jordan's mandatory disclosure regime. To answer, one says that the reason why voluntary disclosure could not be relied upon in Jordan comes from the findings of empirical studies conducted on the disclosure behaviour of Jordanian companies. Among such studies was the one that examined the voluntary disclosure practices

800. Formerly owned by the Royal Jordanian Airlines (RJ).
801. Also formerly owned by RJ. See *Third Annual Report of the Amman Stock Exchange*, Amman Stock Exchange, Amman, 2001, pp. 13–14.
802. Sample consisted of seventy listed companies in the period 1984–1986. See F Gharaibeh et al., 'The Impact of the Content of Annual Reports on the Level of Trading on Listed Jordanian Shareholding Companies', *Dirasat*, University of Jordan, 1989, Vol. 16, No. 1, p.7.
803. See F Haddad, 'The Informational Content of Annual Statements: An Empirical Study of Industrial Public Shareholding Companies in Jordan', *Dirasat*, University of Jordan, 2001, Vol. 16, No. 1, pp. 125–50; and S Haddad, 'The Informational Content of Security Prices in the Amman Bourse', Master's thesis, University of Jordan, 2001.
804. See F Choi, 'Financial Disclosure and Entry to the European Capital Market', *Journal of Accounting Research*, Vol. XI, No. 2, (1973), pp. 159–75; and M Firth, 'Raising Capital and Firms' Corporate Reporting Policies', *Abacus*, Vol. XVI, No. 2, (1980), pp. 100–15.

of fifty listed companies.[805] Using a mixture of empirical research tools, applying a weighed disclosure index[806] and conducting interviews with Jordanian investors, company directors and senior management of the AFM, this substantial study concluded that:

> The statistical findings indicated that the level of disclosure [in Jordan] is associated positively with several company attributes, namely, size, profitability, ownership and gearing...[807] [However] the results indicate that *voluntary disclosure is relatively low and varies widely within the sample of 50 quoted companies*... There is consensus among participants on the *inadequacy of current disclosure practice*.[808] [Italics added.]

Another empirical study also looked at the disclosure practices of twenty-eight listed Jordanian companies when they raised equity capital during 1980–1991[809] – representing almost 60% of the number of listed companies that raised equity capital in that period. This study concluded that although there was a tenuous evidence of marginal increase in the level of voluntary disclosure by Jordanian companies when they raised equity capital, such level was not at all sufficient and legislation was therefore required. It also argued that as requirements for financial reporting were not defined in detail (either legally or professionally), this invited 'uncertainty' as to what constituted *mandatory* or *voluntary* disclosure in Jordan. Indeed, while the need to raise capital was shown to stimulate additional useful disclosure, the study argued that it seemed unlikely that this *alone* would have been sufficient to ensure full and consistent reporting across Jordanian companies:[810]

> The conclusion which must be drawn is that for Jordan... full and consistent reporting will be achieved *only* from legislative action.[811]

Empirical research has also convincingly argued that the Jordanian equity market is still far from being efficient when tested against the standard of a 'semi-strong' market. Such inefficiency is not restricted to the era that preceded the 1997 regulatory regime, where many empirical studies support the argument that Jordan's equity markets were inefficient in that period.[812] It also persists after 1997, especially as studies still point out to the inefficiency of the Amman Bourse when tested

805. This study examined disclosure up until 1986. See El-Issa, *supra* note 761.
806. This consisted of thirty-one items of information.
807. See El-Issa, *supra* note 761, p. 2.
808. *Ibid.*, p. 113.
809. By comparing the disclosure behaviour of such listed companies and the behaviour of other listed companies that did not raise equity capital in that period.
810. See Buckland et al., *supra* note 772, p. 7.
811. *Ibid.*, p. 19.
812. See generally, T Al-Hmoud, 'A Study of the Application of EMH to the Jordanian Stock Market', Ph.D. thesis, University of Wales, UK, 1987; M Yassin, 'The Impact of the Deregulation of Interest Rates on Share Price of Banks in Jordan: An Analytical Study of the Efficiency of Pricing the Shares of the Banking Sector on the Amman Financial Market', Master's thesis, University of Jordan, 1991; M El-Jildah, 'The Impact of Stock Splits on Price Changes: An Empirical Study on the Amman Financial Market', Master's thesis, University of

against a 'semi-strong' form. This was particularly the case in an empirical study that tested the efficiency of the Amman Bourse when listed companies published their annual financial statements in 2002.[813] The qualifying sample comprised of sixty-nine listed companies spread representatively over four sectors: fourteen banking (20%); thirteen insurance (19%); thirteen services (19%); and twenty-nine companies from the industrial sector (42%). The findings were that all the results confirmed the *inefficiency* of the Amman Bourse when tested against a semi-strong form:

> The efficiency of the [Amman] Bourse requires implementing laws to ensure that companies do not delay in publishing their annual statements, so that investors can benefit from the content of such statements when assessing their investments.[814]

Here, as seen from earlier discussion in Chapter 4 on the ECMH, 'weak' capital markets are those characterised by poor informational flow, whereby securities prices do not convey all existing information, whether public or private. This equally supports the argument that disclosure in the particular Jordanian context needs to be *mandatory* so that issuers are compelled to provide investors, in a timely manner, with all relevant information to ensure that price reflects such information. This is especially as (shall be seen below when discussing equity ownership on the ASE) there is a majority of shareholders in Jordan who exceed 800,000 – most of whom are lay investors, thus necessitating the active protection of the law.

After having looked at the catalysts for the structural regulatory changes and the reasons why mandatory disclosure is needed in Jordan, this chapter turns to consider the new structural regulatory changes in substantive terms.[815]

3. THE STRUCTURAL CHANGES AFTER THE 1997 REGIME

One here looks at two areas influenced by the new regulatory regime in Jordan: (1) the structural changes to Jordanian securities markets; and (2) the specific changes to the public offers and listing regimes. However, it must be clearly pointed out that although these structural changes first took place in 1997 after the enactment of the SA 1997, reference in this chapter shall be made to the

---

Jordan, 1996; and A Al-Mutori, 'Testing Semi-Efficiency on the Amman Financial Market: A Trial Test', Master's thesis, University of Jordan, 1996.

813. M Matar, 'Testing the Efficiency of Amman Bourse at the Semi-Strong Level Using Information of Financial Statements Exposure', Master's thesis, Al El-Beit University, Jordan, 2003, pp. 85–86.
814. *Ibid.*, pp. 85–86.
815. It however must be mentioned that the AMIR (USAID) Programme made significant contributions to the modernisation of Jordanian capital markets through training programmes and extensive automation.

provisions of the SA 2002. This is because, although it has essentially kept the new regulatory structure first introduced by the SA 1997, the SA 2002 has since amended many of the provisions of the SA 1997.

3.1. The Structural Changes to Jordanian Securities Markets

The major changes can be seen through the setting up of a securities commission, a depositary centre and introducing radical changes to the AFM. The discussion next outlines these three significant changes.

3.1.1. The Jordanian Securities Commission (JSC)

The regulatory capacity that used to be exercised by the former AFM has now been transferred to the JSC. However, the SA 2002, almost verbatim, repeats many of the provisions of the SA 1997 that set up a securities exchange commission, empowering it with regulatory and supervisory functions.[816]

Reinstating the structure that was first established under the SA 1997, the SA 2002 states that the JSC is a separate juridical person with administrative and financial independence, reporting directly to the Prime Minister.[817] Similarly, the JSC is expected to regulate and monitor the issuance of securities and dealing in them, as well as ensure full and accurate disclosure.[818] It is also expected to regulate, license and monitor the activities of licensed persons, mutual funds and investment companies.[819] The entities directly monitored and supervised by the JSC are: the Amman Bourse (former AFM); the Securities Depository Centre (SDC); financial services companies; public shareholding companies; investment funds; and certified financial professionals.[820]

However, the SA 2002 has on occasions taken away some of the independence that the JSC enjoyed under the SA 1997. This is evident when one, for example, contrasts Article10(b) of the SA 2002 with Article 8(b) of the SA 1997, which relates to the method of appointing and dismissing JSC commissioners.[821] This apparent regression can be attributed to a desire to control the JSC by the Jordanian government. Neither has the SA 2002 addressed earlier doubts about the failure of the SA 1997 to establish proper accountability and transparency mechanisms vis-à-vis the functioning of the JSC.[822]

816. See Art. 7 of the SA 1997 and Arts 7 & 8 of the SA 2002.
817. See Art. 6 of the SA 1997 and Art. 7 of the SA 2002.
818. See Art. 7 of the SA 1997 and Art. 7 of the SA 2002.
819. *Ibid.*
820. See Art. 20 of the SA 1997 and Art. 15 of the SA 2002.
821. Unlike under Art. 8(b) of the SA 1997, JSC commissioners can now be dismissed almost at will by the Prime Minister. See Art. 10(b) of the SA 2002.
822. See, for example, L Al-Rimawi, 'Reform of the Jordanian Securities Commission: A Personal View', *International & Comparative Corporate Law Journal*, Vol. III, No. 4 (2001), pp. 515–33.

For their part, the administrative powers of the JSC concerning the specific question of public offering of shares shall be examined in detail in Chapter 11, when one looks at the liabilities that arise for misleading or inaccurate disclosure in the prospectus.

3.1.2. The Securities Depository Centre (SDC)

The next structural change in Jordanian securities markets was the introduction of a depository centre. For, unlike the AFM under which settlement of trades used to take place, a designated body now conducts settling securities trades outside the remit of the Amman Bourse. Here, the SA 2002 reproduces the SA 1997 provisions that established the SDC in order to, *inter alia*, register, clear and settle trades in securities.[823] Again, the structure of the SDC set by the SA 2002 is identical to the original structure first envisaged under the SA 1997:

> A Centre known as the Securities Depository Centre shall be established in the Kingdom. The Centre shall be a non-profit public entity, and shall have a legal personality with administrative and financial autonomy. As such, it may acquire and dispose of movable and immovable property, and perform all legal acts to realize its objectives, including entering into contracts in its own name. The Centre shall have the right to sue and be sued, and to appoint any attorney to represent it in legal proceedings.[824]

According to its own internal bylaw, the SDC ensures safe custody of ownership of securities listed on the ASE, enacts and implements special rules related to the utilisation of its services, while issuing reports and statistics related to its activities.[825] Membership of the SDC is mandatory for public shareholding companies, public issuers and persons licensed as financial brokers or dealers.[826] For its part, the SDC became operational in May 1999 as a private institution, with complete financial and administrative independence.

3.1.3. The Amman Stock Exchange (ASE)

The Amman Stock Exchange (ASE), or the Amman Bourse, was first set up by the SA 1997 and took over trading from the AFM on 11 March 1999.[827] Like the AFM, it was set up in Amman and has a separate juridical personality with administrative

823. See Art. 29(b) of the SA 1997 and Art. 77 of the SA 2002.
824. See Art. 29(a) of the SA 1997; Art. 76 of the SA 2002; Arts 3–5 of the *Internal Bylaw of the Securities Depository Centre for the Year 2004* – issued in pursuance of Art. 78 of the SA 2002 and came into effect on 11 April 2004.
825. See Arts 4 & 5 of the *Internal Bylaw of the Securities Depository Centre for the Year 2004.*
826. As well as custodians and 'any other entity determined by the Board' of the SDC. See Art. 31(a) of the SA 1997; Art. 82 of the SA 2002; Art. 3 of the *Internal Bylaw of the Membership and Code of Conduct for the Year 2004*. Issued in pursuance of Arts 80 & 83(a) of the SA 2002 and entered into force on 12 May 2004.
827. See Art. 25 of the *2000 Directives for Listing Securities on the Amman Stock Exchange.*

and financial independence.[828] However, the ASE represents a vast improvement on its predecessor, the AFM. Nowhere can this be seen than in modernising its trading systems. Instead of the manual trading system under the former AFM, trading on the ASE is now automated.[829]

However, it would be erroneous to assume that, barring some technological innovations, the ASE is otherwise a replica of the AFM. Administratively, the ASE is subdivided into separate entities. These according to its Administrative Bylaws[830] (which entered into force on 1 April 2004) are: the listing and operations department, the surveillance and inspection department, the legal department, the research and international relations department, the IT department, and the administration and finance department.[831] Additionally, unlike the AFM and its Management Committee mentioned in Chapter 8, the ASE does not anymore enjoy wide-ranging supervisory capacity. For, these powers have now been assigned to the JSC.

As opposed to being a public institution, as was the case under the AFM, the ASE is characteristically a privately owned one.[832] Membership in the ASE is now exclusively restricted to the private sector. Its members consist of financial brokers, dealers and any other entities that maybe designated by the board of the ASE.[833] *Instructions of Financial Services Licensing and Registration for the Year 2005* (entered into force on 4 October 2005[834]) define a broker as any person who buys and sells securities on behalf of others in consideration for a commission.[835] A dealer or market-maker on the other hand is someone who buys or sells securities for their own account.[836]

828. 'As such, it may carry out all legal acts including concluding contracts and acquiring and disposing of movable and immovable property, and authorizing a lawyer to act on its behalf in legal proceedings.' See Art. 23(a) of the SA1997 and Art. 65 of the SA 2002.
829. Started in March 2000, giving licensed brokers the facility to shift to Remote Trading implemented in October 2000. The ASE's order-driven electronic trading system is conducted through matching orders placed by brokers, where trading on the First and Second markets is on a continuous basis, while trading in bonds, mutual fund units and shares on the Third Market used to be in a single price auction.
830. Issued by virtue of Art. 65 of the SA 2002.
831. See Art. 4 (a-f) of the 2004 Admisisrtative Bylaws of the ASE.
832. See Art. 65 of the SA 2002. Cf.: Art. 23(c) of the SA 1997.
833. Membership of the ASE consists of financial brokers, dealers and any other entities designated by the Board [of the JSC]. See Art. 65(b) of the SA 2002; Art. 25(a) of the SA 1997; Art. 7 of the *Internal Bylaws of the Amman Stock Exchange 2004*. Issued by virtue of Art. 65 of the SA 2002.
834. Article (92) specifically states that '*Instructions on Licensing of Activities of Financial Services Companies and Certified Financial Professionals No.1 for the year 1999*, and the *Custodian Licensing Instructions No. (3) for the year 2003* shall be revoked.'
835. Article (12)(1) of the *Instructions of Financial Services Licensing and Registration for the Year 2005* states: 'Financial Broker [is]: any person engaged in the business of buying and selling securities against a commission for the account of others.'
836. Article (12)(2) states: 'Dealer [is]: any person engaged in the business of buying and selling securities directly for his own account through the market.' *Ibid.*

Brokers and dealers are subject to minimum capital adequacy requirements,[837] as well as a number of criteria expected such as being licensed, academic qualification, relevant expertise, etc.[838] Brokers are expected to trade over-the-counter unless of course the trade is exempt due to being a private placement, etc.[839] They equally owe a duty of care to the client to check whether securities transacted are subject to any attachments or restrictions.[840]

For their part, securities listed on the ASE are only traded through brokers *inter se*, each on behalf of themselves or their clients:

> Trading on the Market [ASE] shall be carried out only through trading contracts between brokers, either on behalf of clients or for their own account.[841]
>
> And:
>
> a. Trading with securities at the ASE will take place through trading contracts between brokers for their own account or for the account of their clients. It will be prohibited to agree on a price that violates what is stipulated in the contract.
> b. Trading transactions will be documented in records by the ASE either manually or electronically.[842]

The Jordanian government (and public bodies such as the CBJ) has now no role in the management of the ASE. All questions pertaining to its management are

---

837. For a broker it is expected to be JD 750,000. For a dealer it is expected to be JD 500,000. See Art. (4). *Ibid.*
838. Article (8) of the *Internal Bylaws of the Amman Stock Exchange 2004* states that:

> A. The following conditions must be fulfilled for a broker to submit a membership application to the Stock Exchange:1. The broker must have a valid license to practice. 2. The broker's management and staff must have the necessary academic qualifications, knowledge and expertise to act as a member in the Stock Exchange. 3. The broker must have the needed IT infrastructure to ensure that it carries out trading operations through the Stock Exchange systems in a correct, suitable and uninterrupted manner. 4. The broker must have at least two registered persons working for it. B. The conditions referred to in Paragraph (A) of this Article are continuous conditions that must be met throughout the term of membership of the Stock Exchange. C. Notwithstanding the content of Sub-Paragraph (A) (4) of this Article, it is allowed that only one certified person works for a financial broker in case the license given thereto is limited to a dealer.

839. Article (13) of the *Instructions of Financial Services Licensing and Registration for the Year 2005* states: 'Brokers shall trade in securities of a Public Issuer only through the Market, unless the security is exempted from this condition by the Board.'
840. Article (14) states: 'The broker shall not sell securities before ensuring its title, and that they are not subject to any attachment, pledge, or restrictions on the transfer.' *Ibid.*
841. Article 69(b) of the SA 2002. See also Art. 24(a) of the SA 1997.
842. See Art. 3 of the *Directives for Trading in Securities on the Amman Stock Exchange for the Year 2004.* Issued in pursuance of Art. 67 of the SA 2002 and came into effect on 1 June 2004. However, prior to its amendment on 16 March 2009, Art. 3 used to read: 'Trading on the ASE shall take place through brokers. Trading transactions shall be confirmed in manual or electronic entries on ASE records.'

currently determined by the ASE's bylaws.[843] Such bylaws bind members of the ASE and their clients.[844] Of importance here are the *Internal Bylaws of the Amman Stock Exchange 2004*, as they lay the ground for the management of the ASE – occasionally they are referred to as the *Internal Regulations of the ASE 2004*.[845] The ASE is now managed by a seven-member board of directors and an executive manager who is appointed by the board.[846]

The board of directors itself is chosen by the general assembly of the ASE,[847] which is composed exclusively of all those members (i.e., financial services companies as outlined above) who have paid their subscriptions and have not been disqualified.[848] The seven members must include two bank representatives,[849] two members representing brokers[850] and three members from the private sector who are experts 'in legal, financial and economic fields'.[851] The latter category is however appointed by the board, which elects a chairman and a vice chairman from its ranks for three years tenure.[852] The ASE has equally a set of dispute resolution regulations that deals with any issues arising between members and their clients. These are known as the *Dispute Resolution Directive* and entered into force on 1 September 2004.[853]

In order however to give a rounded discussion, one here shall look at the ASE's primary and secondary markets, together with its volume of trading. One shall equally look at listed companies and capitalisation thereon, equity ownership as well as its membership and management.

3.1.3.1. The Primary Equity Market

Securities issued on the Jordanian primary market are restricted to a limited range of shares and bonds, in which shares constitute a significant bulk. However, the contribution of the equity primary market as a means of funding to Jordanian companies remains modest. For example, the total value of shares issued on the primary market (by new and established companies) in 2002 and 2003 was approximately JD 35.842 million and approximately JD 56.165 million, respectively. This represented the meagre figures of 0.015% and 0.014% of total market capitalisation for that period. Moreover, the contribution of newly established companies to

843. Article 65(c) of the SA 2002, *inter alia*, reads: 'The rules and procedures governing the [ASE] . . . shall be governed by the Amman Stock Exchange's Bylaws and Instructions. . . . '
844. Article 71(a), *inter alia*, reads: 'The Bylaws and Instructions of the [ASE] shall be legally binding upon members and their clients.' *Ibid.*
845. Issued by virtue of Art. 65 of the SA 2002 and entered into force on 1 April 2004.
846. See Art. 17 of the *Internal Bylaws of the Amman Stock Exchange 2004*; Art. 65(c) of the SA 2002; Art. 25(b) of the SA 1997.
847. See Art. 16 of the *Internal Regulations of the Amman Stock Exchange 2004.*
848. Such members all have one vote in general assembly meetings. Art. 13. *Ibid.*
849. See Art. 17(b)(1). *Ibid.*
850. See Art. 17(b)(2). *Ibid.*
851. See Art. 17(b)(3). *Ibid.*
852. Though, no more than two succeeding sessions. See Art. 17(d). *Ibid.*
853. Issued by virtue of the provisions of Art. 24(b)(7) of the ASE Bylaws of 2004.

the depth of the secondary market remained, at best, limited. The value of shares offered on Jordanian primary markets in 2001–2003 reached approximately JD 60.730 million, JD 35.842 million and JD 56.164 million, for 2001, 2002 and 2003, respectively.[854]

However, this situation began to change in the subsequent years when the value of newly issued shares on the primary market in 2004, 2005, 2006, 2007, 2008, 2009 and 2010 was JD 207.066 million, JD 888.825 million, JD 2,408.835 million, JD 883.771 million, JD 827.957 million, JD 317.321 million and JD 119.281 million respectively.[855] Indeed, these figures represent a significant improvement vis-à-vis offering shares on the primary markets, as for example, seen in 2006 when the value of shares issued by new companies reached JD 2,408.835 million.

The reason for the initial low number of shares issued on the primary market was due to Jordanian companies' reliance on bank financing, as it traditionally played a significant role in the Jordanian economy. For example, while the ratio of loans and banking facilities (granted by all Jordanian banks) to GDP constituted almost 70% in 1990, this ratio even reached nearly 80% in 2001.[856] Indeed, industrial, agricultural, commercial and services sectors all relied heavily on bank financing. While bank financing totalled JD 2,741.3 million in 1993, it reached JD 4,948.9 million in 2001.[857] The combined borrowing of public shareholding companies in the industrial and services sectors between 1981 and 1996 was 54% of their total capitalisation – with the majority relying on short-term loans which do not exceed one year.[858] However, as seen above, this reliance on bank loans by newly established Jordanian companies was gradually decreasing as they instead utilised primary markets for funding.

3.1.3.2. The Secondary Market

From a historical viewpoint, formal equity trading in Jordan started in the late 1970s when Law No. 31 of 1976 established the AFM. The AFM initially had one market on which companies could be listed and subsequently traded, known as the *Regular Market*. However, a second market for listing securities on the AFM was later set up in 1982 in order to list the securities of companies that did not qualify for the *Regular Market*. This additional market, with less stringent listing

854. Breaking from this was the large number of shares issued on the primary market in 1994 and 1995 during heightened expectations when Jordan signed a peace treaty with Israel – value of issued shares reached JD 460,920,711 and JD 322,932,733, respectively. See the *Monthly Bulletin*, Amman Stock Exchange (February 1996).
855. Information provided by the Amman Stock Exchange.
856. See J Abu Obaid, 'Non-Performing Loans in Jordanian Commercial Banks: Causes, Effects, and Suggested Solutions: An Analytical Study', Ph.D. thesis, Amman Arab University for Higher Studies, Jordan, (2003). p. 51.
857. *Ibid*., p. 79.
858. See S Hraze, 'The Role of the Banking System in Developing the Primary Capital Market in Jordan', Master's thesis, Al El-Beit University, Jordan 1999, p. 116.

conditions, was known as the *Parallel Market*. The AFM carried on being Jordan's only official exchange until the ASE replaced it in 1999 – following the enactment of the SA 1997. The aforementioned two-tiered structure was maintained under the newly set ASE, which encompasses the *First* and the *Second Markets*.[859]

3.1.3.2.1. Volume of Trading

Equities represent the major trading activity on the Secondary Market. When comparing the volume of bond trading to the volume of equity trading in 2000, 2001, 2002 and 2003 one finds that it only represented 0.02%, 0.01%, 0.01% and 0.006%, respectively. (See Table 9.1 below.) The volume of equity trading has also been rising steadily. It increased from JD 334.7 million in 2000 to JD 668.7 million in 2001. This trend also continued in 2002 and 2003, reaching JD 950.3 million and JD 1,855.2 million, respectively – culminating in 2008, though due to the global downturn in equity trading plummeting in 2009, reaching JD 20.318 billion and JD 9.665 billion, respectively (see Table 9.1).

The above significant improvements in the volume of trading on the Secondary Market is in large part a result of improvements in the general economic conditions in Jordan and legal reforms as shall be seen below. The rising levels of trading volumes have also been accompanied by a steady increase in the ratio of market capitalisation to Jordan's GDP – from 58.4% in 2000 to reach 71.5% in 2001. This trend has also continued reaching 80.4%, 116.8% and 184.7% in 2002, 2003 and 2004, respectively. The ratio continued to increase in more recent years reaching 326.6%, 233.9%, 289.0%, 216.7%, 149.6% and 122.7% in 2005, 2006, 2007, 2008, 2009 and 2010 respectively.[860]

Table 9.1 Equity and Bond Trading Volumes on the Secondary Market (1999–2010)

	1999	*2000*	*2001*	*2002*	*2003*	*2004*	*2005*	*2006*	*2007*	*2008*	*2009*	*2010*
Volume of Equity Trading (JD Million)	389.4	334.7	668.7	950.3	1,855.2	3,793	16,871	14,210	12,348	20,318	9,665	6,689
Volume of Bond Trading (JD million)	4.0	7.2	7.2	9.7	11.4	6.031	3.135	1.868	3.799	0.605.8	2,259.8	140.175

Source: Complied from various *Monthly Statistical Bulletins* issued by the Amman Stock Exchange (1999–2010).

859. Bonds and units in mutual funds are also traded on the ASE – on separate markets called the *Bond Market* and the *Mutual Funds Market*.

860. Information collated from various Amman Stock Exchange *Monthly Statistical Bulletins* (2005–2010).

3.1.3.2.2. Listed Companies and Main Sectors

The number of listed companies on the *First* and *Second Markets* at the end of December 2004 was 192 – 31 more companies than in 2003, when it was 161. Listed companies in 2002 and 2001 numbered 161 and 163, respectively.[861] It must be stated however that the number of listed companies on the ASE has been on the increase over the years. For example, it reached 201, 227, 245, 262 and 272 in 2005, 2006, 2007, 2008 and 2009, respectively.[862] As seen above it increased to 275 by June 2010, decreasing to 249 by September 2011.

Trading in listed companies is concentrated in the three main sectors: financial; services and industry. It is traditionally dominated by the financial sector, which for example in December 2009 reached approximately JD 6.363 billion – nearly 66% of total market trading. (See Table 9.2 below.)

One of the reasons for this increasing domestic interest in the financial sector and local Jordanian banks can be attributed to continuous attention to improving banking regulation in Jordan – culminating in the *Banks Law No. 28 for the year 2000*, which now allows universal banking.[863] Additionally, to the general public, the overwhelming majority of Jordanian banks have proved themselves prudent. For, they remain highly liquid institutions due to their conservative investment policies. Indeed, the state of the Jordanian banking system came in for praise by the IMF in a 2010 report, especially for the CBJ prudential supervision.

Table 9.2 Trading Value of the Listed Companies by Sector (2000–2010) in (JD)

Year	*Financial*	*Services*	*Industry*	*Total*
2000	140,714,325	67,161,208	126,849,101	334,724,634
2001	323,691,265	88,584,016	256,377,393	668,652,674
2002	397,744,122	101,470,613	451,058,259	950,272,994
2003	832,182,588	203,120,441	819,872,983	1,855,176,012
2004	2,403,764,844	379,944,408	1,009,541,799	3,793,251,050
2005	13,200,688,924	1,195,920,637	2,474,442,386	16,871,051,948
2006	11,570,201,564	942,189,854	1,697,479,173	14,209,870,592
2007	8,779,234,370	1,657,992,661	1,910,874,879	12,348,101,910
2008	9,638,936,812	5,422,241,865	5,256,835,871	20,318,014,548
2009	6,363,773,746	2,030,846,061	1,270,692,520	9,665,312,328
2010	4,174,122,697	1,744,663,490	771,210,968	6,689,987,155

Source: Schedule provided by the Amman Stock Exchange in 2011.

861. *Ibid.*
862. Information collated from various Amman Stock Exchange *Monthly Statistical Bulletins* (2005–2010).
863. By 2002 Jordan had 5 investment banks with 51 branches and 9 commercial banks with 315 branches. See *Annual Report of the Central Bank of Jordan* (2002).

For, in its *Jordan—2010 Article IV Consultation, Concluding Statement of the IMF Mission* issued on 17 July 2010, the IMF particularly praised Jordan for its 'sound' and 'resilient' banking sector. It positively highlighted Jordanian banks' conservative funding at 75% ratio, highlighting, *inter alia*, their 'strong' macro-prudential indicators.[864] The CBJ was also praised for its effective banking supervision including – introduction of Basle II (Pillars I and III) regulations in 2008, examining credit risk and concentration risk, etc.[865] Moreover, Jordan's introduction of an automated data collection system to improve off-site monitoring of banks (June 2010) was also highlighted, as well as introducing enhanced cross-border bank regulations through regular supervision and on-site inspections of international branches and subsidiaries of Jordanian banks.[866]

The IMF equally praised the authorities for strengthening Jordan's Anti Money Laundering/Combating the Financing of Terrorism (AML/CFT) framework. These involved: amending the anti-money laundering law in May 2010; issuing regulations that grant the Financial Intelligence Unit greater independence; and adopting a cash declaration system at the borders in March 2010

3.1.3.2.3. Equity Ownership in Listed Companies

Individual investors are increasingly occupying a sizeable role in equity ownership of listed companies traded on the ASE. For, while the number of shareholders in 1978 reached 181,000 it reached 444,450 in 1991.[867] Individual shareholders are now one of the main investors on the ASE, with increasingly diminishing participation by the government.[868] Indeed, while the number of shareholders in Jordan was 493,615 in 2004,[869] it increased to well over 800,000 in 2010.[870] In this respect, the Jordanian government's share in equity ownership of public shareholding companies is also decreasing to the benefit of private investors due to the privatisation programme.[871]

One however must point to the shift that has occurred in the direction of the attitudes of Jordan's pension funds vis-à-vis investing on the ASE. For example, the Social Security Corporation (SSC), which is the only pension fund in Jordan,

864. That is, in terms of banks being well capitalised, liquidity ratios and provisioning reaming high, etc.
865. Reported transparently in the CBJ's *Financial Stability Report*.
866. As well as improvements to the CBJ's early warning system.
867. See B Younes, 'The Effect of New Issues on the Stock Returns in Amman Financial Market', Master's thesis, Jordan University, 1995, p. 30.
868. See, for example, the *Salomon Smith Barney Guide to World Equity Markets 2000, Euromoney* (London) 2000, p. 308.
869. Statistics released by the SDC on 8 July 2004.
870. Information provided by the ASE in 2010.
871. See discussion below on privatisation in Jordan.

invested over 80% of its investments in 1999 in treasury bills, bank deposits, real estate and lending activities – the same investments in 2000 constituted over 75%.[872] This should be taken within the context of its then huge potential vis-à-vis domestic equity market with its accumulative investments in the Jordanian economy in 1999 and 2000 totalling JD 1,291.3 million and JD 1,451.15 million, representing 24.4% and 24.5% of total Jordanian GDP for 1999 and 2000, respectively.[873] Its total assets in 2006 reached JD 3.7 billion, equivalent to 36.0% of GDP.

However, this attitude shifted substantially in later years, where the SSC now holds a substantial portfolio in the ASE. For example, in 2006 alone, the SSC portfolio investment in the ASE reached nearly JD 3.0 billion. However, it must be equally stated that as the value of the ASE dropped steeply in 2006 by nearly 34%, so did the portfolio investment of the SSC thereon – with the SSC's stocks dropping by JD 939 million.[874] However, total assets of the SSC increased in 2008, reaching JD 4.9 billion (USD 6.7 billion).[875] By the end of 2009 the entire investment portfolio achieved growth of 1.5%. (See Table 9.3 below on the investment returns of the Jordanian SSC.)

Table 9.3 Return on the Investment Activities of the Jordanian SSC in 2007–2008

	2008	*2007*	*Last 3 years*	*Last 5 years*
Total real investment return (%)	–20.4%	21.9%	–5.7%	15.24%
Equities (%)	–12.85%	37%	–1.18%	28.38%
Bills and bonds (%)	7.13%	6.45%	6.43%	5.84%
Cash or equivalents (%)	6.5%	6.4%	6.32%	4.96%
Property (%)	–10%	32.19%	28.7%	19.66
Others (%) Loans	7.54%	7.35%	7.15%	7.11%

Source: ISSA Crisis Monitor Project, *Crisis Country Case Study: Jordan*, Geneva (2010), p. 4.

872. See Y Al-Jamal, 'The Impact of Economic Variables on Social Security Indicators in Jordan (1980–2000): An Econometric Study', Master's thesis, Yarmouk University, 2001, p. 54.
873. *Ibid.*, p. 52.
874. See interview with the head of the SSC Investment Unit in 2006. *Jordan Business* 'Securing a Nation', 12 June 2007.
875. See ESMAP (Energy Sector Management Assistance Programme): *Power Sector Financial Vulnerability Assessment Impact of the Credit Crisis on Investments in the Power Sector: Hashemite Kingdom of Jordan*, February 2010, p. 19.

The portfolio investment by banks in the Jordanian equity market remains at best poor. The CBJ estimates that Jordanian banking portfolio on the AFM reached only 3.3% of the total assets deposited in the banking sector between 1993 and 1997, with Jordanian commercial banks holding a large share in such portfolio.[876] Total banking direct investment on the primary market amounted to 10.5% of the value of shares offered for subscription by Jordanian shareholding companies between 1978 and 1997.[877]

In order to counter Jordanian banks' dissatisfactory involvement in this area, the CBJ asked banks to hold some of their reserves in domestic equity portfolios,[878] and equally allowed them to grant loans for the purpose of equity investment. It, for example, allowed investors to borrow upto JD 150,000 for individuals and JD 300,000 for juristic persons in order to invest on the stock exchange, accepting that certain percentage of equities' value could act as a security for the loan – stipulating that loan to value ratio should not exceed 75%.[879] This ratio was later amended in 1993 by the CBJ not to exceed 50% of the total value of equities.[880] However, statistical evidence indicates that the scale of loans given for the purpose of equity investing was not extensive. It did not exceed 0.3% of the total lending granted by the banking sector in Jordan between 1988 and 1997, with subscriptions not exceeding 5.3% of the total value of the primary market in that period.[881]

Having said the above, it however must be stated that empirical studies have found no difference in the return generated by listed Jordanian companies whether they have high or low foreign ownership. This was consonant with the findings of a recent study that looked at two groups of Jordanian listed companies: (1) a group that has high foreign ownership; and (2) a group that has low foreign ownership. The study, which examined forty listed companies on the stock market in 1995–1999, concluded that there were no significant differences between the returns generated by the two groups of listed Jordanian companies.[882]

876. Indeed, it is estimated that between 1978 and 1997, 68.9% of the total Jordanian banks' portfolio holding was held by commercial banks, while investment banks held 21.4% in that period. Specialised banks and foreign commercial banks held 7% and 2.8%, respectively. See Hraze, *supra* note 858, pp. 77–78.
877. The breakdown of this direct banking investment is as follows: Jordanian commercial banks 80.3%; investment banks 16.5%; specialised banks 2.9% and foreign commercial banks 0.3%. *Ibid.*, p. 78.
878. The CBJ in 1984 had asked commercial banks to invest at least 15% of their assets and reserves in public shareholding companies, raising it in 1990 to a minimum of 20%.
879. See *Twenty Third Annual Report*, the Central Bank of Jordan, (1986).
880. See *Thirtieth Annual Report*, the Central Bank of Jordan, (1993). However, such a requirement was abolished in 1995, coupled with lifting the ceiling of borrowing to JD 0.5 million for individuals and JD 1.0 million for juristic persons. See the *Thirty Second Annual Report*, the Central Bank of Jordan, (1995).
881. See Hraze, *supra* note 858, p. 81.
882. See generally R Nazzal, 'The Effect of Foreign Ownership on the Return and Risk in the Amman Bourse', Master's thesis, Jordan university, (2000).

As far as allowing foreign ownership in Jordan is concerned, Jordan in 1997 scrapped the 49% restriction on foreign ownership. Faroise de Consentre[883] and the American United Soft Drinks Production became the first wholly foreign-owned companies operating in Jordan after buying all the shares of Coca-Cola Jordan. Fully liberalised Jordanian sectors, which are now open to foreign investors, include transportation, insurance, banking, telecommunications and agriculture. However, although construction, retail, trading and metallurgy sectors were initially excluded from full liberalisation, the Jordanian government in 2000 cancelled such restriction.[884]

Allowing foreign corporate ownership in Jordan increased foreign equity ownership in listed Jordanian companies. Compared with 1996, non-Jordanian equity purchase in listed Jordanian companies increased dramatically in 1997 and maintained healthy levels thereafter – reaching nearly 40% in 1997 from 32.795% in 1996.[885] However, the issuance of Jordan's first GDRs in London by the Arab Potash Company in 1997 is believed to be the main reason to stimulate added foreign interest in Jordanian corporations. Indeed, the percentage of foreign ownership of Jordanian equities traded on the ASE has been consistently on the increase. For example in 2002, 2003, 2004, 2005, 2006 it was 37.4%, 38.8%, 41.3%, 45.0%, 45.5%, respectively. It further reached 48.9%, 49.2%, 48.9% in 2007, 2008 and 2009, respectively. This percentage of foreign ownership of Jordanian equities traded on the ASE was 49.0% in October 2010.[886]

Having briefly considered the structural changes brought to the microstructure of Jordanian securities markets, one discusses below the changes the new regulatory regime made vis-à-vis the question of public offers and listing.

4. THE SPECIFIC REGULATORY FRAMEWORK FOR PUBLIC OFFERS AND LISTING

This subsection now looks at the specific regulatory regime that occurred in the areas of public offers and listing.

4.1. The New Regulatory Framework for Public Offers

As to the methods of public offers in Jordan, underwriting is traditionally used when issuing debt instruments.[887] As far as equities are concerned, public offers of shares overwhelmingly took place through 'best effort', whereby the issuer promises their best efforts to sell the public issues. Indeed, since the establishment of the AFM in 1978, the 'best effort' method was used in approximately 98.7% of the

883. A French subsidiary of Coca-Cola International.
884. *Non-Jordanian Investments Regulation, No. 54 for the Year 2000.*
885. See *Amman Financial Market Annual Report for the Year 1998*, Amman Financial Market, Amman, 1998, p. 51.
886. Information collated from various Amman Stock Exchange *Monthly Statistical Bulletins* (2002–2010).
887. See Hraze, *supra* note 858, p. 83.

total value of public offers in Jordan until 1997 – with underwriting method used in just over 1.3%.[888] However, 97% of all public issues by underwriting took place in the early 1980s. This was a period when the capital market was still being formed, and public shareholding companies were not confident enough that the Jordanian public would subscribe to their entire issues.[889]

Regulating public offers was mainly found in Chapter VII of the SA 1997,[890] which is now replaced by Chapter V of the SA 2002.[891] Other regulatory aspects were equally found in JSC regulations such as the *Regulations Concerning the Issuance and Registration of Securities No. 2 of 1997*[892] (hereinafter referred to as the *1997 Issuance and Registration Regulations*), which included four important Annexes tackling prospectus requirements. These, however, were replaced by *Instructions of Issuance and Registration of Securities for the Year 2005*, which entered into force on 1 December 2005.[893] Other important regulations are the *2004 Regulations for Disclosure, Accountancy & Audit Standards*.[894] These regulations also address the disclosure requirements that issuers have to provide, together with the more recent *Instructions of the Accounting Principles and Standards Pertaining to the Preparation of Annual and Interim Financial Statements for the year 2007*, which entered into force on 16 December 2007.

In order to formulate a more complete picture, the discussion shall look at all the above regulations (immediate past and present) to assess how they mandate disclosure. It however must be stated here that, in terms of the requirement for registering the offered securities first with the JSC, there is not much difference between the regulatory regimes under the *1997 Issuance and Registration Regulations* and the *Instructions of Issuance and Registration of Securities for the Year 2005*. For, under the former, issuers first of all had to submit an application to register the securities they intended to offer with the JSC, accompanied by a prospectus.[895] Once issued and registered with the JSC, such securities could either be offered through private placement[896] or a public offer.[897]

The latter equally now stipulates that issuers need to submit an application with the JSC to register the securities.[898] It further gives the right to the JSC to reject the registration of such securities if they may cause damage to the issuer's

888. Total number of public issues in Jordan between 1978 and 1997 was 349, with the total value of JD 2,018 million. *Ibid.*
889. *Ibid.*, p. 83.
890. See Arts 53–66 of the SA 1997.
891. See Arts 34–46 of the SA 2002.
892. Issued in accordance with Art. 73(c) of the SA 1997 – became effective on 16 October 1997.
893. Article 21 states that the *Instructions for Issuance and Registration of Securities No. (2) for the Year 1997* shall be repealed.
894. Issued in accordance with Art. 12(p) of the SA 2002 – became effective on 1 March 2004.
895. See Art. 4 of the *1997 Issuance and Registration Regulations.*
896. See brief discussion below.
897. See Arts 5, 8–9 of the *1997 Issuance and Registration Regulations.*
898. Article (3)(a) of the *Instructions of Issuance and Registration of Securities for the Year 2005* state: 'Every Issuer of securities in the Kingdom shall submit an application to the Commission for the registration of those securities therewith in accordance with these Instructions.'

securities or investors.[899] From a first glance this second stipulation appears vague and open to wide interpretation as to what may exactly constitute 'damage' to existing securities or investors. But here the onus is clearly on the JSC when rendering its rejection to justify the grounds on which it judges that such issuance may cause damage to the issuer's securities or investors in general. As mentioned above, similar to the previous regime laid down in the *1997 Issuance and Registration Regulations*, the *Instructions of Issuance and Registration of Securities for the Year 2005* equally envisage that once registered with the JSC, securities can either be sold to the public through a public offer or be sold through private placement.[900] As far as subscription to public offers is concerned, the Jordanian regulatory regime now stipulates that the minimum number of shares in a single application for subscription shall be between 100 and 500 shares.[901]

However, what was striking about the SA 1997 was that it suffered from grave inaccuracy when it dealt with the question of public offers or *Tarh Aam* (the Arabic term for public offers). Chapter VII of the SA 1997 was, for example, entitled *Ifsah* (the Arabic term for 'disclosure'). This was a misnomer, as Chapter VII tackled public offering of securities. Instead of being entitled *Ifsah*,[902] Chapter VII should have been entitled *Tarh Aam* (Public Offers), as 'disclosure' and 'public offers' are not mutually inclusive.[903] Additionally, Chapter VII also makes the conceptual error of confusing public offers with takeover bids.[904] This confusion is carried through in the SA 2002, as Chapter V (which deals with public offers) is equally entitled *Ifsah*, (Disclosure) instead of *Tarh Aam* (Public Offers). The SA 2002 equally confuses public offers with takeover bids.[905] [However, despite the more recent Regulations addressing takeover of public companies that become effective on 6 June 2007[906] and the proposed amendment to the SA 2002 in late 2011,[907] the above inaccuracy still has not yet been addressed.]

899. Article (3)(b) of the *Instructions of Issuance and Registration of Securities for the Year 2005* states: 'The Board may reject the registration and issuance of any securities if it is found that the issuance thereof might cause damage to the owners of the Issuer's securities or the investors in general.'
900. Article (4)(a) of the *Instructions of Issuance and Registration of Securities for the Year 2005* states: 'The Issuer may, after registering its securities with the Commission, offer them for sale through: (1) Public offer for sale of securities, which is the bid directed to more than thirty persons. (2) Non-public offer for sale of securities, which is the bid directed to thirty persons or less.'
901. See Art. (7)(a) (4). *Ibid.*
902. That is, 'Disclosure'.
903. In the UK, for example, although the FSMA touches on the question of public offers and the standard of disclosure required, disclosure is merely a subtopic addressed under s. 80 of the FSMA, not the reverse.
904. See Arts 65–66 of the SA 1997.
905. See Art. 45 of the SA 2002.
906. Referred to as *Public Takeover Bid Procedures*. Issued by the Board of Commissioners by virtue of its Decision No. 372 issued on 6 June 2007.
907. First published on 3 May 2010.

An important difference between the public offers regime prior and post 1997 is that the latter provides a legal understanding of 'public offers'. For, unlike previous company law provisions that addressed this area, the SA 1997 and again the SA 2002 both provided a definition of public offers. This understanding shall be assessed in detail towards the end of this chapter. Additionally, some attention has now been paid to the question of liabilities that may arise from inaccurate or misleading disclosure, particularly under the SA 2002 – something that shall be explored in Chapter 11. Additionally, the disclosure requirements for Jordanian prospectuses have now been revisited – something that shall be tackled in more detail when one looks at the new disclosure regime in the course of this chapter.

4.2. The New Regulatory Framework for Listing

This subsection here briefly considers the important functions of listing as seen from a historical UK perspective, before outlining relevant Jordanian law for listing. When discussing the latter, this subsection shall outline the differences between the regulatory regimes that governed listing in Jordan after 1997.

4.2.1. Brief Account of Historical Functionalities of Listing in the UK

Before discussing the new Jordanian regulatory regime, one must state that regulating listing provides important functionalities, serving as a 'reliable' basis for market evaluation.[908] It equally constitutes an additional (but flexible) layer of control over public shareholding companies.[909] Together with various pieces of legislation regulating companies (particularly company laws), listing is considered as an effective means of regulating listed companies.

There is often a strong historical nexus between investor protection and the regulation of listing. Although this nexus is not apparent in the Jordanian legal context as such, it has been established in many countries. For example, as early as the 1800s in the UK, the 1877 Royal Commission into the Stock Exchange particularly commented on the sense of assurance that lay investors formulate about listed securities: *Inclusion on the Official List gave the security in the mind of the public a stamp of soundness, stability and genuineness to which it was not entitled.*[910] More recently, the Financial Services Authority (FSA) particularly regards compliance with the *Listing Rules* as 'essential to the promotion of investor confidence in the standards of disclosure, in the conduct of listed companies' affairs and in the market as a whole'.[911]

908. See A Hicks et al., *Cases & Materials on Company Law*, Blackstone (1997), p. 549
909. *Ibid.*
910. See D Rosenthal, *Financial Advertising and Marketing Law*, FT Law & Tax (1997), p. 46.
911. See 'The Transfer of the UK Listing Authority to the FSA', CP No. 37, the Financial Services Authority, December 1999, London, p. 22.

4.2.2. Brief Account of the Jordanian Listing Regime

In addition to its capacity to regulate listing, the ASE is also the competent authority entitled to review listing applications and assess the transfer and delisting of securities.[912] As shall be seen below, companies seeking listing must submit to the ASE's board of directors a listing application accompanied by all the required documents. Up until 2004, regulation of listing in Jordan (i.e., under the new regulatory regime) used to be enshrined in the *2000 Directives for Listing Securities on the Amman Stock Exchange* (hereinafter referred to as the *2000 Listing Directives*).[913] The *2000 Listing Directives* had replaced the *1999 Directives for Listing and Suspension of Shares of Public Shareholding Companies* (hereinafter referred to as the *1999 Listing Directives*).[914]

Having said the above, one hastens to add that new listing directives entered into force in Jordan on 1 July 2004. These are the *Directives for Listing Securities on the Amman Stock Exchange for the year 2004* (hereinafter referred to as the *2004 Listing Directives*),[915] which in turn abolish the *2000 Listing Directives.*[916]

In order therefore to present a most accurate account of listing in Jordan, these directives shall be referred to fully in this chapter. For their part, the *2004 Listing Directives* generally maintain the structure of regulation set by the *2000 Listing Directives*. However, in order to clarify the discussion, one briefly outlines the fundamental differences between the three sets of listing directives, which can be summarised as:

(1) The information disclosed by companies listed on the *First* and *Second* markets under the former *2000 Listing Directives* and the *2004 Listing Directives* is now wider in scope than the information disclosed under the *1999 Listing Directives*. This shall become clearer when one looks at the content of disclosure under the new regulatory regime.

(2) As opposed to restricted OTC trading under the supervision of the legal department at the AFM, the former *2000 Listing Directives* had introduced the concept of a *Third Market* on which 'unlisted' securities can be freely traded.[917] However, the *2004 Listing Directives* do not mention anything about 'listing' on the *Third Market*. This is probably because Jordanian regulators eventually realised that to use the term 'listing' for

912. Article 22 (b) of the *2000 Listing Directives* stated: 'The Board of Directors [of the ASE] shall be the competent authority to review listing applications, as well as cases of transfer of listing or delisting, unless otherwise stipulated in the Directives.' For its part, Art. 27 of the recent *2004 Listing Directives* states: 'The Board of Directors shall deal with any event that is not stipulated for in these Directives and shall make the necessary decisions thereon.'

913. Issued by virtue of the provisions of Art. 26 (a) of the SA 1997 – entered into force on 15 June 2000.

914. See Art. 26 of the *2000 Listing Directives*, repealing the *1999 Listing Directives*.

915. Issued by virtue of the provisions of Art. 72 of the SA 2002.

916. Article 29 of the *2004 Listing Directives* repeals the *2000 Listing Directives*: 'Directives for Listing of Securities on the Amman Stock Exchange for the year 2000 shall be repealed.'

917. See Art. 20 of the *2000 Listing Directives*.

unlisted securities such as those which used to be traded on the *Third Market* is a contradiction in functionality and terms. Additionally, unlike other jurisdictions that allow trading in unlisted securities (i.e., AIMs in the UK, launched in 1995 and boasts more than 3,000 unlisted companies), the Jordanian regulatory regime does not tackle this anymore. This is not necessarily a defect on the part of the Jordanian regulatory regime. For, given the size of the Jordanian equity market and for reasons related to investor protection, doing away with such a market may not disadvantage a relatively small market like the Jordanian one.

Undoubtedly, the mere presence of the *Third Market* represented a new development in Jordanian thinking about its securities market. The rationale then was to provide an equal opportunity for less established companies to obtain equity financing from capital markets. The *Third Market* itself was set up in pursuance of Article 20 of the *2000 Directives for Listing Securities* on the ASE, which allowed trading in unlisted securities. The Jordanian understanding of the *Third Market* was 'that part of the secondary market through which trading takes place in securities that are not listed on the ASE'.[918] Companies needed only to have been 'granted the right' to start business and provide the ASE with 'available' financial information.[919] However, trading in an unlisted security on the *Third Market* would have been stopped in the event of liquidating the companies concerned.[920]

However, since June 2000 when it was first set up, the role of the *Third Market* in the Jordanian economy remained very limited. Out of the twenty-nine companies that initially filed for trading thereon, only unlisted securities in sixteen of them were actually traded by the end of 2000. This number decreased to twelve at the end of 2002, with annual trade value of JD 3,569,048 accounting for 6,245,845 unlisted shares traded.[921] It is therefore not a surprise that given its limited impact, this methodology of capital market trading was no longer favoured in subsequent Jordanian regulations post-2004.

(3) When it comes to listing securities which are publicly offered, unlike the *1999 Listing Directives*, which were silent on this subject, the former *2000 Listing Directives*[922] and the *2004 Listing Directives*[923] mandate that if listing is requested by issuer of securities, it must be for the whole issue. This position has equally been entrenched by the SA 2002, which

---

918. See Art. 2. *Ibid.*
919. See Art. 20 (a) & (b). *Ibid.*
920. See Art. 20 (d) *Ibid.*
921. See *Fourth Annual Report*, Amman Stock Exchange, 2002, p. 64.
922. See Art. 22(a) of the *2000 Listing Directives.*
923. Indeed Art. 4 of the *2004 Listing Directives* states: 'The issuer(s) must file the listing application(s) for the entire issue(s) along with all the required documents, as *per* the standard form(s) made for this purpose.'

mandates the listing of the securities that belong to Jordanian public shareholding companies.[924] However, as seen in Chapter 8, the mandatory listing of securities (as a public policy objective that aims at deepening Jordanian securities markets) remains a consistent theme for Jordanian regulators that goes as far back as Article 17 of the AFML 1976.

(4) Unlike the *1999 Listing Directives*, the *2000 Listing Directives* and the *2004 Listing Directives* pay some regulatory attention to listing bonds and units in mutual funds – traded on the *Bond Market* and the *Mutual Funds Market*.[925]

(5) Finally, one must state here that the *2004 Listing Directives* add more clarity and cohesion to the question of listing in Jordan. For, their provisions are much more cohesive and better arranged than both the *1999 Listing Directives* and the *2000 Listing Directives*. As shall also be seen below, they equally introduce some new concepts and widen the disciplinary and administrative powers of the ASE vis-à-vis companies that breach listing rules.[926]

The source of legality that enables the ASE to issue directives to regulate listing in Jordan was first embodied in the SA 1997.[927] The SA 2002 equally gives the ASE the legislative capacity to regulate listing:

> The Market [ASE] shall specify in its Bylaws and Instructions the different sets of standards and conditions for securities to be admitted to trading or listing.[928]

The discussion next shall however elaborate on the substantive listing requirements under the new regulatory regime. These are requirements for listing on the *Second* and *First* markets.

4.2.3. *Listing on the* Second Market

The two-tiered system of the ASE under the new regime has generally remained fundamentally the same as was under the old regime discussed in Chapter 8. The

---

924. 'Every public shareholding company established in the Kingdom, and every public issuer in the Kingdom, is required to apply for listing of its securities for trading on the Market.' See Art. 72(b) of the SA 2002.

925. See, for example, Arts 12–13 of the *2000 Listing Directives* and Arts 20–21 of the *2004 Listing Directives*.

926. Other important changes that the *2004 Listing Directives* bring to Jordanian listing regime is in the area of continuous obligations, which is outside the remit of this book – See Art. 15. These new directives also provide for the listing of private companies if their paid up capital exceed a financial threshold (JD 0.5 million) – see Art. 16(c) of the *2004 Listing Directives*.

927. For example, Art. 26(a) of the SA 1997 stated that 'The Bourse's Board of Directors, upon the [JSC] Board's approval, shall set out the Bylaws and Instructions necessary for . . . (a) The listing and trading of securities . . . '

928. See Art. 72(d) of the SA 2002. Indeed the SA 2002 has given the ASE more defined capacity to regulate its internal affairs and important functions. See, for example, Art. 67(c) (1-8). *Ibid.*

only difference relates to terminology. Under the new regulatory regime the ASE is subdivided into the functionally identical *First* and *Second* markets – that is, instead of *Regular* and *Parallel* markets. There is however no difference whatsoever in Jordanian understanding of what constitutes a *Second Market* between the *2000 Listing Directives* and the *2004 Listing Directives*. Both identically refer to the *Second Market* as:

> That part of the secondary market through which trading takes place in securities that are governed by special listing requirements, in accordance with these Directives.[929]

As seen from the above definition, the *Second Market* refers to that part of the ASE on which shares of less established companies are listed – that is than those listed on the *First Market*. The *Second Market* under the new regime requires less rigorous listing conditions than those expected of companies listed on the *First Market*. However, in a welcome attempt to bring more clarity to the question of listing, the *2004 Listing Directives* now state that securities concerned should be first registered with the JSC and equally deposited with the SDC.[930] The *2004 Listing Directives* also now require that the issuer has an audit committee and that the issuer signs a listing agreement with the ASE.[931]

4.2.4. *Listing on the* First Market

Again there is no difference in Jordanian understanding of what constitutes a *First Market* between the *2000 Listing Directives* and the *2004 Listing Directives*. For, they both identically refer to it as:

> That part of the secondary market through which trading takes place in securities that are governed by special listing requirements, in accordance with these Directives.[932]

The *First Market* is that part of the ASE, on which listed companies have to comply with more rigorous listing conditions than those required from companies listed on the *Second Market*. Article 7 of the *2004 Listing Directives* now largely regulates listing on the *First Market*. However, notwithstanding the new underlying prerequisites and additional sets of information that have now to be provided, the structure of regulation vis-à-vis the *First Market* remains essentially the same.

Similar to what has been seen in Chapter 8, as a general prerequisite for listing on the *First Market*, companies must ensure that their shares are first listed and traded on the *Second Market*. Article 9 of the *1999 Listing Directives* stipulated that to qualify for listing on the *Regular Market* (now the *First Market*), companies had to ensure that they first had listed their shares on the *Parallel Market* (now the

929. Article 2 of the *2000 Listing Directives* and also Art. 2 of the *2004 Listing Directives*.
930. See Art. 3(1) & (2) of the *2004 Listing Directives*.
931. See Art. 3(4) & (5). *Ibid.*
932. Article 2 of the *2000 Listing Directives* and also Art. 2 of the *2004 Listing Directives*.

Second Market) for at least a year. This condition for listing was equally enshrined in the *2000 Listing Directives*.[933] Such condition is now equally found in the *2004 Listing Directives*, which state that:

> Company shares are transferred to the *First Market* if.... (a).... [they are]... listed on the *Second Market* for at least a full year.[934]

However, in order to facilitate the direct listing of formerly state-owned public holding companies, the condition requiring companies to be first listed on the *Second Market* has been modified. The ASE may now instead list newly privatised companies directly on the *First Market*, without their equity being listed and traded on the *Second Market*. This change to listing requirements was first introduced by the *2000 Listing Directives*,[935] and is equally now re-enforced by the *2004 Listing Directives* which state:

> The [ASE's] Board of Directors shall be entitled to list the shares arising from the privatization [*sic*] of public shareholding companies.... on the *First Market*, even if they do not fulfil the listing requirements of the said Market, on the condition that the ASE is provided with the statements and information it requests.[936]

For their part, companies wishing to transfer their listing from the *Second* to the *First Market* must, *inter alia*, ensure that at least 10% of the 'free float'[937] shares has been traded over the last twelve months preceding the listing transfer.[938] Moreover, the minimum days of trading in the shares must not be less than 15% of overall trading days of the same period.[939] Such companies' net shareholders equity must not be less than 100% of the paid-up capital.[940] They also must have no less than 100 shareholders by the end of the fiscal year.[941] Additionally, the company's free float to the subscribed shares ratio by the end of its fiscal year must not be less than (a) 5%, if its paid-up capital is JD 50 million or more or (b) 10% if its paid-up capital is less than JD 50 million.[942]

One however does not consider the above requirements by the Jordanian regulatory regime onerous or indeed burdensome. For, all these safeguards are

933. See Art. 5(e) of the *2000 Listing Directives*.
934. Article 7(a) of the *2004 Listing Directives*.
935. See Art. 23 of the *2000 Listing Directives*.
936. Article 24(a) of the *2004 Listing Directives*.
937. Article 2 of the *2004 Listing Directives* defines 'free float' shares as 'The number of company shares that are available for trading.' The definition excludes a number of shares that are not deemed available for trading. These include: shares owned by the company's board of directors or their relatives; shares owned by holding, subsidiary or affiliate companies; shares owned by shareholders who own 5% or more of the company capital; shares owned by government or public institutions; etc.
938. See Art. 7(f). *Ibid.*
939. *Ibid.*
940. See Art. 7(b). *Ibid.*
941. See Art. 7(e). *Ibid.*
942. See Art. 7(d)(1) & (2). *Ibid.*

put in order to protect the unsuspecting public by ensuring that trading in these companies is as genuine as practicable. They also aim to encourage securities find their true value through the medium of free transactions conducted on the marketplace – thus aiding the process of price accuracy which was addressed in Chapter 4.

In a similar vein, companies must equally establish a record of profitability for two fiscal years out of the last three years preceding the transfer of listing and distributed profits or bonus shares at least once over the last three years.[943] Again this condition is also seen as a measure of protecting investors through weeding out non-performing companies and allowing the ones with proven track record of profit – that is, to progress to the *First Market* given the much wider exposure that securities of such companies will enjoy once quoted freely with higher required levels of transparency. However, shares listed on the *First Market* will also be transferred back to the *Second Market* in certain eventualities, particularly if they no longer meet the aforementioned requirements.[944]

5. SECURITIES DISCLOSURE UNDER THE NEW REGIME

This subsection looks at the new disclosure requirements in the wake of the 1997 regulatory regime. However, one must clearly distinguish between the two types of disclosure that achieve different objectives, albeit being considered complementary from a functional viewpoint.

The *first* is a duty of disclosure when securities are about to be listed/offered to the public. The *second* is disclosure when securities are already listed (i.e., continuing obligations), which arises from a duty to disseminate price sensitive information on a 'continuous' and 'timely' basis. Here issuers are, *inter alia*, under a duty to inform investors of all 'significant' price sensitive changes that may impact on the price of securities.

5.1. The Substantive Content of Mandated Disclosure

Before looking at relevant disclosure requirements this subsection first looks at the applicable law.

5.1.1. The Applicable Law

Applicable law deployed to identify securities disclosure is found in the *2004 Listing Directives*, Chapter V of the SA 2002, the *2004 Regulations of Disclosure*

943. See Art. 7(c). *Ibid.*
944. These are dealt with in Art. 8. *Ibid.*

by Offering Companies, Accountancy & Audit Standards,[945] and the *Instructions of Issuance & Registration of Securities Law (2005)*, which entered into force on 1 December 2005.

However, of particular historical importance to public offers in Jordan were the *1997 Issuance and Registration Regulations*. For, to a large extent, these *Regulations* revolutionised the regime of public offers in Jordan. This is especially as the *1997 Issuance and Registration Regulations* contained four important Annexes – that innovatively addressed the different informational requirements included in prospectuses and registration statements in four different contexts: (1) when issuers publicly offer equities of companies under establishment;[946] (2) when issuers publicly offer equities of existing companies;[947] (3) private placements,[948] and (4) when issuers publicly offer bonds.[949]

Because of their importance in the recent historical development of the new Jordanian regulatory regime of public offers, extensive reference shall be made to the *1997 Issuance and Registration Regulations* – despite the fact that Article (21) of the *Instructions of Issuance & Registration of Securities Law (2005)* abrogated them.[950]

5.1.2. Disclosure When Shares Are About To Be Offered/Listed

From a regulatory viewpoint, differences between disclosure requirements for listing and those for public offers become very small when publicly offered securities are also simultaneously listed on the stock exchanges anywhere in the world. This is no different and equally true in the regulatory context of the ASE. For, as shall be seen below, in practical terms, the informational requirements imposed on issuers when they choose to list their offered securities – as per Article 3 of the *2004 Regulations of Disclosure by Offering Companies, Accountancy & Audit Standards* do not in fact differ much from the requirement of listing securities on the *Second Market* (i.e., as per Article 5 of the *2004 Listing Directives*). Moreover, the *Instructions of Issuance & Registration of Securities Law (2005)* add greater clarity when they, in Article (7)(4) declare that, as far as information required for listing is concerned, the prospectus shall be sufficient.[951]

---

945. Issued by the JSC in pursuance of Art. 12 of the SA 2002 and entered into force on 1 April 2004.
946. See Annex I of the *1997 Issuance and Registration of Securities* entitled: 'Prerequisites for the Registration of Securities Statement of the Issued Stocks Companies under Establishment.'
947. See Annex II of the *1997 Issuance and Registration of Securities* entitled: 'Requirements for the Registration of Securities Shares Prospectus – Existing Companies.'
948. Annex III of the *1997 Issuance and Registration of Securities* entitled: 'Prerequisites for the Registration of Securities Statement of the Issued Stocks Private Offer.'
949. Annex IV of the *1997 Issuance and Registration of Securities* entitled: 'Requirements for the Registration of Securities Bonds Prospectus.'
950. Article (21) of the *Instructions of Issuance & Registration of Securities Law (2005)* states: 'The "Instructions for Issuance and Registration of Securities No. (2) for the Year 1997" shall be repealed.'
951. Article (7)(4) of the *Instructions of Issuance & Registration of Securities Law (2005)* states: 'The effective prospectus shall be considered as substitute for the information required for the

Here, Annex I to the *Instructions of Issuance & Registration of Securities Law (2005)* offers greater clarity than ever before in Jordan. It equally raises the bar of mandated disclosure in the Jordanian prospectus in a considerably much more structured manner – that is, than was the case under Annex I of the *1997 Issuance and Registration of Securities*. For, Annex I to the *Instructions of Issuance & Registration of Securities Law (2005)* combines much of the informational requirements that used to be fragmented. Indeed, to a large extent this new Annex builds up and significantly improves Jordanian securities disclosure regime. This is especially as it was, in large parts, the result of a Jordanian learning curve that evidently took into account much of earlier concerns – incorporating in the process the demands of the Jordanian financial industry of better and more coherent securities disclosure regime.

Accordingly, in order to present a rounded discussion vis-à-vis the Jordanian disclosure regime as set up by Annex I to the *Instructions of Issuance & Registration of Securities Law (2005)*, whenever relevant, extensive reference shall also be made to the informational regime set by Annex I of the *1997 Issuance and Registration of Securities* – that is, when issuers publicly offer securities of companies under establishment: *Prerequisites for the Registration of Securities Statement of the Issued Stocks Companies under Establishment* – and Annex II – that is, when issuers publicly offer securities of existing companies: *Requirements for the Registration of Securities Shares Prospectus –Existing Companies.*

The discussion below shall elaborate on the above.

5.1.2.1. When Shares Are Offered to the Public

In principle, the content of substantive disclosure embodied in the new regulatory regime is not too dissimilar to that under the UK regulatory model. The bulk of the information to be disseminated to investors centres on two main aspects: (1) the offerors; and (2) their securities, as well as all the relevant aspects of the process of issuance itself. In this context, Annex I to the *Instructions of Issuance & Registration of Securities Law (2005)* requires extensive elaboration on eleven broad areas.

However, before elaborating on these eleven broad areas that need to be disclosed in the Jordanian prospectus, one must caution that the categorisation is not mutually exclusive – this is especially as many sub-requirements can be subsumed within others. Notwithstanding this, the depth of required information is a welcome development in the Jordanian regulatory regime for securities disclosure. These eleven broad areas of disclosure are:

(1) Information on offered shares. This includes types of shares, number, price, other securities that may be issued by the offerors, date of board of directors meeting authorising public offer, etc.

---

purposes of listing the securities, and the Stock Exchange shall collect the other listing requirements in accordance with the procedures in force.'

(2) Information on conditions and procedures of the public offer. This includes information on place and period of public offer, its general conditions, methods of returning subscribed funds should public offer not go through (or subscription proves to be less than expected), how to get a copy of prospectus, etc.
(3) Information on registration and objectives of the company making the public offer. These should be as enshrined in the company's Articles of Association.
(4) Information on rights and responsibilities of future shareholders and transfer of property rights. This explains rights of future shareholders in terms of voting rights, entitlement to profit (particularly in the event of liquidation), types of financial reports future shareholders are entitled to receive, detailed explanation of procedures adopted to transfer rights to shares bought, etc.
(5) Information on the purpose of the public offer and the manner in which resultant pecuniary proceeds shall be utilised. Information that need to be disclosed here include amount of funds expected to be raised, purpose of the public offer, what to do if there was a shortage of funds raised and how to prioritise spending funds, elaborating equally on other sources of finance available to the company, etc. As shall be seen below (when discussing the liabilities arising from the prospectus), this is quite an important point and has generated some interesting case law before UK courts. This is especially when companies give false reasons for the purpose of raising funds in their public offer (such as expansion of operation or buying new machineries), when in fact the real reason for raising capital is something else (such as compensating for lost revenue or paying outstanding debt).
(6) Descriptive information about the company. This includes explaining the company's products, services, actual or potential markets, sources of raw material, any patents, exclusive rights, trade marks, etc. Also information needs to be provided regarding company's exporters, suppliers, dealers (whether national or international) especially if they represent 20% or more of the company's sales or purchases. Equally, information needs to be provided on the position of the company in the market relative to that of its main competitors, as well as legal advantages it may have due to legal concessions. If the company had a different legal classification (i.e., private or governmental) before it became public shareholding, it then needs to provide a brief account of the nature of its previous capacity for the last three years. Also, the prospectus is expected to include information on any risks that may be associated with investing in offered equities.

The prospectus under Annex I to the *Instructions of Issuance & Registration of Securities Law (2005)* has equally futuristic elements. It requires information on future projects the company intends to perform. In this context, information needs to be provided on the company's projected work and expansion plans for the coming five years – elaborating in the process on the company's projected sales, nature of future activities (i.e., whether seasonal, permanent or temporary), projected profit margins, period of redeeming invested funds, etc.

The Jordanian prospectus under the new regulatory regime equally expects a detailed description of the company or companies that may be considered as subsidiaries to the company making the public offer. Here information is required regarding their main commercial and trading activities, historical overview that covers the latest five years or more (if necessary) to give investors more accurate understanding of the risks associated in investing in the shares of the (holding) company making the public offer. Such information generally relates to main products and services, availability and place of procuring raw material, patent rights, concessions, trade marks held by such subsidiaries, as well as a five years account of litigation (including pending) against (or for) such subsidiaries. Information on any demands by the tax authorities, any liens or secured assets of such subsidiaries is equally required to be disclosed.

(7) Information on offered equities. This includes disclosure regarding highest and lowest price in the three years preceding the public offer.

(8) Detailed account of sources of financing. This is in terms of the number and percentage of paid up capital by founders of the company making the public offer as well as subscribers for new companies. For existing companies, this information aims to inform investors about the extent of depreciation of the monetary value of shares once the public offer goes ahead – requiring also information on existing company loans, whether short or long term, etc.

(9) Detailed information on the issuing company's financial statements for the latest three years outlining the company's current financial position, loss and profit, periodical statements, including any major event that may impact on the company's finances. Information here should also include an outline of shareholders rights, as well as relevant changes regarding paid-up capital for the last three years. Additionally, the Jordanian prospectus expects offerors to provide information on the company's profitability before tax for the past three years, percentage of profit transferred to paid up capital, share dividend, etc. It equally expects a summary of accounting rules adopted by the issuing company when preparing the prospectus.

(10) Information on the issuing company's management. This includes the names, responsibilities, qualifications, contributions of members of the company's management. Additionally, interest in contracts performed with the company making the public offer as well as membership in the boards of other companies (whether competitors or not) needs to be disclosed.

(11) Information on company founders. This includes their names, nationalities and number of shares they hold. Here, the Jordanian prospectus equally expects information to be disclosed on shareholders (for existing companies) in terms of their nationalities, numbers and proportion of share distribution – including names and percentages of all shareholders who own more than 5% of the company's equities.

As mentioned above, despite the welcome depth of information required by Annex I to the *Instructions of Issuance & Registration of Securities Law (2005)*, one must clarify here that the content of mandated disclosure under the *1997 Issuance and Registration of Securities* was not too dissimilar. For, it too, brought about a commendable Jordanian regulatory regime of securities disclosure. This can be clear when one looks at the disclosure requirements under the *1997 Issuance and Registration of Securities*. For example, information required previously equally concentrated on companies' registration, objectives,[952] main economic and operational activities, etc.[953] Companies were equally expected to provide a brief historical overview accounting for the last five years or, if shorter, from when companies making public offers were first incorporated.[954] Issuers were also expected to disclose changes and events that affected the company's production, assets, liabilities revenues, past, pending or anticipated law suits over the period mentioned above.[955]

Issuers were equally required to provide assessment of the company's development and future business for the coming five years, major expansions, sales policy, dependence on major suppliers or markets, competitive status and estimated volume of business when compared to competitors.[956] Issuers of shares equally needed to provide information on the class of shares, nominal value, number of shares issued, total value of shares offered, types of previously issued shares, or any other securities that were issued and subscribed to. They were also expected (if applicable) to provide investors with information on the number, value and types of future securities they intend to issue.[957] Additionally, issuers were expected to disclose the date of the general assembly meeting (or the date and number of the company's board of directors' resolution approving the share issue), as well as the approval of the Minister of Commerce and Industry.[958]

Indeed, as can be observed from the above discussion, what the latest disclosure regime under the *Instructions of Issuance & Registration of Securities Law (2005)* offers over and above the regime under the *1997 Issuance and Registration of Securities* is greater depth and elaboration – particularly as it equally ensures better investor protection through requiring certain statements and certifications from Jordanian attorneys, accountants, financial advisors and relevant departments

952. That is, as cited in the Articles of Association.
953. See Annex II of the *1997 Issuance and Registration of Securities.*
954. *Ibid.*
955. *Ibid.*
956. *Ibid.*
957. See Annex I of the *1997 Issuance and Registration of Securities.*
958. See Annex II of the *1997 Issuance and Registration of Securities.*

in investment banks to accompany the prospectus. As the categories of information are clearly not mutually exclusive, Annex 1 to the *Instructions of Issuance & Registration of Securities Law (2005)* can certainly benefit from a better structure that avoids unnecessary confusion by apparent repetition of some required information. It can equally benefit from better cohesion in terms of structure -through clear-cut division between the aforementioned eleven categories to amalgamate them into better mutually exclusive categories that delineate underlying conceptual differences in a manner that enhances clarity.

In addition to the aforementioned substantive disclosure requirements, Jordanian regulations now pay more attention to regulating internal auditors and the standards of accounting.[959]

5.1.2.2. When Shares Are Listed on the ASE

The new disclosure regime for listing under the *2004 Listing Directives* is equally wide in scope. However, it must be stated that Jordanian securities laws do not impose additional disclosure requirements per se when companies transfer their listing from the *Second* to the *First Market*. Companies listed on the *First Market* will, however, become subject to more rigorous continuous obligations.[960] Companies seeking listing on the *Second Market* must first ensure that they have acquired the right to commence operations.[961]

They must also provide the ASE with a number of documents including their Articles of Associations (and prospectuses if any),[962] annual reports for the past fiscal year (if applicable),[963] their 'financial statements' and auditors' reports.[964] In another step towards clarifying much of the inaccuracy in this area, the *2004 Listing Directives* now clarify that 'financial statements' refer to items such as balance sheets, income statements, cash flow statements, stockholders equity statements, etc.[965]

Companies seeking listing must also provide the ASE with statements on their relationships with other companies (e.g., subsidiary, affiliate, holding),[966] names of the members of its board of directors, together with number of securities owned by them, etc.[967] They must equally provide the ASE with the names of all those who own 5% or more of their shares,[968] together with statements detailing the names of their shareholders and the number of shares owned by them.[969] Added to

959. See Arts 18–23 of the *2004 Regulations of Disclosure by Offering Companies, Accountancy & Audit Standards*.
960. See, for example, Art. 15(b) of the *2004 Listing Directives*.
961. See Art. 5(a)of the *2004 Regulations of Disclosure by Offering Companies, Accountancy & Audit Standards*.
962. See Art. 5(b)(1). *Ibid.*
963. See Art. 5(b)(2). *Ibid.*
964. *Ibid.*
965. See Art. 5(c). *Ibid.*
966. See Art. 5(b)(4). *Ibid.*
967. See Art. 5(b)(5). *Ibid.*
968. See Art. 5(b)(6). *Ibid.*
969. See Art. 5(b)(7). *Ibid.*

this they must also provide information on the percentage of non-Jordanian equity holding therein.[970]

For their part, issuers, who offer securities and request their listing on the ASE, are also expected to provide the JSC with a report disclosing the following items of information: (1) a briefing of the company's history since incorporation, main objectives and its relation to other companies; (2) description of issued securities; (3) the board of directors' evaluation (supported with figures) of the company's performance, accomplishments, agreements and contracts concluded; (4) disclosure of all significant events that faced or affected the company from its incorporation until the date of submitting the listing application; (5) the company's future plan for the coming three years; (6) names of the board of directors' members, and senior executive managers; and (7) names of owners of securities issued by the company and the number of securities owned by each of them if this constitutes 5% or more of such issued securities.[971]

Additionally, the company's financial statements should also be provided. Such financial statements must include: (1) the annual report of the company for the year preceding the date of submitting the listing application; and (2) periodical financial statements audited by the company's auditors.[972] These disclosure requirements are however similar to those required from companies when they are listed on the *Second Market*, as seen above.

One however must finally mention in this subsection that current Jordanian regulations give the stock exchange similar powers enjoyed by other modern stock exchanges. For example, under the *2004 Listing Directives*, the ASE has the power to suspend the shares if listed companies breach some aspects of the continuing obligations.[973] Here, the ASE can equally impose a number of sanctions for the breach of any of the provisions of the *2004 Listing Directives*.[974] These sanctions include warnings, fines not exceeding JD 5,000, transfer of listing from the *First* to the *Second Market*, suspension and delisting.[975]

6. THE INSTRUMENTS DEPLOYED FOR CONVEYING SECURITIES DISCLOSURE AND DISSEMINATION OF INFORMATION

These are listing particulars (when listing securities) and prospectuses or *nashrat el-esdar* (when offering securities to the public).

---

970. *Ibid.*
971. See Art. 3(a). *Ibid.*
972. See Art. 3(b). *Ibid.*
973. See Art. 12(d) of the *2004 Listing Directives*.
974. See Art. 23. *Ibid.*
975. See Art. 23(1-5). *Ibid.*

6.1. Listing Particulars

Listing particulars in the Jordanian regulatory context refer to the information sheets submitted to the ASE when securities are listed thereon. The content of listing particulars, as seen above, depends on the type of listed securities in terms of being shares or bonds. Additionally, as seen above, when securities are offered to the public and also equally listed on the ASE, disclosure requirements then become very similar.[976] The difference however is that whenever these issuers list their securities on the ASE, they have to provide the JSC with disclosure requirements which otherwise (i.e., in the absence of a public offer) would have been provided only to the ASE.

Having said the above, one must mention a welcome development in this area. For, a loophole that existed in the *Directives on Disclosure Related to the Amman Stock Exchange for the Year 1999*,[977] appears now to have been remedied. This is in the sense that these *Directives* which previously specified the data the ASE was obliged to release, did not contain clear clarification regarding the provisions that gave the public direct access to listing particulars. Under the *Amman Stock Exchange Disclosure Directives for the Year 2004* (which abrogated[978] the above *Directives* and entered into force on 1 September 2004), there is no reason now why investors cannot have access to such information.

For, Article (3) of the *Amman Stock Exchange Disclosure Directives for the Year 2004* gives members of the public the right to information regarding a number of aspects related to listing. Indeed, the ASE has to disclose a number of things. These include the names of issuers of listed securities, names of issuers of securities suspended from trading, names of members of the ASE and names of suspended members, etc. The ASE is also expected immediately to disclose price sensitive information that comes to its position. The public can also have access and copy such information.[979]

---

976. See for example Art. 3 of the *2004 Regulations of Disclosure by Offering Companies, Accountancy & Audit Standards* and Art. (7)(4) of the *Instructions of Issuance & Registration of Securities Law (2005).*
977. Issued by virtue of Art. 26(c) & (d) of the SA 1997 and entered into force on 15 October 1999.
978. Article (7) of the *Amman Stock Exchange Disclosure Directives for the year 2004* states: 'The Amman Stock Exchange/Securities Market Instructions for Disclosure issued by virtue of the provisions of Article 26 of the Securities Law No. 23 of the year 1997 shall be repealed.'
979. Article (3) of the *Amman Stock Exchange Disclosure Directives for the Year 2004* states: '(a) The ASE must disclose the following information: (1) Names of issuers of securities listed on the ASE; (2) Names of issuers of securities suspended from trading; (3) Names and addresses of Members; (4) Names of Members suspended from practice; (5) Names of financial professionals certified to practice as brokers at the ASE; (6) Names of financial professionals suspended from practicing as brokers at the ASE; (7) Daily, weekly, monthly and yearly statements that include trading per company, sector movement in terms of number of traded shares, volume of trading, number of contracts, indices, and main financial indicators; and (8) Financial statements of Members. (b) The ASE must immediately disclose information and data that it receives, which influence the price of securities and trading. (c) The public may have access to and copy information and data referred to in sub-paragraphs A & B of this

Additionally, listing particulars per se are not equally included in Article (4) of the *Amman Stock Exchange Disclosure Directives for the Year 2004* which tackles information obtained by the ASE that is deemed confidential and cannot be released to the public. This generally refers to information and data that the ASE employees access when they enter in the trading system, information related to the names of dealers in securities, the volume of their trading and any information pertaining to their dealings. It also includes information related to the names of owners of securities, as well as information that the ASE obtains through inspection, investigation or dispute settlement, etc.[980] That is why one makes the argument that members of the public are now able to view listing particulars – something which they were not able to do before.

Finally, one must state here that listing particulars in the Jordanian regulatory context are not also expected to be published, whether or not securities are issued for the first time.

6.2. Prospectus or *Nashrat el-Esdar*

The second important instrument for conveying securities disclosure in the Jordanian regulatory context is the prospectus. The prospectus or *nashrat el-esdar*[981] was first introduced in Jordan under the *Internal Regulations of the Amman Financial Markets 1980* – a terminology which has effectively been adopted by all subsequent Jordanian legislation. As seen from the discussion above, the SA 1997 and the SA 2002 prohibit offering securities to the public without having first issued a prospectus or *nashrat el-esdar*.

As mentioned above, the *Instructions of Issuance & Registration of Securities Law (2005)* state that every issuer of securities needs first to register the securities with the JSC. For their part, the *1997 Issuance and Registration Regulations*

Article. (d) Disclosure takes place through ASE bulletins, circulation to Members or announcement in the means deemed appropriate by the ASE.'

980. Article (4) of the *Amman Stock Exchange Disclosure Directives for the Year 2004* states: '(a) The following information, data and records shall be deemed confidential and can only be accessed by the CEO and relevant ASE employees: (1) Information and data that the ASE employees access when they enter in the Trading System; (2) Information related to the names of dealers in securities, the volume of their trading and any information pertaining to their dealings; (3) Information related to the names of owners of securities and their volume of ownership, subject to the provisions of the Disclosure Instructions in force that are passed by the Jordan Securities Commission; (4) Information that the ASE obtains through inspection, investigation or dispute settlement; (5) Information supplied by government organs, the Jordan Securities Commission, and the Securities Depository Centre and that are considered confidential by virtue of their nature; and (6) Board deliberations. (b) The Board shall be entitled to have access to information as needed to perform its duties, which are those cited in sub-paragraphs (1-6) of A of this Article. (c) The Board has the discretion in certain cases to lift the confidentiality from any information, data or record referred to in sub-paragraph A of this Article. (d) The ASE may disclose breaches committed by Members and connected persons with the penalties imposed on them.'

981. The Arabic term of *nashrat el-esdar* literally translates to 'issuance circular'.

equally stipulated that every issuer who wished to offer securities to the public must apply to the JSC for registration, having first submitted a properly prepared prospectus or *nashrat el-esdar*.[982]

The new regulatory regime first initiated under the SA 1997 required offerors to deposit a prospectus or *nasharat al-esdar* with the JSC.[983] The SA 1997 also stated that offerors could not sell their securities to the public without the prospectus first becoming 'effective', and buyers having received a copy of the prospectus.[984] This position was equally repeated in the *Instructions of Issuance & Registration of Securities Law (2005)*.[985] The prospectus or *nasharat al-esdar* became effective after thirty days of being deposited with the JSC. This regime for public offers was repeated verbatim by the SA 2002, whereby the same procedures forwarded by the SA 1997 are followed:

> The prospectus is deemed to be effective thirty days after its submission to the Commission, unless if within this period, the [JSC's] Board declares the prospectus effective or rejected. The Board may specify the period during which the prospectus is considered effective.[986]

The prospectus has to be published at least twice in two local daily newspapers, not less than seven days from the start of the subscription period or sale, having information therein approved by the JSC prior to such publication.[987] The JSC vets the prospectus and can reject it if its informational content does not comply with the SA 2002.[988] It can also reject the prospectus if it deems its contents against public policy or contrary to investors' interests.[989] Equally, if it contains untrue or misleading information.[990]

For their part, the *Instructions of Issuance & Registration of Securities Law (2005)* reinforce the above by equally stating that the JSC can reject or suspend the prospectus if it violates any law or procedures in force, if it is contrary to public interest (or investor protection), or if the fees were not paid. Additionally, in a welcome development in the Jordanian regulatory regime in the sense that it adds

982. See, for example, Annex II to the *1997 Issuance and Registration Regulations 1997.*
983. See Art. 54 of the SA 1997.
984. See Art. 55. *Ibid.*
985. Article (5)(b)&(c) of the *Instructions of Issuance & Registration of Securities Law (2005)* states: '(b) No person shall make a public offer except through an effective prospectus. (c) The sale of securities that are part of a public offer shall not be binding upon the buyer unless the buyer first has received a copy of the effective prospects.'
986. See Art. 57(1) of the SA 1997 and Art. 39 of the SA 2002.
987. Article (5)(a) of the *Instructions of Issuance & Registration of Securities Law (2005)* states: 'The public offer of securities shall come to pass through an effective prospectus, by an advertisement, the text of which, and the data and information included therein shall be approved by the Commission. The advertisement shall be published at least twice in two local daily newspapers, no less than seven days prior to the date set for the commencement of the subscription or sale.' See also Art. 34(b)(2) of the SA 2002. It is also expected to be published at least twice in two dailies, seven days before the subscription date.
988. See Art. 41(b)(1) of the SA 2002.
989. *Ibid.*
990. *Ibid.*

more clarity, the JSC can equally now reject or suspend a prospectus if it contains false, inaccurate or misleading information, or if does not contain material facts that enable investors to make their investment decision. The JSC can equally reject or suspend the prospectus if it contains information presented in a manner that renders it false, inaccurate or misleading.[991] This is especially important and shall be looked at in more detail in Chapter 11 when one addresses the question of regulatory remedies that result from the prospectus.

7. ASSESSMENT OF THE NEW REGULATORY REGIME

This subsection now assesses the Jordanian disclosure regime after 1997 to see how far it protects investors. The discussion here shall tackle three areas:

(i) assessment of Jordanian understanding of public offers;
(ii) assessment of Jordanian general principles of disclosure; and
(iii) assessment of the instruments deployed to convey disclosure to see whether their means of dissemination is conducive to investor protection and legal certainty.

7.1. Assessment of the Jordanian Legal Understanding of Public Offers

This subsection looks at the Jordanian understanding of public offers to see how far it goes in incorporating notions of investor protection. When looking at the Jordanian understanding of the subject matter, some reference shall be made to the EU/UK's understanding of public offers. However, as seen above, an important difference between the public offers regime in Jordan before 1997 and the one enacted after 1997 is that the latter, for the first time, provides a legal understanding of public offers. For, the SA 1997 stated that public offers were those made to more than thirty persons, offering at least 5% of the securities that belong to one offeror:

> For the purposes of this Law [the SA 1997], an offer shall be deemed to be *tarh aam* [public offer] if made to more than 30 persons for the sale of more than 5 percent of the securities of one issuer.[992]

---

991. Article (15) of the *Instructions of Issuance & Registration of Securities Law (2005)* states: 'The Board may reject the prospectus or suspend its effectiveness if it finds: (1) That the prospectus or any of the information attached thereto is not in conformity with the requirements of the Law, regulations, instructions or decisions issued pursuant thereto, or is not in conformity with the requirements of public interest and investor protection; (2) That the prospectus or any of the information attached thereto contains false, inaccurate or misleading data, or that it does not contain material facts that enable the investor to make his investment decision, or if it contains data presented in a way that renders the other information in the prospectus false, inaccurate or misleading; and (3) If the required fees for rendering the prospectus effective have not been paid.'
992. See Art. 64 of the SA 1997.

As shall be seen below, the definition of public offers under the SA 2002 is largely based on the above definition. One therefore asks the question of how consonant was the SA 1997 understanding of public offers with notions of investor protection – that is, in terms of safeguarding those who really require the law's protection?

One argues that the Jordanian understanding of public offers under the SA 1997 left much to be desired. For, restricting public offers to the above two categories did not necessarily safeguard many of the categories that need the law's protection. The above understanding of public offers or *tarh aam* could be criticised on at least two grounds:

(1) The Jordanian regulatory reliance on a numerical threshold to determine what is and what is not a public offer encompasses only *one* of the techniques deployed to identify public offers. It misses utilising other techniques. Thus, resulting in less comprehensiveness in ferreting out the categories that should be included under the law's protection. An arbitrary numerical threshold (whether 30, 40, 50, etc.) does not indicate whether the persons covered are indeed capable of looking after themselves or not.

This is especially as Jordanian understanding of private placements still does not exclude from the law's protection all those who can look after themselves. For, although the *1997 Issuance and Registration Regulations* and the *Instructions of Issuance & Registration of Securities Law (2005)* allowed private placements of securities to limited classes of investors, one cannot consider that those excluded from the definition capable of looking after themselves.

It, however, must be stated here that when addressing the concept of private placements, the *1997 Issuance and Registration Regulations* provided better clarity than under the *Instructions of Issuance & Registration of Securities Law (2005)*. The *1997 Issuance and Registration Regulations* stated that private placements took place:

> Through direct selling of securities to either of the following: (1) the company's shareholders at the end of the tenth day from when the JSC registers the securities concerned; (2) specific investors including strategic investors or underwriters; and (3) investors who pay in kind.[993]

On the other hand, the *Instructions of Issuance & Registration of Securities Law (2005)* had a less precise definition of private placements in that they were considered as any sales of shares to thirty persons or less:

> The Issuer may, after registering its securities with the Commission, offer them for sale through . . . (2) Non-public offer for sale of securities, which is directed at thirty persons or less . . . [994]

993. Article 11(a) of the *1997 Issuance and Registration Regulations*.
994. Article (4)(a)(2) of the *Instructions of Issuance & Registration of Securities Law (2005)*.

Nevertheless, despite the fact that the *1997 Issuance and Registration Regulations* had provided better clarity, generically including certain categories in the definition of private placements (such as shareholders 'at the end of the tenth day from when the JSC registers the securities concerned'), it nevertheless invited some uncertainty.[995] For, it did not clearly indicate whether such a provision is meant to cover promoters or may have included ordinary shareholders – i.e., in a rights issue when the company increased its authorised capital by issuing new shares. Additionally, the clarity of the understanding of private placements in the Jordanian regulatory context had equally been somewhat compromised by the fact that the *1997 Issuance and Registration Regulations* did not provide a definition of who 'strategic investors' were.

On the other hand, the definition provided in the more recent *Instructions of Issuance & Registration of Securities Law (2005)* is simplistic. It does not address in detail the various categories subsumed within the understanding of private placements that do not necessarily require the law's protection. For, there will be instances when shares are offered to significantly larger number of investors that by far exceed thirty, who due to technical expertise or otherwise, equally do not necessarily require the law's protection. As such, issuers should be exempt from the onerous requirements that result in preparing a prospectus and the extensive disclosure requirements therein.

The answer that Jordanian public offers are directed at significantly different types of investors than, for example, in the EU may be partially correct. But this very answer carries within it the complacency that the Jordanian regulatory context should not concern itself with expanding its understanding of public offers. For, this is an evolving process. This is especially as the Jordanian financial services industry is gaining significant momentum – achieving higher levels of sophistication that were unimaginable only few years ago. The Jordanian regulatory approach in this vital area therefore needs to be much more proactive and widen its understanding of those who do not need the law's protection when public offers are made – as shall be seen below when one briefly discusses the EU/UK regulatory understanding of public offers.

(2) The threshold of 5% of 'securities belonging to one offeror' as it appeared in the definition of public offers under the SA 1997 was also problematic. For, it was couched in vague terminology, especially as it used the generic term 'securities' and issuers may indeed offer shares, bonds and convertibles all in one issue. Neither, did the SA 1997 explain how to calculate the 5% ratio if the public offer included a mixture of financial instruments. However, although more recent definitions of public offers under the SA 2002 and the *Instructions of Issuance & Registration of Securities Law (2005)* do away with the 5% requirement, they still fully incorporate the first limb of the definition.

---

995. Article 36 of the SA 2002 does not aid much in clarifying what a private placement is.

The SA 2002 states that:

> Public offer is any bid for the sale of any security to more than 30 members of the public, including public issuance and public subscription.[996]

The *Instructions of Issuance & Registration of Securities Law (2005)* state that:

> The Issuer may, after registering its securities with the Commission, offer them for sale through . . . (1) Public offer for sale of securities, which is directed at more than thirty persons . . . [997]

It is evident that the SA 2002 and the *Instructions of Issuance & Registration of Securities Law (2005)* understanding of public offer is based on the first limb of the definition under the SA 1997 –with its exclusive reliance on the thirty members of the public threshold.

As mentioned above, the position in Jordan contrasts, for example to the UK, in which an understanding of public offers is instead reached through eliminating what is *not* a public offer – through excluding from the law's protection those who are deemed capable of looking after themselves in terms of being able to assess investment risks.

But how is it determined who is and who is not able to look after themselves? For its part, the Jordanian regulatory regime does not address this question as mentioned above – even at a basic level. In the EU/UK regulatory model, for example, one finds that there are a number of techniques used to identify the persons deemed capable of looking after themselves. These techniques are:

(a) The'professionals' or 'qualified investors' technique. This simply refers to exempting offers made to professionals whose ordinary business activity involves acquiring, holding, managing, disposing of investments, etc.[998] The rationale behind this is that legal protection becomes superfluous vis-à-vis those who do not need the law to compel the disclosure of information. For, by virtue of their profession, they are capable of asking for and obtaining such information for themselves.

Such 'qualified investors' are equally able to understand the risks intrinsic in their investment activities. This category generally refers to legal entities such as authorised fund managers and investment banks. Indeed, it would be very difficult from a regulatory viewpoint to justify protecting professionals such as brokers, dealers, underwriters, fund managers, etc., whether they act as principals or agents. They therefore do not require the law's unnecessary (over)protection. It, however, must be stated here that this category is not rigid and is quite flexible – that is, in terms of being open for expansion when certain conditions are met. For, EU Member States can, when requested to do so, include within this category of

996. Section 2. *Ibid.*
997. Article (4)(a)(1) of the *Instructions of Issuance & Registration of Securities Law (2005).*
998. See for example s. 86(1)(a) of FSMA.

'qualified persons' those who fulfil at least two criteria. Those who have carried out at least ten transactions of significant size per quarter over the previous four quarters; working or having worked for a year in the financial services sector in a position requiring knowledge of securities investment; or having a securities portfolio of at least half a million euros.[999] Finally, most recent amendments to EU law also point out that the definition of 'qualified investors' in Article 2 of the Prospectus Directive shall include those classified as professional clients or eligible counterparties.[1000]

Having said the above, one must add that another technique which was not too dissimilar to the 'qualified' persons technique was the 'restricted circle' technique. However, given its proneness to vagueness and misinterpretation this technique is no longer applied in the UK as evidenced by section 86 of the FSMA.[1001]

(b) The 'minimum' retail monetary value technique. This minimum monetary value was EUR 50,000 – in light of Article 2(c) of EU (Prospectus) Directive No. 2003/71/EC. However, it must be stated here that important

999. See for example Davies, *supra* note 18, pp. 873–75.
1000. That is, in accordance with Annex II of MiFID.
1001. Indeed, another technique that was deployed was the 'restricted circles' technique. One must state that the techniques adopted to exclude offers from being considered public may have overlapped. For, such techniques did not result in a neat methodological compartmentalisation – in the sense of producing conceptually discrete categories of exempted public offers. Here, non-public offers extend to all securities offers made to 'restricted circles' of persons whom the offeror believes to be knowledgeable of the risks involved. However, while it was true that this technique of identifying non-public offers appeared to overlap with the 'qualified investor' technique, one can nevertheless point to some differences. The main difference between them was that the 'restricted circles' technique was more discretionary, encompassing those whom the offeror deemed to understand the investment risks involved. Also, unlike the above situation where a presumption of knowledge was automatically made by virtue of the 'professional' status of an offeree, the onus of proving that a member of a 'restricted circle' was knowledgeable lied squarely with the offeror. Such an onus of proof was not rigid, though. (*See para. 6 of the now repealed Sched. 11 of the FSMA*):

i. Offerors needed first and foremost to demonstrate the 'reasonability' of their assumption, depending of course on each situation in hand.
ii. Once point (i) above was satisfied, offerors then needed only to demonstrate two interrelated requirements:
   1) Their mere *belief* that;
   2) The offerees were *sufficiently* knowledgeable of the risks inherent in the investment. As 'absolute' knowledge was not required, the threshold for determining 'sufficient' knowledgeability became significantly lower – i.e., in terms of offerors being able to at least benefit from any doubt concerning the level of offerees' awareness of investment risks. For, they only needed to prove that they had reasonably believed that offerees were *sufficiently* knowledgeable. However, in determining whether or not a person was knowledgeable (i.e., to understand the risks), regard should have been had to both: (a) information supplied by the offeror about the issuer; and (b) information about other issuers if the offer also conferred the right to acquire their securities.

One hastens to add that applying this in practice was not completely non-problematic. For, 'sufficiently knowledgeable' to understand the risks might have implied both a

changes to the Prospectus Directive were approved by the EU Parliament on 17 June 2010. Indeed, the Prospectus Directive (Directive 2003/71/EC) (PD) has now been amended after Directive 2010/73/EU (the Directive) came into force on 31 December 2010. EU Member States are required to implement such changes into their respective national law within eighteen months following entry into force – by 1 July 2012 at the latest. Accordingly, the minimum monetary value shall now be raised to EUR 100,000 for issuers of debt securities.

The rationale behind this is that when investors opt for investing in securities, which require a threshold of high retail monetary value, then such investors are deemed able to look after themselves. For, small or lay investors would not normally be expected to engage in such securities transactions – which more often than not require pecuniary clout and financial sophistication.[1002] The 'monetary value' technique can be applied in two practical manners. The first is when the actual minimum *consideration* paid for securities exceeds a predetermined monetary threshold. The second is if the securities themselves are *denominated* in indivisible blocks, whose value also exceeds a predetermined minimum monetary threshold.

(c) The 'maximum' monetary value or the 'small offer' technique. Here, offers of securities are considered non-public if they are relatively small and the total consideration does not exceed a maximum monetary value. The rationale behind this exemption is that small offers do not necessarily justify the potentially huge costs associated with issuing a prospectus. Currently this threshold includes any public offers of transferable securities which are less than EUR 2.5 million. Having said this, one must hasten to add that under the amendments to the Prospectus Directive mentioned above, this threshold shall become EUR 5.0 million. However, one must clearly state that this rationale[1003] is not present in the maximum consideration (exempted) offers. For, such offers are deemed to be small enough to the extent that they do not warrant triggering the need for statutory protection. The maximum consideration offer is to be taken together with any other offer with the same securities made by the same offeror and open at any time within twelve months.

(d) The technique of designating a 'predetermined number' of the public to whom securities are offered as a numerical threshold determining what is and what is not a public offer. Again, this technique is premised on the rationale that issues, which are more akin to private placements, should be

---

knowledge of the business activity of the issuer (e.g., biotechnology) and of investment activity (see *Public Offering of Securities: Proposals for Consultation by HM Treasury*, UK Treasury, 20 August 1998, p. 7) – something which might not have always presented a workable definition in practice. This was especially the case as other EU jurisdictions implemented this differently. France, for example, at one stage, deemed it to be within the restricted circles anything up to 300 persons – including collective funds.

1002. The mustering of which is characteristically beyond ordinary investors.

1003. That is, on which the 'minimum consideration' and 'minimum denomination' are predicated.

exempted from the regulations concerning public offers. It initially exempted all public offers of securities when members of the public were less than 50. This was later raised to 100. However, according to the amendments mentioned above (which EU Member States must implement by no later than 1 July 2012), this threshold shall become 150 members of the public.

A crucial point to bear here is that the calculation of the 150 persons/individuals threshold is reached according to the number of persons/individuals to whom the securities are *offered* – not to those who eventually *subscribe* to such an offer, as the number of subscribers is of no consequence.[1004] In order for this technique to apply, a number of requirements need to be present: The same person (offeror) must make the offer to investors (part, or all of which are situated) in the UK; the offer must be open at any time for twelve months; and offers made to trustees of a partnership in their capacity as such and offers to persons jointly, are to be treated as making an offer to a single person. Of course 'qualified investors' are not taken into account when reaching this numerical threshold.

It however must be stated clearly that the rationale behind exempting certain offers from the onerous obligations resulting from being characterised as public offers has generally varied.[1005] In addition to what has been mentioned above, other categories equally deemed not in need of 'prospectus information' are those investors who are expected to receive such disclosure through different means – such as targeted shareholders in a share-exchange takeover bid as well as shareholders in merger situations.[1006] Exemptions equally apply to situations when the offer is made in a context other than that of raising funds – that is, when shareholders receive new shares in substitution for existing ones when there is no increase in share capital.[1007]

7.1.1. Implications of the EU Criteria of Public Offers for Jordan

As far as Jordan is concerned, as mentioned above the sole reliance of the Jordanian regulatory regime on one technique when determining what is a public offer does not take into account many other determinants. Indeed, as was argued above, although the Jordanian market is markedly different in size and structure from that of the EU, there is no reason not to contemplate a more comprehensive

1004. See *Public Offering of Securities: Proposals for Consultation by HM Treasury*, UK Treasury, 20 August 1998, p. 10.
1005. Other UK grounds for exempting securities offers from being considered 'public' could have also been because certain offers were deemed to be outside the regulations. Examples of such offers included those made to employees (or members of their families) by a private company offering its securities. (See *para. 16 of the now repealed Sched. 11 of the FSMA*.) Offers made to clubs and associations (in which members could reasonably have been regarded as having common interest with each other and with the club) were also exempt. (See *para. 5 of the now repealed Sched. 11 of the FSMA*.)
1006. See for example Davies, *supra* note 18, pp. 873–75.
1007. *Ibid.*

Jordanian understanding of public offers. This is especially as the numerical limit of over thirty investors remained static since the implementation of the new regime in 1997. Indeed, as has been seen in the UK context, this numerical threshold has evolved from 50 to 100 and shall become 150 by 1 July 2012. For, this is an area of dynamic change – especially in light of the increasing reliance on public offers when raising capital in Jordan as has been witnessed since 2005.

Additionally, Jordanian financial regulation can benefit from appreciating the rationales behind the 'minimum retail value' technique and 'small offer technique', which clearly aim to obviate the need to issue a prospectus in needless circumstances. This equally applies when offers are made to qualified investors who do not necessarily require a prospectus. Indeed, as well as the need for general examination of the question of public offers in Amman, given the significant costs associated with preparing and issuing a prospectus, this exclusive Jordanian threshold (of over thirty investors) needs to be raised to a more accommodating level – with extensive consultation with the Jordanian financial services industry.

7.2. Assessment of the Jordanian General Principles of Securities Disclosure

General principles of disclosure aid in understanding the conceptual thrust of securities laws in the area of regulating listing and public offers, and serve as a yardstick to assess whether or not resultant regulations comply with such thrust. One accordingly looks here at the Jordanian regulatory regime's general principles vis-à-vis securities disclosure.

There is little difference between the old and new regimes in Jordan when it comes to articulating clear and sufficient general disclosure principles. The SA 1997 did not articulate general principles to address the purpose of Jordanian securities disclosure when listing/offering shares to the public. Only in passing did it enunciate what may loosely be interpreted as a disclosure principle, stating rather vaguely that a prospectus may contain:

> Any . . . information required or allowed by the Commission in accordance with the Instructions issued by the Board [of the JSC], *and which may be of assistance to investors in making their decision regarding investing in the said securities.*[1008] [Italics added.]

For its part, the SA 2002 does not equally pay enough attention to formulating general principles for disclosure when listing/offering shares to the public and merely paraphrases the above provision, stating:

> No person shall make a public offer unless a prospectus is filed with the Commission, together with such additional information and data that *enables the investor to make his investment decision.*[1009] [Italics added.]

1008. See Art. 56(4) of the SA 1997.
1009. See Art. 34(a)(1) of the SA 2002.

This is inadequate, particularly as the above provisions give the misguided impression that disclosure's functionality lies in aiding investors reach *any* investment decision and providing them with information they *may* need. The implication is that the threshold to providing such information can be significantly lower than that needed to enable investors reach an *informed* decision.

However, in a positive development much of these shortcomings were remedied by the aforementioned two Annexes to the *Instructions of Issuance & Registration of Securities Law (2005)* and the four Annexes to the *1997 Issuance and Registration Regulations*. These Annexes in effect represent the prospectus requirements. Preamble to Annex II to the *1997 Issuance and Registration Regulations* and Annex I to the *Instructions of Issuance & Registration of Securities Law (2005)* for example, provides that:

> The main aim of preparing this prospectus is to present all the information that helps investors make suitable decision concerning the investment in the shares offered for sale.

Indeed, the above positive development in delineating the objective of Jordanian securities disclosure is not too dissimilar to, for example, the position under the EU regulatory model – which clarifies in no unclear terms that issuers need to provide all information necessary for investors to reach an *informed* decision.

In this context, general principles of disclosure in the EU regulatory context do not only aim at helping investors reach *any* investment decision, but also to provide them with all the necessary information to reach a correct investment decision. For example, the EU's Prospectus Directive acknowledges the inherent risks in transferable securities and requires that investors are provided with *full knowledge of the facts* in order to make an *informed assessment* of the risks. Thus, achieving better level of investor protection:

> Investment in transferable securities, like any other form of investment, involves risks. Safeguards for the protection of the interests of actual and potential investors are required in all Member States in order to enable them to make an *informed assessment* of such risks *so as to be able to take investment decisions in full knowledge of the facts*.[1010] [Italics added.]

The UK regulatory system equally pays due attention to advisors' need for adequate disclosure. For example, the FSMA imposes a wide-ranging general duty of disclosure. It therefore requires that listing particulars contain all such information that not only investors, but also their professional advisors would *reasonably* require in order to reach an informed assessment:

> Listing particulars submitted to the competent authority . . . must contain *all* such information as investors and their *professional advisors* would *reasonably* require, and reasonably expect to find there, for the purpose of making an *informed assessment* . . .[1011] [Italics added.]

1010. See para. 19 of Preamble to EU Directive No. 2003/71/EC.
1011. Section 80(1) of the FSMA.

Furthermore, information disclosed on issuers and their securities should be 'sufficient' and 'objective'. In this context, the Prospectus Directive specifically states that:

> Such information, which needs to be *sufficient* and as *objective* as possible as regards the financial circumstances of the issuer and the rights attaching to the securities . . . [1012] [Italics added.]

The above general principle is important as it clarifies that the sufficient provision of information on issuers and their securities should be as far as is objectively possible. For, requiring that issuers' endeavours should be *as objective as possible* has practical implications on the degree of issuers' liability vis-à-vis investors in terms of it being strict or not – which it is clear that it is not strict.

Another important general principle to which Jordanian general principles have recently paid attention is that information disclosed should be provided in an easily analysable and comprehensible format. In this respect, Annexe I to the *Instructions of Issuance & Registration of Securities Law (2005)* states that information provided to investors need to be legible and under clear subheadings. This requirement is equally embodied in the EU's general principles on securities disclosure:

> [Information disclosed] should be provided in an easily analysable and comprehensible form.[1013]

Indeed, the above general principle is of particular significance as the whole objective of securities disclosure is not only to provide information in a standardised format, regardless of comprehensibility. But rather to provide such information in a manner that renders it amenable to being easily accessible to lay investors. As the objective is to enable investors to reach an informed decision, this necessitates that securities disclosure needs to steer away from overcomplicating the presentation of facts and figures pertaining to issuers and their offered securities.

Finally, an important general principle is that disclosure should not arbitrarily include all items of information regardless of its impact on the company's position. Here, Annexe I to the *Instructions of Issuance & Registration of Securities Law (2005)* states that information provided in the Jordanian prospectus should be relevant, non-rambling and without repetitions so that investors would not be bombarded with confusing sets of information. They equally accept that non-sensitive information may not be disclosed if this proves detrimental to issuers. Under the EU regulatory context the omission of disclosing sensitive information is equally allowed:

> Omission of sensitive information to be included in a prospectus should be allowed through derogation granted by the competent authority in certain circumstances in order to avoid detrimental situations for the issuer.[1014]

1012. See para. 20 of Preamble to EU Directive No. 2003/71/EC.
1013. *Ibid.*
1014. See para. 25 *Ibid.*

When applying the above general principle, the UK, for example, implements a number of exemptions limited to few situations under which the United Kingdom Listing Authority (UKLA) may authorise the omission of information from prospectuses. These relate to exempting:

(1) disclosure of information deemed contrary to public interest;[1015]
(2) disclosure of information that causes serious detriment to issuers, providing that it is not likely to mislead investors;[1016] and
(3) disclosure is unnecessary for the type of persons expected to deal in the securities concerned.[1017]

Unlike the situation under the first or the third categories, exemption from disclosing information that may cause serious detriment to issuers shall not however be in respect of 'essential' information.[1018] 'Essential' information here refers to information without which investors would be misled about the facts enabling them to make informed assessments.[1019]

7.3. Assessment of the Instruments Deployed to Convey Securities Disclosure

This subsection here briefly assesses some of the issues related to instruments deployed to convey securities disclosure in Jordan. Though, one must mention that the SA 1997 and SA 2002 have both placed disproportionate importance on *nashrat al-esdar* becoming *effective*, as opposed to its contents being *disseminated* properly.

7.3.1. Potential Loophole due to Statutory Insistence on Delivery of Prospectus

The condition that buyers must also physically receive *nashrat el-esdar* 'prior to the sale' may on occasions be impractical. For, unlike the position, for example, under the EU regulatory model where investors in some circumstances may be entitled to *request* a hardcopy of the prospectus,[1020] the SA 2002 states quite categorically that the sale would not be binding *unless* the investor receives a copy of the 'effective' prospectus:

> The sale of securities that are part of a public offer *shall not* be binding upon the buyer *unless* the buyer first has received a copy of the effective prospectus.[1021] [Italics added.]

1015. See s. 82(1)(a) & (3) of the FSMA; Art. 8(2)(a) of EU Directive No. 2003/71/EC.
1016. See s. 82(1)(b) of the FSMA; Art. 8(2)(b) of EU Directive No. 2003/71/EC.
1017. See s. 82(1)(c) of the FSMA; Art. 8(2)(c) of EU Directive No. 2003/71/EC.
1018. See s. 82(2)(b) of the FSMA.
1019. See s. 82(6). *Ibid.*
1020. See Art. 14(7) of EU Directive No. 2003/71/EC.
1021. See Art. 34(c) of the SA 2002.

Taken literally, the problem with the above Jordanian provision is that it potentially gives rise to loopholes inviting transactional instability, as investors can claim that they never received a copy of the prospectus, thus invaliding the sale – although Annexe I to the *Instructions of Issuance & Registration of Securities Law (2005)* makes this quite difficult as investors must sign the standard template when subscribing to shares confirming that they in fact received a copy of the prospectus.

7.3.2. Conflict between Laws and Regulations until December 2005

Although the SA 1997 has now been replaced by the SA 2002, it was still not without legal effect for a considerable number of years. For, many of the regulations were issued in pursuance to its provisions. The main argument here is that when one looks closely at the treatment of public offers of securities under the SA 1997 and the *1997 Issuance and Registration Regulations*, one finds conflict between the two respective regimes laid by them. Indeed, not only was there an evident fundamental flaw in the Jordanian regulatory understanding of the rationale for regulating public offers. The whole regulatory regime itself was at times no more than a composite of inconsistent pieces of legislation. Such an argument becomes apparent when one juxtaposes some of the provisions of the SA 1997 next to the *1997 Issuance and Registration Regulations*.

To begin with, Article 54 of the SA 1997 stated that public offers took place either 'verbally', 'through a prospectus', a 'subscription advertisement' or by means of a 'text' attached to, or preceding a prospectus –providing such prospectus became *effective*:

> An issuer, an affiliate thereof, or an underwriter of either one of them shall not offer any securities of the issuer before *submitting* the prospectus to the [JSC's] Commission and *paying* the requisite fees. In all circumstance, the offer shall be made in one of the following ways: (1) *verbally*; (2) by *means of a prospectus*; (3) by means of *a proclamation containing a summary of the prospectus* and any other information required or allowed by the Commission in accordance with the Instructions approved by the [JSC's] Board; and (4) by means of a *text attached to*, or *preceding* the prospectus, provided the prospectus has come into effect.[1022] [Italics added.]

However, when one juxtaposes the above to the regime laid by subsequent JSC regulations, one finds evident inconsistency that persisted up until December 2005, when the *Instructions of Issuance & Registration of Securities Law (2005)* came into force. Nowhere could this be more evident than under the former regulatory regime laid by the *1997 Issuance and Registration Regulations*. For, oblivious to the fact that provisions in bylaws could not repeal or amend provisions in primary legislation, Article 7 of the *1997 Issuance and Registration Regulations* appeared to have amended Article 54 of the SA 1997. Article 7 solely relied on subscription

1022. Article 54 of the SA 1997.

advertisements or 'announcements' as the only means to effecting a public offer. Excluding all the methods mentioned in Article 54 of the SA 1997, Article 7 of the *1997 Issuance and Registration Regulations* stated that public offers:

> Take place through an effective prospectus *via* the means of subscription advertisement, the format and contents of which are approved by the JSC.[1023]

This inconsistency would have been remedied had the SA 1997 itself been subsequently amended to accommodate such changes in the modalities of disseminating public offers in Jordan. But no such amendment took place. Indeed, even after the promulgation of the SA 2002, new regulations for public offers were issued only by late 2005. Moreover, even after hypothetically having remedied the above inconsistency between provisions in bylaws and primary legislation, Article 7 of the *1997 Issuance and Registration Regulations* would have still posed a problem. For, its exclusive reliance on the JSC to determine the format and contents of subscription advertisements could itself have been criticised on a number of grounds. One of such grounds would have been that, primary Jordanian law, as it stood then, contained no guidance on how the JSC should determine the format or contents of subscription advertisement and left this question entirely vague. This lacuna was overlooked by the SA 2002.[1024]

7.3.3. No Obligation to Publish a Supplementary Prospectus until December 2005

Another criticism of the post 1997 Jordanian regulatory regime was that up until December 2005 there was no obligation on issuers immediately to publish supplementary prospectuses (or supplementary subscription advertisements). It is important to inform investors and their advisors about changes to information in the prospectus during the period of subscription. Mechanisms should be in place to ensure that issuers publish supplementary material immediately to inform investors of such changes. For their part, issuers under Article 57(b) of the SA 1997 had only 'promptly' to inform the JSC in *writing* if there was any change in the information supplied in *nashrat el-esdar* or prospectus:

> The issuer must promptly inform the Board [of the JSC] in writing of any changes to the information included in *nashrat el-esdar*.[1025]

This position was repeated by the SA 2002:

> The issuer shall inform the Commission in *writing* or *electronically* of any changes to the information in the prospectus as soon as they occur, whether or not the prospectus has been declared effective.[1026] [Italics added.]

The above requirement could be criticised on a number of grounds.

1023. Article 7 of the *1997 Issuance and Registration Regulations*.
1024. See Art. 34(b) of the SA 2002.
1025. Article 57(b) of the SA 1997.
1026. Article 40 of the SA 2002.

First, it was confused with Article (5)(b) of the *1997 Issuance and Registration Regulations*, which did not require that the JSC be informed in writing or electronically. It merely stated:

> Issuers must promptly inform the JSC of any changes to the information mentioned in *nashrat el-esdar* as soon as they occur.[1027]

For, as seen above, although it mandated that the JSC must be promptly notified of changes to the prospectus or *nashrat el-esdar*, Article (5)(b) nevertheless did not state that issuers had to notify the JSC in writing (or electronically) of such changes. This was inconsistent with the aforementioned SA 1997 and SA 2002 provisions, which state that the modality of informing the JSC is at least in writing.

Second, all the above provisions failed for a number of years to address how to remedy the problem of disseminating new information that came into light after submitting the prospectus or publishing the subscription advertisement. Indeed, without paying any consideration to investors' right to be promptly informed of such changes, they implied that issuers' duty in this eventuality was fulfilled once they have informed the JSC. This was however untenable.

For, investors and their investment advisors were entitled to be informed of the changes that took place in the period when subscription advertisements were published until the passing of the subscription date. 'Promptly' informing the JSC should not be viewed as a substitution to directly informing investors. It only added needless bureaucratic complications in the sense of additional compliance procedures, resulting in unnecessary delays. For, instead of promptly publishing the new additional information that had arisen, issuers had to write to the JSC advising on such changes, which in turn would decide whether or not to pass them to the public.

Third, there was no guidance as to what happens to investors who have already subscribed to the shares before they have learnt about the new significant information, which affected the securities or their issuers.

The above situation which lasted until the *Instructions of Issuance & Registration of Securities Law (2005)* came into force in December 2005[1028] could be

1027. Article (5)(b) of the *1997 Issuance and Registration Regulations*.

1028. The *Instructions of Issuance & Registration of Securities Law (2005)* now state in Article (16):

> A- The Issuer shall inform the Commission in writing or electronically of any change to the information in the prospectus as soon as it occurs, whether or not the prospectus has been declared effective. B- If the Commission finds that a material change has occurred in the data in the prospectus or that a new material fact has developed and has not been disclosed in due course, the Board may take the measures it deems appropriate including the suspension or cancellation of the public offer.

It equally states in Art. (17):

> A- If a material change occurs in the data in the prospectus, or a new material fact develops during the public offer period and before the period of subscription or sale, the Issuer shall inform the Commission of such change and prepare a (prospectus appendix) which shall be approved by the Commission in order to be attached to the prospectus

contrasted to the UK, where issuers have to publish supplementary prospectus if significant new matters rose at any time after the prospectus was submitted to the FSA and before the commencement of dealing in securities.[1029] Moreover, as far as the EU regulatory system is concerned, investors who have already agreed to subscribe to the securities before publishing the supplementary prospectus can (within no more than two days after publishing the supplementary prospectus) withdraw their acceptances.[1030]

Prior to December 2005, a solution to the need to inform investors and their investment advisors of new changes in Jordan would have been a 'simultaneous approach'. Under such an approach, issuers would have informed the JSC of the changes that occurred since the submission of the prospectus (or the publication of the subscription advertisement), and at the same time published supplementary *nashrat el-esdar* so that investors would have received this information as quickly as possible. Therefore, instead of segmenting the process into two stages, where – (1) the JSC first received the additional information from issuers; and (2) subsequently (and rather bureaucratically) determined whether or not such additional information would have been important, investors and their investment advisors could have made assessment of such information more speedily as they directly received it when it was published by issuers.

Additionally, Jordanian laws needed to address the position of aggrieved investors who had already agreed to subscribe for the securities before the publication of the supplementary prospectus. Here, such investors needed to have been given an opportunity to withdraw their acceptances within a prescribed period after publishing the supplementary prospectus.

7.4. No Investment Promotion Regime

The new Jordanian regulatory regime still conspicuously lacks an investment promotion regime. But why is it important to have a financial promotion regime in the first place? Here, although general advertising controls focus on accuracy, they will not provide adequate investor protection – especially as mentioned in Chapter 4 lay investors make high-risk commitments. Additional statutory controls can therefore ensure the accuracy of [financial] advertising, requiring the disclosure of risks associated with an investment and also 'full disclosure of terms and charges'.[1031]

---

before the subscription or sale process is commenced. B- The (prospectus appendix) shall be advertised in the same newspapers wherein the public offer has been advertised and before starting the subscription or sale. C- If the material change occurs or the material fact develops during the period of public subscription, the Issuer shall immediately suspend the public subscription and inform the Commission thereof, provided the public subscription shall be resumed after the Issuer completes the procedures specified in Paragraphs (A) and (B) of this Article.

1029. See s. 81 of the FSMA.

1030. See Art. 16(2) of EU Directive No. 2003/71/EC.

1031. See M Blair et al., *Blackstone's Guide to the Financial Services & Markets Act 2000*, Blackstone (London), 2001, p. 56.

In order to attain some appreciation of the regulatory importance of this area, one here briefly looks at the position in the UK – where investment promotion when offering securities to the public is not a new phenomenon, dating back almost 350 years ago.[1032] The new regulatory regime is now embodied under section 21 of the FSMA:

> Section 21 consolidates into a single new legislative framework three legislative regimes concerning the advertising and marketing of deposits, insurance, and financial services in the UK.[1033]

Section 21 contains a prohibition on financial promotion by unauthorised persons when: (1) the promotion is made in the course of business; (2) the communication amounts to an invitation or inducement to engage in investment activity; and (3) the communication does not fall within an exemption.[1034] It specifically states that a person must not, in the course of business, communicate an invitation or induce to engage in an investment activity, if the issuing person was not an authorised person[1035] or an authorised person does not approve the content.[1036]

Moreover, the FSMA specifically states that no advertisement or other information in conjunction with an application for listing may be issued unless the contents of such advertisement or information have been submitted and authorised/approved by the UKLA.[1037] Those who contravene this provision are liable to a criminal offence, as well as being civilly liable.[1038]

In the case of a communication originating outside the UK, the above applies only if the communication is capable of having an effect in the UK. This is relevant in the case of, for example, Internet promotion of securities.[1039] However, the interpretation of the new promotion regime is now restricted and applies to communications which amount to an invitation or inducement to engage in an investment activity – applying therefore to communications which contain a degree of 'incitement', not to communications made up of purely factual information.[1040]

1032. Indeed, the earliest paid-for prospectus advertisement was first published in 1657 in Cromwell's newspaper *Mercurius Pollіticus*. This was under the heading 'An Advertisement of very Great Importance', and related to the then reconstructed East India Company's subscription advertisement. See K Newman, *Financial Marketing and Communications*, Holt Rineheart and Winston Ltd (1984), p. 49. Here, the Bubble Act of 1720 particularly declared that companies formed without a Royal Charter or Act of Parliament were illegal and those convicted of their promotion could face life imprisonment and forfeiture of all property. *Ibid.*, p. 52.
1033. See HM Treasury, *Financial Promotion*: *Third Consultation Document*, October 2000 [hereinafter Treasury 2000], Part I, para. 1.1.
1034. Treasury 2000. *Ibid.*, Annex C, para. 3.
1035. For authorisation and exemptions, see Pt. III of the FSMA (ss 31–39).
1036. See s. 21(2)(a)(b). *Ibid.*
1037. See s. 98(1). *Ibid.*
1038. See s. 98. *Ibid,*
1039. See s. 21(3), the *Investment Advertisement on the Internet Order No. GR2/98* (May 1998).
1040. Where the facts presented do not amount to an invitation. Treasury 2000, *supra* note 1033, para. 4.4.

Here, in order to protect investors, unless an exemption applies, companies listing/offering their securities must have their investment advertisements approved or issued by an authorised person[1041] – exemption exclude, *inter alia*, none 'real-time' communications and 'solicited' real-time promotions in connection with listing applications, promotions included in listing particulars and promotions included in prospectus for public offer of unlisted securities.[1042]

8. CONCLUSION

Due to external exhortations and structural adjustment programmes, Jordan was galvanised to pay considerable attention to reforming the regulation of its equity markets. This reform has brought structural changes as well as more reliance on disclosure as a tool of investor protection. However, although in substantive terms the disclosure requirements in Jordan are now not too dissimilar to those in advanced economies, a closer analysis reveals many shortcomings.

1041. See generally the Financial Services and Markets Act 2000 (Financial Promotion) Order 2005 (*SI 2005/1529*) (as amended) (FPO). It came into force on 1 July 2005 (replacing the original Financial Services and Markets Act 2000 (Financial Promotion) Order 2001 (*SI 2001/1335*) (as amended)). Previously, the relevant exemptions could be found in Arts 69–73 of the Financial Services and Markets Act 2000 (Financial Promotion) Order 2001. See Statutory Instrument No. 1335, on 2 April 2001in conjunction with Sched. 1 (paras 3–11, 14, 15, 17, 18) & Sched. III (Parts I-III) of that Order.

1042. To elaborate one says that according to the Financial Services and Markets Act 2000 (Financial Promotion) Order 2005 (*SI 2005/1529*) (as amended) these exemptions encompass six broad categories: (1) Types of communication. These include: follow-up communications (*Art. 14*); introductions (*Art. 15*); generic promotions (*Art. 17*); and one-off communications (*Art. 28 and 28A*). (2) Communications to certain recipients. These include: overseas recipients (*Art. 12*); investment professionals (*Art. 19*); persons in the business of placing promotional material (*Art. 38*); persons in the business of disseminating information (*Art. 47*); certified high net worth individuals (*Art. 48*); high net worth companies, unincorporated associations etc. (*Art. 49*); sophisticated investors (*Art. 50*); self-certified sophisticated investors (*Art. 50A*); and associations of high net worth or sophisticated investors (*Art. 51*). (3) Communications from certain persons. These include: exempt persons (*Art. 16*); mere conduits (*Art. 18*); journalists (*Art. 20*); overseas communicators (*Arts 30 to 33*); government and central banks (*Art. 34*); nationals of EEA states other than the UK (*Art. 36*); financial markets (*Art. 37*); and communications by members of a profession (such as firms of solicitors which are not authorised persons) (*Arts 55 and 55A*). (4) Communications relating to securities and listing matters. These include: promotions required or permitted by market rules (*Art. 67*); promotions in connection with admission to certain EEA markets (*Art. 68*); promotions of securities already admitted to certain markets (*Art. 69*); promotions included in listing particulars etc. (*Art. 70*); and material relating to prospectus for public offers of unlisted securities (*Art. 71*). (5) Company communications. These include promotion broadcast by company director (*Art. 20A*); members and creditors of certain bodies corporate (*Art. 43*); group companies (*Art. 45*); annual accounts and directors' report (*Art. 59*); and participation in employee share schemes (*Art. 60*). (6) Communications relating to corporate transactions. These include: sale of body corporate (*Art. 62*); and takeovers of relevant unlisted companies (*Arts 63 to 66*).

For example, when looking at the Jordanian legal understanding of public offers under the new regime, one sees that it is not entirely based on the notion of investor protection – in terms of excluding from the law's protection those capable of looking after themselves. This is especially as the Jordanian regulatory reliance on a numerical threshold to determine what is and what is not a public offer encompasses only one of the techniques deployed to identify public offers. It does not utilise other techniques, thus resulting in less comprehensiveness in ferreting out the categories that should be included under the law's protection.

The above can potentially be problematic, as the Jordanian understanding of private placements still does not exclude from the law's protection all those who can look after themselves. Indeed despite the phenomenal growth of the Jordanian financial services industry and significantly increased sophistication the numerical threshold for determining public offers in Jordan is still more than thirty – adding considerable costs to offering companies. This threshold needs to be re-examined in consultation with the Jordanian financial services industry.

However, a positive development has taken place in the Jordanian general principles vis-à-vis securities disclosure under the new regime. For, under Jordanian latest regulations they now make a significant effort to emphasise the notion of investor protection. In this context, general principles aid in formulating the conceptual thrust, and serve as a yardstick to assess whether resultant disclosure complies with such a thrust. When contrasting the position to that under the EU one equally finds similar emphasis. Another similarity now is that EU and Jordanian general principles on securities regulation pay attention to the requirement that information disclosed should be provided in an easily analysable and comprehensible format.

An area that needs further elaboration in the Jordanian context is how to address disclosing information deemed contrary to public interest or disclosure that may cause serious detriment to issuers. The Jordanian regulatory regime can in this area benefit from the UK/EU experience in this regard.

When looking at the instruments deployed to convey securities disclosure, one finds that the SA 1997 and SA 2002 place disproportionate importance on *nashrat el-esdar* becoming effective, as opposed to its contents being disseminated properly. Additionally, the condition that buyers must also physically receive a copy of *nashrat el-esdar* 'prior to the sale' may give rise to a potential legal loophole that may result in transactional instability. Needless to say, up until December 2005 there was apparent inconsistency between the regime laid by the SA 1997 and the one laid by subsequent JSC regulations, which on occasions, invited uncertainty.

Neither was there any provision for supplementary prospectuses or supplementary subscription advertisements prior to December 2005. Indeed, the SA 1997 and the SA 2002 both failed adequately to deal with this question. For, the modality of 'promptly' informing the JSC of new changes and leaving it to the JSC to decide whether such new information required publishing, only added needless layers of bureaucracy. There was equally no guidance as to what exactly would happen to investors who already subscribed to the shares before they had learnt about the new significant information. To have left this un-redressed for a considerable number of years (1997–2005) was a serious oversight.

Added to all the above is the criticism that the Jordanian regulatory regime does not pay adequate attention to the question of investment promotion in the context of listing/offering securities to the public.

The next question to be addressed relates to liability resulting from inaccurate or misleading disclosure under both the general law and the regulatory regime in Jordan.

Chapters 10 and 11 next examine this in detail.

Chapter 10

Liabilities for Fraudulent or Negligent Misstatements under the Jordanian General Law: Selected Comparative Aspects with the UK General Law

INTRODUCTION

Chapter 10 now discusses liabilities for fraudulent and/or negligent misstatements under the Jordanian general law. The discussion shall first look at liability for fraud under the general law before looking at negligent liability – where one asks how far has Jordanian law moved beyond liability for fraudulent misstatements to include liability for either negligent or innocent misstatements.

One must however emphasise at the beginning that the reason for discussing civil liability under the Jordanian general law stems from the fact that this area is beset with conceptual inconsistencies – and therefore cannot be taken for granted. The picture here is especially confusing given that the JCC is itself inconsistent about tortious liability in terms of whether it is based on *injury* or *fault*. This is because when drafting the JCC, Jordanian legislatures were contradictory about the question of civil liability. For, as shall be seen below, they unsuccessfully attempted to harness *Shari'a's* principles of civil liability (often based on *injury*) with modern secular notions – under which civil liability is generally based on *fault*. The problem is further exacerbated by the fact that liability for negligence as such is not coherently addressed by the JCC. It is rather developed by Jordanian judges, who predominantly rely on the ECC, which bases tortious liability on *fault not injury*.

The discussion here tackles the general rules that protect shareholders who were induced to buy shares by fraudulent or negligent statements in the prospectus. One shall therefore identify these rules, before looking at their application under the JCC. One shall equally assess the effectiveness of shareholders remedies for fraudulent or negligent misstatements under the Jordanian general law.

1. LIABILITY FOR FRAUD ARISING FROM *GHUBIN* AND *TAGHREER*

Before proceeding any further one must point out that, unlike the position in the UK, the main bulk of Jordanian rules on civil liability[1043] when offering shares to the public has not historically been found in specialised statutory law.[1044] Moreover, whilst under English general law fraudulent statements of facts that induce the contract will invariably justify some form of legal relief,[1045] as shall be seen below, fraud under the general law in Jordan may not result in granting any remedy – particularly if it is accompanied by minor financial loss.

As seen in Chapter 6, the JCC leans heavily towards the *Hanefite* juristic school. This is a result of it being largely modelled on the Ottoman *Majallat*, which itself was strongly influenced by the *Hanefite* School. For its part, the *Hanefite* School does not recognise misrepresentations as understood under the general law in the UK.[1046] It instead refers to *ghubin*[1047] and *taghreer*,[1048] the combination of which constitutes a defect of consent in contracts for consideration. However, as the analysis shall reveal there are some similarities between the concept of *taghreer* and fraudulent misrepresentation.[1049]

Having said the above, one must clearly point out that *taghreer* accompanied with *ghubin* that induces a contract is a pre-contractual remedy and is not considered as a contractual wrong as such. One must equally emphasise that the rules on *ghubin*

1043. Generally speaking, the objective of civil liability is largely remedial. One says 'largely' as the inhibitive economic cost of civil liability can be a deterrent in itself. See, for example, G Williams, 'The Aims of the Law of Tort' (1951) 4 CLP 137 and more recently *Smith v. Scrimgeour*, as per *Lord Steyn*, [1996] 4 All ER 769 at 790.

1044. That is, Directors' Liability Act 1890, which is arguably the origin of modern prospectus liability in the UK.

1045. As per Lord Campbell in *Walton v. Morgan* (1861), 3 De. G., F. & J. 718, at 723.

1046. Misrepresentations refer to unambiguously, untrue pre-contractual statements of material fact made by one party to a transaction (the representor) that induce another party (the representee) to enter into a contract. See generally: J Beatson, *Anson's Law of Contract*, Oxford University Press, 27th edn, Oxford, 1998, pp. 232–57; D Allen *Misrepresentation*, Sweet and Maxwell, London, 1988; G Treitel, *The Law of Contract*, Sweet & Maxwell, 10th edn, London, (1999), pp. 305–74; A Grubb, *The Law of Contract*, Butterworths, London, 1999, pp. 568–633; G Appleby, *Contract Law*, Sweet & Maxwell, London, 2001, pp. 309–27.

1047. *Ghubin* refers to imbalance in a transaction, where one party makes a profit and another makes a loss. See discussion below on *ghubin*.

1048. *Taghreer* refers to deceiving a contracting party by words or acts. See discussion below on *taghreer*.

1049. A nod, wink, shake of the head, smile, photograph, etc., may give rise to a misrepresentation. *E.g.: Marylebone Property Co. Ltd v. Payne* [1994] 45 EG 156; *R v. Lambie* [1982] AC 449 & *R v. Gilmartin* [1983] QB 953. The distinction between what is and what is not a misrepresentation is not often clear, however – *Kleinwort Benson Ltd v. Malaysia Mining Corporation Berhad* [1989] 1 WLR 379.

and *taghreer* were developed through completely different routes than those of negligence under tort. As shall be seen below, *ghubin* and *taghreer* were developed through *mu'awadah* contracts (or contracts for consideration). As both evolved *via* different routes, one shall therefore address *ghubin* and *taghreer* separately from the general rules on negligence under tort. For their part, the combination of *taghreer* and *ghubin fahish*,[1050] as shall be seen below, entitles the aggrieved party to rescind the contract –who can claim for damages once they have rescinded the contract.

However, before discussing these concepts one points out to the difficulties in presenting a consistent application of the Islamic doctrine of fraud. Indeed a doctrine of fraud under Islamic jurisprudence can be constructed from the pooling of the numerous exegeses of Islamic jurists concerning general principles. Where application is concerned, however, the doctrine becomes more subjective. This is especially as each juridical school must be consulted at length in order to ferret out its particular construction of the doctrine:

> An example considered to constitute fraud by one school, or even one disciple of that school, may not always be deemed so by the jurists of another school . . . The nice distinctions of Common Law, based on precedent, are not to be found in the *Shari'a* texts . . . .[1051]

As far as the substantive discussion is concerned, one first considers the meaning of *ghubin* and *taghreer* under *Shari'a*, before explaining their juridical impact. Once this is achieved one then discusses shareholders suing on the grounds of *ghubin* and *taghreer* in Jordan, looking at how such shareholders can establish them. One then moves to addressing how effective are the general Jordanian remedies based on *ghubin* and *taghreer* for shareholders induced to buy shares by fraudulent or misleading statements.

1.1. Meaning of *Ghubin* and *Taghreer* under *Shari'a*

Together, *ghubin* and *taghreer* represent Islamic theory of fraud when forming *mu'awadah* contracts. Linguistically, *mu'awadah* means 'compensatory' and the noun *ta'wid* means 'compensation'. *Mu'awadah* contracts relate to contracts for consideration, under which one party gives a consideration in exchange for goods or services. This subsection starts the discussion by explaining the connotations of *ghubin* and *taghreer*.

1.1.1. The Concept of *Ghubin*

Linguistically, *ghubin* means depreciation, shortfall or folding to make smaller as in to '*ghubin* a dress' which means to fold a dress to make it shorter or tighter.[1052]

1050. *Ghubin fahish* refers to excessive imbalance in the benefits of a given transaction. See discussion on *ghubin fahish* below.

1051. See Rayner, *supra* note 568, p. 243.

1052. See A Zarqa, *El-Fiqh El-Islami fi Thoubeh El-Jadid: El-Juz' El-Awal: El-Madhkal El-Fiqhi El-Aam* 9th edn, Damascus (1967–1968), p. 378.

Juridically, it refers to imbalance in the value between the subject matter of a contract and the consideration paid for it in a manner that makes the interests of one party more dominant than the other.[1053] So, if the subject matter of a contract has been exchanged for a consideration either above or below the market price, then *ghubin* takes place. In this context, Islamic jurists have defined *ghubin* as:

> From the viewpoint of the person who commits *ghubin*: it [*ghubin*] is to acquire an item paying less than its value. From the viewpoint of the aggrieved party: it [*ghubin*] is to acquire an item paying more than its value.[1054]

Jurists have further subdivided *ghubin* into two types, *yaseer* and *fahish*.

1.1.1.1. Ghubin Yaseer

The term *yaseer* means simple or easy. *Ghubin yaseer* refers to imbalance in a given exchange under which small financial loss or gain accrues. An example is if an item is exchanged for 10 Dinars, but on assessment by experts was valued at 9 or 11 Dinars. This estimation is said to be within the reasonable valuation of assessors or experts.[1055]

1.1.1.2. Ghubin Fahish

Fahish literally means excessive, exorbitant or grave. *Ghubin fahish* refers to imbalance in a given exchange under which excessive financial loss results or big gain accrues. As far as quantifying *ghubin fahish* is concerned, fixed ratios have been advanced such as a fifth for real estate, twentieth for movables (or goods) and tenth for animals – the *Majallat* employed this method.[1056] Another method of quantifying *ghubin fahish* is to consider it as anything that is outside the reasonable estimation of experts or assessors. As shall be seen below, this is the view adopted by the JCC.[1057]

1.1.2. The Concept of *Taghreer*

Taghreer linguistically connotes danger in the sense of leading someone to a perilous situation. *Taghreer*, which is the term for fraud used by the *Hanefite* School, is also synonymous with the Arabic term *tadlis*, which is mainly used by the *Maliki* School. However, these two terms are used interchangeably in virtually all classical and even modern texts on the subject matter.

It is argued that the term *tadlis* is an Arabised form of the Greek Byzantine *Dolos* as an example of classical Islamic thought being influenced by other

---

1053. *Ibid.*
1054. See G Taha, *Al-Wajeez fe El-Nathariat El-Ammah fe El-Tizam, El-Kitab El-Awal: Masadar El-Eltizam* (Baghdad) 1971, p. 202.
1055. *Ibid.*
1056. See Art. 165 of the *Majallat.*
1057. See Art. 146 of the JCC.

contemporaneous civilisations.[1058] *Dolos* is believed to have entered Arabic vernacular through commerce and trade with foreign nations. It is argued that through their contacts with the Byzantines on the Syrian frontier the pre-Islamic Arabs became familiar with Graeco-Latin terms and institutions. This was mostly in relation to military, administrative and legal aspects. It is furthermore argued that:

> The Arabic verb *dallas* . . . is derived from Latin *dolus*; the word entered Arabic through the channel of commercial practice at an early date, but it did not become a technical term for fraud in early Islamic law.[1059]

However, regarding the difficulty of pinning down the concept of *tadlis*, it has been rightly argued that irrespective of its possible 'eclectic' origins:

> *Tadlis* does not form a neat parallel concept of fraud with equivalent institutions elsewhere as may perhaps have been expected. Indeed, it remains somewhat removed conceptually from the Roman system of *Dolus*, the French Civil Law concept of *Dol*, or English Common Law Fraud.[1060]

Juridically, *taghreer* or *tadlis* refers to inducing others to contract by false or deceptive means.[1061] It must be stated that *taghreer* takes place at the time of forming the contract. Hence, its juridical impact, as shall be seen below, is to vitiate the consent of the aggrieved party. Islamic jurists have therefore defined it as:

> [*Taghreer* is] . . . for one party to cheat another deploying misleading means, whether *verbal* or by *action*, which make him consent to transact when he would have not consented had such means not been deployed.[1062] [Italics added.]

As shall be seen below, the above definition adopted by Islamic jurists is almost identical to the definition of *taghreer* adopted by the JCC. Islamic jurists further subdivide *taghreer* into *taghreer qawli*[1063] (verbal) and *taghreer fi'li*[1064] (by action).

For its part, the JCC does not recognise the practical implications from distinguishing between *taghreer qawli* and *taghreer fi'li* as outlined by Islamic jurists. In this respect, the majority of jurists view *taghreer fi'li* as more serious than the *Hanefite* School. They accordingly grant an option to rescind contracts induced by *taghreer fi'li*, if they suffer *ghubin yaseer.* Those who recourse to *taghreer fi'li* demonstrate malice and serious bad faith, as they engage in deceptive actions and manoeuvres – not only fibs or exaggerations as under *taghreer qawli.* Also a main reason for transacting is often the missing attribute.

1058. See N Coulson, *A History of Islamic Law*, 1978, p. 28.

1059. See J Schacht, *An Introduction to Islamic Law*, Clarendon Press, Oxford, 1964, p. 9.

1060. See Rayner, *supra* note 568, p. 205.

1061. See M Salameh, *Nathariat Al-Aqid fi El-Fiqh El-Islami min khilal Aqid El-Bay'*, Moroccan Ministry of Religious Affairs, 1994, p. 233; A Hakeem, *Al-Wajeeze fi Sharh El-Qanoon El-Madani: El-Juz' El-Awal: Masader El-Iltizam*, 4th edn (Baghdad), pp. 163–65.

1062. See Zarqa, *supra* note 1052, p. 374, who also refers to *taghreer* as *khilabeh*.

1063. Takes place through deceptive or false verbal attributions aimed at inflating the qualities of the subject matter of a contract.

1064. Takes place through false or deceptive manoeuvres that aim at tempting others to enter into a contract.

So, the purchaser should be entitled to rescind the contract. The majority of the *Maliki* School stipulates that in order to rescind a contract, the purchaser must have trusted the vendor's disclosure of the price – under *bay' al-amanat* or *bay' el-mustarsil.* The *Shafi'te* School holds a similar view, focusing on the deceit deployed by the defendant, regardless of *ghubin yaseer* or *ghubin fahish.* So, if deceptive means were deployed, then this alone entitles aggrieved parties to rescind the contract.

The *Hanbali* School gives rescission only to those not experienced in the market who might suffer from *ghubin fahish.* Experienced buyers have no right to rescind even when suffering from *ghubin fahish.* The *Hanefite* School retorts by saying that there still should not be a right to rescind the contract due to *taghreer fi'li* as far as there is neither *ayib khafii* (latent defect), which the deceptive manoeuvres aimed to hide, or *ghubin fahish.*[1065]

1.2. The Juridical Impact of *Taghreer* and *Ghubin* under *Shari'a*

One first discusses the juridical impact of *ghubin* before tackling the concept of *taghreer.*

1.2.1. The Juridical Impact of *ghubin*

Ghubin does not warrant rescinding *mu'awadah* contracts or awarding damages, as people are expected to lose and gain from their contracts.[1066] However, only on very limited occasions will transactions be subjected to juridical scrutiny on the grounds of *ghubin yaseer.*[1067] Islamic jurists will also rarely interfere on public policy grounds to protect the public from *ghubin fahish.* Examples of when Islamic jurists will interfere include *ghubin fahish* in contracts concerning properties that belong to *waqf,*[1068] *Beit El-Mal*[1069] or orphans.[1070] Such contracts are voidable at the discretion of the courts or guardians, as the case may be. However, as shall be

1065. See generally Salameh, *supra* note 1061, p. 234.
1066. Indeed, the Prophet Muhammad said: 'Leave people to be provided by the Almighty God [through making profit] from each other'; and 'The Almighty God favours those men who are easy to sell and easy to buy.' Taha, *supra* note 1054, p. 203.
1067. The exception is in *bay' al-amanat* (the buyer trusts the seller's disclosure of the original purchase price) and *bay' el-mustarsil* (the buyer or seller confides to the other that they are ignorant about the price and asks to buy or sell at market price). This is similar to the Common Law contracts of *uberrimae fidei.*
1068. Juridically, to *waqf* something is to hold it for the benefit of all or to donate its revenues. It can also refer to properties held in trust for private beneficiaries. See Z Yakan, *Al-Waqf fi Al-Shari'a wa Al-Qanoon*, Dar al-Nahda, 1388 H, pp. 7–9.
1069. *Beit El-Mal* is a historic term that relates to the treasury, or a modern social security department.
1070. The *Malki* School adds to this category sales in which one declares their ignorance of the price and requests to buy and sell according to market price.

seen below, *ghubin* under the JCC renders consent defective only if accompanied by *taghreer* and was excessive (*fahish*).

1.2.2. The Juridical Impact of *Taghreer*

According to the *Hanefite* School, *taghreer* without *ghubin fahish* does not provide an automatic right to rescind a contract of sale.[1071] The requirement of *ghubin fahish* as the sole grounds for rescinding such contracts when induced by *taghreer* is not necessarily the view of other juristic schools.[1072] However, if *ghubin yaseer* occurs due to *taghreer*, instead of rescinding the contract, some opinions of the *Hanefite* School is prepared to give a right to damages only.[1073] For its part, the JCC, as shall be seen below, has not adopted this view. It therefore does not take account of *ghubin yaseer* in *mu'awadah* contracts,[1074] and will allow rescission only when *taghreer* is accompanied by *ghubin fahish*.

1.3. Shareholders Suing on the Grounds of *Ghubin Fahish* and *Taghreer* under the JCC

This subsection now discusses the conditions to sue under the JCC for shareholders induced by *taghreer* to buy shares in public offering. However, although Jordanian shareholders, like shareholders in the UK, will have recourse in the regulatory regime, there nevertheless may be situations where it is more beneficial for them to sue under the general law. This for example can be in situations where they do not seek damages as such but rather rescission, where they want to be put in the same position that they would have been had they not bought the shares. In such circumstances shareholders do not seek damages of pecuniary remedies for the loss that resulted from fraudulent/negligent misstatements, while keeping the shares. Rather, they seek to return the shares they originally bought in exchange for the sums of money they paid for such shares.

As far as the Jordanian general law is concerned, one says that the influence of the Ottoman *Majallat* in the area of *taghreer* and *ghubin* is evident in the JCC.[1075] For example, the *Explanatory Memorandum to the JCC*[1076] [hereinafter referred to

1071. '... The Islamic jurist is not generally concerned with the psychological impact of fraud. What counts for him are the effects of the fraud in the form of the lesion caused, so that the equivalence of the benefits may be maintained. This means that unless there is lesion, even if it has been the deciding factor for the will of the contracting party, it has no effect on the validity of the juridical act.' See Comair-Obeid, *supra* note 557, p. 107.
1072. See, for example, the discussion above on the divergent approach of Islamic jurists on *taghreer fi'li* and *qawli*.
1073. See Sanhuri, *Masadir El-Haqq*, Pt.11, pp. 143–46, 160–89; Mahmasani, *General Theory*, Pt. II, p. 426.
1074. Excluding some of the exceptions mentioned above.
1075. The *Majallat* refers extensively to the *Hanefite* School in this area.
1076. The *Explanatory Memorandum to the JCC* is the official commentary on the JCC. It was published simultaneously with the Civil Code – *Law No. 43 for the Year 1976*.

as the *Explanatory Memorandum*] explains that the JCC reproduced many of the provisions of the *Majallat* concerning *taghreer* and *ghubin*.[1077] In this respect, only *taghreer* accompanied with *ghubin fahish* entitles the aggrieved party to rescind the contract. Moreover, neither the JCC nor the Court of Cassation will allow rescission or even damages in the case of *taghreer* and *ghubin yaseer*. For, unlike other Arab civil codes, the JCC has adopted a strict view that does not allow damages if fraud has not resulted in excessive loss.

However, as unconvincing as it may be, the reason for this Jordanian position is its purported minimal desire to interfere in contractual relations, giving 'maximum freedom' to contracting parties:

> The general rule states that even if they [*taghreer* and *ghubin*] influence consent in terms of it being given on erroneous grounds, this does not detract from the fact that such erroneous consent was the result of one party . . . not being careful enough. This *should not* negate contracts, as the deceived party would have had ample time to consider his decision. This is the *maximum freedom and choice* given to contracting parties. So, if one party makes a mistake, then that is human nature and who does not err? Legislation *should not* protect people from their mistakes. So, in order to preserve the sanctity of contracts and stability in dealings, such contracts *must be upheld* . . . [1078] [Italics added.]

However, one strongly argues that the above statement by the *Explanatory Memorandum* appears to be misplaced when explaining the general position vis-à-vis the question of *taghreer* coupled with *ghubin fahish*. For, it appears to generalise the requirement of *ghubin* and *taghreer* to all contracts, rather than restricting it to *mu'awadah* contracts only. One therefore contends that it contravenes the approach of Islamic exegetes.[1079] Indeed, the Ottoman *Majallat* mostly dealt with *taghreer* and *ghubin* under the rubric *Matters Related to the Contract of Sale which Contains Five Chapters*. It gave no indication that their combined applicability would apply outside *mu'awadah* contracts.[1080] Furthermore, some modern Arab civil codes even specifically mention *mu'awadah* contracts when discussing *ghubin* and *taghreer*.[1081]

For its part, the juridical impact of the combination of *ghubin fahish* and *taghreer* is to render *mu'awadah* contracts *fasid*. As mentioned in Chapter 6, *fasid* means 'corrupt' or 'rancid'. Juridically, a *fasid* contract means that, although

1077. See generally the *Explanatory Memorandum* Vol. I, pp. 144–50.
1078. *Ibid*, pp. 144–45.
1079. See, for example, classical Islamic works such as: *El-Hattab* Pt. IV, pp. 437–38; Ramlie: *Nehayat El-Muhtag Ella Sharh El-Manahej; El-Sharh El-Kabeer Alla Mutin El-Muqanna'* Pt. IV, pp. 80–81, *El-Mukana'* Ibin Qudama, Vol. II, p. 42. Also, Sanhuri, *Massader El-Haqq*, Pt. II pp. 160–66.
1080. See, for example, Arts 356, 357 and 441 of the *Majallat*.
1081. See, for example, Art. 213 of the *Lebanese Law of Obligations and Contracts*.

it is originally legitimate, such a contract is nevertheless liable to rescission due to defects in its form.[1082] Article 170(1) of the JCC defines a *fasid* contract as:

> *Fasid* contract is what is legitimate in its origin, but not in its form. If the reason that renders it *fasid* is removed then it becomes a valid contract.

Having introduced the juridical impact of *ghubin* and *taghreer* under the JCC, one now turns to look at how shareholders can establish *ghubin fahish* and *taghreer*.

1.3.1. Establishing *Ghubin Fahish*

The JCC does not provide a definition for the generic term of *ghubin fahish* as such. It rather quantifies it in general terms, assuming that whatever lies outside such quantification is *ghubin fahish*. When quantifying *ghubin fahish*, the JCC does not accept the fixed ratio adopted by the *Majallat*. It opts instead for associating it with what lies outside the valuation of experts. Article 146 states:

> *Ghubin fahish* in real estate or otherwise is what would be outside the estimation of assessors.

Such adoption by the JCC is justified on the grounds that it offers more 'simplicity and flexibility' than rigid, pre-determined ratios. The *Explanatory Memorandum* states:

> *Ghubin* can either be *yaseer* or *fahish*. There are different methods to determine them. For example, Art. 165 of the *Majallat* states that '*ghubin fahish* is at least twentieth of goods, tenth of animals and fifth of real estates.' Others . . . state that '*ghubin fahish* in real estate or otherwise is what lies outside the valuation of assessors.' The Jordanian draft adopted the latter due to its *simplicity* and *flexibility*.[1083] [Italics added.]

In order to establish *ghubin fahish*, shareholders in Jordan must therefore prove that the depreciation in the price of the shares they were offered in the prospectus lies well below the valuation of market experts. This they can establish by, for example, relying on experts' reports. For its part, the Court of Cassation has ruled that accepting experts' reports is a matter left entirely to courts of substance:

> The experts' report is the evidence for which the court of substance has exclusive jurisdiction in terms of weighing and assessing, without any supervision from the Court of Cassation as long as the report fulfils its conditions and purpose.[1084]

1082. However, 'Due to the importance placed upon intention and mutual consent in Muslim nominate contracts, the system is generally free from the fetters of external formalism which are to be found for instance, in the formalistic institutions of *Mancipatio* and *In Iure cessio* in the early Roman classical law of contract, and other archaic legal systems, as well as early European law.' Formalism however remains important in few Islamic contracts such as pledge, gift, marriage, barter, etc. See Rayner, *supra* note 568, pp. 161–66.
1083. See *Explanatory Memorandum*, p. 148.
1084. CCD No.786/99, *LSJ*, 2000, p. 3898, at 3901–02.

1.3.2. Establishing *Taghreer*

In order to establish *taghreer*, shareholders need to look at the definition of *taghreer* in Article 143 of the JCC, which states:

> *Taghreer* is for one party to deceive another by manipulative verbal or actual means that lead them to consent to transact, when they would have not consented without such manipulative means.

In order for shareholders to be able to sue on the grounds of *taghreer* and rescind the contract of sale, they must prove a number of things:

First, the subjective element of an intention on the part of the offeror or those responsible for the prospectus deceptively to induce shareholders to buy shares. However, if defendants base their inducing fraudulent statements on false information, which they genuinely believed to be true without any intention to deceive, then there is no *taghreer*. Here, a similarity between *taghreer* (as seen from the definition above) and fraudulent misrepresentation (as understood by the general law in the UK) is that if a party deliberately misstates their intentions, which they know are false, then they can be liable.[1085] In *Edgington v. Fitzmuaurice*,[1086] a fraudulent misrepresentation arose when the prospectus stated that the debentures were issued for obtaining funds to develop the company's business, when in fact they were intended to pay off its debt.[1087]

Second, the material element of deploying deceitful/manipulative or false means, whether verbal or otherwise, is required. The Court of Cassation accepts the importance of the *material* element in fraud, stipulating that a defendant needs to make a positive effort to deceive the aggrieved party. For example, the mere presence of a latent defect in goods without interference from the seller does not automatically amount to fraud:

> The mere presence of a latent defect in the merchandise is not sufficient to prove fraud .... Fraud requires the seller to undertake deliberate actions which confuse the buyer ....[1088]

A similarity between *taghreer* and fraudulent misrepresentation here is that they must be material, affecting the judgement of any reasonable person in terms of whether to enter or not to enter into an agreement to buy the shares concerned. This is apparent from the above Jordanian definition, which clearly states that *taghreer* has the effect of inducing the contracting parties *to consent to transact, when they would have not consented without such manipulative means*. This is indeed similar

1085. *Smith v. Price* (1862) 2 F & F 748, at 752.
1086. [1885] 29 Ch D 459.
1087. As per Bowen LJ, 'The state of a man's mind is as much a fact as the state of his digestion. It is true that it is very difficult to prove what the state of a man's mind at a particular time is, but if it can be ascertained it is as much a fact as anything else. A misrepresentation as to the state of a man's mind is, therefore, a misstatement of fact.' *Ibid.*, at 483.
1088. CCD No. 127/85, 1985 *LSJ*, p. 1886, at 1890.

to the general law in the UK, where Lord Mansfield, for example, stated in *McDowell v. Fraser*[1089] that:

> A representation is material when its tendency, or its natural and probable result is to induce the representee to act on the faith of it in the kind of way in which he is proved to have in fact acted.[1090]

One must however emphasise that the *material* element in Jordanian general law should be read in conjunction with other provisions of the JCC, which accept that *taghreer* can also take a negative form in terms of reticence. Therefore, shareholders induced to buy shares by hiding a particular fact in the prospectus can equally sue on the grounds of *taghreer*. Here, the key word is 'deliberate'. If silence or omission is not deliberate but rather innocent or negligent then there is no *taghreer* as such.[1091] Article 144 of the JCC states:

> Deliberate silence about an incidence or circumstance is considered *taghreer*, if it is proven that the aggrieved party would have not entered into the contract had he known of such incident or circumstance.[1092]

The above provision is not exclusive to the JCC and can be seen in the ECC[1093] and other Arab civil codes, influenced by it such as the Syrian[1094] and Libyan[1095] civil codes. The deceptive assertions/manoeuvres (or deliberate silence) resulting in *taghreer* must be made by a contracting party or their agents. Accordingly, there would be no liability if a third party makes false or deceptive assertions/manoeuvres inducing the shareholder to contract without the knowledge of the defendant. However, the defendant would be caught by *taghreer* if, even though they were not party to it, they nevertheless were aware of the false assertions/manoeuvres made by a third party.[1096] The burden of proof is of course on shareholders to substantiate this claim.[1097]

A similarity between *taghreer* and misrepresentation here is that they are distinguished from exaggerations,[1098] puffs[1099] or vague misstatements.[1100] For,

1089. (1779) 1 Dougl 247.
1090. *Ibid.*, at 248. Here, the test for materiality is an objective one, determined by whether or not in any similar context a statement would have reasonably been considered as material. Nevertheless, if a representee was induced to enter into a contract when a reasonable person may have not been induced, the representee would be entitled to a relief. *Museprime Ltd v. Adhill Properties Ltd* (1991) 61 P & CR 111 at 124; *Goff v. Guathier* (1991) 62 P & CR 388; *Smith v. Land and House Property Corporation*, per Bowen LJ (1884) 28 Ch D 7 at 16.
1091. There however may be negligent liability which is discussed below.
1092. Article 144 of the JCC.
1093. See Art. 125(2) of the ECC.
1094. See Art. 126 of the Syrian Civil Code.
1095. See Art. 125(2) of the Libyan Civil Code.
1096. See Art. 148 of the JCC.
1097. *Ibid.*
1098. See *Smith v. Land and House Property Corp* (1884) 28 Ch. D7.
1099. See *Scott v. Hanson* (1829) 1 Russ. & M 128.
1100. That is, as per Turner LJ in *Dimmock v. Hallett.* (1866) LR Ch App 21. C.f., *Carlill v. Carbolic Smoke Ball Co* [1893] 1 QB 256.

Islamic jurists equally accept that sellers may recourse to exaggerations to sell their products.[1101] However, under the UK general law, if misstatements are reasonably amenable to being interpreted in different contexts in a manner that does not necessarily render them misleading, then it is incumbent upon the representee to prove that the context in which they understood them was misleading.[1102] It is equally argued that even if the representor's interpretation was an unreasonable one, they would not be liable as long as they can prove that they honestly believed in it.[1103]

Another similarity is that *taghreer* and misrepresentation result from misstatements of fact, not simply expressions of opinion. For, as seen above, the definition of *taghreer* requires that one party deceives another by manipulative verbal or actual means, excluding statements that express (subjective) honest opinion. Equally, actionable misrepresentation results from misstatements of facts not expression of opinion.[1104] However, under the UK general law, if at the pre-contractual stages a party, who has special knowledge and expertise, makes a professional forecast or opinion, with the intention of inducing another party to enter into a contract, then there are grounds for misrepresentation – even if such forecast is made in good faith.[1105]

Third, there must be reliance by shareholders on the above manipulative means. Their consent must have been vitiated by *taghreer*. If however they were aware that such assertions/manoeuvres were false or deceptive prior to buying the shares, then *taghreer* does not materialise.[1106] Additionally, those claiming *taghreer* on the grounds of facts hidden from the prospectus must prove that had they known of them, they would have not bought the shares.[1107]

1101. This is seen most clearly when looking at Islamic jurists' approach regarding *taghreer qawli* or *taghreer* by verbal means as mentioned above. See, for example, *supra* note 1063.
1102. See, for example, *Shroeder v. Mendl* (1877) 37 LT 452; *Arkwright v. Newbold* (1881) 17 Ch D 301; *Akerhielm v. De Mare* [1959] AC 789; *Piggott v. Stratton* (1859) 1 De GF & J 33 at 50; *The Siboen and the Sibtree* [1976] 1 Lloyds Rep 293 at 318.
1103. See Treitel, *supra* note 1046, p. 310.
1104. See, for example, *Economides v. Commercial Union Assurance Co. plc*. [1997] 3 WLR 1066; *Bisset v. Wilkinson* [1927] AC 177, where the court, *inter alia*, held that despite its factual incorrectness, the appellant's erroneous statement concerning the capacity of land to carry sheep was that of an honest opinion, not a misstatement of fact. Therefore, no misrepresentation was found.
1105. In *Esso Petroleum Ltd v. Mardon* [1976] QB 801, the plaintiff, who relied on Esso's estimation of petrol throughput, succeeded in a claim of misrepresentation. Equally, a statement of opinion could amount to misrepresentation if a party who has close knowledge made the opinion knowing that the statement they are making was false. Per Bowen LJ in *Smith v. Land and House Property Corporation* (1884) 28 Ch D7 at 15: 'If the facts are not equally known to both sides, then a statement of opinion by the one who knows the facts best involves very often a statement of material fact, for he impliedly states that he knows facts which justify his opinion.'
1106. See A El-Saddeh, *Nathariat El-Aqud fi El-Bilad El- Arabia*, Dar El-Nahdah, 1974, pp. 254–65.
1107. See Art. 144 of the JCC.

The importance of reliance in *taghreer* is equally similar to its importance in actionable misrepresentation. For, as far as inducement is concerned, a representor would not be liable if the representee was not *induced by* and in fact did not rely on misstatements made by them. However, it must be noted that the meaning of inducement under the UK general law includes both: (1) having actually been induced to enter into an agreement; or (2) even though a representee may have entered into an agreement, they nevertheless would have not entered it on the same terms had misrepresentations not taken place.[1108]

The above position of the general law in the UK is however not too inconsistent with the concept of *taghreer*. For, it refers to the aggrieved party not giving their consent without the manipulative means, which would have partially or totally induced them to give such consent. Here, like the situation under *taghreer*, there would be no actionable misrepresentation if representees were not aware of, did not take much notice of misstatements, or if such misstatements were not essential in inducing them to contract. For example, in *Horsfall v. Thomas*[1109] and *Re Northumberland and Durham District Banking Co. ex. p. Bigge*[1110] there was no actionable misrepresentation, as the respective representees were unaware of the existence of the misstatements. In *Smith v. Chadwick*[1111] it was equally held that there was no misrepresentation as the misstatement was unimportant to the representee.[1112]

Fourth, in order to be able to rescind the contract, shareholders in Jordan must also prove the objective element of *ghubin fahish* concerning the shares bought. This element is independent from *taghreer* and is assessed objectively outside the will or intention of the contracting parties. Article 145 of the JCC states:

> If one party to a contract subjects another to *taghreer* and this results in *ghubin fahish*, the aggrieved party has the right to rescind the contract.

In its insistence on *ghubin fahish*,[1113] the JCC has distinguished itself from the majority of Arab civil codes.[1114] In such codes, shareholders only need to prove that *taghreer* seriously affected their consent and that they would have not bought the shares had they not been induced by *taghreer*. Here, *taghreer* becomes not too dissimilar to the French concept of fraud *Dol*, which takes place at the formation of the contract.[1115] For example, Article 125 of the ECC states:

1108. See *Pulsford v. Richards*, (1853) 17 Beav 87, as per Sir John Romilly at 96. See also *Pan Atlantic Insurance Co Ltd v. Pine Top Insurance Co Ltd* [1995] 1 AC 501; *JEB Fasteners Ltd v. Marks Bloom & Co* [1983] 1 All ER 583; *Atlantic Lines Ltd v. Hallam Ltd, The Lucy* [1983] 1 Lloyd's Rep 188 per Mustill at 201.

1109. (1862) 1 H & C 90.

1110. (1859) 28 LJ Ch 50.

1111. (1884) 9 App Cas. 187.

1112. Recent cases on inducement include *Museprime Properties Ltd v. Adhill Properties Ltd* [(1991) 61 P & CR 111] and *County NatWest v. Barton* (*The Times* 29 July 1999).

1113. This position is however identical to the position of the Iraqi Civil Code – see Art. 121.

1114. The Jordanian requirement is matched only by few Arab civil codes, such as the Iraqi Civil Code (Art. 124) and the UAE Civil Code (Art. 182).

1115. See, for example, Art. 1116, *alinea* 1 of the French Civil Code.

> A contract becomes voidable on the grounds of *tadlis*, when the manoeuvres exercised by one party or their representatives are of such seriousness that without them the aggrieved party would have not entered into the contract.[1116]

The position of the ECC is repeated by many Arab civil codes including the Syrian[1117] and Kuwaiti[1118] civil codes. For their part, Jordanian courts strictly follow the JCC in its insistence on the combined requirement of *taghreer* and *ghubin fahish*. They therefore will not award damages on the grounds of *ghubin yaseer* even with *taghreer*. Thus, refusing to uphold the contract and award damages at the same time.[1119] Indeed, from reviewing the rulings of the Court of Cassation in the past fifty years (1963–2011), one has not found a single case in which the Court has awarded damages for *taghreer* and *ghubin yaseer*. This approach of Jordanian courts is identical to its attitude towards the 'option of defect' or *khayar al-ayyb*, where purchasers can either accept the contract without compensation or rescind it with compensation.[1120] The Court of Cassation upholds this strict view:

> The Court finds that Art. 513 of the Civil Code states that if there is an old defect, the purchaser has the option to rescind the contract or accept it according to the agreed price. He *cannot* hold the item and *at the same time claim the depreciation of value*.[1121] [Italics added.]

In this respect, the above position of the general law in Jordan is not too dissimilar to that under the general law in the UK when shareholders had first to dispose off their shares in order to sue for damages. However, in contrast to the position under the general law in Jordan it is worth adding here that this historic position under the UK Common Law has long been addressed to the benefit of shareholders. For, existing shareholders in the UK are no longer required to dispose of their equity holdings in order to start civil proceedings against the company – as was established under *Houldsworth v. City Glasgow*.[1122]

Another marked difference between the general law in Jordan and that under the Common Law is that the Jordanian Court of Cassation will neither award rescission nor damages when *ghubin yaseer* is present. Rather, it will rescind *mu'awadah* contracts only on the grounds of *taghreer* accompanied by *ghubin fahish*.[1123] Reinforcing this, the Court stated in an important case:

1116. Law No. 131 of 1948.
1117. See Art. 126 of the Syrian Civil Code.
1118. See Art. 151 of the KCC.
1119. Although this is allowed under some opinions of the *Hanefite* School as mentioned above.
1120. See Art. 513(1) of the JCC.
1121. See CCD No. 196/91, *LSJ* (1992), p. 2104, at 2106–07.
1122. (1880) 5 App. Cas. 317.
1123. However, see CCD No. 121/73, 1973 *LSJ*, p. 1023, at 1023–29, where the Court did not require *ghubin* as the contract was not *mu'awadah*: 'To claim that the bill of exchange was obtained by fraud is different from claiming that it was obtained under duress. . . . The law has equated between both of them *in the sense of rendering the legal act void*.' [Italics added]

> After considering and re-examining the relevant provisions of the *Majallat*... we find that it is decided in Arts. 356 and 357 ... [that] rescinding a contract of sale will take place if it suffered from both *ghubin fahish* and *taghreer*.... Given the fact that the appellant has based his claim for rescission on the grounds of *ghubin* [*fahish*] only and did not claim *taghreer*, the Court rejects such claim.[1124]

However, the above requirement of *ghubin fahish* is one of the clearest distinctions between the general law in Jordan and the general law in the UK. For, the general law in the UK does not prescribe such a requirement. But, what about the question of bars to rescission?

1.3.3. Bars to Rescission: Comparative UK and Jordanian Aspects

As far as bars to rescission are concerned, one says that they are not too dissimilar to those under the general law in the UK, especially as the Court of Cassation has ruled on many occasions that injured parties must not cause the injury or contribute to it.[1125] Here, the main limitation to rescission generally relates to *restitutio in integrum*, as parties to a contract must be restored to the position they were in, had the contract not existed. In this context, *restitutio in integrum* may become impossible if disposal of shares takes place before investors have become aware of the misrepresentation.

As far as the JCC is concerned, one says that although there is no direct answer to the question of what happens if shares were disposed off before the buyer becomes aware of *ghubin fahish* accompanied with *taghreer*, one says that two provisions in the JCC remain of interest here. The first is Article 150, which states that the right to rescind a contract would be lost if the buyer has disposed of the subject matter in a manner that indicates that they have allowed the contract. The inference here is that such disposition would have taken place with the knowledge that *ghubin fahish* and *taghreer* have taken place. This is especially as the JCC does not seem to be absolute, denying the right of rescission whether or not the buyer has known of the *taghreer* accompanied with *ghubin fahish*:

> The right to rescind the contract induced by *taghreer* accompanied by *ghubin fahish* is lost and the contract becomes binding ... if the subject matter had been consumed or disposed of (wholly or partially) in a manner that indicates that the buyer has allowed the contract ...[1126]

The second provision is Article 248, which states that if rescission becomes impossible due to the fact that it is no longer feasible to put the contracting parties in the

1124. CCD No. 414/76, 1977 *LSJ*, p. 492, at 494–95.
1125. See, for example, CCD No. 510/95, *LSJ* (1995), p. 3402.
1126. Article 150 of the JCC.

position in which they were (as is the case above), then the JCC awards damages for the financial loss incurred:

> If the contract was rescinded then the contracting parties must be put in the position in which they were before the contract. If that was impossible then the court may order damages instead.[1127]

So, given the above, one argues that if shares were disposed off before the buyer knew of *taghreer* accompanied with *ghubin fahish* then such a buyer would be entitled to damages. However, the burden of proof in these circumstances would be on the buyer to prove their lack of knowledge of *taghreer* before they disposed of the shares. Moreover, there is nothing in the JCC that specifically states that considerable depreciation in shares' value will bar rescission when it is still possible to return them – as long as the buyer has not allowed the contract with their knowledge of *taghreer* accompanied by *ghubin fahish.*

The above is incidentally the broad view under the general law in the UK, which does not necessarily bar rescission if shares have suffered considerable depreciation in their value. For example, in *Armstrong v. Jackson,*[1128] McCardie J stated that: *It is only . . . where the plaintiff has sustained loss by the inferiority of the subject matter or a substantial fall in its value that he will desire to exert his power of rescission . . .* [1129] Commenting that barring rescission in certain occasions of depreciation of value can be undesirable, McCardie J added, *If mere deterioration of the subject matter negatived the right to rescind, the doctrine of rescission would become a vain thing.*[1130]

Similar to the position under the general law in the UK,[1131] Jordanian shareholders will also lose their right to rescind the contract if time lapses, as this is seen as an implicit evidence of affirmation. However, the JCC grants shareholders one year to effect rescission:

> Rescission cases . . . shall not be heard by court if a year lapsed since the delivery of the subject matter.[1132]

This period of one year is long and can equally jeopardise *bona fide* transactions, as shares may by then have exchanged hands several times over. This raises the prospect of more claims for rescission, thus further diluting transactional stability. However, a difference between the general law in Jordan and that of the UK is that

1127. Article 248. *Ibid.*
1128. [1917] 2 KB 822.
1129. *Ibid.*, at 829.
1130. *Ibid.* See also *Smith New Court Securities Ltd v. Scrimgeour Vickers (Asset Management) Ltd* [1996] 4 All ER 769, as per Lord Browne-Wilkinson at 774.
1131. See, for example, *Leaf v. International Galleries* [1950] 2 KB 86. Indeed, as Mellor J stated in *Clough v. LNW* that lapse of time 'without rescinding will furnish evidence that he has determined to affirm the contract, and, when the lapse of time is great it would probably in practice be treated as evidence to shew [*sic*] that he has so determined.' (1871) 7 Exch. 26, at 34–35.
1132. See Art. 493 of the JCC. However, a claim based on latent defect must be within six months from delivery, unless the buyer has deliberately hidden such defect. See Art. 521(1) & (2). *Ibid.*

the latter adopts a more flexible approach. For, it does not adopt a rigid application of time-lapse rule concerning shares.[1133] It instead assumes that there is no acid test that accurately measures what amounts and what does not amount to time lapse when shareholders wish to rescind a contract for the purchase of shares. This is especially as what is a reasonable time is a question of fact, the circumstances of which will inevitably vary between different cases.[1134] Indeed, as Baggallay LJ stated in *Re Scottish Petroleum Co*:[1135]

> The delay of a fortnight in repudiating the shares makes it to my mind doubtful whether the repudiation in the case of a going concern would have been in time. No doubt where investigation is necessary some time must be allowed... But where, as in the present case, the shareholder is at once fully informed of the circumstances he ought to lose no time repudiating.[1136]

Additionally, similar to the position under the UK general law, shareholders in Jordan are also likely to lose their right to rescission if the company is liquidated.[1137] Equally, if third party rights are involved,[1138] as a *bona fide* purchaser for value without notice of fraud under Jordanian general law can, too, pass good title.[1139] Moreover, similar to the position under the general law in the UK, shareholders in Jordan may not equally be able to rescind the contract if they accept dividends[1140] or sell their shares.[1141] There is also no reason why Jordanian courts should not equally deny rescission if, following their knowledge of *taghreer*, shareholders fail to remove their names from the register of shareholders[1142] – especially if this is interpreted as affirming the contract.

Having looked at the above, the next question to ask is how effective are shareholders remedies under *ghubin* and *taghreer*? This question shall be tackled next.

1.3.4. How Effective Are Shareholders Remedies under *Ghubin* and *Taghreer*?

The above discussion has revealed important differences between the general law in Jordan when compared to that in the UK under the Common Law. The most

1133. On lapse of time in the context of shares see, for example, *Scholey v. Central Ry of Venezuela* (1869) LR 9 Eq. 266, where a shareholder sought rescission after reading that another shareholder had succeeded in rescinding his own contract after learning of the misrepresentation.
1134. While in *Re Christineville Rubber Estates* [1911] WN 216, four months was judged to be the limit before time lapses; such period was not the same in the *Taite's Case* (1867) LR 3 Eq 795.
1135. (1883) 23 Ch D 413.
1136. *Ibid.*, at 434.
1137. See *Oakes v. Turquand and Harding* (1867) LR 2 HL 325. See also *Re Scottish Petroleum Co* (1883) 23 Ch D 413; *Tennet v. The City of Glasgow Bank* (1879) 4 App. Cas 615.
1138. *Lewis v. Averay* [1972] 1 QB 198.
1139. See Art. 248 of the JCC. Equally, s. 23 of the Sale of Goods Act 1979.
1140. See *Scholey v. Central Ry of Venezuela.* (1869) LR 9 Eq 266; attend general meetings: *Sharply v. Louth and East Coast Railway Company.* (1876) 2Ch D 663.
1141. See *Ex. P. Briggs.* (1866) LR 1 Eq 483.
1142. See *First National Reinsurance Co Ltd v. Greenfield* [1921] 2 KB 260, and *Re Scottish Petroleum Co* (1883) 23 Ch D 413.

important difference is that while the Common Law recognises both pecuniary damages as well as the right to rescind the contract, the Jordanian general law under the theory of *gubin* and *taghreer* seems to recognise only rescission. This however does not mean that Jordanian shareholders cannot recourse to tort law in order to recoup any losses incurred.

As shall be seen below, the position seems to be dissatisfactory as Jordanian general law rules on inducing a contract through fraud, negligence or mere omissions need to take account of the need that shareholders may need to keep their shares and sue for damages simultaneously. In order to achieve this, wider Jordanian examination of its Civil Code regarding this question is required. This examination is not only restricted to issues related to offering shares through fraudulent/negligent misstatements or mere omissions. Rather, it is relevant to assess how adequate the general law in Jordan is in addressing circumstances that may require that investors or buyers would like to keep the merchandise but sue for damages at the same time.

Furthermore, remedies under the general law in Jordan for shareholders induced by fraudulent misstatements in the prospectus are inadequate. For, as seen above, fraud alone in *mu'awadah* contracts will not suffice to rescind sales contracts (or award damages) and *ghubin fahish* is required. Here, in its insistence on *ghubin fahish*, the general law in Jordan differs significantly from the general law in the UK, which does not insist on such a requirement. It instead recognises fraudulent misrepresentation as a reason serious enough to justify rescinding the contract.[1143] Indeed, under the general law in the UK, claming rescission on the grounds of fraudulent misrepresentation is not contingent on excessive loss as required under the JCC, though it requires a high level of proof.[1144]

For their part, Jordanian courts' general approach is either the buyer accepts the contract in its entirety, or rescinds it and demand they are put back in the position in which they were before transacting. In other words, Jordanian courts will not generally accept that shareholders keep their shares and sue for damages at the same time. In this context, the JCC has adopted a less practical approach than the majority of Arab civil codes. Indeed, its inadequate approach in this area is less satisfactory even than those Arab civil codes which are equally based on *Shari'a*. For, such codes still award damages while *allowing* the contract if *taghreer* was accompanied by *ghubin yaseer*. For example, the JCC has no parallel provisions like that of the Iraqi Civil Code which state that *ghubin yaseer* and *taghreer* will entitle the victim to receive damages *in lieu* of rescission.[1145]

1143. See *Angus v. Clifford* [1891] 2 Ch 449; *Polhill v. Walter* (1832) 3 B & Ad 114; *Bedford v. Bagshaw* (1859) 4 H & N 538 (Ex); *Hughes v. Clewley 'The Siben'* [1996] 1 Lloyd's Rep. 35; *Downs v. Chappell* [1997] 1 WLR 426.

1144. As per Lord Herschell '. . . . fraud is proved when it is shown that a false representation has been made (i) knowingly, or (ii) without belief in its truth, or (iii) recklessly, careless whether it be true or false.' See *Derry v. Peek* (1889) 14 App Cas. 337 at 373. English law imputes to authors the natural consequences of the results of their actions. Per Lord Selbonre in *Smith v. Chadwick* [1884] 9 App Cas. 187, at 190.

1145. See Art. 123 of the Iraqi Civil Code.

As mentioned above, when aggrieved shareholders in Jordan decide to rescind the contract they will subsequently revert to the *status quo ante.* Once the contract has been set aside, they can then claim damages in tort,[1146] taking account of actual loss suffered and missed profit.[1147] However, the above Jordanian solution that focuses on rescission and excludes damages *in lieu* of it is extremely dissatisfactory. For, the threat of rescission by shareholders upsets the stability of transactions. There is also the risk that shareholders may try to rescind the contract if it has turned out to be unattractive to them. This is especially as, unlike the position under the general law in the UK, innocent misrepresentation does not exist in the Jordanian legal system where Jordanian courts can substitute rescission for damages.[1148]

Having looked at shareholders' claims under the general law of *ghubin* and *taghreer*, one discusses next their claims under the Jordanian general law of negligence.

2. LIABILITY FOR NEGLIGENCE

The central question here is how far has Jordanian law moved beyond liability for fraudulent misstatements to include liability for either negligent or innocent misstatements, and whether it ties remedies to the ability to rescind the contract. For, as seen above, under the concepts of *taghreer* accompanied by *ghubin fahish*, the aggrieved party has first to rescind the contract in order to be able to receive remedies.

However, one cannot state that Jordanian tort law renders examining the rules on fraud discussed earlier irrelevant. For, although shareholders can use the tortious route directly without basing their claims on *taghreer* accompanied by *ghubin fahish*, this practice is not entirely always guaranteed – at least at a conceptual level. It is true that on the surface it appears that the JCC has moved to including liability for negligent misstatements. However, a deeper analysis reveals that its position is based on incompatible sets of *Shari'a* and non-*Shari'a* legal grounds.

Indeed, because of the flawed structure of civil liability under the JCC, there is nothing to stop a majority of Jordanian judges with entrenched Islamist views to insist on characterising public subscriptions as essentially contracts of *mu'awadah*. They accordingly can insist (supported by the relevant provisions of the JCC mentioned above) that the only route that applies for compensation would therefore be *taghreer* accompanied with *ghubin fahish*. This argument shall however become clearer in the course of this chapter.

The picture is further muddled due to the JCC's failure to harness a consistent legal theory of civil liability. Indeed, as shall be seen below, the JCC simultaneously adopts two incompatible basses of tortious liability – oscillating between *Shari'a* principles of strict liability and secular notions that do not adopt strict liability as the predominant basis for tortious liability. For their part, the roots of the

1146. See Art. 259 of the JCC.
1147. See discussion below on damages.
1148. That is, akin to s. 2(2) of the Misrepresentation Act 1967.

law of negligence in Jordan are different from those of *ghubin* and *taghreer*, which arise under Islamic contract law as seen above – and therefore need to be addressed in a different subsection. Part of the problem here is also due to the fact that Islamic notions of tortious liability adopted by the JCC, which distinguish between direct tortfeasor (*mubasher*) and indirect tortfeasor (*mutasabib*), contradict with the very same JCC that adopts a negligence liability regime that does not take into account such distinctions.[1149] This argument shall again become clearer when one briefly touches upon the basis of tortious liability under *Shari'a* in the course of this chapter.

Moreover, what confounds matters more (at least at a conceptual level) is also the fact that Jordanian judges have chosen not to acknowledge that the JCC is deeply contradictory vis-à-vis the fundamental question of the basis of tortious liability. As far as the question of negligence is concerned, Jordanian judges have simply chosen to brush aside the inconsistencies of the JCC. They instead have adopted the Egyptian negligence liability regime – which as shall be seen below, is incidentally in contradiction with the JCC in this area.[1150]

In order therefore to provide a deeper analysis, the methodology here is briefly to introduce the concept of tort under *Shari'a*. One shall equally look at the constituent elements of liability that shareholders in Jordan need to establish in order to be able to sue for negligent misstatements in the prospectus. Having done this, one then examines the question of how effective shareholders remedies under Jordanian law of negligence are.

2.1. Brief Discussion of Tortious Liability under *Shari'a*

As the JCC has based its theory of tort on *Shari'a*, the objective here is to provide a summary of *Shari'a's* general approach vis-à-vis the question of tortious liability. One shall therefore introduce basic terminology and the basis of liability as understood by the *Majallat*. The term for tort under *Shari'a* is *fi'il dar*, which literally translates to 'harmful act'.[1151] There are many Islamic rules that forbid inflicting harm or *fi'il dar* against persons or properties.[1152] Tortious acts can be committed against persons (*ashkas*) or properties (*amwal*). The Islamic term for liability is *daman*, which has many nuances.[1153]

1149. See discussion below.
1150. See discussion below.
1151. See classical Arab dictionary *Al-Mughni Al-Kabier*, p. 1487; *Farouqi's Law Dictionary*, p. 259.
1152. That is, the Prophet's saying: 'No harm nor reciprocation of harm' [*Al-Muwatta'*, p. 529] and 'A Muslim refrains from harming others with tongue or hands' [*Sahih Al-Bukhari*, Vol. 1, p. 18].
1153. These include 'responsibility', 'accountability', 'compensation' and 'warranty'. Equally, a duty to pay a pecuniary reward against injury incurred upon tortfeasor. *Daman* is also synonymous with *kafalah* (suretyship), though admittedly wider in application. See Mosmar, *supra* note 510, pp. 38–39. The *Majallat* defined *daman* as: 'To compensate by providing like-for-like or market value.' See Art. 415 of the *Majallat*.

For its part, the Ottoman *Majallat* loosely bases tort on the notion of strict liability and the materialisation of injury without the need for fault.[1154] This is predicated on Islamic legal maxims adopted verbatim by the *Majallat* such as: 'No harm and no reciprocation of harm'[1155] and 'Injury must be removed.'[1156] *Shari'a* further subdivides tortfeasors into those who cause the injury directly (*mubasher*) and those who cause it indirectly (*mutasabib*), holding *mubasher* strictly liable while requiring *ta'adi* or *ta'amud* from *mutasabib*.[1157]

Ta'adi means that the tortfeasor is transgressing without a legal right.[1158] Negligence and omissions that result in injury will generally be considered *ta'adi*.[1159] *Ta'amud* means that the tortfeasor was intent on inflecting the damage or injury.[1160] The rules relating to *mubasher* and *mutasabib* are found in Islamic legal maxims embodied in the *Majallat* such as '*Al-Mubasher* is liable even if he is not *muta'amid*',[1161] and '*Al-Mutasabib* is not liable unless he is *muta'amid*'.[1162] If both *mubasher* and *mutasabib* are together responsible for a tortious act, then it is the former who is liable under the *Majallat*.[1163]

Finally, *Shari'a* requires financial equivalence between injury and compensation, based on the legal maxim that 'Injury must be removed'. This is achieved by either replacing damaged items or by offering their market value. The inference that has traditionally been made is that damages should not go above the actual loss.[1164] For their part, *Hanefite* jurists leave out lost profits from damages awarded to victims.[1165] When items cannot be replaced like-for-like, damages are calculated in relation to the actual value at the date of the action for tort. Jurists of all schools accept this view.[1166] The *Majallat*, too, limits compensation to actual loss suffered by injured parties.[1167]

Having briefly discussed tortious liability under *Shari'a*, one considers next the constituent elements of liability shareholders need to establish in order to be able to sue for negligent misstatements in the prospectus.

1154. Some authors mistakenly exchange 'strict liability' for 'personal liability'. See, for example, A Al-Qadir *Al-Tashri' Al-Jina'i*, Vol. I, p. 394, Wahbah, *Nathariyat Al-Daaman*, p. 251; F Fayd Allah, *Nathariyat Al-Daaman*, p. 158.
1155. See *Majallat*, Art. 19.
1156. See Art. 20. *Ibid.*
1157. See Zarqa, *Al-Fi'il Al-Dar*, *supra* note 506, p. 78.
1158. The tortfeasor who commits such transgression is called *muta'adi*.
1159. However, Islamic jurists have not developed a theory of duty of care. See *Al-Mughni* Vol. IX, p. 577; *Al-Fatawi Al-Khiariyyah*, Vol. II, p. 179.
1160. The tortfeasor who harbours such intent is called *muta'amid*. Islamic jurists have exchanged *muta'amid* with *muta'adi*. See, for example, Baghdadi, *Majma' Al-Damanat*, pp. 146, 165; Wahbah *Nathariyat Al-Daman*, p. 196. Cf. Sarkhasi *Al-Musbah*, Vol. XXVII, p. 22; Mhmassani, *Al-Mujibat wa Al-Uqood*, p. 197.
1161. See *Majallat*, Art. 92.
1162. See Art. 93. *Ibid.*
1163. See Art. 90. *Ibid.*
1164. See Ibin Abdeen *Radd Al-Muhtaar*, Vol. VII, pp. 184–85.
1165. See Mosmar, *supra* note 510, p. 210.
1166. *Ibid.*
1167. See *Majallat*, Art. 596.

2.2. Shareholders Suing for Negligent Misstatements in the Prospectus under the JCC

This subsection discusses liability for negligence. In order to claim damages, shareholders in Jordan need to establish the general constituent elements of liability, which are discussed next.

2.2.1. Constituent Elements of Liability

Constituent elements of tortious liability are found in Article 256 of the JCC, which states:

> Every injury against others renders the tortfeasor liable for compensation, even if such tortfeasor lacks discernment.

The above provision represents the general rule regarding tortious liability, which is strict.[1168] Article 256 is based on Islamic jurisprudence, a fact buttressed by the *Explanatory Memorandum*, which explicitly states that it is modelled on what 'is decided by *Shari'a*'.[1169] The *Explanatory Memorandum* equally refers, *inter alia*, to Articles 19 and 20 of the *Majallat* as the grounds for such a general rule of tortious liability[1170] – Articles 19 and 20 of the *Majallat* are formally incorporated by the JCC under Article 62.[1171] The *Explanatory Memorandum* identifies the elements of tortious liability as 'injurious act', 'injury' and a 'causal connection':

> In a clear and succinct statement, the above provision [Article 256] identifies tortious liability in its three constituent elements. It prescribes compensation for 'every injury'. Injury requires an action (or inaction) . . . and causal connection between them.[1172]

The above identification of tortious liability is highly significant as it imposes liability based on injury *not* fault. The JCC has equally adopted the *Shari'a* view on subdividing tortfeasors into *mutasabib* and *mubasher*. Article 257 states:

> 1. Injury takes place either through *mubasharah* [directly] or *tasabub* [indirectly].
> 2. If it [injury] was through *mubasharah* then the tortfeasor is held unconditionally liable. If it took place through *tasabub*, then *ta'adi* or *ta'amud* is required or that the injurious act has led to injury.

The above requires that *mutasabib* is either in a state of *ta'adi* or *ta'amud*, while it holds *mubasher* strictly liable. On the face of it, the meaning of *ta'adi* or *ta'amud*,

---

1168. The Court of Cassation occasionally interpreted Art. 256 as requiring fault, injury and causal connection. See, for example, CCD No. 380/88, *LSJ* (1990), p. 1406.
1169. See the *Explanatory Memorandum*, p. 288.
1170. *Ibid.*
1171. Article 62 of the JCC states: 'No harm nor reciprocation of harm. Injury must be removed.'
1172. *Ibid.*

in the Jordanian general law appears to be straightforward. For, concerning the former, the *Explanatory Memorandum* states that: 'Fault under [secular] law is equivalent to the concept of *ta'adi* under Islamic jurisprudence.'[1173] Concerning the latter, the *Explanatory Memorandum* states that: '*Ta'amud* refers to intention or wilfulness to inflict injury not the act per se.'[1174] However, when one looks at Jordanian judicial interpretations of *ta'adi* and *ta'amud*, one finds that they refer to a variety of often loose and confusing meanings. This is something that does not necessarily aid legal clarity in this area.

Regarding the meaning of *ta'adi*, the Court of Cassation widely accepts that it is akin to fault.[1175] Yet, it equally states that *ta'adi* is causing 'injury without fault',[1176] a 'constituent element of fault',[1177] acting 'without legal justification',[1178] or even 'negligence'.[1179] Regarding the meaning of *ta'amud*, the Court of Cassation accepts that if the inevitable result is to cause harm, then tortfeasors will be liable on the ground of *ta'amud*.[1180] Yet, it equally grants *ta'amud* a meaning akin to *ta'adi*, thus blurring the difference between them.[1181] *Ta'amud* is even occasionally exchanged for fault '... what is meant by *ta'amud* here is *mere* fault, not the intention to cause injury'.[1182]

For its part, keeping up with *Shari'a*, the JCC also prescribes that if an injury was caused by the combined tortious acts of a *mutasabib* and a *mubasher*, then the latter is liable.[1183] Article 258 states:

> If the *mubasher* and *mutasabib* are simultaneously responsible for a tortious act, then the *mubasher* is held liable.

However, the JCC later on contradicts itself, effectively setting aside Article 258.[1184] Under Article 265, it prescribes that if injury is caused by a number of tortfeasors, then all are liable according to their contribution to the injury:

1173. See the *Explanatory Memorandum*, p. 290.
1174. *Ibid.*, pp. 293–94.
1175. See, for example, CCD No. 209/72, *LSJ* (1972), p. 1237; CCD No. 129/73, *LSJ* (1973), p. 1029; CCD No. 350/73, *LSJ* (1974), p. 412; CCD No. 283/77, *LSJ* (1977), p. 1461; CCD No. 313/79, *LSJ* (1980), p. 319; CCD No. 1471/98, *LSJ* (1999), p. 1474.
1176. See, for example, CCD No. 730/99, *LSJ* (2000), p. 3221. Also, CCD No. 1664/97, *LSJ* (1999), p. 1310; CCD No. 34/98 *LSJ* (1998), p. 1479; CCD No. 218/98 *LSJ* (1998), p. 3637.
1177. See, for example, CCD 170/75 *LSJ* (1976), p. 202.
1178. See, for example, CCD No. 3027/99, *LSJ* (2003), p.778. Also, CCD 170/75, *LSJ* (1976) p. 202, at 204–05; CCD No. 658/91, *LSJ* (1992), p. 2096, at 2097.
1179. See, for example, CCD No. 466/93, *LSJ* (1995), p. 301, at 304; CCD No. 2/98, *LSJ* (1998), p. 3550.
1180. See, for example, CCD No. 213/72, *LSJ* (1972), p. 1241.
1181. See, for example, CCD No. 372/79, *LSJ* (1980), p. 627.
1182. See, for example, CCD No. 251/70, *LSJ* (1970), p. 923, at 933. Also, CCD No. 480/66, *LSJ* (1967), p. 49.
1183. The Court of Cassation has occasionally accepted this view. See, for example, CCD No. 988/89, *LSJ* (1990), p. 2238.
1184. The reason for the above inconsistent rule is copying the ECC's position under Art. 169. See Art. 169 of the ECC and its *Preparatory Works*, Vol. II, pp. 283–84. See discussion below regarding the Egyptian influence on the Jordanian concept of fault.

> If there are many tortfeasors responsible for an injurious act, then every one of them is responsible in a manner proportional to their contribution. However, the court, at its own discretion, can hold such tortfeasors *equally* or *jointly* liable.[1185] [Italics added.]

The Court of Cassation has ignored the contradiction between Articles 258 and 265, holding tortfeasors jointly or severally liable.[1186] However, there are irreconcilable conceptual differences between the notion of *mubasher* on the one hand and the notion of fault on the other. For, although fault might be relevant when dealing with *mutasabib*, it is not with *mubasher*, whose liability is unconditional. This means that negligence will be irrelevant when harm is caused by *mubasher*, as such category is always strictly liable regardless of fault. Yet, although this may be good news from the viewpoint of shareholders, this is not from the perspective of issuers and offerors whose activities would be stymied by such draconian application. Moreover, they cannot contractually exclude their liabilities beforehand, as this would be illegal under the JCC, which states:

> Every condition that stipulates excluding liability from injurious acts is null and void. [1187]

Although it has no firm legal basis, the approach of Jordanian courts however can be generally summarised in confining the application of the unconditional liability of *mubasher* to car accidents.[1188] One therefore argues that if there is a general approach that tentatively[1189] characterises the Court of Cassation, it is that it holds *mubasher* unconditionally liable when they are car drivers.[1190] Liability for negligence has therefore been applied in cases outside car accidents.[1191]

Having briefly considered the constituent elements of negligent liability, one turns next to discussing how shareholders can establish such elements.

1185. See Art. 265 of the JCC.
1186. See, for example, CCD No. 298/67, *LSJ*, 1967, p. 1198; CCD No. 963/86, *LSJ*, 1987, pp. 210–11; CCD No. 114/92, *LSJ* (1993), p. 1902; CCD No. 816/94, *LSJ* (1995), p. 1297; CCD No. 819/94, *LSJ* (1995), p. 1265; CCD No. 1037/94, *LSJ*, 1996, pp. 1042–45.
1187. See Art. 270 of the JCC.
1188. See, for example, CCD No. 157/79, *LSJ* (1979), p. 1494; CCD No. 391/79, *LSJ* (1980), p. 746; CCD No. 988/89, *LSJ* (1990), p. 2238, at 2240; CCD No. 453/90, *LSJ* (1991) p. 2089; CCD No. 466/93, *LSJ* (1995), p. 301; CCD No. 1198/93, *LSJ* (1995), p. 312; CCD No. 741/97 *LSJ* (1997), p. 4611.
1189. Drivers have occasionally been held liable on the basis of fault. See, for example, CCD No. 388/76, *LSJ* (1977), p. 453, at 455; CCD No. 965/90, *LSJ* (1992), p. 1052.
1190. See, for example, CCD No. 152/68, *LSJ* (1968), p. 582, at 584; CCD No. 14/75, *LSJ* (1975), p. 1222; CCD No. 388/76, *LSJ* (1977), p. 453; CCD No. 986/89, *LSJ* (1991), p. 1298; CCD No. 925/90, *LSJ* (1992), p. 1021.
1191. See, for example, CCD No. 251/70, *LSJ* (1970), p. 923; CCD No. 104/74, *LSJ* (1974), p. 1126; CCD No. 744/99, *LSJ* (1999), p. 3355, at 3361; CCD No. 1869/99, *LSJ* (2000), p. 1755; CCD No. 2572/99, *LSJ* (2002), p. 1746; CCD No. 2677/99, *LSJ* (2002), p. 1751; CCD No. 772/2000, *LSJ* (2002), p. 1782.

2.2.1.1. *Establishing Injurious Act*

In explaining what constitutes 'injurious acts', the *Explanatory Memorandum* refers generically to 'unlawful acts' or 'acts that breach the law', [1192] stating that tortious acts incorporate 'negative acts' whether they are deliberate or negligent.[1193] The *Explanatory Memorandum* leaves determining 'injurious acts' to the judge, who should be guided by the principle that:

> People owe a duty of care in their acts equivalent to what is expected of ordinary people.[1194]

The above interpretation of injurious acts by the *Explanatory Memorandum* however comes as a deep contradiction and in effect represents *the* source of inconsistency under the JCC. For, the *Explanatory Memorandum* without any prior warning is in effect talking about Article 1297 of the Austrian Civil Code, which is based on fault, rather than injury as stated by Article 256. This inconsistency which has serious legal ramifications is due to the simple fact that the draftsmen of the JCC were copying word-for-word the explanation of 'injurious act' provided by the *Preparatory Works of the Egyptian Civil Code*. The reason behind the persistent influence of the ECC on the JCC is attributable to the formative impact of the ECC on Arab civil codes. Equally, three of the five experts who had significant input in drafting the JCC were Egyptians.[1195] Here, the drafters of the ECC forwarded Article 1297 to explain the standard of care under the ECC.[1196]

Indeed, the stance of the draftsmen of the JCC is even more bewildering, given that tortious liability under the ECC is based on fault, *not* injury.[1197] Article 164 of the ECC states:

> Every fault that causes injury to others renders the tortfeasor liable for compensation.

The above is symptomatic of the conceptual confusion, which filters through to the Court of Cassation. The influence of the Egyptian legal system, which is based on fault not injury, was no stronger than among Jordanian judges, most of who studied

1192. The *Explanatory Memorandum*, pp. 288–89. If injurious acts are 'lawful', then there is no tortious liability. See, for example, CCD No. 143/71, *LSJ* (1972), p. 352; CCD No. 304/73, *LSJ* (1973), p. 1614; CCD No. 160/75, *LSJ* (1976), p. 192; CCD No. 242/75, *LSJ* (1976), p. 573; CCD No. 249/75, *LSJ* (1976), p. 599; CCD No. 435/76, *LSJ* (1977), p. 518; CCD No. 319/79, *LSJ* (1980), p. 746; CCD No. 656/85, *LSJ* (1987), p. 1953; CCD No. 1134/88, *LSJ* (1989), p. 205; CCD No. 244/89, *LSJ* (1990), p. 679; CCD No. 602/91, *LSJ* (1992), p. 2076; CCD No. 1455/96, *LSJ* (1997), p. 1536; CCD No. 373/97, *LSJ* (1998), p. 1901.

1193. See, for example, the *Explanatory Memorandum*, p. 289.

1194. *Ibid.*, p. 288.

1195. These were M Zaki Abdel Bir, M Mustafa Al-Manfalouti and Ali Al-Khafif.

1196. See, for example, *Preparatory Works of the Egyptian Civil Code*, Vol. II, pp. 354–55.

1197. This in turn is based on Latin codes, particularly the French Civil Code – Art. 1382.

in Egypt. Indeed, in one of the few insights into the legal thinking of Jordanian judges on this question, one clearly sees the full impact of the Egyptian legal system – no clearer presented than in a rare study on the subject matter by a Jordanian judge.[1198] What adds to the considerable conceptual legal confusion here is that, as shall be seen below, Jordanian courts have simply, on many occasions, taken the extraordinary decision completely to ignore the JCC. They instead apply *fault* as the criterion for liability for negligence not *injury* as prescribed by Article 256[1199] – aided of course by the contradictory commentary of the *Explanatory Memorandum* on what constitutes an 'injurious act' as seen above.

2.2.1.2. Establishing Injury

Tortious injury relates to harm inflicted on *persons*, their *properties*, legitimate interests or rights, whether or not they are *financial rights*. The JCC accepts that persons can relate to individuals[1200] or non-individuals alike.[1201] Concerning 'properties', the JCC accepts that they are everything that has a material value in dealings.[1202] Article 53 prescribes:

> Property is every item or right, which in dealings has a material value.

As to 'financial rights', the JCC elaborates that all items which can be possessed morally or materially can be the subject matter of financial rights. Article 54 states:

> Everything that can be possessed either materially or morally and benefited from legitimately, and is not excluded from dealing because of its nature or law can be the subject matter of financial right.

From the above, one observes that shares offered in a public offer are included in the definition of property under the JCC. However, including shares, as a recognised form of property, should not be taken for granted. For, this is not necessarily the unanimous view of *Shari'a*, particularly the *Hanefite* School.[1203] It has therefore been particularly argued that the JCC, unlike other Arab civil codes, has

---

1198. See, for example, Judge A Al-Essess 'Intention in Fault: As Fault is a Constituent Element in Tortious Liability', *LSJ* (1971), pp. 827–74.

1199. The requirement of fault in tortious acts was pervasive even before the JCC. The Court of Cassation often referred to tortious liability as 'fault liability', requiring 'fault', 'injury' and 'causal connection between them'. See, for example, CCD No. 3/71, *LSJ* (1971), p. 182, at 184. See also CCD No. 137/72, *LSJ* (1972), p. 717; CCD No. 258/72, *LSJ* (1972), p. 1285; CCD No. 320/72, *LSJ* (1972), p. 1522; CCD No. 384/72, *LSJ* (1972), p. 1604; CCD No. 334/75, *LSJ* (1976), p. 927.

1200. See Arts 30–49 of the JCC.

1201. Such as companies, public bodies, etc. See Arts 50–52. *Ibid.*

1202. See Arts 53–60. *Ibid.*

1203. Indeed, the *Hanefite* jurists are averse to loosening the definition of property, restricting it only to items that can be hoarded in a material sense.

expanded its understanding of property so that it would not be restricted by the narrow *Majallat* definition.[1204] However, as well as material harm, the concept of injury under the JCC also incorporates moral harm.[1205] The Court of Cassation has supported this view.[1206]

Tortious injury should be *certain*, even if it were to take place in the future.[1207] The victim must provide evidence of the injury,[1208] and prove before the court of substance that the particular injury is the direct result of the injurious act committed by the tortfeasor, not other factors.[1209] Shareholders can prove injury through all means of evidence,[1210] most common of which is experts' report submitted to the court of substance.[1211] The depreciation of shares' value due to tortious acts would be considered as injury. However, unlike the situation under *taghreer* that requires the combination of *ghubin fahish*, shareholders here do not have to prove that the loss in the value of the shares was excessive or *fahish*.[1212]

2.2.1.3. Establishing Causal Connection

To prove negligence, victims must establish causal connection between the fault of the tortfeasor and the injury they have suffered. Shareholders therefore need to prove that they relied on the negligent statements in the prospectus that resulted in

---

1204. See M Sewar, '*Ahkam Al-Uqood wal Daman al Waredah fi Qanoon Usuol Al-Muhakamat Al-Huqookiya*', *LSJ* (1980), p. 170, at 180–81.
1205. See Art. 267(1) of the JCC.
1206. See, for example, CCD No. 71/78, *LSJ* (1978), p. 1128; CCD No. 382/79, *LSJ* (1980), p. 915; CCD No. 29/80, *LSJ* (1981), p. 1239; CCD No. 247/81, *LSJ* (1981), p. 1922; CCD No. 656/81, *LSJ* (1982), p. 644; CCD No. 153/97, *LSJ* (1998), p. 2517; CCD No. 1260/97, *LSJ* (1998), p. 1147; CCD No. 1685/97, *LSJ* (1998), p. 131; CCD No. 2065/98, *LSJ* (1999), p. 3174.
1207. See CCD No. 273/75, *LSJ* (1976), p. 820; CCD No. 844/95, *LSJ* (1995), p. 3430. The Court refuses to accept future harm that is not certain. See, for example, CCD No. 131/74, *LSJ* (1974), p. 1173; CCD No. 2584/98, *LSJ* (2000), p. 2274. It draws attention to 'possible injury' and 'future injury that is nevertheless certain'. See, for example, CCD No. 1366/99, *LSJ* (2002), p. 2693, at 2698. On expanding the meaning of *certainty* to include events that are probable to a *very high degree*, see for example CCD No. 768/82, *LSJ* (1983), p. 625; CCD No. 480/86, *LSJ* (1989), p. 1980; CCD No. 1527/96, *LSJ* (1997), p. 1566.
1208. See, for example, CCD No. 256/97, *LSJ* (1998), p. 2568; CCD No. 200/99, *LSJ* (2000), p. 2483.
1209. See, for example, CCD No. 3/71, *LSJ* (1971), p. 182 at 185; CCD No. 334/75, *LSJ* (1976), p. 92. If injury was the fault of victims or due to their acts, then there may not be liability on tortfeasors. See, for example, CCD No. 216/79, *LSJ* (1979), p. 1686; CCD No. 741/97, *LSJ* (1997), p. 4611.
1210. See CCD No. 981/87, *LSJ* (1990), p. 987.
1211. See CCD No. 537/99, *LSJ* (2000), p. 1812, at 1816.
1212. For example, depreciation in the value of the car is considered injury [CCD No. 48/73, *LSJ* (1973), p. 975]; So is depreciation in the value of the land [CCD No. 2338/99, *LSJ* (2001), p. 2241]. See also CCD No. 97/84, *LSJ* (1984), p. 701; CCD No. 827/86, *LSJ* (1989), p. 2457.

the loss they suffered. Negligence here is based on fault, when people deviate from the obligation not to injure others:[1213]

> If he [the tortfeasor] deviates from this standard of behaviour with his awareness of such deviation, then this deviation constitutes fault, giving rise to tortious liability.[1214]

Therefore, if all the necessary precautions have been taken, then there is no negligent liability. The Court has accordingly ruled that if the hairdresser has informed the customer of the potential risks and has taken all necessary precautions, then there is no tortious liability if the hair was damaged:

> The hair treatment was undertaken by the respondent with the consent of the appellant, despite the warning of the former of the potential serious consequences. *The respondent has observed the necessary precautionary measures and has not committed a fault that renders her liable.*[1215] [Italics added.]

From the above ruling one argues that shareholders in Jordan can (under the general law) hold company directors liable for negligence.[1216] For its part, the Companies Law 1997 states that directors and members of the board of directors are responsible for all faults or breaches committed by them.[1217] They can also be held personally or jointly liable for the damage that results from their breaches.[1218] Shareholders can equally hold auditors responsible for the damage that results from their fault or negligence in auditing financial statements on which they relied to buy the shares. For, the Companies Law 1997 also holds auditors responsible before the company they audit, its shareholders and *all those who use its financial statements.*[1219]

1213. Duty of care pre-dates the JCC. Those who owe such a duty would be held liable for negligence if they 'do not exert the required efforts'. See, for example, CCD No. 267/65, *LSJ* (1966), p. 267; CCD No. 507/65, *LSJ* (1966), p. 396; CCD No. 31/66, *LSJ* (1966), p. 418; CCD No. 37/66, *LSJ* (1966), p. 611; CCD No. 46/66, *LSJ* (1966), p. 620; CCD No. 73/66, *LSJ* (1966), p. 652; CCD No. 171/66, *LSJ* (1966), p. 894; CCD No. 132/77, *LSJ* (1977), p. 1052.
1214. See CCD No. 809/86, *LSJ* (1989), p. 267, at 269.
1215. See CCD No. 1001/96, *LSJ* (1997), p. 1500, at 1503. Equally, as the damage to the goods was caused by an electric spark due to static electricity generated from strong hot winds, not the fault or negligence of the warehouse management, they were not held liable. CCD No. 1164/99, *LSJ* (2000), p. 682.
1216. Particularly if they bought the shares in good faith. Indeed, Art. 156(a) of the Companies Law 1997 states that directors' acts are obligatory vis-à-vis third parties with good faith. Here, the law presumes that such third parties are of good faith, and those who claim otherwise must prove it. There is equally no positive duty on third parties to search whether directors' acts are *ultra virus* or not. Art. 156(b). *Ibid.*
1217. That is, violating the Companies Law 1997, its regulations, the company's articles of associations, shareholders general meetings' decisions, and other relevant laws and regulations. Art. 157(a). *Ibid.*
1218. See Art. 157(b). *Ibid.*
1219. See Art. 201. *Ibid.* If the company has more than one auditor, then all are jointly liable. *Ibid.*

Regarding professional fault expected from professionals such as directors or auditors, the Court of Cassation states that it is based on the behaviour expected from a person with similar expertise:

> As far as professional fault is concerned, it has been decided that the benchmark against which it is measured is a technical one. Accordingly, it is a personal benchmark based on the professional standards expected from such professional persons. From the viewpoint of a particular profession and its practitioners, such a professional person is not allowed to commit the fault in question.[1220]

However, Jordanian law expects a reasonable standard of behaviour from victims in the sense of whether or not an average member of the public would have behaved in the same manner. Here, the courts will look to see if an ordinary person would have been reasonable in their reliance on the negligent statements to buy the shares. Nevertheless, Jordanian courts are not likely to demand that shareholders who buy shares possess special expertise that would make them understand financial statements better than the lay person.[1221]

Management is responsible for the negligent acts of its employees, when they are performing tasks related to their jobs.[1222] Employers however can hold such employees liable and recover compensation from them only if the injury caused was due to their negligence or fault.[1223]

As far as the quantification of damages is concerned, the JCC contains a general provision regarding damages for tortious acts that allows for lost profit.[1224] Article 266 states:

> Damages are valued according to the actual injury infliected or lost profit on the condition that it is a natural result to the injurious act.[1225]

1220. CCD No. 380/88, *LSJ* (1990), p. 1406, at 1409.
1221. Victims in tortious claims must behave like an 'ordinary person'. See, for example, CCD No. 466/93, *LSJ* (1995), p. 301, at 305. C.f., CCD No. 741/97, *LSJ* (1997), p. 4611, at 4615.
1222. See, for example, CCD No. 321/73, *LSJ* (1974), p. 366; CCD No. 429/79, *LSJ* (1980), p. 942; CCD No. 222/84, *LSJ* (1984), p. 737; CCD No. 224/84, *LSJ* (1984), p. 840; CCD No. 655/84, *LSJ* (1985), p. 413; CCD No. 343/87 *LSJ* (1990), p. 893; CCD No. 25/88 *LSJ* (1990), p. 1135; CCD No. 477/89, *LSJ* (1991), p. 845; CCD No. 1061/90, *LSJ* (1992), p. 1660; CCD No. 247/94, *LSJ* (1995), p. 2464; CCD No. 1952/97 *LSJ* (1998), p. 3099; CCD No. 2363/97 *LSJ* (1998), p. 1487; CCD No.2606/98, *LSJ* (2000), p. 874.
1223. CCD No. 406/79, *LSJ* (1980), p. 776.
1224. However, not only has the Court of Cassation fully upheld Art. 266 of the JCC, it has equally accepted that specific performance can also be part of damages. See, for example, CCD No. 86/73, *LSJ* (1973), p. 1004; CCD No. 211/73, *LSJ* (1973), p. 1334; CCD No. 72/77, *LSJ* (1977), p. 808; CCD No. 550/87, *LSJ* (1990), p. 638; CCD No. 616/99, *LSJ* (2000), p. 326.
1225. The JCC does not explain what it means by 'natural result'. This, for example, can be contrasted from the approach of the ECC, which states: '... losses shall be considered as normal result, if the injured party cannot avoid such losses by making a reasonable effort.' See Art. 221 of the ECC.

The Court of Cassation has applied the above provision faithfully. It has therefore established through numerous cases that compensation is measured according to direct harm, including lost profit and subsequent loss – as long as it is a natural consequence of the injurious act:

> It is agreed judicially and jurisprudentially that damages for *fi'il dar* [injurious act] are estimated on the basis of direct injury caused by *fi'il dar*. Direct injury includes subsequent profit and loss, which the injured party missed. The condition for the aforementioned is that it is a natural consequence to the *fi'il dar*, as prescribed by Art. 266 of the Civil Code.[1226]

Determining the amount of damages is incumbent on victims and is decided by the court of substance.[1227] However, the court of substance can reduce damages if it finds that the injured party has contributed to the injury.[1228] Shareholders therefore need to establish the amount of loss suffered. They again are most likely to rely on the estimates of experts to determine the level of damages.[1229] This can be awarded through a lump sum, or paid in instalments for a definite or an indefinite period.[1230]

2.2.2. How Effective Are Shareholders Remedies under Negligence?

The situation is no more satisfactory for shareholders induced by negligent misstatements or omissions in the prospectus than for those induced by fraud. For, shareholders in Jordan will need to recourse to the general law in order to establish their claims. Those induced to buy shares by negligent statements will be able to receive damages only if they establish fault, injury and causal connection between them. These, as seen above, are onerous requirements and the burden of proof is on shareholders.

In this context, unlike the position under the general law in the UK, the Jordanian general law does not go as far as the Common Law[1231] or statutory

1226. CCD No. 827/86, *LSJ* (1989), p. 2457, at 2459. See also: CCD No. 320/72, *LSJ* (1972), p. 1522; CCD No. 384/72, *LSJ* (1972), p. 1604; CCD No. 144/87, *LSJ* (1990), p. 41; CCD No. 268/87, *LSJ* (1990), p. 66; CCD No. 122/89, *LSJ* (1990), p. 2181; CCD No. 1969/97 *LSJ* 1998, p. 315; CCD No. 1211/98 *LSJ* (1998), p. 3200; CCD No. 2370/98, *LSJ* (1999), p. 2200; CCD No. 200/99, *LSJ* (2000), p. 2483; CCD No. 786/99, *LSJ* (2000), p. 3898; CCD No. 3027/99, *LSJ* (2003), p. 778.

1227. See, for example, CCD No. 830/86, *LSJ* (1989), p. 1752; CCD No. 2149/98, *LSJ* (1999), p. 1267; CCD No. 1775/98, *LSJ* (1999), p. 1505.

1228. Indeed: 'The court [of substance] can reduce compensation or not award it at all if the injured party has contributed to the injury or increased it.' See CCD No. 510/95, *LSJ* (1995), p. 3402; CCD No. 22/93, *LSJ* (1994), p. 2080.

1229. 'Determining the level of damages that is owed to victims is . . . a factual matter under the jurisdiction of the court of substance based on evidence, of which is experts' opinion.' See CCD No. 2021/99, *LSJ* (2000), p. 1840, at 1846.

1230. See CCD No. 1760/98, *LSJ* (1999), p. 1469.

1231. Where a 'special relationship' between the representor and the representee exists. See *Candler v. Crane, Christmas and Co.*[1951] 2KB 164; *Hedley Byrne v. Heller* (1964); *Esso Petroleum v. Mardon* 1976.

law vis-à-vis the question of negligent misstatements. For, the position of litigants who utilise the general law in the UK has long been improved since a statuary right of civil action for negligent misrepresentation was provided. This is especially as section 2(1) of the Misrepresentation Act 1967 does away with the requirement of the 'special relationship' under *Hedley Byrne v. Heller*[1232] – particularly pointed out in *Gosling v. Anderson*,[1233] which shifts the burden of proof to representors. However, it may still be difficult under section 2(1) to sue directors, experts or advisors as the right to sue under it extends only to misstatements made by a party to the subsequent contract.[1234]

Indeed, when compared with the UK's Common Law, shareholders in Jordan suing under the general law of negligence will not benefit from anything similar to section 2(1) of the Misrepresentation Act 1967 which reverses the burden of proof in favour of shareholders vis-à-vis the remedy of negligent misstatement. Neither will misrepresentors under Jordanian general law equally benefit from anything similar to section 2(2) of the Misrepresentation Act 1967 which gives the courts the discretion in certain circumstances to substitute damages for rescission. This is in circumstances where shareholders are claiming damages but the courts may suspect that the collapse in shares prices is due to deteriorating market conditions as opposed to actions by alleged misrepresentors.

Shareholders in Jordan equally remain vulnerable when they have been induced to buy shares by omissions in the prospectus. For, under the general law, they will be able to receive damages if they prove that such omissions were either negligent or fraudulent as seen earlier. The former requires that shareholders prove the constituent elements of tortious liability under the general law. The latter requires that shareholders prove that such omissions were 'deliberate' and that they would have not bought the shares had they known of the hidden facts. Here, unlike the general law in the UK, the Jordanian general law does *not* recognise innocent misstatements that result from inducing a representee to enter into a contract by a misstatement that is neither fraudulent nor negligent.[1235] This is especially disconcerting to shareholders in Jordan. For, under the Jordanian

1232. [1964] AC 465.

1233. [1972] EGD 709. However, the measure of damages under s. 2(1) is that of fraudulent misrepresentation. See *Royscott Trust Ltd v. Rogerson*. [1991] 3 All ER 294. This however is not without reservations. See, for example, *Smith Court Securities Ltd v. Citibank* [1997] AC 254; *Avon Insurance plc v. Swire Fraser Ltd* [2000] 1 All ER (Comm) 573.

1234. Or agents – making the principal liable, though. See, for example, Davies, *supra* note 18, p. 437. The position under the Common Law following *Hedley Byrne v. Heller* would be slightly more favourable to representees if they want to sue company directors in cases of negligent misrepresentation. It is not restricted by the statutory wording of s. 2(1). Representors will also disentangle themselves from liability if they prove they had reasonable grounds to believe (and did believe) that the statements they made were true. *Howard Marine and Dredging Co v. A Ogden and Sons*. [1978] QB 574.

1235. Historically, there were innocent and fraudulent misrepresentations. Damages were not awarded in the former, limiting remedies to rescission only. See *Heilbut Symons & Co v. Buckleton* [1913] AC 30.

general law, they will not be able to receive damages for misstatements that are neither fraudulent nor negligent.

However, the inadequate position of the general law in Jordan regarding the question of omissions is not too dissimilar to the general law of the UK, which often adopts a restrictive approach. For example, as far as omissions are concerned, the general law does not prima facie provide an automatic right to rescind the contract for non-disclosure, unless there is a duty of disclosure under *uberrimae fidie* contracts. This is so even if omissions take place in prospectuses – *Re South of England Natural Gas and Petroleum Ltd.*[1236]

Nevertheless, the UK general law remains generally more sympathetic to shareholders than the general law in Jordan. For, as seen in *R. v. Keelson,*[1237] if omissions render particulars and prospectuses (as a whole) misleading, then it grants remedies. Indeed, in *Peek v. Gurney*[1238] Lord Cairns even stated that: *There must, in my opinion, be some active misstatement of fact, or, at all events, such a partial and fragmentary statement of fact, as that the withholding of that which is not stated makes that which is stated absolutely false.*[1239] Equally, half truths inserted in prospectuses to mislead investors also warrant remedies under the general law in the UK – for example, as per Lord Macnaghten in *Gluckstein v. Barnes*:[1240] *Everybody knows that half a truth is no better than a downright falsehood.*[1241]

It is also questionable that aftermarket traders would be able to benefit from the Jordanian general law on negligence, as they would have bought the shares from other shareholders, not directly from those who issued the prospectus. Aftermarket traders who were induced by fraud will equally be unable to utilise the rules on *taghreer* and *ghubin fahish* to rescind the contract. For, as seen earlier, such a right is strictly given to the original parties to the contract or their guardians.[1242]

However, the above Jordanian approach is not too dissimilar to the general law in the UK regarding aftermarket traders. For, admittedly, the restrictive rule in *Peek v. Gurney*[1243] was somewhat tempered in *Andrews v. Mockford.*[1244] But, it must be cautioned that the application of *Andrews v. Mockford* is limited to cases with similar facts. Indeed, the position has only slightly changed since

1236. [1911] 1 Ch 573.
1237. [1932] 1 KB 442.
1238. (1873) LR 6 HL. 377.
1239. *Ibid.*, at 403.
1240. [1900] AC 240 HL.
1241. *Ibid.*, at 250–51.
1242. Under *taghreer*, the right of rescission, for example, expires with the death of those who have the right to rescind. See Arts 150 & 248 of the JCC.
1243. (1873) LR 6 HL. 377. The plaintiff (an aftermarket trader), who bought shares in a company months after having obtained and relied on a copy of the prospectus, failed to rescind the contract when the prospectus turned out to be fraudulent.
1244. [1892] 2 QB 372. For, the Court of Appeal here held that the existence of other documents was an evidence of issuers' intention to extend the misrepresentation in the prospectus to aftermarket traders.

Peek v. Gurney as the High Court in *Al Nakib Investments (Jersey) Ltd v. Longcroft*[1245] dismissed a claim for prospectus misrepresentation by aftermarket traders. Having said this, one nevertheless should not overlook the more recent case *Possfund Custodian Trustee Ltd and Another v. Diamond*,[1246] where Lightman J accepted the wider role of prospectuses at least in unlisted securities markets.[1247]

Added to the above, is the JCC's inherent contradiction concerning the basis of liability, in terms of whether it is strict or not, as evidenced by Article 256 and the conflicting interpretations of the *Explanatory Memorandum*. This, as seen earlier, impacts on applying negligent liability, particularly on *mubasher*, whose liability is unconditional. For, this implies that negligence will be irrelevant when caused by *mubasher*, as such category is always strictly liable regardless of fault. Indeed, the JCC's attempts at constructing a homogeneous legal system of tortious liability were almost doomed from the start due to the many inconsistencies discussed earlier. Neither has the Court of Cassation resolved these inconsistencies, opting instead to ignore them altogether.

3. CONCLUSION

One examined above how far does the general law in Jordan go in protecting shareholders induced to buy shares by fraudulent, negligent statements or omissions. The investigation has shown that there are no simplistic answers. For, although the Jordanian general law appears to have moved towards including liability for negligent misstatements (without necessarily tying remedies to the ability to rescind the contract), the legal basis for such a move remains at best precarious. Indeed as mentioned earlier, one cannot state that Jordanian tort law renders examining the rules on fraud irrelevant. For, although it was seen that shareholders could use the tortious route directly without basing their claims on *taghreer* accompanied by *ghubin fahish*, this practice was not entirely always guaranteed at a conceptual level.

Because of the flawed structure of civil liability under the JCC, Jordanian judges with entrenched Islamist views can potentially insist on characterising contracts for the sale of shares as *mu'awadah* contracts – demanding that the only route for compensation would be *taghreer* accompanied by *ghubin fahish*. Indeed, it is quite conceivable that such judges may become more literal in applying the JCC –particularly Articles 145, 256-57, all of which contain the seeds of conceptual contradictions.

This is because the JCC simultaneously adopts two incompatible bases of tortious liability. Indeed, part of the problem here is also due to the fact that Islamic notions of tortious liability adopted by the JCC, which distinguish between direct tortfeasor (*mubasher*) and indirect tortfeasor (*mutasabib*), contradict with the very

1245. [1990] 1 WLR 1390.
1246. [1996] 2 All ER 774.
1247. *Ibid.*, at 788.

same JCC. For, it adopts a negligence regime that does not often take into account such distinctions.

Neither has the JCC moved far enough to provide remedies for shareholders who have been induced to buy shares by innocent misstatements in the prospectus. Added to this is the fact that Jordanian general law denies granting damages *in lieu* of rescission when shareholders are induced to buy shares by fraudulent misstatements in the prospectus. This is especially as Jordanian general law and the Court of Cassation will insist on the buyer either allowing the contract without remedies, or rescinding it with the right to apply for damages. There are however three solutions to addressing all the above.

The *first* is fundamentally to reform the JCC in a manner that removes problematic provisions (such as Articles 145, 256, 257) and makes it consistent with other Arab civil codes. For, the majority of such civil codes do not require that *taghreer* is accompanied by *ghubin fahish* and will offer damages/rescission upon proof of fraud. They equally, construct a more consistent tortious liability regime based on fault. Thus, removing the confusing twin-liability system of *mubasher* and *mutasabib*. However, such a reform may prove difficult due to the political sensitivity of appearing to be de-Islamising the JCC – especially by abolishing Article 256, which is seen as *Shari'a's* general rule on tortious liability.

The *second* solution would however be to look within *Shari'a* itself to find rules that are more accommodating to modern needs. For example, as seen earlier, some Islamic exegetes are agreeable to granting damages and/or rescission on the grounds of fraud alone, if such fraud was sophisticated enough to vitiate consent. This as mentioned earlier is applied successfully in the Iraqi Civil Code, which is equally based on *Shari'a*. However, an attempt such as this may in the end prove to be limited in its reach. For, modern notions of civil liability may not necessarily always go in tandem with *Shari'a*, which addressed different historical needs and less complicated legal relations.

The *third* solution would be to bypass the JCC altogether by enacting specialised securities laws. Such securities laws would construct a civil liability regime that provides a clearer basis of liability together with awarding damages, without shareholders having to rescind the contract. Equally, to demand less onerous requirements for proving negligent misstatements or omissions. However, although this may offer immediate makeshift solutions, it is again based on precarious legal grounds. This is due to ignoring the inconsistencies that exist in the general law and the JCC, as well as the wider juridical risks that were discussed in Chapter 6.

As precarious as it may be, Jordanian policy makers have opted for the third solution. One shall therefore in Chapter 11 look at the liability regime constructed by Jordanian securities laws to examine how successful they are in addressing the problems discussed in this chapter.

Chapter 11

Regulatory Liabilities for Misleading or Inaccurate Disclosure: Selected Comparative Aspects with the UK

INTRODUCTION

Chapter 10 assessed the general law in Jordan in terms of how inadequate it is in protecting shareholders induced to buy shares by misleading or inaccurate information in the prospectus. Chapter 11 now concludes this book by looking at available remedies under the new Jordanian regulatory regime. There is however still no judicial involvement at this stage that would illuminate on how the SA 2002 (which came into force on 31 December 2002) may be applied by Jordanian courts. For, no cases have yet been brought by shareholders claiming compensation for being induced to buy shares by misleading or inaccurate statements. However, from analysing its relevant provisions one argues that aggrieved shareholders' position has improved under the SA 2002.

In order to present a rounded assessment of the Jordanian regulatory regime in this area, one shall look at the civil and criminal liability regimes that arise under the SA 2002 when offerors, issuers etc., get ahead of the prospectus by offering shares to the public without having published a prospectus. Thus, *diluting the impact of the prospectus*. Equally, when they provide information that is misleading or inaccurate. Thus, *undermining the informational probity of the prospectus*. The discussion here shall also look at the administrative remedies, which the SA 2002 grants to the JSC. In order to give a wider comparative picture, when assessing the Jordanian regulatory regime, reference shall be made to the UK regulatory system.

1. CIVIL LIABILITY

This subsection looks at the civil liability regime constructed under the SA 2002 and subsequent regulations. It first looks at the civil liability regime for *diluting* the impact of the prospectus before looking at the civil consequences for *undermining* its informational integrity.

1.1. Civil Liability for Diluting the Impact of the Prospectus

The Jordanian regulatory regime now creates civil liability for diluting the impact of the prospectus. This new regime is somewhat similar to the one created under the UK regulatory regime. Both, the SA 2002 and the FSMA prescribe publishing the prospectus before offering shares to the public. For its part, the Jordanian civil liability regime is a two-staged one.

Under Article 42(4), the SA 2002 first prescribes that offering shares to the public through a public offer without the prospectus or *nasharat el-esdar* having become effective constitutes a 'breach of this Act'.[1248] Then, it under Article 110(f) declares that those found committing a 'breach of the Act', either because of *intentional* actions or due to *negligence*, would be liable for damages incurred by such a breach.[1249] The liability regime constructed here is not a strict one, as Article 110(f) clearly excludes actions that are neither intentional nor negligent. So, generally speaking, if the offerors' actions were, for example, accidental or innocent then there is no liability under the Jordanian liability regime constructed under Article 110(f). However, liability here would arise under Jordanian law of tort.

The elements of liability here involve offering shares to the public without the prospectus having become *effective*.[1250] Anyone offering shares to the public without the prospectus having become effective is civilly liable. However, if the offer of shares was not public (e.g., through a private placement), then there is no liability. Shareholders need to prove they have lost financially due to issuers' offering shares to the public without the prospectus having become effective.

For its part, the UK gives a direct statutory civil action to shareholders who suffer financial loss due to the non-publication of the prospectus.[1251] Here, section 85 of the FSMA renders those who offer shares to the public in the UK (before the required prospectus is published) civilly liable, at the suit of investors who suffer loss as a result.[1252]

1248. Article 42(4) of the SA 2002 states: 'The following constitutes a breach of this Act: . . . (4) the person who sells securities through a public offer without an effective *nasharat el-esdar* [prospectus].'

1249. Article 110(f) states: 'A person who is convicted of a violation, whether intentional or negligent shall be held liable for the damages incurred commensurate to the amount of loss suffered or profit made.' *Ibid.*

1250. See Art. 3. *Ibid.*

1251. Section 85(1) of the FSMA states: 'It is unlawful for transferable securities to which this subsection applies to be offered to the public in the United Kingdom unless an approved prospectus has been made available to the public before the offer is made.'

1252. Section 85(4) of the FSMA, *inter alia*, states: 'A contravention . . . is actionable, at the suit of a person who suffers loss as a result of the contravention, subject to the defences and other incidents applying to actions for breach of statutory duty.' Those who equally fail to publish supplementary listing particulars are also subject to civil liability. See s. 90(4). *Ibid.*

1.2. Civil Liability for Undermining the Informational Probity of the Prospectus

Jordanian securities laws now impose civil liability on those who undermine the informational integrity of the prospectus. SA 2002 contains Article 111(b), which grants an independent cause of action to shareholders induced to buy shares by inaccurate information or misstatements in the prospectus:

> Every investor who has suffered financial loss due to inaccuracy or incompletion of disclosure contained in *nasharat el-esdar* [prospectus], its attachments or reports that should be submitted to the Commission in compliance with this Act, can ask any person who singed such documents for damages incurred. This is on the condition that he proves the following:
>
> 1. That *nasharat el-esdar*, its attachments or reports did not contain *material information* which is essential for reaching a suitable decision regarding buying, selling or retaining thc securities concerned.
> 2. That *nasharat el-esdar*, its attachments or reports contains misleading or inaccurate statements, which has *influenced the decision* regarding buying, selling or retaining the securities concerned.[1253] [Italics added.]

Additionally, Annex I to the *Instructions of Issuance & Registration of Securities Law (2005)* contains a mandatory proviso in which investors state that they do not forgo their legal remedies for damages that they may incur due to their subscription in the shares offered. However, similar to the position under Article 111(b), such investors must also prove reliance on the prospectus when making their investment decision to purchase the shares:

> I do not forgo my legal right to sue the [issuing] company for damages that I sustain due to the insertion of incorrect or incomplete information in the prospectus or as a result of omitting information that influence my decision to subscribe to the shares . . . [1254]

The above represents an improvement from the position under the general law, which as seen in Chapter 10, is inadequate to protect shareholders induced to buy shares by misleading or inaccurate statements. For, it shifts the burden of proof to defendants to disprove their negligence or intent. This is especially as, in order to receive compensation under the general law, the burden of proof is on shareholders in Jordan to prove that the acts of defendants were either negligent or fraudulent.

The position of the SA 2002 is also an improvement on the SA 1997, which never tackled the question of civil remedies for misleading or inaccurate disclosure as such. All the SA 1997 contained was Article 70(f), which compensated for 'breaches of the Act' that were either *intentional* or *negligent*.[1255] For their part,

1253. Article 111(b) of the SA 2002.

1254. See Annex I to the *Instructions of Issuance & Registration of Securities Law (2005)*.

1255. Article 70(f) of the SA 1997 stated: 'A person who is convicted of a violation, whether intentional or negligent shall be held liable for the damages incurred commensurate to the amount of loss suffered or profit made.'

as shall be seen below, Jordanian courts are most likely to accept disproving negligence by defendants as a defence when applying Article 111(b).

As far as Article 111(b) of SA 2002 is concerned, aggrieved shareholders must prove three constituent limbs of liability:

(1) That *nasharat el-esdar*, its attachments or reports contain misleading or inaccurate statements.[1256] Here, the burden is on aggrieved shareholders to prove the inaccuracy of such information – who in turn are likely to rely on experts' reports.[1257]
(2) The above misleading or inaccurate statements are *material*.[1258] The SA 2002 explains that 'material information' refers to any incident or information that impacts on investors' decisions in terms of whether to buy the security, keep it, sell it or deal with it in any manner.[1259] Here, shareholders must establish that they have *relied* on such information when they bought the shares.[1260]
(3) Aggrieved shareholders must also prove that they have suffered financial loss due to such misleading or inaccurate disclosure, which *induced* them to buy the shares.[1261] They, however, have to make their claim within two years from when the prospectus became effective, after having been properly submitted to the JSC.[1262]

Additionally, Article 111(b) also widens the scope of regulatory liability to include omissions of 'material information'.[1263] In a similar vein, all 4 Annexes to the *1997 Issuance Regulations* contained the same provision, which specifically held issuers liable for omissions. The requirement here was that such omissions or 'deletions' would render the prospectus as a whole misleading.[1264] The same position is now equally espoused by the *Instructions of Issuance and Registration of Securities for the Year 2005*. For example, Annex I includes a clear statement that specifically

1256. See Art. 111(b) of the SA 2002.
1257. In order to expedite trials resulting from such claims, the SA 2002 prescribes that shareholders' claims receive Fast Track treatment from Jordanian courts. See Art. 113. *Ibid.*
1258. See Art. 111(b)(1). *Ibid.*
1259. See Art. 2. *Ibid.*
1260. See Art. 111(b)(2). *Ibid.*
1261. See Art. 111(b). *Ibid.*
1262. 'A person incurring damages shall institute the action for restitution before the competent Court no later than two years following: (1) the date of the sale, where the damages have resulted from sale of a security; or (2) the effective date of the prospectus or the date of filing the report or the date at which it should have been filed, as the case may be.' Art. 111(c)(1) & (2). *Ibid.*
1263. For its part, Art. 2 widens its understanding of its own concept of 'misrepresentation' to include 'untrue statements', 'omissions' or 'concealment of material facts' in the prospectus. It, *inter alia*, reads: 'Misrepresentation: [is] any untrue statement of a material fact, or any omission or concealment of a material fact or any other datum required to ensure that a statement made is true and accurate.' *Ibid.*
1264. Indeed, all four Annexes contained the following statement: 'The Company shall be fully responsible concerning the information contained in this Statement, and ascertains the non-existence of other information which deletion would render the information misleading.' See, for example, Annex II of the *1997 Issuance and Registration of Securities*.

says that investors do not forgo their rights of legal remedies for damages that they may sustain as a result of the prospectus containing information that is incorrect, incomplete or due to omissions.[1265] So, as long as omissions are material to the decision of shareholders (rendering the prospectus misleading) then issuers, offerors, etc., would be civilly liable under the SA 2002. Here, too, the burden is on defendants to disprove negligence or fraudulent intent.

Liability under the UK regulatory system differs from liability under the Jordanian regulatory regime in at least *four* major ways:

(1) The *first* is that under section 90 of the FSMA there is no requirement of reliance/proximity vis-à-vis fraudulent/negligent misstatements by those who have acquired the shares suffering financial loss due to such fraudulent/negligent misstatements or omissions in the prospectus.

(2) The *second* major difference between the Jordanian regulatory regime and the UK statutory liability regime relates to the treatment of aftermarket traders – in terms of those who have bought shares in the immediate aftermath of a public offer. In this respect, aftermarket traders are able to sue for damages under the UK liability regime if they suffer financial loss due to fraudulent/negligent misstatements or omissions in the prospectus – unlike the situation under the Jordanian regulatory regime, where aftermarket investors have no statutory recourse.

(3) Though not directly related to public offers, the *third* major difference relates to the newly enacted regulatory regime in the UK which has replaced the original section 90A of the FSMA. This regime addresses civil liability that results from misleading statements or omissions when discharging transparency obligations vis-à-vis annual financial reports, half-yearly, quarterly financial reports, interim management statements or some ad hoc announcements – something which is not yet addressed under the civil liability rules of the Jordanian regulatory regime.

    In this respect, the Financial Services and Market Act (Liability of Issuers) Regulations came into force on 1 October 2010, inserting a new section 90A and Schedule 10A into the FSMA.[1266] It, *inter alia*, extended the range of statements and markets to which the statutory regime applies. In this sense, the new *Regulations* apply to all issuers, regardless of whether or not having been incorporated in the UK, whose securities are admitted to a market situated or operating in the UK.[1267]

1265. Annex I to the *Instructions of Issuance and Registration of Securities for the Year 2005* contain an explicit proviso in which the investor 'Agrees to subscribe to the shares of the offering company and that [he] has received a copy of the prospectus.... That [he] has examined and understood the content. That [he] has accordingly completed [his] subscription in the shares. And that [he] does not forgo [his] right for legal recourse against the offering company due to any damages resulting from incorrect or incomplete information or omissions in the prospectus...'

1266. See P Davies, 'Liability for Misstatements to the Market', 5 *Capital Markets Law Journal*, (2010) p. 443.

1267. *Ibid*, pp. 444–46.

(4) The *fourth* major difference between the regulatory regimes of the UK and that of Jordan is that the UK regulatory regime now recognises the new liability to compensate for damages arising from dishonest delays in making announcements.[1268] It is worth mentioning here that much of the above recent legal developments largely resulted from the UK Treasury commissioning a review on whether the revision power contained in section 90B of the FSMA should be exercised – culminating in the 2007 *Davies Review of Issuer liability*,[1269] with the Treasury responding with a Consultation Paper in 2008[1270] and subsequent implementing regulation in 2010.

To elaborate on some of the above, one states that section 90 of the FSMA grants a right of civil action to shareholders who suffer financial loss arising from false/misleading information or omissions in the prospectus when buying shares. For its part, section 90(1) of the FSMA states:

> Any person responsible for listing particulars is liable to pay compensation to a person who has:
>
> (a) acquired securities to which the particulars apply; and
> (b) suffered loss in respect of them as a result of:
>   i. any untrue or misleading statement in the particulars; or
>   ii. the omission from the particulars of any matter required to be included [by relevant sections of the FSMA.]

As is evident from the above, section 90(1) of the FSMA does away with the requirements of the Common Law of proximity, causation, and foreseeability as seen when discussing liability under the general law in the UK. The parameters of the regulatory civil liability regime constructed under section 90 are:

(1) Investors should have acquired the securities to which the particulars apply. This means that the holder of such securities can be either 'primary' (e.g., who bought the securities directly in a public offer from the issuer or offeror) or 'secondary' (e.g., who bought the securities in subsequent trading and not necessarily in a public offer such as aftermarket traders).[1271]
(2) Investors have suffered a loss in respect of securities exchanged in accordance with the circumstances mentioned above.

1268. See generally Davies, *supra* note 1266, pp. 295–313.
1269. See HM Treasury 'Davies Review of Issuer Liability, Liability for Misstatements to the Market: A Discussion Paper' (March 2007). HM Treasury 'Davies Review of Issuer Liability, Liability for Misstatements to the Market: Final Report' (June 2007).
1270. See HM Treasury, 'Extension of the Statutory Regime for Issuer Liability', (July 2008).
1271. Section 67 of the Companies Act 1985 placed restrictions on aftermarket traders' right to civil action.

(3) The loss is a result of either an *untrue* or *misleading* statement in the prospectus,[1272] or equally as a result of an *omission* of information which the person responsible for the particulars should have disclosed.[1273]

Unlike Article 111(b) of the SA 2002, section 90 of the FSMA widens the ambit of liability, as direct reliance by investors on prospectuses is not required.[1274] This position, as seen above, can be contrasted to that under the general law in the UK, which requires plaintiffs to prove that they were *induced* by and in fact *relied* on misstatements made by representors. In *Pulsford v. Richards*,[1275] for example, Sir John Romilly stated that:

> To use the expression of the Roman Law . . . it must be a representation *dans locum contractui* that is, a representation giving occasion to the contract: the proper interpretation of which appears . . . to be the assertion of a fact on which the person entering into the contract relied, and in the absence of which, it is reasonable to infer, that he would not have entered into it; or the suppression of a fact, the knowledge of which it is reasonable to infer, would have made him abstain from the contract altogether.[1276]

Indeed, the requirement of *reliance* under the Jordanian regulatory regime, which is akin to the position of the general law in the UK, is a significant drawback. For, although Article 111(b) of the SA 2002 has improved shareholders' position who in the past would have had to rely on the Jordanian general law,[1277] it nevertheless does not go far enough. This is especially as not every aggrieved shareholder who buys shares in a public offering will be able to prove that they relied on the prospectus when they bought the shares. Indeed, Jordanian lack of attention to this important point defeats the object of regulating this aspect of civil liability by securities laws. For, the very reason behind tackling this area under specialised securities laws is precisely to bypass the requirement of reliance required by the general law.

Moreover, insisting that aggrieved shareholders prove that they actually relied on the prospectus when they bought the shares means that it would be difficult for aftermarket traders to receive compensation. For, such traders would have generally bought their shares on the secondary market (most probably for an inflated price impounding the inaccurate or misleading information), without having

1272. See s. 90(1)(a), (b)(i) of the FSMA.

1273. Broadly speaking, according to the FSMA, the 'necessary information' is the information necessary to enable investors to make an informed assessment. These largely relate to the assets and liabilities, financial position, profits and losses, and prospects of the issuer of the transferable securities and of any guarantor. They equally relate to the rights attaching to the transferable securities.

1274. The above grounds for liability are also applicable should the *untrue*, *misleading* statement or *omission* occur in supplementary prospectuses – subject to the same exemptions contained in Sched. 10 of the FSMA. Section 90(10). *Ibid.*

1275. [1853] 17 Beav 87.

1276. *Ibid.*, at 96.

1277. Which as seen above proved highly problematic.

necessarily seen or considered the prospectus. This is particularly significant. For, as seen in Chapter 10, the position of aftermarket traders is overlooked under the Jordanian general law, which effectively leaves them without remedies.[1278]

As far as the original version of section 90A of the FSMA is concerned, one states that this was relevant to transparency obligations enforcing the EU Transparency Obligations Directive.[1279] As mentioned above, in light of the *Davies Review of Issuer Liability* and subsequent enforcing legislation, some of the restrictions that applied in the past to this section have now been removed. These namely relate to excluding ad hoc disclosure requirements such as trading up-dates, notifications about contract wins, revisions (upwards or downwards) of earning expectations. In this respect, the *Regulations* apply to information published by the issuer of securities by 'recognised' means, or by other means where the availability of the information has been announced by the issuer through recognised means. It is also deemed immaterial whether the information is required to be published (by recognised means or otherwise).[1280]

Additionally, the original version of section 90A of the FSMA equally excluded issuers trading on non-regulated markets – for example issuers on AIMs were not covered. Breaking away from this somewhat rigid position, the *Regulations* now apply to securities that are, with the consent of the issuer, admitted to trading on a securities market, where – (a) the market is situated or operating in the UK or (b) the UK is the issuer's home state.[1281]

As mentioned above, reliance on such periodic statements need to be demonstrated by those who suffered loss. Additionally, those eligible to claim compensation were restricted to those who acquired the shares – thus excluding sellers, holders and non-acquirers of shares.[1282] The basic framework for issuer liability under the *Regulations* remains the same requiring fraud/recklessness and dishonest

1278. Neither will aftermarket traders be able to receive compensation if such prospectuses equally contained omissions unless they prove that they too have relied on the prospectus.

1279. 2004/109/EC.

1280. See para. 2(1)(a)(b) & (2) of the Financial Services and Market Act (Liability of Issuers) Regulations. [There is however an evident error in the enumeration in the *Regulations* as this should be para. 2. Instead it erroneously appeared as para. 4.] As far as 'recognised' means are concerned, the *Regulations* state: 'The following are 'recognised means' – (a) a recognised information service; (b) other means required or authorised to be used to communicate information to the market in question, or to the public, when a recognised information service is unavailable.' As far as 'recognised information service' is concerned, the *Regulations* state: 'A "recognised information service" means – (a) in relation to a securities market situated or operating in the EEA, a service used for the dissemination of information in accordance with Article 21 of the transparency obligations directive; (b) in relation to a securities market situated or operating outside the EEA, a service used for the dissemination of information corresponding to that required to be disclosed under that directive; or (c) in relation to any securities market, any other service used by issuers of securities for the dissemination of information required to be disclosed by the rules of the market.' See para. 2(3)(a)(b) & (4)(a)(b)(c), *ibid.*

1281. See para. 1(1)(a)(b) of the Financial Services and Market Act (Liability of Issuers) Regulations.

1282. See Davies, *supra* note 1266, pp. 446–48.

concealment of information when suffering financial loss due to omissions in such periodic statements. In this respect, an issuer of securities to which the *Regulations* apply is liable to pay compensation to a person who does the following:

(a) Acquires, continues to hold or disposes of the securities in reliance on published information to which this Schedule applies.
(b) Suffers loss in respect of the securities as a result of:
  (i) any untrue or misleading statement in that published information; or
  (ii) the omission from that published information of any matter required to be included in it.[1283]

As mentioned above, these *Regulations* equally for the first time recognise liability of issuer for dishonest delay in publishing information. To elaborate one says that issuers under the *Regulations* are now liable to pay compensation to persons who acquire, continue to hold or dispose of the securities, and suffer loss in respect of the securities as a result of such delay by the issuer in publishing such information.[1284] It however must be clearly stated that the issuer is liable only if a person discharging managerial responsibilities within the issuer acted *dishonestly* in delaying the publication of the information.[1285] They are liable in respect of an untrue or misleading statement and/or dishonest concealment of material fact only if a person discharging managerial responsibilities within the issuer knew the statement to be untrue or misleading, or was reckless as to whether it was untrue or misleading.[1286]

As far as the Jordanian regulatory regime is concerned, as mentioned above, there are no equivalent Jordanian provisions that address the above aspects of liability vis-à-vis periodical disclosure. Indeed, if issuers delay the publication of important periodic information (even fraudulently) and that results in financial loss, the regulatory regime appears to stand rather impotent. However, this does not mean that investors in Jordan will not have the right to recourse to general Jordanian law of tort to sue for compensation. But this, as seen above, is a rather complicated route and it would be a much more favourable solution if it was addressed *via* the regulatory regime.

Attention therefore needs to be given in Jordan to such aspect of liability in order to provide better investor protection in Amman for those who suffer loss due to fraudulent/negligent misstatements or dishonest concealments or delays of material facts when discharging transparency obligation on the ASE.

1.3. Persons Liable and Defences

The SA 2002 now states that shareholders induced to buy shares by misleading or inaccurate statements in the prospectus can seek compensation from ‘any person

1283. See para. 3(1)(a)(b) of the Financial Services and Market Act (Liability of Issuers) Regulations.
1284. See para. 5(a)(b). *Ibid.*
1285. See para. 5(2). *Ibid.*
1286. See para. 3(2). *Ibid.*

who signed such documents'.[1287] From the wording of the SA 2002, one finds that shareholders in Jordan have a wide range of potential defendants. This is especially as it now enlists the persons who should sign the prospectus when a public offer is made. These include:

(1) chairman of the board of directors;
(2) general director or executive director;
(3) financial director;
(4) company founders if it is being formed;
(5) members of the board of directors; and
(6) the auditor who verified the financial statements, which are included in the prospectus.[1288]

Such persons appear to be caught by the SA 2002, as it holds 'any person' who signs the prospectus liable for the financial loss caused to shareholders if loss results 'from incorrect, inaccurate or inadequate disclosure'.[1289] The only condition that the SA 2002 sets for responsibility here is that aggrieved shareholders must establish the three limbs of liability discussed above. However, if the person responsible for the incorrect, inaccurate or inadequate disclosure in the prospectus is a corporate entity, then members of its board of directors or board of executives, general partners and concerned employees are equally liable for the violation.[1290]

Jordanian regulations add further clarification and give practical expression to the above. For example, Annex I to the *Instructions of Issuance & Registration of Securities Law (2005)* states that the financial director (or chief executive officer), the general manager (or the chairman of the committee of directors), the chairman of the board of directors as well as members of the board (founders or partners) must all certify that:

> [We] take full responsibility for the correctness, accuracy and completeness of the information contained in the prospectus. [We] confirm that there is no

1287. See Art. 111(b)(1) of the SA 2002.
1288. Article 37(a) of the SA 2002 states:

> The prospectus shall be submitted in the written or electronic form specified by the Commission in accordance with the instructions issued by the Board, and shall be signed by the chairman of the board of directors or the chairman of the executive board and each of the chief executive officer or the chief operating officer and the chief financial officer of the issuer, in addition to the following: 1. If a company is in the process of being established, the majority of the founders; 2. If the company is a public shareholding company or a private shareholding company, the majority of the members of the board of directors of the issuer; 3. If the issuer is a limited liability company, the majority of partners; 4. The underwriter or underwriters, as the case may be; and 5. The auditor who certified financial reports attached to the prospectus.

1289. See Art. 111(b)(1) of the SA 2002.
1290. See Art. 110(e). *Ibid.* However the new *Amendment Law to the SA 2002* (mentioned below) maintains this understanding. It for example under Art. 12 (which abrogates Art. 110 of the SA 2002) states that: 'Unless proven otherwise, members of the board of directors, members of the board of executives, partners and concerned employees are vicariously liable on behalf of the corporate body.'

> information the withholding of which renders the prospectus misleading or the omission of which impacts on the decision of the investors in terms of whether to buy the securities offered – or equally impact upon the price of such securities. [We] affirm our commitment to provide the prospective investor with this prospectus before he accepts to subscribe in the offered securities and to provide the JSC with any information that may arise after the prospectus has been submitted to the JSC or after it having been deemed effective by the JSC.

As seen from the above, the list of officers responsible for the prospectus under section 37(a) of the SA 2002 is evidently more exhaustive than the one included in Annex I to the *Instructions of Issuance & Registration of Securities Law (2005)*. One however does not think that there is necessarily a contradiction as such. For, shareholders can sue all those included in the primary law and subsequent regulation. Indeed, what the subsequent regulation appears to do is to focus the minds of those who certify the mandatory statement mentioned above – which clearly has serious legal consequences in terms of potential civil liability should there be incorrect, misleading information or omissions that may render the prospectus misleading or inaccurate.

In addition to the above list, disclosure regulations in Jordan also require that a lawyer/legal consultant certify the prospectus – in the sense that the public offer complies with company laws, securities laws as well as the articles of association of the issuing company, etc. Equally, that the offeror does not face any existing or pending litigation.[1291] Furthermore, Annex I to the *Instructions of Issuance & Registration of Securities Law (2005)* mandates that an issuance managers (usually an investment bank) should certify the prospectus – in the sense that it was prepared according to the information provided by the offeror and that the issuance manager has no knowledge of any other information that would impact on the veracity, correctness, accuracy and completeness of information contained in the prospectus. However, this mandatory requirement has contributed to enhancing the role of investment banking in Jordan as prospectuses must be prepared and certified by an issuance manager.

The above list of persons liable under the Jordanian regulatory regime is however not too dissimilar to those liable for misleading or inaccurate information in the prospectus in the UK.[1292] These include issuers, directors of the issuer, and each person who has authorised himself to be named, and is named, in the particulars as a director or as having agreed to become a director of that body either immediately or at a future time. Added to this, is each person who accepts and is stated in the prospectus as accepting responsibility for it.[1293]

1291. See generally Annex II to the *1997 Issuance and Registration of Securities* and Annex I to the *Instructions of Issuance & Registration of Securities Law (2005)*.

1292. They are determined by Treasury regulations. See s. 79(3) of the FSMA.

1293. Paragraph 5.5.3 of the Prospectus Rules, *inter alia*, states: Each of the following *persons* are responsible for the *prospectus*:

   (a) the *issuer* of the *transferable securities;*

A noticeable difference here between the Jordanian and the UK approach is that under the UK regulatory system, a person may accept responsibility in relation to certain specified parts of the prospectus, or only in certain specified respects. This approach gives confidence, for example, to experts to state their professional opinions about certain matters knowing full well that their liability will not stretch beyond their area of expertise – in terms of what they actually certify. Additionally, in other cases where sometimes it would be difficult to delineate the responsibility of various parties to the prospectus, this approach serves as a means to 'compartmentalise' the prospectus in terms of the liability of different parties.

From the above, one finds that the list of potential defendants is quite wide-ranging in both the Jordanian and the UK regulatory systems. This is in order to widen the scope of investor protection due to the potential involvement of significant numbers of parties. However, a critique that can be levelled against the Jordanian system when contrasted to the UK is that the former does not pay adequate attention to the defences that can be forwarded by defendants.

The only ground for avoiding liability under the Jordanian regulatory regime is that defendants must establish that they had 'no knowledge of the violation' that resulted in providing incorrect, inaccurate or inadequate disclosure in the prospectus.[1294] Moreover, as observed in Chapter 10, liability under the Jordanian general law is based on fraudulent intent or negligence. Jordanian courts are therefore likely to accept the important ground for avoiding liability in the UK regulatory regime when defendants prove that they reasonably believed (and after having made inquiries) that the untrue or misleading information was true and not misleading.[1295]

Here, defendants in the UK must prove that they continued with their belief until the shares were acquired or until after the commencement of dealings

---

(b) if the *issuer* is a *body corporate*:
  (i) each *person* who is a *director* of that *body corporate* when the *prospectus* is published; and
  (ii) each *person* who has authorised himself to be named, and is named, in the *prospectus* as a *director* or as having agreed to become a *director* of that *body corporate* either immediately or at a future time;
(c) each *person* who accepts, and is stated in the *prospectus* as accepting, responsibility for the *prospectus*;
(d) in relation to an *offer*:
  (i) the *offeror*, if this is not the *issuer*; and
  (ii) if the *offeror* is a *body corporate* and is not the *issuer*, each *person* who is a *director* of the *body corporate* when the *prospectus* is published;
(e) in relation to a request for the *admission to trading* of *transferable securities*:
  (i) the *person* requesting admission, if this is not the *issuer*; and
  (ii) if the *person* requesting admission is a *body corporate* and is not the *issuer*, each *person* who is a *director* of the *body corporate* when the *prospectus* is published; and
(f) each *person* not falling within any of the previous paragraphs who has authorised the contents of the *prospectus*. . . .

1294. See Art. 110(e) of the SA 2002.
1295. Or omissions (if applicable) were rectified. See para. 1(2), Sched. 10 of the FSMA.

following their admission[1296] or listing.[1297] Additionally, issuers under the UK regulatory regime and in Jordan will be able to avoid liability if they can prove that claimants bought the shares with knowledge that the information contained in the prospectus was false or that it contained omissions that rendered it inaccurate.

The above however is not too dissimilar to the position of defendants under the general law in Jordan, where, as seen in Chapter 10, negligence is based on fault when people deviate from the obligation not to injure others.[1298] In order to avoid liability, it would therefore be a defence for defendants in Jordan to claim that they were not at fault. Indeed, as seen in Chapter 10, if all the necessary precautions were taken, the Jordanian Court of Cassation would find no negligent liability.[1299]

One therefore argues that there is no reason to expect that Jordanian judges would not apply the *criterion* of fault when they apply specialised laws such as the SA 2002. For, as seen in Chapter 10, the notion of fault features heavily as a constituent element in the liability of other specialised Jordanian laws such as the Companies Law 1997 – for example, liability of directors, auditors, etc.[1300] In this context, the Court of Cassation is likely to base the behaviour of professionals such as directors and auditors on the behaviour expected from likewise professionals.[1301] It would accordingly be a defence if directors and auditors disprove fault by establishing that they have indeed behaved in a manner consonant with the behaviour expected from persons with similar expertise.

However, the Jordanian regulatory system can benefit from the UK's defences regarding the question of when prospectuses contain experts' statements, which turn out to be misleading or inaccurate. Here, defendants in the UK must prove that such statements were made (or they reasonably believed that they were made) by or on the authority of experts with their consent.[1302] Defendants in the UK must equally have either continued to believe that the information was true until the time the shares were acquired,[1303] or that it was not practicable for them to bring to investors' attention that the expert was not competent or that they had not consented.[1304]

1296. That is, to the Official List in the UK. And they were acquired after such a lapse of time that the defendant ought in the circumstances to be reasonably excused. See para. 1(3)(a)(d), Sched. 10. *Ibid.*
1297. There will also be no liability in the UK if the shares were acquired before it was reasonably practicable for defendants to bring corrections to investors, or that they have taken all reasonable steps to secure that such corrections were brought to investors. See para. 1(3)(b)(c), Sched. 10. *Ibid.* It is also a defence if defendants reasonably believed that the change or the new matter did not warrant a supplementary listing particular. See Sched. 10, para. 7. *Ibid.*
1298. See CCD No. 809/86, *LSJ* (1989), p. 267, at 269.
1299. See CCD No. 1001/96, *LSJ* (1997), p. 1500, at 1503.
1300. See, for example, Arts 156(a) & (b), 157(a) & (b), 201 of the Companies Law 1997.
1301. See CCD No. 380/88, *LSJ* (1990), p. 1406, at 1409.
1302. See para. 2(1) & (2), Sched. 10 of the FSMA.
1303. Or for a reasonable period after the shares have been admitted to the official list.
1304. They will also escape liability if they took all reasonable precautions to secure that the fact was brought to investors' attention. See para. 4(2)(a)(b), Sched. 10 of the FSMA.

Defendants under the UK regulatory system will also avoid liability if they prove that before the shares were acquired, corrections had been published in a manner calculated to inform investors – or that they took all reasonable steps to secure such publication and reasonably believed that it had taken place before the shares were acquired. In order to extricate themselves from liability, experts can of course argue that they did not consent to their statements being included in the prospectus.[1305]

Another area that is equally ignored by the SA 2002 is issuers' defence when the prospectus contains misstatements quoted from official information. Defendants in the UK may not be liable if such official statements, quoted in the prospectus, turned out to be false or misleading. Here, defendants must prove that such statements were accurately and fairly reproduced, and made by an official or contained in a public official document.[1306]

As far as knowledge is concerned, persons responsible for listing particulars in the UK are under a duty to provide information about changes of which they are aware and it would be reasonable for them to attain such knowledge. However, in both the Jordanian and UK regulatory systems a director is not to be treated as responsible for any particulars if they are published without their knowledge or consent[1307] and on becoming aware of their publication they give reasonable public notice that they were published without their knowledge or consent.[1308] Additionally, defendants will not equally be liable if they can prove that the plaintiff had knowledge that the statement was false or misleading, or knew of the omission or the change.[1309]

Having looked at civil liability under the SA 2002, the subsection next shall look at criminal liability.

2. CRIMINAL LIABILITY

This subsection now turns to look at criminal liability under the SA 2002 for diluting the impact of the prospectus and undermining its informational probity.

2.1. Criminal Liability for Diluting the Impact of the Prospectus

The SA 2002 now makes diluting the impact of Jordanian prospectuses a criminal offence, something that was not criminalised under the SA 1997. In this context, Article 110(b)(2) renders it a criminal offence punishable by a prison sentence for

1305. See para. 1(4), Sched. 10. *Ibid.*
1306. See para. 5(a)(b), Sched. 10. *Ibid.*
1307. See Art. 110(e) of the SA 2002.
1308. See para. 6(2), Sched. 10 of the FSMA.
1309. See para. 6(a)(b)(c), Sched. 10. *Ibid.*

up to one year to violate Article 34(a)(1) and Article 42(d).[1310] For its part Article 34(a)(1) prohibits offering securities to the public without 'filing a prospectus with the Commission',[1311] and Article 42(d) prohibits 'selling securities to the public without an effective prospectus'.[1312] So, anyone who offers or sells shares to the public without filing a prospectus with the JSC or ensuring that it has become effective would be committing a criminal offence punishable by a prison sentence for up to one year. It must be mentioned here that a new *Amendment Law to the SA 2002* has now entered into its final stages in Jordan. Article 12 of this Amendment Law abrogates Article 110. However, as far as the prison stance mentioned above is concerned, the maximum limit of one year has remained the same.

The above is somewhat different from the UK, where the emphasis is on whether the prospectus was published prior to offering shares to the public. For, it is a criminal offence in the UK to offer new securities to the public before publishing a prospectus as required by the *Listing Rules*.[1313] The punishment varies between imprisonment for a term not exceeding three months or a fine,[1314] or imprisonment for a term not exceeding two years or a fine or both.[1315] Additionally, Jordanian regulations still do not address the question of advertising when offering securities to the public. This oversight is however addressed in the UK regulatory system, where it is a criminal offence to issue unauthorised advertisements.[1316] Persons responsible for prospectuses will accordingly be criminally liable if they issue unauthorised advertisements, if listing particulars are (or to be) published in connection with an application for listing. Consequences for contravening the above restriction result in a fine,[1317] imprisonment[1318] or both.[1319]

1310. Article 110(b)(2) of the SA 2002, *inter alia*, states:

> (b) Without prejudice to any stricter penalties imposed by any other legislation, and in addition to the fines specified in Paragraph (a) of this Article, any person violating the provisions of the Articles mentioned hereunder shall be subject to the following penalties. . . . Imprisonment of up to one year for violations of the provisions of Subparagraph (1) of Paragraph (a) of Article (34), Paragraph (d) of Article (42). . . .

1311. Article 34(a)(1) reads: 'No person shall make a public offer unless a prospectus is filed with the Commission, together with such additional information and data which enables the investor to make his investment decision.' *Ibid.*

1312. Article 42(d) reads: 'The following shall be considered a violation of the provisions of this Law. . . . (d) Any person who sells securities *via* a public offer without an effective prospectus.' *Ibid.*

1313. See s. 85(1) & (2)(a) and (b) of the FSMA.

1314. If summarily convicted.

1315. If convicted on indictment.

1316. See ss 21 & 98 of the FSMA.

1317. On summary, conviction not exceeding the statutory minimum. See s. 98(2)(a). *Ibid.*

1318. On conviction on indictment for a term not exceeding two years. See s. 98(2)(b), *ibid.*

1319. On conviction on indictment. See s. 98(2)(b). In order to avoid liability, defendants must either prove that: (a) the FSA actually approved or authorised the contents of the advertisement prior to their publication; or (b) they had reasonable grounds to believe that the UKLA authorised the publication of the advertisement. See s. 98(3) of the FSMA.

2.2. Criminal Liability for Undermining the Informational Probity of the Prospectus

Surprisingly, Jordanian securities laws commit a grave oversight by not criminalising actions that undermine the informational probity of the prospectus. Instead, as shall be seen below they are subject to administrative fines. For, when one surveys the newly enacted SA 2002 one finds that it fails to criminalise providing information that is misleading or deceptive. This, as shall be seen below, contrasts with the regulatory regime in the UK, which criminalises *intentional* and *reckless* acts that undermine the informational probity of the prospectus. For its part, the SA 2002 declares that submitting false or misleading data in any document filed with the JSC is a 'violation of the provisions of this Act'.[1320] It also equally declares the same concerning offering or selling securities on the basis of false or misleading data.[1321] However, despite this prohibition, the SA 2002 does not declare any of the above criminal as such. All it does is rather generically declaring a fine for all acts that violate the 'provisions of this Act'.[1322] Thus reverting this question to general criminal law in Jordan.

For its part, general criminal law in Jordan does not adequately address the question of undermining the informational probity of the prospectus. For, all it contains is the potentially relevant offence of 'criminal deception'.[1323] Criminal deception is dealt with by Article 417 of the Jordanian Penal Code 1960.[1324] It punishes all those who deceptively induce others to part with their monies through making victims believe, *inter alia*, in 'false projects or events, untrue matters, or creating hope in false profit'.[1325] The punishment here is a custodial sentence between three months to three years,[1326] and is doubled if the offender is an issuer who deceptively issues shares or bonds as outlined above.[1327]

1320. See Art. 107(a) of the SA 2002.
1321. See Art. 107(b). *Ibid.* This concerns: (1) the rights and privileges conferred by the security being offered or sold [s. 107(b)(1)]; and (2) the nature of issuers' businesses, their profit, financial conditions or future prospects [s. 107(b)(2)]. *Ibid.*
1322. Article 110(a) reads: 'Any person who violates the provisions of this Law or the Regulations, Instructions or Decisions issued pursuant thereto shall be subject to a fine of not more than one hundred thousand (100,000) Dinars, in addition to a fine of not less than twice the amount, and not more than five times the amount, of profit made or loss avoided by the person committing the violation.' *Ibid.*
1323. Less significantly through the offence of 'forgery'. See Arts 260–72 of the Penal Code 1960. The Court of Cassation treats forging foreign documents as forging Jordanian ones. See CCD 169/79, *LSJ* (1979), p. 1119; CCD 69/85, *LSJ* (1985), p. 1270. The Court however does not require that forged documents be done to a high standard, but rather enough to deceive lay persons. See CCD 118/80, *LSJ* (1980), p. 1570; CCD 840/98 *LSJ* (1999), p. 3227. The onus however is on the prosecution to prove that offenders intended to use forged documents to achieve their objectives. See, for example, CCD 24/71 *LSJ* (1971), p. 995.
1324. Law No. 16 for the year 1960.
1325. See Art. 417(1)(a) of the Jordanian Penal Code 1960.
1326. See Art. 417(1). *Ibid.*
1327. See Art. 417(2)(b). *Ibid.*

However, reliance by aggrieved shareholders on the above general provision remains highly inadequate. For, in order to succeed, not only Jordanian prosecution must first prove that the offender deployed the above deceptive means, they equally need to establish that they have done so with the *intention* to defraud shareholders.[1328] For its part, the Court of Cassation adopts a strict approach towards criminal intent and requires a high level of proof to this effect.[1329] However, although it acknowledges that 'criminal intent is an internal matter', the Court of Cassation nevertheless states that 'it can be manifested through overall external evidence [and circumstances]'.[1330]

Moreover, Jordanian prosecution also needs to prove that the offender took possession of the money with their full *knowledge* that they are not entitled to such possession.[1331] Prosecution equally needs to establish a causal connection between the acts of offenders and victims' decision to part with their monies in terms of being influenced by the deceptive acts of offenders. As far as the impact of the deceptive actions on shareholders is concerned, the yardstick is an objective one seen through the behaviour of the lay person in terms of whether or not they would have fallen for the deception. In this context, the Court of Cassation stated in one of its landmark judgements:

> The Court finds that the respondent's act does not reach the standard prescribed in Art. 417 of the Penal Code, as it only contained mere lies to which the appellant fell and was not buttressed by external means which would have deceived the lay person.[1332]

The above Jordanian position under general criminal law, with its demands of high level of proof as seen above, is highly dissatisfactory to shareholders induced to part with their monies by criminal deception. Indeed, the position under the Jordanian regulatory system can be contrasted to that of the UK, which criminalises undermining the informational probity of the prospectus. For, it is a criminal offence under section 397(1) & (2) of the FSMA,[1333] knowingly or recklessly to make a statement, promise, forecast, or conceal material fact in order to induce a person to enter into (or refrain from entering) an investment agreement. The three limbs of liability under section 397(1) & (2) therefore relate to *intention*, *dishonest concealment* and *recklessness*, as it targets a person who:

(1) Makes a statement, promise or forecast, which they know is misleading, false or deceptive in a material particular. The defendant, who is *intent* on

1328. See CCD 140/83, *LSJ* (1983), p. 223.
1329. See CCD 482/99, *LSJ* (1999), p. 975; CCD 214/2000, *LSJ* (2000), p. 1298.
1330. See CCD 823/99, *LSJ* (1999), p. 2601 at 2606.
1331. If the offender *genuinely* believed that they were entitled to take possession of the money, they do not commit the offence of criminal deception. See Art. 417(1)(b) of the Jordanian Penal Code 1960.
1332. CCD 13/76, *LSJ* (1976), p. 990, at 992; see CCD 135/85, *LSJ* (1986), p. 1388.
1333. Section 397(1) & (2) of the FSMA is similar to s. 47(1) of the FSA 1986 – s. 47(1) replaced s. 13 of the Prevention of Fraud (Investments) Act 1958, which itself replaced s. 12 of the Prevention of Fraud (Investments) Act 1939.

deceiving, must have had actual *knowledge* of the falsehood or deceptiveness of the statements, forecasts or promises made.

(2) Dishonestly conceals any material fact whether in connection with a statement, promise or forecast made by them or otherwise. Here, the requirement is *dishonestly to conceal*. If it turns out that the concealment is not dishonest but rather, for example, negligent then there is no criminal liability under this limb.[1334]

(3) *Recklessly* makes (dishonestly or otherwise) a statement, promise or forecast which is misleading, false or deceptive in a material particular.[1335]

Such a person, according to section 397(2), is guilty of a criminal offence if he or she commits the above in order to induce[1336] another to enter[1337] into an agreement, or to exercise (or refrain from exercising) any rights conferred by a 'relevant agreement'.[1338] A person guilty of this offence in the UK is liable on summary conviction to imprisonment for a term not exceeding six months or a fine,[1339] or both. A person convicted on indictment is punishable by imprisonment for a term not exceeding seven years or a fine, or both.[1340]

Finally, one must briefly mention here a drawback in the powers of the JSC when, for example, compared to the FSA in terms of its inability directly to prosecute offenders. One says a 'drawback' because many prosecutions will require financial expertise that is better handled by specialised regulatory bodies. This is addressed in the UK, where, *inter alia*, proceedings for an offence may be

1334. The test for 'dishonesty' can be inferred from relevant judicial interpretations such as Lord Lane CJ in *R v. Ghosh* [1982] QB 1053. Here, the term has 'objective' and 'subjective' undertones. The former in the sense that 'dishonesty' relates to what members of the public would view as dishonest. The latter in that the person committing the offence should also know that they are committing a dishonest act.

1335. *Recklessness* finds much of its roots in earlier anti-fraud provisions. Judicial interpretation of 'recklessness' is therefore instrumental. Indeed, when tackling the meaning of 'recklessness' under s. 47 of the FSA 1986, the Court of Appeal in *R v. Page* [(1996) Crim LR 821] countenanced Paull J's interpretation [i.e., under s. 13 of the Prevention of Fraud Act 1958] in *R. Grunwald* [(1963) 1 QB 935] – construing 'recklessness' as a 'rash statement or promise . . . made heedless of whether the person making it has any real facts on which to base'. This carries the day-to-day meaning of 'recklessness', denoting statements whose authors are careless or indifferent to their veracity.

1336. Or is reckless as to whether it may induce, another person whether or not the person to whom the statement, promise or forecast is made.

1337. Or offer to enter into or to refrain from entering or offering to enter into.

1338. 'Relevant agreement' is defined in s. 397(9) of the FSMA. It means an agreement to enter into or performance of which by either party constitutes an activity of a specified kind or one that falls within a specified class of activity; and relates to relevant investment, which falls within a prescribed class of investment.

1339. Not exceeding the statutory maximum.

1340. See s. 397(8) of the FSMA. As far as the territorial scope is concerned, s. 397(1)&(2) gives rise to a criminal offence if: (1) the facts, arrangements, statement, promise or forecast (or the facts to be concealed) are all made in the UK; or (2) the person on whom the inducement is intended is in the UK, or the agreement is (or would be) entered into or the rights are (or would be) exercised in the UK. See s. 397(6). *Ibid.*

instituted[1341] by the Secretary of State, by (or with the consent) of the Director of Prosecutions,[1342] or the FSA[1343] – who equally has extensive information gathering and investigative powers. Yet, while some provisions empower the FSA to gather and ask for information from authorised persons only,[1344] other provisions widen this power to encompass non-authorised persons.[1345] Section 168 of the FSMA specifically grants the FSA the power to investigate circumstances 'suggesting' that a criminal offence under section 21[1346] or section 397[1347] has been committed – regardless of authorisation.[1348] However, when deciding to prosecute, the FSA will consider the seriousness of the misconduct, whether breach was dishonest, carried by a group, the number of victims, etc. It will also consider the extent of loss, impact on the market, whether civil or administrative sanctions would be enough to deter future breaches and previous disciplinary record. Another important factor is the impact of criminal prosecution on the prospects of securing redress to injured investors. For example, if criminal prosecution is likely to have adverse effects on the solvency of the offending firm, then the FSA may decide that criminal proceedings are not appropriate. The FSA may issue a caution under Home Office Circular 18/1994. When prosecuting it applies the Code for Crown Prosecution, considering: (1) whether there is sufficient evidence – i.e., where a jury or a bench of magistrates is 'more likely than not' to convict; and (2) whether criminal prosecution is in the public interest – i.e., seriousness of the offence, whether premeditated or carried out by a group, previous convictions, recurrences, etc. The FSA also has the power to apply to a magistrate for a warrant to search for and seize documents or information.[1349]

3. ADMINISTRATIVE REMEDIES

Investor protection requires that regulatory bodies enjoy administrative powers. This is especially as lay investors may be the victims of widespread infractions that

1341. In England and Wales.
1342. Private persons can obviously apply for the consent here to prosecute under this section.
1343. See s. 401(2)(a) of the FSMA. Other offences the FSA can prosecute include carrying on regulated activity without authorisation or exemption (s. 23), making false claims to be authorised or exempt (s. 24), promoting investment activity without authorisation (s. 25), breaching a prohibition order (s. 56), Money Laundering Regulations 1993 (s. 402), and insider dealing Pt V Criminal Justice Act 1993 (s. 402). However, one must caution that the FSA will not be the only prosecuting authority. Other agencies include the Serious Fraud Office, the Department of Trade and Industry, the Police, HM Customs and Excise, Office of Fair Trading, Local Authority, Trading Standards Departments, etc.
1344. See, for example, ss. 165 and 166 of the FSMA.
1345. The FSA can require information not only from authorised persons. It can also ask for information from all those who were 'at the relevant time, carrying on business'. See s. 166(2)(d) of the FSMA.
1346. See s. 168(2)(a). *Ibid.*
1347. See s. 168(2)(c). *Ibid.*
1348. See generally 'Financial Services Regulation: Enforcing the New Regime', FSA, CP 25 (July 1999).
1349. See s. 176 of the FSMA.

affect large numbers of investors. Likewise, they may suffer huge financial losses that could shake the public's confidence in financial markets or may equally not be able to take action against powerful financial institutions on their own. It is therefore important that regulatory agencies are able to take action on behalf of such lay investors. Additionally, proactive regulatory measures may also be necessary to stop repeated encroachments.[1350]

When determining whether or not to impose sanctions it can equally be crucial to look at practical factors such as the level of compliance of offending firms, their disciplinary record and measures taken to remedy the breach, etc. This task of rigorous regulatory supervision and monitoring is better performed by specialised regulatory agencies, not the courts.

For their part, the administrative powers enjoyed by regulatory agencies are *disciplinary* and *civil enforcement*. While the former generally aims at punishing authorised firms which violate statutory procedures, the latter aims at pre-empting violations and/or securing financial redress for injured consumers. The reason however why they are termed 'administrative powers' is because they enable the regulatory body itself, rather than the courts, to determine the appropriate course of action vis-à-vis offending firms or individuals.[1351]

Indeed, as the application of administrative remedies depends entirely on regulatory bodies' independent characterisation of the relevant issues and facts, disciplinary actions taken by such bodies will accordingly be tailored to dovetail with their stated regulatory objectives.[1352] Additionally, such powers equally enable regulatory bodies to determine beforehand whether or not to invoke the courts' assistance.

One however must clearly point out here that the SA 2002 was the first Jordanian statutory instrument to look at the question of administrative remedies of the JSC. For, the former SA 1997 did not pay any serious consideration to such important question and the JSC was almost toothless.[1353] However, one must hasten to add that although there are now some similarities between the administrative powers enjoyed by the JSC and the FSA, Jordanian securities laws remain inadequate. The discussion below shall elaborate on this.

A positive development that has taken place under the new Jordanian regulatory regime in this area is the ability of the JSC to investigate breaches of Jordanian securities laws and subsequent regulations. In this respect, the *2004 Instructions of Investigating Violations of Securities Law*, which entered into force

1350. Or equally pre-empt a new breach that is in the offing.

1351. See 'Financial Services Regulation: Enforcing The New Regime', FSA, CP 17 (December 1998), p. 11.

1352. The stated objectives of the JSC are (1) protecting investors in securities; (2) regulating and developing the capital market to ensure fairness, efficiency and transparency; and (3) protecting the capital market from the risks that might face it. See Art. 8(a) of the SA 2002. The stated objectives of the FSA are achieving: (1) market confidence; (2) public awareness; (3) the protection of consumers; and (4) the reduction of financial crime. See ss 2(2), 3-6 of the FSMA.

1353. This is evident from the provisions of the SA 1997. See Ch. II of the SA 1997, Arts 6–22.

on 12 May 2004, are highly relevant.[1354] They, *inter alia*, set the *modus operandi*[1355] for the JSC when it investigates regulated persons[1356] in order to determine whether breaches or attempted breaches have taken place.

3.1. Disciplinary Measures

In strict terms, the objective of disciplinary measures is to ensure the compliance of authorised firms and approved persons with the regulatory requirements under legislation. An important development in this area is that the JSC can now under the SA 2002 impose financial fines on those who provide it with misleading or inaccurate information. This is equally considered as a new development under the UK regulatory regime. Yet, neither the JSC nor the FSA can create criminal penalties. They instead can only impose civil sanctions.[1357] Limiting regulatory agencies' power to impose civil, rather than criminal sanctions is justified on the grounds that civil sanctions can be decided on the balance of probabilities, not proof beyond reasonable doubt as criminal charges require.[1358]

1354. Issued by the Board of Commissioners of the Securities Commission pursuant to Articles (12/Q), (17) and (21) of the Securities Law No. (76) for the Year 2002.

1355. Article (4) of the *2004 Instructions of Investigating Violations of Securities Law* states: 'In order to undertake investigation procedures, the competent department may carry out the following: A- Inspect any of the entities subject to the Commission's monitoring, audit its records and registers, and acquire any information or documents relevant to the investigation matter. B- Acquire primary statements from any person whether in the entities subject to the Commission's monitoring, or otherwise and acquire any relevant information, documents or records. Such statements shall be in writing and shall be signed by the person who made the statement. C- Request any documents or papers relevant to the investigation matter. D- Summon witnesses and hear their testimony under oath. E- Recommend to the Chairman to serve the person to whom the violation is ascribed with a notice, including a description of the violation ascribed, an invitation for a hearing of statements and submission of any evidence at the time set by the competent department. F- The competent department may substitute hearing by a request for the addressee's written response to the notice. G- The competent department may seek the assistance of any of the Commission's employees.'

1356. Article (3) states: '(A) The competent department shall undertake the investigation under the supervision of the commissioner assigned by the Chairman as its supervisor. (B) The competent department shall investigate any person to determine whether such had committed, or taken preparatory measures to commit a violation. As well as any information, circumstances or practices that the Commission deems necessary to execute the provisions of the Law and Regulations, Instructions and Decisions issued pursuant thereto. (C) The Chairman may instruct the competent department to undertake investigation procedures on the basis of information, reports or complaints presented to the Commission or as he otherwise deems necessary to uncover any violation – or preparatory measures thereto – of the provisions of the Law or Regulations, Instructions or Decisions issued pursuant thereto.' *Ibid*

1357. For the UK, see 'Designing the FSA Handbook of Rules and Guidance', CP.08 (April 1998), p. 13.

1358. This view is clear from almost all official debates on the FSMB. See, for example, *Minutes of Evidence Taken Before the Joint Committee on Financial Services and Markets* (Second Report), UK Parliament, 19 May 1999.

3.1.1. Monetary Fines Imposed by the JSC

The JSC can now impose monetary fines[1359] on those who violate the provisions of the SA 2002, its regulations, instructions or decisions,[1360] and those who wilfully aid, abet, counsel or instruct others to commit such breaches.[1361] It can equally impose fines for providing misleading or inaccurate information in the prospectus.[1362] Article 22(a)(3) of the SA 2002 states:

> A) The Board [of the JSC] may impose monetary fines of no more than JD 50,000 (Fifty thousand Jordan Dinars) on any person in any of the following circumstances . . . . If the person makes, or causes to be made, in any application or report to be filed with the Commission, any information which is false or misleading with respect to any *material* fact, or has omitted to state in any such application or report a *material* fact that should have been stated. [Italics added.][1363]

From the above provision one finds that Jordanian securities laws now impose a civil penalty on those who provide the JSC with misleading or inaccurate information. However, the criterion here is that the misleading or inaccurate information must be *material*. As seen earlier, the Jordanian regulatory understanding of *material* is that it refers to information that would impact on investors' decision in terms of whether to buy, sell, keep or deal in the security.[1364] From Article 22(a)(3) one also finds that a civil fine would be applicable if a person has equally omitted to disclose such material information in particulars submitted to the JSC.

As mentioned above there are certain amendments that are due to be implemented vis-à-vis the SA 2002. Articles (8)&(9) now abrogate Articles (21)&(22) of the SA 2002. However, as this new regime has not been implemented yet one only needs to point to any possible changes, if any. As far as Article 22 is concerned Article 9 of the *Amendment Law to the SA 2002* does away with the first limb as mentioned above. It is here assumed that any breach or attempted breach of the Act can be first addressed through a formal notice issued by the JSC in which the breach is investigated and the accused is given opportunity to address the situation

1359. This should be no more than JD 50,000.
1360. See Art. 22(a)(1) of the SA 2002.
1361. See Art. 22(a)(2). *Ibid.*
1362. See Art. 22(a)(3). *Ibid.*
1363. Article 22 of the SA 2002, *inter alia*, states:

> A- The Board may impose monetary fines of no more than JD 50,000 (Fifty thousand Jordan Dinars) on any person in any of the following cases: 1. If the person violates the provision of this Law and the Regulations, Instructions and Decisions issued pursuant thereto; 2. If the person wilfully aids, abets, counsels or commands any other person to commit the violation; 3. If the person makes, or causes to be made, in any application or report to be filed with the Commission, any information which is false or misleading with respect to any material fact, or has omitted to state in any such application or report any material fact that should have been stated.

1364. See Art. 2. *Ibid.*

with the possibility to appeal before Jordanian administrative courts – as mentioned in the newly amended Article 21 which has not yet come into force. As to applicable fines, once the *Amendment Law to the SA 2002* enters into force, the ceiling shall become JD 100,000 instead of JD 50,000.

As far as the UK is concerned, section 91 of the FSMA is the counterpart to Article 22(a)(3) of the SA 2002, which imposes a civil fine on those who violate the *Listing Rules*.[1365] For their part, both provisions have potentially wide-ranging applications. While Article 22(a)(3) is applicable to all those who 'make' misleading information or omissions or 'cause' such statements or omissions to be made, section 91 imposes financial penalties for contravening 'any provision' of the *Listing Rules*.

Indeed, from Article 22(a)(3) of the SA 2002, it is evident that the JSC has extensive discretionary powers when imposing financial fines. However, like the position under the FSMA,[1366] such discretionary powers are tempered by a number of guidelines. For, in determining whether to impose financial fines, and if yes, what the appropriate level should be, the JSC must take into account the following factors:

(1) That the fine shall be commensurate with the requirements of *public interest*.[1367] The SA 2002 does not explain what it means by 'public interest' and uses this term rather generically. However, one argues that the meaning of public interest here includes achieving the stated regulatory objectives of the JSC in terms of 'protecting investors' and ensuring 'fairness and efficiency' in the marketplace.[1368] The FSA recourses to the less generic criterion of 'proportionality', in the sense that it should not overburden market participants and lessen market efficiency by overregulation.[1369]
(2) The *nature of the breach* in terms of whether it involves fraud, deceit, manipulation or gross negligence.[1370] This criterion is also applied by the FSA, which looks at whether the breach is deliberate or reckless, its duration and frequency, etc. Here, under the Jordanian and UK regulatory regimes, fines are, for example, likely to be larger if breaches were deliberate or deceitful.

1365. Section 91(1)(a)(b) of the FSMA states: 'If the competent authority considers that (a) an issuer of listed securities, or (b) an applicant for listing, has contravened any provision of the *Listing Rules*, it may impose on him a penalty of such amount as it considers appropriate.' The FSA can particularly impose financial penalties on directors of the issuer or applicants if they, at the material time, enjoyed such capacity and had knowledge of the contravention. Section 91(2). *Ibid*. See also s. 91(3)(6)(7)(a)(b). *Ibid*.

1366. See 'Financial Services Regulation: Enforcing The New Regime', FSA, CP 17 (December 1998), pp. 35–36; 'Financial Services Regulation: Enforcing The New Regime', FSA, CP 25 (July 1999), pp. 10–12; *FSA Handbook*, ENF 11.4.1.

1367. See Art. 22(b) of the SA 2002.

1368. See Art. 8. *Ibid.*

1369. See s. 2(3)(2)(c) of the FSMA.

1370. See Art. 22(b)(1) of the SA 2002.

(3) The *nature of harm* that results from the violation, where the JSC is likely to impose a larger fine if breaches resulted in harm to investors in large-scales.[1371] The FSA equally looks at the degree of damage to the orderliness and confidence in financial markets, costs on market users, the size of systemic risks caused by the breach, the amount of profit accrued or loss avoided by violators, etc.
(4) The JSC will also consider the *behaviour of those who commit the breaches*, taking into account any restitution made to persons injured by such a violation.[1372] The FSA also adopts this criterion, equally looking at important factors such as the speed with which breaches have been identified, the degree of cooperation during investigation and remedial steps undertaken.
(5) The JSC is also likely to consider 'any other matters dictated by fairness and justice'.[1373] This, for example, includes the previous disciplinary record and compliance history of violators.

A person subject to a fine can appeal to the JSC within two weeks of issuing the fine, and the JSC has to make its decision regarding the appeal within a period of two weeks from receiving the appeal.[1374] Failure by the JSC to decide on the appeal is regarded as a decision to turn it down, and such a person has the right to appeal against it before the High Court of Justice.[1375]

Other disciplinary actions that can be taken by the JSC when offering shares to the public also include suspending the public offer of a security if investor protection requires such a measure.[1376] Additionally, the JSC can equally cease or suspend any activity related to all securities traded by a company or a specific security.[1377] Added to this are the powers that the ASE now enjoys in terms of its ability to impose sanctions on those who violate the *2004 Listing Directives*.

For its part, the FSA has similar powers which include refusing to list new securities,[1378] suspend and/or delist traded ones.[1379] However, under section 118 of the FSMA a person who breaches the *Listing Rules* may also be committing market abuse,[1380] where the FSA can impose civil sanctions on such a person.[1381]

1371. See Art. 22(b)(2). *Ibid.*
1372. See Art. 22(b)(3). *Ibid.*
1373. See Art. 22(b)(4) & 22(c). *Ibid.*
1374. See Art. 22(c). *Ibid.*
1375. *Ibid.*
1376. See Art. 19(a)(2). *Ibid.*
1377. See Art. 19(a)(1). *Ibid.*
1378. See s. 75 of the FSMA.
1379. See ss 77 and 78. *Ibid.* The FSA can also disqualify auditors [ss 345 and 249. *Ibid.* Regulations made by the Treasury pursuant to ss 342(5) and 343(5) of the FSMA are the *Financial Services (Communication by Auditors) Regulations 2001.*] It can equally withdraw its approval under s. 63.
1380. Compliance with the *Listing Rules* under s. 118(8) of the FSMA however provides a safe harbour vis-à-vis disclosure of information.
1381. Market abuse refers to a behaviour likely to be regarded by a regular user of the market as a failure [s. 118(1). *Ibid.*]. Such failure is seen through three categories: (1) misuse of

In this context, the market abuse regime will be useful to impose civil regulatory sanctions (fines or censures) against those who provide false or misleading information, particularly when handling price sensitive information.[1382]

Having considered the disciplinary powers enjoyed by the JSC when offering shares to the public, one now turns to discuss the question of civil powers in this area.

3.2. Civil Enforcement Powers

Regulatory agencies need to enjoy civil enforcement powers in order to carry out their regulatory mandate effectively. These enforcement powers aim at enabling them to (1) restrain a course of conduct and secure assets of offenders; and (2) ensure redress for investors. However, the JSC has limited civil enforcement powers vis-à-vis violators when contrasted to the FSA. The ensuing discussion shall look at the above in more detail.

3.2.1. Restraining a Course of Conduct and Securing Assets of Offenders

It is important for regulatory bodies to be able to stop violators from issuing securities when they flout statutory procedures.[1383] However, regulatory bodies will not involve themselves in every infraction. Rather they generally will prohibit serious violations that result in huge financial losses, threaten the systemic stability of financial markets, impact upon wide scale investors, undermine confidence in the marketplace, etc. When deciding on such a course of action, regulatory bodies may also consider other important factors such as the ability of investors to take civil actions on their own.

For its part, although as seen earlier the JSC cannot prosecute offenders, it nevertheless has the capacity to sue – represented by what is equivalent in the UK to the Solicitor General (the Civil Attorney General).[1384] Under the newly enacted SA 2002, the JSC has wide investigative powers. It, for example, can conduct any investigation, inspection, hearing or auditing to determine if any person has violated or has taken preparatory measures to violate any of the provisions of the SA

---

information which is not generally available but, if available, would be considered relevant when deciding the terms of the transaction in question [s. 118(2)(a). *Ibid.*]; (2) giving a false or misleading impression as to the supply, demand, price or value [s. 118(2)(b). *Ibid.*]; and (3) market distortion [s. 118(2)(c). *Ibid.*].

1382. See H Davies, former Chairman of the FSA, 'N2 Plus 3', speech at the Worshipful Company of Chartered Secretaries & Administrators Annual Lecture, 5 March 2002.

1383. Regulatory bodies will probably first withdraw their approval or make prohibition orders against individuals who are not approved persons.

1384. See Art. 7(a) of the SA 2002, which states: 'The Commission shall have the right to sue and be sued, and may be represented in legal proceedings by the Civil Attorney General or any attorney it appoints for this purpose.' Also Art.22(d). *Ibid.*

2002 or its regulations.[1385] It can audit and make copies of the documents, records and registers of any licensed or registered person, or any entity subject to its monitoring and supervision, and inspect such bodies with or without prior notice.[1386] It can also summon witnesses to testify under oath, and request documents pertaining to the investigated matter.[1387] In carrying out this duty, the JSC can enlist the services of experts and specialists in conducting the investigations, inspections and audits.[1388]

If as a result of such investigations the JSC finds that any person has violated, or taken steps to violate the above, it can publish the findings.[1389] It can equally issue an order requiring such a person to desist from committing, attempting to commit, or causing such breach, or requiring elimination of the breach, as the case may be.[1390] It can equally impose a fine and/or order the cessation of issuance or trading in any security to which the offence relates.[1391]

In addition to the above if the violator is an authorised person, it can suspend or revoke their license or registration.[1392] The JSC can also adopt a temporary order to cease and desist the activities of a licensed or registered person who commits or attempts to commit any violation that is likely to result in dissipation or conversion of assets.[1393] These temporary orders are important as they enable the JSC to freeze the violators' assets, while it conducts its investigation. Once the case is being tried by a court, the SA 2002 leaves Jordanian courts to freeze offenders' assets:

> The Competent Court may sequester the assets of a person who stands trial before the Court to ensure that sufficient funds are available for possible future fines or restitution the Court may order, and may appoint a judicial custodian over such assets.[1394]

For its part, the FSA can make prohibition orders against individuals who are not approved persons.[1395] If this is not complied with,[1396] it under section 380 of the

1385. See Art. 17(a) & Art. 21(a). *Ibid.*
1386. See Art. 17(c)(1). *Ibid.*
1387. See Art. 17(c)(2). *Ibid.*
1388. See Art. 17(d). *Ibid.*
1389. See Art. 21(b)(1). *Ibid.*
1390. See Art. 21(b)(2). *Ibid.*
1391. See Art. 21(b)(3) & 21(4). *Ibid.*
1392. See Art. 21(b)(5). *Ibid.*
1393. See Art. 19(b). *Ibid.* However, such temporary order shall remain effective pending the completion of due proceedings by the JSC, unless the order is otherwise cancelled or set aside by the JSC.
1394. See Art. 110(g). *Ibid.*
1395. See s. 56 of the FSMA. This is carried through prohibition orders, where the FSA deems it necessary to prevent or restrict an individual from carrying out any function related to regulated activities or from restricting or preventing their employment by any firm. See *FSA Handbook*, ENF, 8.1.2. However, when considering whether or not to make a prohibition order, the FSA will consider if the person was guilty of misconduct.
1396. See s. 56(4) of the FSMA.

FSMA can then apply to the High Court[1397] for an injunction where there is a reasonable likelihood that a person will contravene a 'relevant requirement' or that a violation is likely to continue.[1398] The FSA can also apply to courts for an injunction[1399] directing a person to remedy a breach of 'relevant requirement'.[1400] It can also apply for freezing or *Mareva* injunctions to freeze offenders' assets.[1401] When applying for a *Mareva* injunction, the FSA must satisfy the court of two things: (1) a person may have breached the relevant provisions of the FSMA;[1402] and (2) such a person is reasonably likely to dispose of, or otherwise deal with, the assets that are to be the subject of the restraint.[1403]

3.2.2. Ensuring Redress for Investors

Ensuring redress for aggrieved investors is increasingly becoming an important function for modern regulatory agencies. Indeed, this is especially the case if the number of injured customers is significant and their financial losses are grave. Moreover, modern regulatory agencies are also likely to be galvanised into action to ensure redress for injured investors if such investors are unable to institute legal proceedings against powerful offending firms.[1404]

However, despite this important functionality by modern regulatory agencies, investors' redress is an area in which the JSC is still lacking. For, there are no measures under the SA 2002 that would enable it to seek redress for aggrieved investors. Additionally, this area does not appear to have been addressed in the expected amendments to the SA 2002. For, Articles (8)&(9) of the *Amendment Law to the SA 2002* (which in turn abrogate and replace Articles (21)&(22) of the SA 2002 Act) have not paid attention to this question.

The above situation can, for example, be contrasted to the FSA, which can apply to courts for restitution orders where a person (whether authorised or not) has breached relevant requirements such as section 397 of the FSMA or the *Listing Rules*.[1405] Here, section 382 of the FSMA states that the FSA may apply to the court for an order if it is satisfied that a person has contravened a relevant requirement or been knowingly concerned in the contravention of such a requirement, and: (a) that profits have accrued to him as a result of the contravention; or (b) that

1397. The Court of Session for an interdict in Scotland.
1398. See s. 380 of the FSMA.
1399. See s. 380(2). *Ibid.*
1400. Sections 380(6)(a) and (7)(a) of the FSMA state that relevant requirement means a requirement: (1) which is imposed by or under the Act; or (2) which is imposed by or under any other Act and whose contravention constitutes an offence which the FSA has power to prosecute.
1401. See s. 380(3). *Ibid.*
1402. Or may have been knowingly concerned in such a breach.
1403. See s. 380(2) of the FSMA.
1404. Such criterion is, for example, applied by the FSA, which also looks at the likelihood of success, the costs incurred by the FSA to secure redress, the size of sums likely to be recovered, willingness of contraveners to make informal restitution, etc. See, FSA 1999, *supra* note 1346, p. 23.
1405. See s. 382 of the FSMA.

one or more persons have suffered loss or have been otherwise adversely affected as a result of the contravention.

The FSA under section 384(5) of the FSMA can also require restitution through an administrative order from a firm which has breached a relevant requirement – without necessarily referring it to the court.[1406] The FSA will utilise its administrative powers under section 384 before applying to the court for a restitution order – though it may opt for a restitution order first if there was a risk of non-compliance by a firm with the administrative order, especially as such a firm will be liable to contempt of court.[1407]

4. CONCLUSION

The liability regime for misleading or inaccurate disclosure under Jordanian securities laws remains somewhat inadequate. The position under the new regulatory liability regime vis-à-vis the question of diluting the informational probity of the prospectus is an improvement on both the Jordanian general law and the SA 1997. For, it now reverses the burden of proof placing the onus on defendants to disprove their negligence or intent. Nevertheless, the requirement of *reliance* under the SA 2002 remains a significant drawback. For, it will not be always possible for shareholders to prove that they have relied on the prospectus when they purchased the shares. This requirement further complicates matters for aftermarket traders – as they would have bought their shares on the secondary market without having necessarily seen or considered the prospectus.

Another area that the Jordanian regulatory regime equally fails to tackle is defences from liability. Jordanian securities laws, for example, do not adequately address issuers' and offerors' defences when prospectuses contain misleading information by experts or quotations from official statements.

Other criticisms can also be levelled against the criminal liability regime for diluting the impact of the prospectus. It is acknowledged that, unlike the SA 1997, the new regulatory regime now makes diluting the impact of the prospectuses a criminal offence. However, a persistent drawback is that it still does not address the question of advertising when offering shares to the public. It significantly also still does not criminalise actions that undermine the informational probity of the prospectus. This is especially problematic, as general criminal law in Jordan will not help. Here, the regulatory Jordanian regime needs to criminalise undermining the informational probity of the prospectus through *intentional* or *reckless* actions, as well as *dishonest concealment* of information.

1406. Here, the FSA must give the person against whom it decided to exercise an administrative order a *warning notice* followed by a *decision notice* and a *final notice*.

1407. For other conditions see *FSA Handbook*, ENF 9.7.3. Restitution orders that the FSA will require violators to: (1) disgorge illicit profits made by such violators as a result of their breaches; and/or (2) compensate losses caused by violators' breaches. In both instances the money is paid directly to the FSA, not the victim – though the FSA must pay the funds back to the victims as courts may direct. See, FSA 1999, *supra* note 1346, p. 21.

Additionally, in order to have more regulatory clout the JSC needs to have prosecutory powers, where more complex cases require to be dealt by specialised personnel. Another drawback in the SA 2002 is that it still does not pay adequate attention to the role of the JSC in ensuring redress for investors on *par* with what is applicable in the UK. This is especially important if lay investors are unable to institute legal proceedings against powerful offending firms, or if there are widespread infractions.

To address all the above, proper amendments to Jordanian securities laws need to be made in order to provide better investor protection for shareholders in Jordan.

Appendix

Oman:

As far as Oman is concerned, the stock exchange there is known as the Muscat Securities Market (MSM) that started its activities in 1989, with sixty-eight joint stock companies.[1408] The number of listed companies has risen substantially since then, sub-divided into banking, services, insurance and industrial (manufacturing) sectors. By the end of December 2006, such a number of listed companies reached 121 companies, with total market capitalisation of USD 13.037 billion.[1409] The capitalisation of the MSM reached a healthy increase the following year, estimated at USD 16.27 billion by the end of September 2007.[1410] Regarding 2010, and 2011, the capitalisation of the Muscat Securities Market in June 2010 was USD 24.031 billion, increasing to USD 26.646 billion in June 2011.[1411] For its part, the number of listed companies equally increased to 133 by June 2011.[1412]

Oman also has a *Parallel Market*, which trades stocks of companies that do not qualify for listing on the MSM, together with a *Third Market*.[1413] The number of companies traded on the *Parallel Market* has also increased, allowing more joint-stock companies to tap into equity markets.

However, unlike the majority of Arab countries that established securities markets in the 1970s and 1980s, the establishment of the MSM was accompanied

---

1408. See Azzam, *supra* note 777, p. 169.
1409. See *Quarterly Bulletin*, Arab Monetary Fund, No. 48 (4th Quarter, 2006), p. 33.
1410. See *Quarterly Bulletin*, Arab Monetary Fund, No. 51 (3rd Quarter, 2007), p. 77.
1411. See *Quarterly Bulletin*, Arab Monetary Fund, No. 65 (2nd Quarter, 2011), p. 109.
1412. *Ibid.*
1413. Under 'General Definitions', Law No. 80/98 defines the *Third Market* as: 'That section of the Secondary market where off-floor dealings takes place at the broker's office in respect of companies' shares to which the specific listing rules for trading on the floor do not apply, or where ownership of securities is transferred off-floor without a broker.'

from its inception by a securities law [the Securities Market Law of 1988 (No. 35/88)]. Although it introduced a regulatory structure into the MSM, it, *inter alia*, did not initially separate between the management and supervisory branches of the exchange. In the late 1990s Oman promulgated a new Securities Markets Law – Royal Decree No. 80/98.[1414] It came into force on 15 January 1999. This new law replaced the 1988 law. Its most important feature is that it separates the supervisory and management roles of the MSM by setting up the Capital Market Authority (CMA).[1415] In this context, Oman was the first Arab Gulf country to set up a designated regulatory body, known as the Capital Market Authority (CMA). The board of directors of the CMA is headed by the Minister of Commerce and Industry and currently includes eight other members.[1416]Among its important regulations was *Administrative Decision 1/2003 Approving the Rules for Listing Securities on Muscat Securities Market.*[1417] Additionally, on 13 July 2011 the CMA issued Decision No. 5/2011 entitled the *Issuance, Clearance and Settlement Regulation.*[1418]

Royal Decree No. 82/98 dated 25 November 1998 established the Muscat Depository and Securities Registration Company. It, however, must be stated here that former settlement mechanism involved only three parties in the clearance and settlement, MSM, Muscat Clearing and Depository Company and the broker. The newly introduced settlement mechanism is now through a Settlement Bank with a Settlement Guarantee Fund (SGF).[1419]

1414. Published in *Official Gazette* No. 635 of 15 November 1998.

1415. See Arts 46–63 of Law No. 80/98.

1416. These are the Under-Secretary for Economic Affairs, an executive president, a director general, representative of the Ministry of Commerce and Industry, representative of the Central bank of Oman, and three other members.

1417. Issued on 23 April 2003.

1418. The Decision came into force after two months of its publication in the *Official Gazette*.

1419. See Royal Decree No. 72/2010, *Amending the Name of Muscat Depository and Securities Registration Company*.

Bibliography

General English

Abdalla M, 'Partnership (*musharakah*): A new option for financing small enterprises?', *Arab Law Quarterly*, Vol.14, No. 3 (March 1999), pp. 256–267.

Abdel-Hadi A, *Stock Markets of the Arab World: Trends, Problems and Prospects for Integration*, Routledge (UK), 1988.

Abdel-Hadi A, 'The role of capital markets in underdeveloped countries with particular reference to South Korea, Brazil and Nigeria', Ph.D thesis, Exeter University, 1989.

Abdel-Haq M, 'The relationship between Islamic banking theory and practice', Ph.D thesis, Oxford Brookes University, 1993.

Abu Obaid J, 'Non-performing loans in Jordanian commercial banks: Causes, effects, and suggested solutions: An analytical study', Ph.D thesis, Amman Arab University for Higher Studies, Jordan, 2003.

Agtmael A, *Emerging Securities Markets: Investment Banking Opportunities in the Developing World*, Euromoney Publications (London), 1984.

Ahmed E, 'Islamic banking: Distribution of profit', Ph.D thesis, Hull University, 1990.

Ajayi O, 'Regulatory techniques in internationalisation and emerging capital markets', Ph.D thesis, Cambridge University, 1990.

Al-Bader A, 'Economic liberalisation: A developmental must for Kuwait', paper presented in a seminar entitled 'Economic liberalisation: Efficiency, growth and employment in a Kuwaiti context' 22 February 1997, Kuwait.

Al-Harran S, 'Introduction: Cases in Islamic finance', *Arab Law Quarterly*, Vol.14, No. 3, (March 1999), pp. 193–202.

Al-Hmoud T, 'A study of the application of EMH to the Jordanian stock market', Ph.D thesis, University of Wales, UK, 1987.

Al-Jamal Y, 'The impact of economic variables on social security indicators in Jordan (1980–2000): An econometric study', Master's thesis, Yarmouk University, Jordan, 2001.

Al-Kuhaimi S, 'Contract law and the judicial system in Saudi Arabia', Ph.D thesis, London University, 1982.

Allen D, *Misrepresentation*, Sweet and Maxwell, (London), 1988.

Al-Moqatei M, 'Introducing Islamic law in the Arab Gulf states: A case study of Kuwait', *Arab Law Quarterly*, Vol.4, No. 2, (May 1989), pp. 138–148.

Al-Mutori A, 'Testing semi-efficiency in the Amman Financial Market: A trial test', Master's thesis, University of Jordan, 1996.

Al-Rimawi L, 'Relevance of *Shari'a* as a legislative source in modern Arab legal context: A brief constitutional synopsis with emphasis on selected commercial aspects', *Company Lawyer*, Vol. XXXII, No. 2, January 2011, pp. 58–65.

Al-Rimawi L, 'Reform of the Jordanian Securities Commission: A personal view', *International & Comparative Corporate Law Journal*, Vol. III, No. 4 (2001), pp. 515–533.

Al-Rimawi L, 'Securities markets: Instruments, globalization and benefits for emerging economies', *Arab Bank Review,* Vol. 3, No. 2, (October 2001), pp. 33–44.

Al-Rimawi L, 'Jordanian, Kuwaiti and Omani securities regulation: Can they be the subject-matter of a viable comparative study with EU securities regulation? (Part Two)', *Journal of Financial Regulation and Compliance*, Vol. IX, No. 3, August 2001, pp. 253–273.

Al-Rimawi L, 'Jordanian, Kuwaiti and Omani securities regulation: Can they be the subject-matter of a viable comparative study with EU securities regulation? (Part One)', *Journal of Financial Regulation and Compliance*, Vol. VIII, No. 4, November 2000, pp. 349–357.

Al-Rimawi L, 'Emerging financial markets in the Middle East: A critique of selected issues in Arab securities regulation', *Journal of Financial Regulation and Compliance,* Vol. VII, No. 2, June 1999, pp. 149–176.

Al-Rimawi L, 'Arab regulation of fraud, insider dealing, market manipulation and possible contractual remedies', *Journal of Financial Crime*, Vol. VI, No. 4, May 1999, pp. 303–310.

Al-Rimawi L, 'Combating fraud in Arab securities regulation', *European Financial Services Law*, Vol. VI, No. 3, March 1999, pp. 110–116.

Al-Rimawi L, 'The Jordanian definition of "financial security" in light of British and American definitions', *European Financial Services Law*, Vol. V, Nos. 5&6, May/June 1998, pp. 127–130.

Al-Rimawi L, 'Middle Eastern review: Recent company and financial legal reforms in selected Arab jurisdictions', *European Financial Services Law*, Vol. V, Nos. 1&2, Jan/Feb 1998, pp. 40–44.

Al-Rimawi L, 'Jordan's financial laws: An introduction to an Arab model in securities regulation', *Yearbook of Islamic and Middle Eastern Law*, Vol. IV, 1998, pp. 73–98.

Al-Rimawi L, 'An overview of Jordanian investment laws set in a larger regional context', *European Business Law Review*, Vol. VIII, No. 9, September 1997, pp. 198–201.

Al-Rimawi L, 'Middle East report: Why Arab interest has turned to its securities markets?', *European Financial Services Law*, Vol. IV, No. 3, March 1997, pp. 106–107.

Al-Yahya M, *Kuwait: Fall and Rebirth*, Kegan Paul International (London), 1993.

Amin S, *Islamic Banking and Finance: The Experience of Iran*, Vahid Publications (Iran), 1986.

Anwar M, 'Islamicity of banking and modes of Islamic banking', *Arab Law Quarterly*, Vol.18, No. 1, (February 2003), pp. 62–80.

Appleby G, *Contract Law*, Sweet & Maxwell, (London), 2001.

Arif M, *Monetary and Fiscal Economics of Islam*, King Abdulaziz University Press, (Saudi Arabia), 1982.

Asimakopoulos I, 'Stock prices, exchange rate and market efficiency', Research Paper No. 97/4, Institute of European Finance, University of Wales, 1997.

Atiyah P, *An Introduction to the Law of Contract,* Clarendon Press, Oxford, 1981.

Atiyah P, *The Rise and Fall of Freedom of Contract*, Clarendon Press, Oxford, 1979.

Atje R et al., 'Stock markets and development', *European Economic Review*, Vol.37, (June 1993), pp. 632–640.

Awadallah S, 'Privatisation and economic development: A Study on the effect of privatisation on the economic efficiency in developing countries: Egypt –as a case study under Law No. 203 for 1991', *Arab Law Quarterly*, Vol.18, No. 1, (February 2003), pp. 34–61.

Azzam H, *The Emerging Arab Capital Markets: Investment Opportunities in Relatively Underplayed Markets*, Kegan Paul International (London), 1997.

Ballantyne W, 'The second Coulson memorial lecture: Back to the Shari'a?', *Arab Law Quarterly*, Vol.3, No. 4, (November 1988), pp. 317–328.

Ballantyne W, *Commercial Law in the Arab Middle East: The Gulf States*, Lloyd's of London, London, (1986)

Baloglu A, 'Law of sales in the works of Marwazi, Quduri and Sarakhsi', Ph.D thesis, Manchester University, 1991.

Bananga A et al., *External Audit and Corporate Governance in Islamic Banks*, Athenaeum Press Ltd., (UK), 1994.

Barfield C, *International Financial Markets: Harmonization versus Competition*, Washington, D.C: AEI Press, 1996.

Barsellah S, 'Mandatory disclosure regulation, insider trading and the economics of information', MPhil thesis, York University, 1989.

Baumol W, *The Stock Market and Economic Efficiency*, Fordham University Press (New York), 1965.

Beatson J, *Anson's Law of Contract*, Oxford University Press, 27th Ed., 1998.

Benston G et al., 'The appropriate role of bank regulation', *Economic Journal* (May 1996), pp. 688–697.

Benston J, 'The value of the SEC's accounting disclosure requirements', 44 *Accounting Review* (1969), p. 515.

Bernham A et al., 'The securities markets: Findings and recommendations of a special staff of the Twentieth Century Fund', Twentieth Century Fund, Inc. (New York) 1935.

Bill J, 'Resurgent Islam in the Persian Gulf', *Foreign Affairs*, (Fall 1984).

Billah M, '*Caveat emptor* versus *khiyar al-aib*: A dichotomy', *Arab Law Quarterly*, Vol.13, No. 3, (1998), p. 287.

Birds J et al., *Boyle & Birds' Company Law*, Jordans, 3rd Ed. (UK), 1995.

Black B, 'The core institutions that support strong securities markets', Stanford Law School, John M. Olin Programme in Law and Economics, Working Paper No. 200, June 2000.

Blair M et al., *Blackstone's Guide to the Financial Services & Markets Act 2000*, Blackstone, (London), 2001.

Blair W et al., *Banking and Financial Services Regulation*, Butterworths, (London), 2002.

Briault C, 'Revisiting the rationale for a single national financial services regulator', London School of Economics, Financial Markets Group, Special Paper No. 135, 2002.

Buang A, 'The prohibition of gharar in the Islamic law of contracts: A conceptual analysis with special reference to the practice of Islamic commercial contracts in Malaysia', Ph.D thesis, London University, 1995.

Buckland R et al., 'Companies' voluntary disclosure behaviour and raising equity capital on the Amman Financial Market', *Aberdeen Papers in Accountancy, Finance & Management Working Paper 98-2*, (1998).

Cagatay N, 'Riba, interest concepts and banking in the Ottoman Empire', *Studia Islamica*, (1970), p. 2.

Carazzai E, 'The internationalisation of the financial market and its impact on direct and indirect investment on Brazil', M.Phil thesis, Manchester University, 1990.

Cartwright P, *Consumer Protection in Financial Services*, Kluwer Law International, 1999.

Choi F, 'Financial disclosure and entry to the European capital market', *Journal of Accounting Research,* Vol. XI, No. 2, (1973), pp. 159–175.

Clarke M, *Citizen's Financial Futures: The Regulation of Retail Investment Financial Services in Britain*, Brookfield (USA), 1998.

Coffee J, 'Market failure and the economic case for mandatory disclosure system', 70 *Virginia Law Review* (1984), p. 717.

Comair-Obeid N, 'Particularity of the contract's subject-matter in the laws of the Arab Middle East', *Arab Law Quarterly*, 1994, p. 335.

Comair-Obeid N, *The Law of Business Contracts in the Arab Middle East*, Kluwer Law International, 1996.

Cooper J, 'Do the merits matter? A study of settlements in securities class actions', *Stanford Law Review* 43 (1991), p. 497.

Cotter A, *Banking & Corporate Financial Services*, London, Cavendish, 2003.

Coulson N, *Conflicts and Tensions in Islamic Jurisprudence*, University of Chicago Press, 1969.
Coulson N, *A History of Islamic Law*, Edinburgh University Press, (1978).
Coulson N, *Commercial Law in the Gulf States: The Islamic Legal Tradition*, Graham & Trotman, (Boston, London), 1984.
Cunningham L, 'Capital market theory, mandatory disclosure, and price discovery', 51 *Washington & Lee Law Review* (1994), p. 843.
Davies P, 'Liability for misstatements to the market', 5 *Capital Markets Law Journal* (2010) pp. 443–451.
Davies P, 'Liability for misstatements to the market: Some reflections' 9 *Journal of Corporate Law Studies* (2009), pp. 295–313.
Davies P, *Gower's Principles of Modern Company Law*, Sweet & Maxwell, (London), 8th Edition (2008).
Davies P, 'Institutional investors in the United Kingdom' in D Prentice et al., *Contemporary Issues in Corporate Governance* (Oxford University Press), 1993, 49.
Dowd K, 'The case for financial *laissez-faire*', *Economic Journal* (May 1996), pp. 679–87.
Downes et al., 'The efficient market reconsidered', 4 *Journal of Portfolio Management* (1977), p. 4.
Drake P et al., 'IPO underpricing and insurance against legal liability', *Financial Management* (Spring 1993), 64.
Dwyer D, *Law and Islam in the Middle East*, Bergin & Garvey Publications, (UK), 1990.
EASRA, *Summary Project Completion Report: Advice on achieving compliance with IOSCO MMoU*. The East African Securities Regulatory Authorities, (February 2007).
Easterbrook & Fischel, *Economic Structure of Corporate Law*, Harvard University Press, 1991.
Edge I, *Islamic Law and Legal Theory*, (Dartmouth Publishing Company Ltd.), 1996.
Edge I, 'Comparative commercial law of Egypt and the Arabian Gulf', *Cleveland State Law Review*, 34, 1985–1986.
El-Ashker A, *The Islamic Business Enterprise,* Croom Helm, 1987.
El-Issa Y, 'The usefulness of corporate financial disclosure to investors in the Amman Financial Market', Ph.D thesis, Lancaster University, 1988.
El-Jildah M, 'The impact of stock splits on price changes: An empirical study on Amman Financial Market', Master's thesis, University of Jordan, 1996.
El-Naggar S, 'Prospects and problems of privatisation: The case of Egypt', paper presented to the Thirteenth Annual Symposium, Centre for Contemporary Arab Studies, Georgetown University, April 1988.
El-Sharif B, 'Law and practice of profit-sharing in Islamic banking with particular reference to mudarabah and murabaha', Ph.D thesis, Exeter University, 1990.
ESMAP, *Power Sector Financial Vulnerability Assessment Impact of the Credit Crisis on Investments in the Power Sector: Hashemite Kingdom of Jordan*, (Energy Sector Management Assistance Programme). February 2010.

Fabozzi F, *Capital Markets: Institutions and Instruments*, Prentice Hall New Jersey, 1996.
Fama E, 'Efficient capital markets: A review of theory and empirical work', 25 *Journal of Finance* (1970), p. 383.
Ferran E, *Principles of Corporate Finance Law*, Oxford University Press, 2008.
Ferran E, *Regulating Financial Services and Markets in the Twenty First Century*, Oxford University Press, 2001.
Ferran E, *Company Law and Corporate Finance*, Oxford University Press, 1999.
Firth M, 'Raising capital and firms' corporate reporting policies', *Abacus,* Vol. XVI, No. 2, (1980), pp. 100–115.
Firth M, *Share Price and Mergers: A Study of Stock Market Efficiency*, Saxon House, 1976.
FSA, 'Response paper to CP 30: the FSA's regulation of professional firms', Financial Services Authority, 2000.
FSA, 'Response to consultation paper 31: The FSA's approach to setting prudential standards', Financial Services Authority, 2000.
FSA, 'Proposed amendment to the compensation rules', Financial Services Authority, Consultation Paper 44, 2000.
FSA, 'Customer classification', Financial Services Authority, Consultation Paper 43, 2000.
FSA, 'The FSA's approach to regulation of the market infrastructure', Financial Services Authority, (Discussion Paper), 2000.
FSA, 'Financial Services Authority: A new regulator for the new millennium', Financial Services Authority, 2000.
FSA, 'The transfer of the UK Listing Authority to the FSA', Financial Services Authority, Consultation Paper 37, 1999.
FSA, 'The FSA's approach to setting prudential standards', Financial Services Authority, Consultation Paper 31, 1999.
FSA, 'Enforcing the new perimeter', Financial Services Authority, Consultation Paper 25, 1999.
FSA, 'Response to consultation paper 17: Financial services regulation: Enforcing the new regime', Financial Services Authority, 1999.
FSA, 'Financial services regulation: Enforcing the new regime', Financial Services Authority, Consultation Paper 17, 1998.
FSA, 'Designing the FSA Handbook of rules and guidance', Financial Services Authority, Consultation Paper 08, 1998.
FSA, *FSA Handbook,* Financial Services Authority.
Furmston M, *Cheshire, Fifoot & Furmston's Law of Contract*, 2nd Ed., Butterworths, (London), 1991.
Garbade K, *Securities Markets*, McGraw-Hill (USA), 1982.
Ghanem I, 'The role of Islamic law in commercial litigation in North Yemen' Ph.D thesis, University of London, 1987.
Gharaibeh F et al., 'The impact of the content of annual reports on the level of trading on listed Jordanian shareholding companies', *Dirasat*, University of Jordan, 1989, Vol.16, No. 1, p. 7.

Gilligan G, 'The origins of UK financial services regulation', *The Company Lawyer*, Vol. 18, No. 6, 1997, pp. 167.
Goodheart C et al., *The Operation and Regulation of Financial Markets*, Macmillan (London), 1987.
Group of Ten, 'Financial stability in emerging market economies a strategy for the formulation, adoption, and implementation of sound principles and practices to strengthen financial systems: Report of the working party on financial stability in emerging markets economies'. Basle, Bank of International Settlements (April 1997).
Grubb A, *The Law of Contract*, Butterworths, (London), 1999.
Gust A, *Anson's Law of Contract*, Oxford University Press, 1984.
Habachy S, 'Commentary on the decision of the Supreme Court of Egypt given on 4 May 1985 concerning the legitimacy of interest and the constitutionality of Article 226 of the new Egyptian Civil Code of 1948', *Arab Law Quarterly*, Vol.1, No. 2 (1986), p. 240.
Haddad F, 'The informational content of annual statements: An empirical study of industrial public shareholding companies in Jordan', *Dirasat*, University of Jordan, 2001, Vol.16, No. 1, pp. 125–150.
Haddad S, 'The information content of security prices in the Amman Bourse', Master's thesis, University of Jordan, 2001.
Hallaq W, *A History of Islamic Legal Theories: An Introduction to Sunni Usul Al-Fiqh*, Cambridge University Press, 1997.
Hamad H, 'Privatisation of Jordanian electric companies: A field study of its managers' attitudes', Master's thesis, Jordan University, 1999.
Hamid M, 'The role of consent in formation of contracts: A comparative study in English and Islamic law', Ph.D thesis, London University, 1971.
Harris M et al., 'The theory of capital structure', *Journal of Finance*, Vol.46 (1991), pp. 297–355.
Heimann J, 'Global institutions, national supervisions and systemic risk', *Financial Stability Review*, No. 3, (Autumn 1997), pp. 82–91.
Hertig G et al., 'Issuers and investor protection' in R Kraakman et al., *The Anatomy of Corporate Law: A Comparative and Functional Approach*, Oxford University Press, (2004).
Hicks A et al., *Cases & Materials on Company Law*, Blackstone, (London), 1997.
Hidayatullah M, *Mulla's Principles of Mahomedan Law*, N M Tripathi Private Ltd., Bombay, 1990.
Hirshleifer J, 'The analytics of uncertainty and information' 17 *Journal of Economic Literature*, (1979), p. 1375.
Hirshleifer J, 'The private and social value of information and the reward of incentive activity', 61 *American Economic Review*, (1971), p. 561.
Hjerppe R, 'Provision of public and merit goods: Towards an optimal policy mix?', Helsinki: United Nations University, World Institute for Development Economics Research, (Research in progress 10), 1997.
Hraze S, 'The role of the banking system in developing the primary capital market in Jordan', Master's thesis, Al El-Beit University, Jordan, 1999.

Hudson A, *The Law on Financial Derivatives*, Sweet & Maxwell, (London), 1998.
Ibbotson R, 'The market's problem with the pricing of initial public offerings', *Journal of Applied Corporate Finance*, Vol.7, 1994, p. 67.
Idris F, 'Islamic banks' financial reporting and its usefulness to investors: A case study of Bank Islam Malaysia Behrad, Malysia', Ph.D thesis, Cardiff University, 1995.
Ireland P, 'Company law and the myth of shareholder ownership', *The Modern Law Review*, Vol.62, No. 1, January 1999, p. 37.
ISSA, *Crisis Monitor Project, Crisis Country Case Study: Jordan*. Geneva (2010).
Jaffar Z, 'The concept and application of daman in Islamic commercial law', Ph.D thesis, Edinburgh University, 1994.
James K, 'Waiting for Ariadne: A suggestion for reforming financial services regulation, Centre for the Study of Financial Innovation, London, 2002.
Jasay A De, *Social Contract, Free Ride: A Study of the Public Goods Problem*, (Oxford Press), 1989.
Jensen & Meckling, 'Theory of the firm: Managerial behaviour, agency costs and ownership structure', 3 *Journal of Finance and Economics* (1976), p. 305.
Jeunemaitre A, *Financial Markets Regulation: A Practitioner's Perspective*, Macmillan, (London), 1997.
Johnson et al., 'The impact of securities litigation reform on the disclosure of forward-looking information by high technology firms', 39 *Journal of Financial Accounting*, 297 (2001).
Kahan M, 'Securities laws and the social costs of "insurance" stock prices', 41 *Duke Law Journal*, (1992), p. 979.
Kamali M, 'Methodological issues in Islamic jurisprudence', *Arab Law Quarterly*, Vol. II, No. 1, 1996, p. 3.
Keane S, *Stock Market Efficiency: Theory, Evidence and Implications*, Philip Allan (Oxford), 1983.
Khan T, 'An analysis of risk sharing in Islamic finance with reference to Pakistan', Ph.D thesis Loughborough University, 1996.
Kirsch C, *The financial Services Revolution: Understanding the Changing Role of Banks, Mutual Funds, and Insurance Companies*, Chicago: Irwin Professional Pub., 1997.
Kitch E, 'The theory and practice of securities disclosure', 61 *Brooklyn Law Review*, (1995) 763.
Kraakman R et al., *The Anatomy of Corporate Law: A Comparative and Functional Approach*, Oxford University Press, (2004).
Kremers J, *Financial Supervision in Europe*, Cheltenham: Edward Elgar Pub, 2003.
Kripke H, *The SEC and Corporate Disclosure: Regulation in Search for Purpose* (New York: Law and Business Inc.) Harcourt Brace Jovanovich Publishers, 1979.
Kumar M, *Growth, Acquisition and Investment*, Cambridge University Press, Cambridge, 1984.

Llewellyn D, 'The economic rationale for financial regulation', FSA, Occasional Papers, No. 1, (April 1999).

Llewellyn D, 'Consumer protection in retail investment services: Protection against what?', *Journal of Financial Regulation and Compliance*, Vol. III No. 1, p. 45, (1995).

Loss L, *Fundamentals of Securities Regulation*, Little Brown & Company (Canada), 1988.

Madi S, 'The concept of unlawful gain and legitimate profit in Islamic law', Ph.D thesis, London University, 1989.

Mahoney P, 'Mandatory disclosure as a solution to agency problems', 62 *University of Chicago Law Review*, (1995), p. 1047.

Mallat C, *Islamic Law and Finance*, Graham & Trotman Ltd., (Boston, London), 1988.

Mallat C, 'The renaissance of Islamic law: Constitution, economics and banking in the thoughts of Muhammad Baqer As-Sadr', Ph.D thesis, London University, 1990.

Mankabady S, 'Insurance and Islamic law: The Islamic insurance company', *Arab Law Quarterly*, Vol.4, No. 3, (August 1989), pp. 199–205.

Mannan M, *Mulla's Principles of Mahomedian Law* (Pakistan Edition), P.L.D. Publications, Lahore, 1991.

Matar M, 'Testing the efficiency of Amman Bourse at the semi-strong level using information of financial statements exposure', Master's thesis, Al El-Beit University, Jordan, 2003.

Mayer A, 'The regulation of interest charges and risk contracts: Some problems of recent Libyan legislation', *International and Comparative Law Quarterly*, Vol.28, No. 4, October (1979), pp. 541–553.

McElwee M, 'Leviathan at large: The new regulator for the financial markets', Centre for Policy Studies, London, 2000.

McMeel G, *Financial Advice and Financial Products: Law and Liability*, Oxford University Press, 2001.

Mendez R, 'The provision and financing of universal public goods' London School of Economics. Centre for the Study of Global Governance, Discussion paper 7, 1993.

Moghaizel F, 'Insurance in the light of Islamic legal principles', Ph.D thesis, London University, 1991.

Mohamad A, 'The Islamic law of tort', Ph.D thesis, University of Edinburgh, 1997.

Mondellini L, 'Putting out green shots', *Euromoney*, (September 1998).

Moore P, *Islamic Finance: A Partnership for Growth*, Euromoney Publications, 1997.

Moore P, 'Saudi Arabia: Pressure builds up for change', *Euromoney*, June 1997.

Moran M, *The Politics of the Financial Services Revolution: The USA, UK and Japan*, Macmillan, London, 1990.

Mosmar M, 'Civil liability in the Jordanian Civil Code: A comparative study with the Shari'a', Ph.D thesis, London University, 1998.

Mullin J, 'Emerging equity markets in the global economy', *Federal Reserve Bank of New York Quarterly Review*, Summer 1993.
Muslehuddin M, *Insurance and Islamic Law*, New Delhi, 1982.
Namethy L, 'KIA's privatisation: A pioneering experience', paper presented in a seminar entitled 'Privatisation programme: Review and prospects', Kuwaiti Investment Authority, 17 December 1996.
Napiah M, 'The theory of the contract of agency (*al wakilah*) in Islamic law', Ph.D thesis, Glasgow Caledonian, 1995.
Nazzal R, 'The effect of foreign ownership on the return and risk in the Amman Bourse', Master's thesis, Jordan university, 2000.
Newman K, *Financial Marketing and Communications*, Holt Rineheart and Winston Ltd., 1984.
Norton J et al., *Emerging Financial Markets and the Role of International Financial Organisations*, Kluwer Law International, 1996.
OECD, 'Securities markets in OECD countries: Organisation and regulation', OECD Documents, (1995).
Padoa-Schioppa T, *Regulating Finance: Balancing Freedom and Risk*, Oxford University Press, 2004.
Page A et al., *Investor Protection*, Weidenfield & Nicolson (London), 1992.
Perry J, *The Financial Services and Markets Act: A Practical Legal Guide*, Sweet & Maxwell, (London), 2001.
Peters R, 'Divine law or man-made law? Egypt and the application of the Shari'a', *Arab Law Quarterly*, Vol.3, No. 3, (August 1988).
Posner R et al., *Economics of Corporation Law and Securities Regulation*, (Little, Brown and Company –Boston and Toronto), 1980.
Prentice D, *Contemporary Issues in Corporate Governance*, Oxford University Press, 1993.
Rahman A, *Banking and Insurance*, London, 1979.
Ramanov J, 'Saudi Arabia and Kuwait: Closed-economy cousins', *Euromoney* (May 1999).
Ray N, *Arab Islamic Banking and the Renewal of Islamic Law*, Graham & Trotman, (Boston, London), 1995.
Rayner S, *The Theory of Contracts in Islamic Law: A Comparative Analysis with Particular Reference to the Modern Legislation in Kuwait, Bahrain and the United Arab Emirates*, Graham & Trotman, (Boston, London), 1991.
Rider B et al., *Guide to Financial Services Regulation*, CCH Editions, (UK), 1997.
Roberts G, *Law Relating to Financial Services*, Canterbury: Financial World Publishing, (UK), 2001.
Rogoff, K, 'International institutions for reducing global financial instability', *Journal of Economic Perspectives*, Vol.13, No. 4, (1999), pp. 21–42.
Rosenthal D, *Financial Advertising and Marketing Law*, FT Law & Tax (UK), 1997.
Ross J, 'The globalisation of financial markets and its impact on the financial services industry', MSc thesis, Heriot-Watt University, 1995.

Rutterford J, *Introduction to Stock Exchange Investment*, Macmillan, (London), 1993.

Sabalot D, *A Guide to the Financial Services and Markets Act 2000*, Butterworths, (London), 2000.

Sabri N, 'Cross-listing of stocks among European-Arab (Mediterranean) markets', *Finance India*. Vol. XVI, No. 1, March 2002.

Saeed A, *Islamic Banking and Interest: A Study of the Prohibition of Riba and its Contemporary Interpretation*, E.J. Brill, (New York), 1996, p. 34.

Sala-i-Martin X, et al., 'Economic Growth and Investment in the Arab World', Columbia University Department of Economics Discussion Paper No. 0203–08, 2002, (New York: Columbia University).

Saleh N, *Unlawful Gain and Legitimate Profit in Islamic Law: Riba, Gharar and Islamic Banking*, Graham & Trotman (Boston, London), 1992.

Saleh N, 'Freedom of contract: What does it mean in the context of Arab Laws?' *Arab Law Quarterly*, Vol.16, No. 4, (April 2001), pp. 346–357.

Salomon Smith Barney Guide to World Equity Markets 2000, Euromoney, (London), 2000.

Schacht J, *An Introduction to Islamic Law*, Oxford, (1964).

Schacht J, *The Origins of Muhammadan Jurisprudence*, Clarendon Press, 1979.

Schmidtz D, *The Limits of Government: An Essay on the Public Goods Argument*, (Boulder, London, Westview), 1990.

Seznec J, *The financial Markets of the Arabian Gulf*, Croom Helm, (London), 1987.

Shachmurove Y, 'Introduction for the special issue on emerging financial markets of the Middle East', *International Journal of Business*, Vol. 8, No. 3, (2003), pp. 227–41.

Shoker T, 'The internationalisation of the Arab Gulf banks', Ph.D thesis, University of Wales, Bangor, 1989.

SIB, 'Regulation of the United Kingdom equity markets: Report by the Securities and Investment Board', the Securities and Investment Board (SIB), June 1995, London.

SIB, 'Regulation of the United Kingdom equity markets, market views: A digest of responses to SIB's discussion paper', SIB, June 1995, London.

Siddiqi M, *Insurance in an Islamic Economy*, The Islamic Foundation, (UK), 1985.

Sloane P, 'The status of Islamic law in the commercial world', *International Lawyer*, (Fall, 1988), Vol.22, No. 3, p. 747.

Smith-Highes A, 'Parliament, the City and financial regulation: A review of the passage of the Financial Services and Markets Act 2000', London: Hansard Society, 2001.

Thani N, 'Legal aspects of the regulatory framework of the Malaysian financial system', Ph.D thesis, London University, 1993.

Tobbal Y, 'Islamic banks and investment depositors: Their relationship and accounting implications under the profit and loss sharing *mudaraba*', Ph.D thesis, Kent University, 1988.

HM Treasury (UK), 'Extension of the statutory regime for issuer liability' (July 2008).
HM Treasury (UK), 'Davies review of issuer liability, liability for misstatements to the market: Final report' (June 2007).
HM Treasury (UK), 'Davies review of issuer liability, liability for misstatements to the market: A discussion paper' (March 2007).
HM Treasury (UK), 'Financial promotion: Third consultation document', Her Majesty's Treasury, 2000.
HM Treasury (UK), 'Guidance note on public offers of securities amendment regulations 1999', Her Majesty's Treasury, 1999
HM Treasury (UK), 'Competition and regulation in financial services: Striking the right balance', Her Majesty's Treasury, 1999.
HM Treasury (UK), 'Public offering of securities: Proposals for consultation', Her Majesty's Treasury, 1998.
HM Treasury (UK), 'Guidance note: Public offers of securities regulations 1995', Her Majesty's Treasury, 1995
Treitel G, *The Law of Contract*, Sweet & Maxwell, 10th Ed., London, 1999.
Underhill G, 'Keeping governments out of politics: The internationalisation of securities markets and the question of regulation', Working Paper No. 118, University of Warwick, (August 1993).
Usher J, *The Law of Money and Financial Services in the European Community*, Oxford University Press, 2000.
Usmani M, 'The concept of *musharakah* and its application as an Islamic method of financing', *Arab Law Quarterly*, Vol.14, No. 3, (March) 1999, pp. 203–220.
Wasserfallen W, 'Macroeconomic news and the stock market' *Journal of Banking and Finance*, Vol.13, No. 4, 1989, pp. 613–626.
Watson A, *Legal Transplants: An Approach to Comparative Law*, University of Georgia Press (USA), 1993.
Wilhelmsson T, *Social Contract Law and European Integration*, (Aldershot, Dartmouth), 1994.
Willett E, *Fundamentals of Securities Markets*, New Century (New York), 1971.
Wilson R, 'The issue of interest and the Islamic financing alternative', *Journal of International Banking*, Issue 1 (1998), pp. 23–25.
Wilson R, *Banking and Finance in the Arab Middle East*, Macmillan Publishers Ltd. (London), 1983.
Yago G, *Restructuring Regulation and Financial Institutions*, Kluwer Law International, 2001.
Yassin M, 'The impact of the deregulation of interest rates on share prices of banks in Jordan: An analytical study of the efficiency of pricing the shares of the banking sector on the Amman Financial Market', Master's thesis, University of Jordan, 1991.
Younes B, 'The effect of new issues on the stock returns in Amman Financial Market', Master's thesis, Jordan University, 1995.

Zahraa M et al., 'The validity of contracts when goods are not yet in existence in the Islamic law of sale of goods', *Arab Law Quarterly*, Vol.17, No. 4, (December 2002), pp. 379–397.

Zahraa M et al., 'Characteristic features of Islamic law: Perceptions and misconceptions', *Arab Law Quarterly*, Vol.15, No. 2, (February 2000), pp. 168–196.

Zineldin M, *The Economics of Money and Banking: A Theoretical and Empirical Study of Islamic Interest-Free Banking*, Almqvist & Wiksell International (Stockholm), 1990.

Zohny A, 'The suitability of US security laws and regulations to serve as a model law for Egyptian financial markets', *Arab Law Quarterly*, Vol.15, No. 1, (January 2000), pp. 5–47.

United Nations, IMF and World Bank Publications

Abisourour A, 'The emerging Arab capital markets: Status, role and development prospects', in S El-Naggar, *Financial Policies and Capital Markets in Arab Countries*, IMF, 1994.

Alonso-Gamo P, 'Globalisation and growth prospects in Arab countries', Middle Eastern Department, IMF, WP/97/125, September 1997.

Amsden A et al., 'Republic of Korea's financial reforms: What are the lessons?', UNCTAD, Discussion Paper No. 30, April 1990.

Annual Report 1995, Central Asia, Middle East and North Africa, IFC, (Washington).

Aylward A et al., 'Primary securities markets: Cross country findings', IFC, Washington D.C., Discussion Paper No. 39, 1999.

Blommestein H et al., 'The role of financial institutions in the transition to a market economy', Research Department, IMF, WP/93/75, October 1993.

Cashin P et al., 'Informational efficiency in developing equity markets', WP/95/58, Research Department and Middle Eastern Department, IMF, June 1995.

Chami R et al., 'The stock market channel of monetary policy', IMF Institute, WP/99/22, February 1999.

Chuppe M et al., 'Regulation of securities markets', World Bank, WPS/829, January 1992.

Claessens S, 'Corporate governance and equity prices: Evidence from the Czech and Slovak republics', Policy Research Working Paper No. 1427, World Bank, February 1995.

Creane S, *et. al.*, 'Financial sector development in the Middle East and North Africa', Middle East and Central Asia Department, WP/04/201, (October 2005), p. 4.

Dasgupta D, et al., 'Reform and elusive growth in the Middle East – What has happened in the 1990s?' World Bank Working Paper No. 25, 2002.

Dattels P, 'The microstructure of government securities markets', Monetary and Exchange Affairs Department, IMF, WP/95/117, November 1995.

Demirguc D et al., 'Stock market development and financial intermediary growth: A research agenda', Policy Research Department, World Bank, WPS 1159, July 1993.

Dittus P et al., 'Corporate control in Central Europe and Russia: Should banks own shares?' Transition Economics Division, Policy Research Working Paper No. 1481, World Bank, June 1995.

Egerer R, 'Capital markets, financial intermediaries and corporate governance: An empirical assessment of the top ten voucher funds in the Czech Republic', Policy Research Working Paper No. 1555, World Bank, December 1995.

El-Naggar S, *Financial Policies and Capital Markets in Arab Countries*, IMF, 1994.

Errico L et al., 'Islamic banking: Issues in prudential regulations and supervision', Monetary and Exchange Affairs Department, IMF, March 1998.

Fasano U, et al., *GCC Countries: From Oil Dependence to Diversification*, International Monetary Fund, 2003.

Feldman R et al., 'Emerging equity markets: Growth, benefits and policy concerns', Research Department, IMF, PPAA/94/7, March 1994.

Fouad M, et. al., 'Public debt and fiscal vulnerability in the Middle East', IMF, WP/07/12, (January 2007).

Galibs V, 'Financial sector reforms in eight countries: Issues and results', IMF, WP/95/141, Policy Development and Review Department, December 1995.

Glen J, 'An introduction to the microstructure of emerging markets', Discussion Paper No. 24, IFC, Washington, November 1994.

Hakura D, et al., 'Growth in the Middle East and North Africa', Research Department, IMF, WP/04/56, (April 2004).

He D, 'Stock market development and financial deepening in developing countries: Some correlation patterns', Country Economic Department, World Bank, WPS 1084, February 1993.

Heller P et al, 'The fiscal impact of privatisation, with some examples from Arab countries', in S El-Naggar *Financial Policies and Capital Markets in Arab Countries*, IMF, 1994.

IMF, '*World Economic and Financial Surveys: Regional Economic Outlook, Middle East and Central Asia*', International Monetary Fund, Washington DC, (October 2011).

IMF, '*World Economic and Financial Surveys: Regional Economic Outlook, Middle East and Central Asia*', International Monetary Fund, Washington DC, (October 2010).

IMF, '*World Economic Outlook: Recovery, Risk and Rebalancing, World Economic and Financial Surveys*', International Monetary Fund, Washington DC, (October 2010).

IMF, '*Jordan: Article IV Consultation, Concluding Statement of the IMF Mission*', (July 17, 2010).

IMF, '*World Economic Outlook: Financial Systems and Economic Cycles*', World Economic and Financial Surveys, IMF, September 2006.

IMF, *Jordan: Selected Issues and StatisticalAppendix*, IMF, IMF Country Report No. 04/121, (May 2004).

IMF, *World Economic and Financial Surveys*, 'World economic outlook: Advancing structural reforms', IMF, Washington, April 2004.

IMF, *World Economic and Financial Surveys*, 'World economic outlook: International financial contagion', IMF, Washington, October 1999.
IMF, *World Economic and Financial Surveys*, 'International capital markets: Developments, prospects, and key policy issues', IMF, Washington, September 1999.
IMF, *World Bank Annual Report,* Middle East & North Africa, IMF, Washington, 1998.
IMF, *World Bank Middle East and North Africa Economic Studies*, 'Egypt in the global economy, strategic choices for savings, investments, and long term growth', No. 19, World Bank, Washington DC, 1998.
Kalotay K, 'Emerging markets and the scope for regional cooperation', UNCTAD/OSG/DP/79, February 1994.
Knight M, 'Developing countries and the globalization of financial markets', Monetary and Exchange Affairs Department, IMF, WP/98/105, July 1998.
Kumar M, 'Emerging equity markets in Middle Eastern countries', Middle Eastern and Research Departments, IMF, WP/94/103, September 1994.
Long M et al., 'Financial regulation: Changing the rules of the game', Country Economic Department, World Bank, WPS 803, November 1991.
Mauro P, 'Stock returns and output growth in emerging and advanced economies', IMF, WP/00/89, 2000.
Mayer C, 'Myths of the West: Lessons from developed countries for development finance', Policy, Planning and Research in Development Economics, IMF, November 1989.
Pardy R, 'Regulatory and institutional impacts of securities market computerization', Country Economic Department, World Bank, WPS 866, February 1992.
Pardy R, 'Institutional reform in emerging securities markets', Country Economic Department, World Bank, WPS 907, May 1992.
Singh A et al., 'Corporate financial structure in developing countries', Technical Paper No. 1, IFC, May 1992.
Smith T, 'Markets for corporate debt securities', Research Department, IMF, July 1995.
Sylla R, 'The rise of securities markets: What can governments do?', The World Bank, Policy Research Working Paper No. 1539, November 1995.
Vittas D, 'Policy issues in financial regulation', Country Economics Department, World Bank, WPS 910, May 1992.

Selected Arabic

El-Saddeh A, *Nathariat El-Aqud fi El-Bilad El-Arabiah*, Dar El-Nahdah, 1974.
Hakeem A, *Al-Wajeeze fi Sharh El-Qanoon El-Madani: El-Juz' El-Awal: Masader El-Iltizam*, 4th Ed. (Baghdad).
Salameh M, *Nathariat Al-Aqid fi El-Fiqh El-Islami min khilal Aqid El-Bay'*, Moroccan Ministry of Religious Affairs, 1994.
Sanhuri A, *Masadir El-Haqq*, Pts.I-III, 1957–1962.

Taha G, *Al-Wajeez fe El-Nathariat El-Ammah fe El-Tizam, El-Kitab El-Awal: Masadar El-Eltizam* (Baghdad) 1971.
Yakan Z, *Al-Waqf fi Al-Shari'a wa Al-Qanoon*, Dar al-Nahda, 1388 H.
Zarqa M, *El-Fiqh El-Islami fi Thoubeh El-Jadid: El-Juz' El-Awal: El-Madhkal El-Fiqhi El-Aam*, 9th Ed., Damascus (1967–1968).
Zarqa M, *Nazam Al-Ta'min*, Beirut, 1984.

Amman Stock Exchange & Amman Financial Market Publications

(a) Annual Reports:

Fourth Annual Report of the Amman Stock Exchange, Amman Stock Exchange, Amman, the Hashemite Kingdom of Jordan, 2002.
Third Annual Report of the Amman Stock Exchange, Amman Stock Exchange, Amman, the Hashemite Kingdom of Jordan, 2001
Amman Financial Market Annual Report for the Year 1998, Amman Financial Market, Amman, the Hashemite Kingdom of Jordan, 1998.
Amman Financial Market Annual Report for the Year 1982, Amman Financial Market, Amman, the Hashemite Kingdom of Jordan, 1982.

(b) Monthly Statistical Bulletins:

Monthly Statistical Bulletin of the ASE (until November 2010), Amman Stock Exchange, Amman, the Hashemite Kingdom of Jordan.
Monthly Statistical Bulletin of the ASE (February 2004), Amman Stock Exchange, Amman, the Hashemite Kingdom of Jordan, 2004.
Monthly Statistical Bulletin of the ASE (January 2001), Amman Stock Exchange, Amman, the Hashemite Kingdom of Jordan, 2001.

Central Bank of Jordan Publications

(a) Annual Reports:

39th Annual Report of the Central Bank of Jordan, Central Bank of Jordan, Amman, the Hashemite Kingdom of Jordan, 2002.
30th Annual Report of the Central Bank of Jordan, Central Bank of Jordan, Amman, the Hashemite Kingdom of Jordan, 1993.
23rd Annual Report of the Central Bank of Jordan, Central Bank of Jordan, Amman, the Hashemite Kingdom of Jordan, 1986.
15th Annual Report of the Central Bank of Jordan, Central Bank of Jordan, Amman, the Hashemite Kingdom of Jordan, 1978.

(b) Monthly Statistical Bulletins:

Various *Monthly Statistical Bulletins* by the Central Bank of Jordan, Amman, the Hashemite Kingdom of Jordan, 1975–2002.

Jordanian Securities Commission Publications

The Fifth Annual Report, Jordanian Securities Commission, Amman, the Hashemite Kingdom of Jordan, 2003.

The Fourth Annual Report, Jordanian Securities Commission, Amman, the Hashemite Kingdom of Jordan, Amman, 2002.

The Third Annual Report, Jordanian Securities Commission, Amman, the Hashemite Kingdom of Jordan, 2001.

The Second Annual Report, Jordanian Securities Commission, Amman, the Hashemite Kingdom of Jordan, 2000.

The First Annual Report, Jordanian Securities Commission, Amman, Amman, the Hashemite Kingdom of Jordan, 1999.

Various World Wide Web resources from JSC Official Website –until December 2011.

Arab Monetary Fund Publications

Various *Quarterly Statistical Bulletin* by the Arab Monetary Fund, Abu Dhabi, United Arab Emirates (1995–2011).

Bolbol A, et al., 'Arab stock markets and capital investment', Economic Policy Institute. The Arab Monetary Fund, AMF Economic Papers No. 8, (February 2004).

Table of Selected Cases

(1) Jordan

(2) United Kingdom

Table of Statutory Instruments and Regulations

(1) Jordan

A) Statutory Instruments

B) (Jordan) Bylaws and Regulations

The Sale of Goods Act 1979

Kuwait

Lebanon

Book/Author Index

I

J

K

L

M

N

P

R

S

Index

K

L